T0331187

RADICAL POLITICAL ECONOMICS

This collection of essays engages in the analysis of key concepts, concerns, and cutting-edge insights in radical political economy.

Offering a robust critique of capitalist institutions as well as of mainstream economics, radical political economics reveals the structures and dynamics of global capitalism. The attention to method, ideology, and institutions differentiates it from mainstream approaches to economics, which often obfuscate how capitalism actually works. While maintaining a central focus on capitalism, the analyses in this book encompass a variety of issues from racial discrimination, gender inequality, to economic development and imperialism. Capitalism is an economic system based on the exploitation of workers to generate surplus value (profit) which is then appropriated by the owners of capital. Under global capitalism, profit maximization precedes other social concerns such as protection of the environment. Political economy understands that social relations are shaped by class, race, geography, and gender. Capitalism skews social relations of production and reproduction. It perpetuates inequalities along classed, gendered, racialized, and geographic lines.

Radical political economy offers ideas and policies to change capitalism, in ways that are more beneficial for people and the planet. Incorporating insights from a range of disciplines including history, philosophy, political science, anthropology, sociology, and law, the wide range of topics, diverse set of scholars, and consideration of future political-economy formations offers readers a deeper understanding of the contours of contemporary global capitalism and post-capitalist possibilities in the twenty-first century.

Mona Ali is Associate Professor of Economics at the State University of New York. Her research on international political economy has been published in the *Cambridge Journal of Economics*, the *International Review of Applied Economics*, and *Géopolitique, Réseau, Énergie, Environnement, Nature (GREEN)* among elsewhere. Her popular writing for *Phenomenal World* has been translated into four languages and featured in the *Financial Times*. She received her PhD from the New School for Social Research and she has served on the steering committee of Union for Radical Political Economics.

Ann E. Davis is Associate Professor of Economics (retired) at Marist College and served as chair of the Department of Accounting, Finance, and Economics, and chair of the Faculty. She has published articles in the *Review of Radical Political Economics, Cambridge Journal of Economics, Critical Historical Studies*, and *Journal of Economic Issues*. She has published four books and various book chapters and served in leadership roles in heterodox economic associations.

RADICAL POLITICAL ECONOMICS

Principles, Perspectives, and Post-Capitalist Futures

Edited by Mona Ali and Ann E. Davis

Routledge
Taylor & Francis Group

LONDON AND NEW YORK

Designed cover image: Leontura © Getty Images

First published 2025
by Routledge
4 Park Square, Milton Park, Abingdon, Oxon OX14 4RN

and by Routledge
605 Third Avenue, New York, NY 10158

Routledge is an imprint of the Taylor & Francis Group, an informa business

British Library Cataloguing-in-Publication Data
A catalog record for this book is available from the British Library

ISBN: 978-1-032-43302-8 (hbk)
ISBN: 978-1-032-43301-1 (pbk)
ISBN: 978-1-003-36669-0 (ebk)

DOI: 10.4324/9781003366690

Typeset in Times New Roman
by SPi Technologies India Pvt Ltd (Straive)

CONTENTS

PART III
Post-Capitalist Futures **235**

FIGURES

CONTRIBUTORS

Ilias Alami is University Assistant Professor in the Political Economy of Development in the Centre of Development Studies and the Department of Politics and International Studies at the University of Cambridge. Prior to joining Cambridge, he held research and teaching positions at Uppsala University, Maastricht University, and Manchester University. He also held visiting positions at the Getulio Vargas Foundation in Sao Paulo, the University of Johannesburg, and Sciences Po Paris.

John Peter Antonacci is a PhD Candidate (ABD) in Sociology at the University of Binghamton, New York, and Adjunct Professor of Sociology. His dissertation, tentatively titled "Climates of Coercion, Climates of Capital: Military Revolutions in the Capitalist World-Ecology, 1492–1815," situates military revolutions as turning points in the environmental history of early modern capitalism.

Al Campbell is a Professor Emeritus of Economics at the University of Utah. He is the author of many articles and book chapters regarding economic alternatives and macroeconomics analysis.

C. P. Chandrasekhar was formerly Professor at the Centre for Economic Studies & Planning, Jawaharlal Nehru University, New Delhi. His areas of interest include the role of finance and industry in development. He has published widely and among his recent publications are two books titled *Demonetisation Decoded: A Critique of India's Currency Experiment* (Routledge) and *Karl Marx's Capital and the Present: Four Essays* (Tulika Books). He is a regular columnist for *Frontline* (Economic Perspectives), *Business Line* (Macroscan), and the *Economic and Political Weekly*.

Jayati Ghosh taught economics at Jawaharlal Nehru University, New Delhi, for nearly 35 years, and since January 2021 she has been Professor of Economics at the University of Massachusetts Amherst, USA. She has authored and/or edited 20 books and more than 200 scholarly articles. Recent books include *The Making of a Catastrophe: Covid-19 and the Indian Economy*, Aleph Books, 2022; *When Governments Fail: Covid-19 and the Economy*, Tulika Books and Columbia University Press, 2021 (co-edited); Women *Workers in the Informal Economy*, Routledge, 2021 (edited); *Never Done and Poorly Paid: Women's Work in Globalising India*, Women Unlimited, New Delhi, 2009; *Elgar Handbook of Alternative Theories of Economic Development*, 2014 (co-edited); *After Crisis*, Tulika, 2009 (co-edited); *Demonetisation Decoded*, Routledge, 2017 (co-authored).

Barry Herman has served as a Visiting Scholar (from July 2016) and visiting faculty at the Julien J. Studley Graduate Program in International Affairs, The New School, New York. He has served at the United Nations in various capacities, including United Nations Department of Economic and Social Affairs (DESA), and the Financing for Sustainable Development Office. He has also served at the IMF as a member of the Consultative Group on Social Spending (2018–2019), to assist the International Monetary Fund develop an "institutional view" on social protection.

Michael G. Hillard is a Professor of Economics at the University of Southern Maine, Portland. He is the author of *Shredding Paper: The Rise and Fall of Maine's Mighty Paper Industry*, Cornell University Press, 2022. He has published widely in the fields of labor relations, labor history, and the political economy of labor in academic journals including *Labor: Studies in Working Class History of the Americas, Labor History, Review of Radical Political Economics, Advances in Industrial and Labor Relations, Journal of Economic Issues,* and *Historical Studies in Industrial Relation* and is co-editor with Jonathan Goldstein of *Heterodox Macroeconomics: Keynes, Marx, and Globalization* (Routledge Press, 2009).

David M. Kotz is an Emeritus Professor of Economics at the University of Massachusetts at Amherst. He is the author of several books and articles regarding the Social Structure of Accumulation approach, including the *Rise and Fall of Neoliberal Capitalism*, Harvard University Press, 2015.

William Lazonick is an Emeritus Professor of Economics at the University of Massachusetts, at Lowell. He is co-founder and president of the Academic-Industry Research Network, a 501(c)(3) non-profit research organization, based in Cambridge, Massachusetts. He is an Open Society Fellow and a

Canadian Institute for Advanced Research Fellow. His publications include widely cited articles in the *Harvard Business Review* regarding stock buy backs, and books regarding innovation. In January 2020, Oxford University Press published his book, co-authored with Jang-Sup Shin, *Predatory Value Extraction: How the Looting of the Business Corporation Became the U.S. Norm and How Sustainable Prosperity Can Be Restored.*

Richard McIntyre is a Professor of Economics at the University of Rhode Island where he also teaches in the International Studies and Diplomacy BA program. He is on the advisory board for the Schmidt Labor Research Center and the URI Global Ed Steering Committee. He was economics department chair from 2015 to 2020, Associate Director of the URI Honors Program from 2003 to 2006, and Director from 2006 to 2013. From 2015 to 2020, he co-directed URI Study Abroad programs in Cuba. He edits the *New Political Economy* book series for Routledge Press.

Jason W. Moore is an environmental historian and historical geographer at Binghamton University, where he coordinates the World-Ecology Research Collective. He is author or editor, most recently, of *Capitalism in the Web of Life* (Verso, 2015), *Capitalocene o Anthropocene?* (Ombre Corte, 2017), *Anthropocene or Capitalocene? Nature, History, and the Crisis of Capitalism* (PM Press, 2016), and, with Raj Patel, *A History of the World in Seven Cheap Things* (University of California Press, 2017). His books and essays on environmental history, capitalism, and social theory have been widely recognized, including the Alice Hamilton Prize of the American Society for Environmental History (2003), the Distinguished Scholarship Award of the Section on the Political Economy of the World-System (American Sociological Association, 2002 for articles, and 2015 for *Web of Life*), and the Byres and Bernstein Prize in Agrarian Change (2011). He coordinates the World-Ecology Research Network.

Erik K. Olsen is an Associate Professor and Chair of the Economics Department at the University of Missouri at Kansas City. He is a Research Fellow at the Rutgers University School of Management and Labor Relations, USA. He has published widely on the topic of group or cooperative ownership and is a co-editor of the *Routledge Handbook of Marxian Economics*, 2017.

Prabhat Patnaik joined the Faculty of Economics and Politics of the University of Cambridge, UK, in 1969 and was elected a fellow of Clare College, Cambridge. In 1974, he returned to India as an associate professor at the newly established Centre for Economic Studies and Planning (CESP) at the Jawaharlal Nehru University (JNU), New Delhi. He became a professor at the Centre in

1983 and taught there till his retirement in 2010. He obtained his Bachelor of Philosophy and his Doctor of Philosophy degrees from Oxford. His specialization is macroeconomics and political economy, areas in which he has written a number of books and articles. Some of his books include *Time, Inflation and Growth* (1988), *Economics and Egalitarianism* (1990), *Whatever Happened to Imperialism and Other Essays* (1995), *Accumulation and Stability Under Capitalism* (1997), *The Retreat to Unfreedom* (2003), *The Value of Money* (2008), and *Re-envisioning Socialism* (2011). He is the editor of the journal *Social Scientist*.

Robert Pollin is a distinguished university professor of economics and co-director of the Political Economy Research Institute (PERI) at the University of Massachusetts Amherst. His books include *The Living Wage: Building a Fair Economy*; *Contours of Descent: U.S. Economic Fractures and the Landscape of Global Austerity*; and *Back to Full Employment*, as well as *Green Growth* (2014), *Global Green Growth* (2015), and *Greening the Global Economy* (2015). He has worked as a consultant for the U.S. Department of Energy, the International Labour Organization, the United Nations Industrial Development Organization, and numerous non-governmental organizations in several countries and US states and municipalities on various aspects of building high-employment green economies. He was selected by *Foreign Policy* magazine as one of the "100 Leading Global Thinkers for 2013."

Smita Ramnarain's research interests lie at the intersection of political economy, development, and feminist economics. Her work has focused on the gendered political economy of development in the global South, particularly in South Asia. In her work, she examines the gendered impact of economic policies and programs in contexts of economic, social, political, or environmental upheaval (war, complex emergencies, climate change, and/or agrarian crisis) and the consequences of these changes on women's well-being. Her work has been published in diverse and interdisciplinary fora – such as *Development and Change, Feminist Economics, Gender Pace & Culture*, the *Community Development Journal*, and the *Forum for Social Economics* – and in edited volumes, including the *Handbook of Gender in Asia* and the *Handbook of Research Methods and Applications in Heterodox Economics*.

Smriti Rao is Department Chair, Economics, Finance and Accounting, Professor of Economics, and Global Studies Program Director at the Worcester Assumption College. Dr. Rao's teaching and research interests lie in the areas of development economics, gender and development, and feminist economics. Her research is particularly focused on understanding gendered patterns of labor and migration in India. Among many other publications, she has published, with Haroon Akram-Lodhi, 2021, a chapter on "Feminist Political Economy" in *The Routledge Handbook of Feminist Economics*, edited by Günseli Berik and Ebru Kongar. New York: Routledge.

Michael Roberts worked in the City of London as an economist for over 40 years. He has closely observed the machinations of global capitalism from within the dragon's den. At the same time, he was a political activist in the labor movement for decades. Since retiring, he has written several books, including *The Great Recession – A Marxist View* (2009); *The Long Depression* (2016); *Marx 200: A Review of Marx's Economics* (2018), and jointly with Guglielmo Carchedi as editor of *World in Crisis* (2018). He has published numerous papers in various academic economic journals and articles in leftist publications.

Paulo L. dos Santos is Associate Professor of Economics and Director of Undergraduate Studies and Departmental Faculty Advisor, Economics at the New School for Social Research. He is a mathematical political economist. His research engages with the social content of market outcomes and institutional structures in contemporary capitalism and includes work on economic and mathematical methodology, the use of concepts and tools from information theory in social inquiry, the measurement of inequality in economic outcomes, and on central themes in Classical political economy His research interests include the nature and content of contemporary financial systems and relations; "financial inclusion"; the functioning and problems of the present international monetary system; and the economic effects of systems of racial, ethnic, and gender subordination. He received his PhD in Economics from the University of London.

Geoffrey Schneider is Professor of Economics at Bucknell University. He is the Executive Director of ICAPE, the International Confederation of Associations for Pluralism in Economics. Professor Schneider recently published new editions of two textbooks, *Economics: A Tool for Critically Understanding Society* (with Jean Shackelford, Steve Stamos, and Tom Riddell), and *Introduction to Political Economy* (with Charles Sackrey and Janet Knoedler). His current research projects include papers on comparative institutional advantage and economic systems. He was recently selected as the recipient of the Class of 1956 Lectureship Award for Inspirational Teaching.

Farwa Sial is a Research Associate with the Department of Economics at SOAS University of London, an Honorary Research Fellow at the Global Development Institute at the University of Manchester, and a steering group member of Diversifying and Decolonising Economics (D-econ). In addition to development finance, her research interests and publications also cover the evolution of capitalism in developing countries, specifically in relation to corporate transformations, the role of industrial policy, and changing technology. She holds a PhD in Development Studies from the School of Oriental and African Studies (SOAS).

Elaine Tontoh, PhD, is based at Austin Peay State University. She was previously at Belmont University Faculty Fellow in Economics, Nashville, Tennessee. In 2021, Dr. Tontoh won the Heterodox Economics with the Best Early Career Research Prize for her work on "Theorizing Motherhood within the Capabilities Approach and Social Reproduction Theory," and The New School for Social Research with the Edith Henry Johnson Memorial Award in Economics, Civil Affairs, and Education for dissertation, "The Triple Day Thesis: Three Theoretical Essays on The Capability Perspective and Economics of Motherhood." She holds BA and MPhil degrees in Economics from the University of Ghana, and MA, MPhil, and PhD degrees in Economics from the New School for Social Research.

Ramaa Vasudevan is a Professor of Economics at Colorado State University, which she joined in 2007. Her PhD in economics from New School University, New York, focused on the political economy of international trade and finance, while her MPhil at the Centre for Development Studies, Trivandrum, India, was a study about the evolution of labor markets in colonial India. Her main research interests are in international finance, open economy macroeconomics, and the political economy of development and finance. Her books and papers on finance include *Things fall Apart: From the Crash of 2008 to the Long Slump*, Sage: India, 2013 to many publications in *Review of Keynesian Economics, Metroeconomica, Journal of Post Keynesian Economics, Structural Change and Economic Dynamics*, 2014. (with Daniele Tavani), *Cambridge Journal of Economics, Review of Political Economy* and *International Review of Applied Economics*, among elsewhere.

PREFACE

The aim of this book is to introduce readers to radical political economics from a variety of diverse disciplines and perspectives. Radical political economics (RPE) reveals the structures and dynamics of global capitalism. Offering a robust critique of capitalist institutions as well as of mainstream economics, RPE is distinctly different from orthodox economic thought, which often obfuscates how capitalism actually works. The attention to method, ideology, and institutions differentiates RPE from mainstream approaches to economics. While maintaining a central focus on capitalism, the analyses in this book encompass a variety of issues from racial discrimination, gender inequality, as well as economic development and imperialism.

Capitalism is an economic system based on the exploitation of workers to generate surplus value (profit), which is then appropriated by the owners of capital. Under global capitalism, profit maximization precedes other social concerns such as the protection of the environment. Political economy understands that social relations are shaped by class, race, geography, and gender. Capitalism skews social relations of production and reproduction. It perpetuates inequalities along classed, gendered, racialized, and geographic lines. Radical political economy offers ideas and policies to change capitalism, in ways that are more beneficial for people and the planet.

This edited volume includes contributions by established and younger economists working in the RPE tradition. We also include essays by sociologists and legal scholars. Broadly interdisciplinary, the authors in this volume attend to history, philosophy, political science, anthropology, sociology, and law.

The organization of the book is to provide some key concepts in RPE in Part I, discuss some key RPE issues and debates in Part II, and elaborate on the future of capitalism in Part III. Part I is organized as follows. There is a central focus on the role of labor in the capitalist system, and how the dynamics of labor coalitions impact the operation of the capitalist economy. The first chapter offers a definition of class conflict, a key element of social change. Michael Hillard and Richard McIntyre offer a definition based on an awareness of class consciousness, rather than objective criteria for defining class, such as ownership of the means of production. They review case studies in US history, emphasizing the role of the state and ideology, as well as gender and race, in developing cohesive social movements. The second chapter by Ann Davis focuses on the role of ideology in the formation of class consciousness. Mainstream economics focuses on the idealization of the market as an efficient system, whereas radical political economics focuses on specific markets, like land, labor, and money, and examines the interactions between them as well as their role in driving economic fluctuations. The specific lens of the perfect market of mainstream economics obscures the inherent instability and inequality that radical political economics reveals. William Lazonick examines more closely the typical firm in the mainstream economic model, which is "perfectly competitive." As Lazonick shows in Chapter 3, such a model would have no profit and no innovation. A characterization of the "innovative firm" is necessary to understand the actual operation of the capitalist system. As the capitalist system has evolved, there have been different "social structures of accumulation," based on relationships among firms and workers. As David Kotz describes in Chapter 4, the capitalist system has operated differently in different periods, with more competition in the nineteenth century, a capital/labor accord in the twentieth century, and a turn to neoliberalism in the twenty-first century. In Chapter 5, Ramaa Vasudevan continues the discussion of neoliberalism to the financial sector. Differentiating between Post-Keynesian and Marxian approaches to financialization, she explains how they shed light on the distinctive features of contemporary financial globalization.

The operation of the capitalist system tends to disadvantage countries with a colonial legacy, as well as discriminate along gendered and racialized lines within the labor force. In Chapter 6, Smita Ramnarain discusses the unique role of the household in the reproduction of the labor force, and how special consideration of gender is required for a holistic analysis of capitalism. She also reviews debates within the field of "feminist radical political economy" and prospects for future alliance formation. In Chapter 7, Prabhat Patnaik describes the role of imperialism in capitalism and how the drive to colonize in various forms to secure cheap access to raw materials and reserve labor is necessary to capitalist growth and stability for the core.

Part II addresses some compelling issues, subject to debate and discussion, in radical political economics. The ordinary operation of the capitalist system reproduces inequality and instability, by race, gender, and geography. The resulting divisions lead to polarization as well as alliance formation. In Chapter 8, Michael Roberts assesses the causes of economic crises, within, before, and, more speculatively, even beyond capitalism. He considers whether there are irreconcilable contradictions within capitalism, between capitalism and nature, and within socialism. Inequality with respect to gender is the subject of two additional chapters. In Chapter 9, Elaine Tontoh argues that the existing system imposes a triple burden on women, at the workplace, in the household, and in restoring her own capabilities. The exhaustion of the triple day erodes the capacity of the household, the labor force, and the society. Global inequities are further explored in Chapter 10 where Barry Herman examines the issue of social protection. There are efforts by global institutions and NGOs to provide support for those unable to work, such as elderly, children, the injured, and disabled. So far, these efforts have been limited and uneven, although they are necessary for global stability and human well-being. In Chapter 11, Smriti Rao examines the patterns of cross-border migration and finds inequities across differentiated Global North and South divide. She theorizes migration as not only deleterious to human flourishing but also imbued with radical potentiality. In Chapter 12, Farwa Sial investigates how international development aid is a channel of capitalist internationalization. The question of whether aid facilitates development or invokes dependency on the wealthy North is examined.

The role of government is further explored in Chapter 13 by Ilias Alami. He inquires the changing nature of state interventionism in the shape of sovereign wealth funds, industrial policies, and state-owned enterprises. What do more assertive state capitalisms mean for transformations in global capitalism and progressive politics? In Chapter 14, Robert Pollin also explores the role of the government in helping to provide renewable energy alternatives, as well as green infrastructure. He argues that a global Green New Deal not only promotes planetary viability but also promotes economic growth as well as jobs in new industries. In Chapter 15, Paulo dos Santos rejects reductionist individualist approaches in favor of emergent approaches to understanding complex systems, which he argues, are better aligned with the historical materialism that undergirds radical political economy. Extending the analysis to statistical inference, he argues that innovations in information theory offer promising statistical approaches that are compatible with the social and systemic nature of radical political economy.

Part III considers future possibilities and various visions of alternatives to capitalism. In Chapter 16, Campbell notes that the definition of socialism has been shaped historically by the critique of capitalism. The goals of socialism would consist of human betterment rather than profit. A discussion of various definitions of "human nature" and flaws in actually existing socialist experiments provides a useful background for assessing the viability of this conception of an economic alternative. In Chapter 17, Erik Olsen reviews the experience of worker cooperatives. While this form of the firm is more resilient, productive, and equitable, their small scale not yet provided the sense of a realistic alternative. He reviews the literature to discern the shortcomings and the potential of worker cooperatives. The question of whether social democracy provides a meaningful alternative to capitalism is considered by Geoff Schneider. In Chapter 18, he reviews the structure of existing models, with large public sectors and regulated capitalism, along with the pressures for change. As a middle way, social democracy may be subject to pressures to resort to the alternatives of capitalism or socialism. What should economic development for the Global South entail? In Chapter 19, this question is considered by C.P. Chandrasekhar and Jayati Ghosh, within the limits of existing capitalism, in the context of climate change and the potential promise of new technologies and trade relations. Jason Moore and John P. Antonacci examine the "Capitalocene" and the ways in which capitalism engenders the exhaustion of earth's resources to produce cheap inputs for capitalist production in Chapter 20. As the planetary crisis leads to slower economic growth and instability, the need to envision new ecological relations between humans and the earth is essential.

While maintaining a coherent focus on capitalism as a complex system, subject to continuing and renewed challenges, Radical Political Economy addresses a wide range of current issues and debates. This broad understanding is essential in addressing the issues of the twenty-first century, including climate change, various forms of inequality, instability, and the possibilities of alternative economic systems.

ACKNOWLEDGMENT

Thanks to all the scholars included in these pages for their brilliant contributions. Ann and Mona would also like to thank Geoff Schneider for initiating a project on the URPE Steering Committee regarding the formulation of the principles of radical political economics.* We would also like to thank Andy Humphries, Publisher at Routledge, for inviting us to work with Routledge on this edited collection to extend the radical political economy principles project in a new direction. Many thanks to URPE for countless invaluable experiences for learning and collaboration over five-plus decades (in Ann's case). Ann would also like to thank her family for their constant support, encouragement, and willingness to critically discuss and provide challenging counterarguments for any idea at any time. She would also like to thank Mona for being a splendid collaborator and proficient co-editor. Mona thanks Ann for being a wonderful collaborator and interlocuter. She would also like to thank her research assistant Alex Ardieta.

* The members of that project were Al Campbell, Ann Davis, David Fields, Paddy Quick, Jared Ragusett, and Geoffrey Schneider. They presented their findings at several economic associations meetings and published their findings, in Campbell A., A. Davis, D. Fields, P. Quick, J. Ragusett, and G. Schneider (2019). "The Principles of Radical Political Economics", *American Review of Political Economy* 14(1). doi: https://doi.org/10.38024/arpe.212

PART I

Principles of Radical Political Economics

1

CLASS CONFLICT

Michael G. Hillard and Richard McIntyre

Introduction

Economists mostly ignore class and class conflict. Most economics departments do not include its study in their curriculum. And yet class relations and class conflict are clearly important for understanding the development of economic life.

Classes and class conflict exist. As Warren Buffet famously said in 2006, "There's class warfare, all right," Mr. Buffett said, "but it's my class, the rich class, that's making war, and we're winning" (Stein 2006). Smith, Ricardo, and Marx saw classes – workers, capitalists, and landowners – as the fundamental actors in the economy. Yet neoclassical economics, the kind that most economics students are familiar with, focuses on individuals in isolation. Neoclassical economics, first developed in the 1870s, replaced labor with utility, classes with individuals, and production and distribution with consumption, at a time when strikes and unions were on the rise.

Sociology students are more likely to study class conflict. Sociology embraces Marx as a major influence and includes much recent work on how class and class conflict work in contemporary societies (Wright 2015). When mentioned at all, economists tend to use "class" to designate people at different income levels but ignore what class and class conflict actually mean. Since the 2008 economic crisis, more attention has been paid to class and class conflict, influenced especially by French economist Thomas Piketty's book *Capital in the 21st Century*, itself stimulated by rising inequality and the one-sided class war evoked by Warren Buffet. Nonetheless, this work is largely statistical, ignoring theories of class analysis or class conflict (Piketty 2014).

DOI: 10.4324/9781003366690-2

We lay out a theoretical approach to class conflict and use that approach to interpret the development of the US economy since the Great Depression, omitting developments outside the United States in this short essay. Class conflict is taken for granted as a driver of social changes in most countries, but people in the United States are often uncomfortable talking about class, for many reasons – the "American Dream" of individual success, the Red Scares, and the Cold War, which made discussion of class appear to be "Un-American." Yet class and class conflict are on the agenda in the US today, and they have crucially shaped modern economic development.

Theories of Class and Class Conflict

Adam Smith, the founder of modern economics, saw profits as a distribution from the total product and not part of rent or wages, and as an outcome of production not of exchange. Smith famously saw the division of labor and the extension of the market as key to the wealth of a nation, but he also saw the division of labor as making workers stupid because of the repetition of tasks and as homogenizing skills and wages. Smith assumed the existence of three classes – laborers, masters, and landlords – and to some extent documented conflict between them. Marx, writing 75 years later during the early modern socialist movement, developed class analysis more explicitly.

The Neoclassical economists of the late 19th century evacuated class as an economic concept. Some were explicit in denying the salience of class. For Stanley Jevons, producer–consumer conflict was most important. Lionel Robbins claimed that classes are communities of interest, but that the working class is not one. Monopoly and access to resources are sources of conflict in neoclassical economics, but even in the labor market class is missing – only individuals maximizing their utility by supposedly choosing whether or not to work and if so, how many hours to offer. The landmark introductory textbook, Samuelson and Nordhaus's *Principles of Economics*, mentions class once, in a passing quote from the sociologist W.J. Wilson about the debate over the so-called "underclass" (Munoz de Bustillo and F. Rafael Estella Mura 2022).

Karl Marx is a major figure in Sociology, seen as one of the founders of the discipline alongside Emile Durkheim and Max Weber. In economics, Marx functions like a specter, someone whose insights hover around many discussions, but who is rarely analyzed in any serious way.

Marx used "class" in three different ways depending on his audience. In *The Communist Manifesto*, a popular pamphlet meant to unify different branches of the mid-19th-century socialist movement, he argued along with his co-author Friedrich Engels that the bourgeoisie, or capitalists, were a revolutionary class that had transformed the economy, culture, and the entire world. In doing so, however, they had produced their opponent, the proletariat, or working class, who were destined to overthrow the bourgeoisie. Marx and Engels argued that the complex class structure of 19th-century European societies was simplifying, leaving only the capitalist and working classes, whose interests were utterly opposed. While Marx's own later work emphasized a more complex notion of class, and subsequent research continues to find a variety of class relationships existing in virtually all societies, Marx and Engels' emphasis in the *Manifesto* on how classes emerge and are made by social events are similarly notable.

Marx's journalism used a loose, context-specific definition of social classes, including descriptions of not only capitalists and workers but also landlords, financiers, peasants, "petit" or small bourgeois, the professional middle classes, and the "dangerous" classes or lumpen proletariat. In his famous pamphlet on the 1851 French coup d'etat, "The 18th Brumaire of Louis Bonaparte," Marx intended to "demonstrate how the class struggle in France created circumstances and relationships that made it possible for" a mediocre dictator to emerge when the ruling classes were split among themselves (Marx 1852). This idea of the state as an important aspect, site, or object of class struggle will be emphasized below.

Marx also saw class as a relationship between groups of people in which economic surplus is produced and distributed. By surplus, he meant what is left over after the direct producers have been paid and machinery and raw materials have been replaced. In capitalism, this relationship is exploitive: those who receive the surplus, for example, the boards of director in large corporations, do no real work, and those who do work have no say in how the fruits of their labor are distributed. Marx and Engels, in *The Communist Manifesto* and elsewhere, argued that this exploitation would cause collective resistance, that is, class conflict, and eventually the overthrow of capitalism.

This was more a wish or a hope than a careful prediction. Still, class understood in this way, and the conflicts it involves, is a basic tool to understand how capitalism works. In the *Manifesto*, Marx and Engels discussed qualitative class struggle – a change from capitalism to socialism. However, in *Capital* and elsewhere, Marx discussed what is defined as quantitative class struggle, a change in the distribution of income and power within capitalism. Because revolution hasn't generally been on offer in the United States' particular history of class conflict, quantitative class conflict is this chapter's focus (1977). *Capital*, Volume 1, examined capitalists and workers, at least until the last part of the book, which tells the story of the historical emergence of capitalism. In Volumes II and III, he lays out a richer theory of class relationships including merchants, bankers, landlords, and managers, and how they compete for shares of the surplus (Marx 1978; 1981). This research adds the state and the "thinkers" (ideologists) of the capitalist class "who make the perfecting of the illusion of the capitalist class about itself their chief source of livelihood" (Tucker 1978). Following modern Marxian economists Stephen Resnick and Richard Wolff, we call these subsumed classes (with their receipt of a portion of this surplus value, or "SV," identified as "SC"). We use the following equations to express their positioning in the class structure (Resnick and Wolff 1987, 170-226):

$$SV = \text{Total output} - \left(\text{wages} + \text{depreciation} + \text{raw materials}\right)$$

$$SV = SC_{\text{investment}} + SC_{\text{supervision}} + SC_{\text{advertising}} + SC_{\text{R\&D}} + SC_{\text{lobbying}}$$
$$+ SC_{\text{free market propaganda}} + SC_{\text{taxes}} + SC_{\text{dividends}} + SC_{\text{other.}}$$

The twofold character of capitalist classes is identified by these equations. The first-class relationship is the creation of surplus value through the exploitation of the worker, where she/they get paid for only part of the working day but the fruits of the rest of the day are appropriated by the capitalist. The second-class relationship stems from the use of surplus value – that is, how, in order to secure and successfully reproduce capitalists' class position, they must distribute portions of the surplus to various groups: to managers for investment and workplace supervision, to merchants for advertising and distribution of products, etc. Of course, corporate boards may work together with some or all of these groups to increase the surplus through technology, speed up of work, globalization, union busting, lobbying or buying politicians, endowing professorships to teach the virtues of free markets, etc. The relationship between the active capitalist – the corporate board in most cases – and these various subsumed classes can be cooperative, but it is also competitive, and thus in conflict, as they each work to increase their share and power over others. Similarly, corporate boards and some subsumed classes may find it convenient to cooperate with some parts of the working class, say skilled workers, or with other classes such as small, owner-operated businesses, but they often find themselves in conflict with those groups as well.

Similarly, workers do not automatically act together as a class. Labor historians have emphasized that classes are made not born (Thompson 1963). Classes form as conscious social subjects at some times but not at others. Active capitalists, and their ideological allies in the media, academia, and elsewhere are generally able to achieve hegemony, a term developed by the Italian trade union leader Antonio Gramsci (Jones 2006). Capitalist hegemony occurs when their interests come to be understood as common sense and in the general interest of society; for example, the 20th century notion that the point of being a factory worker is to enable consumption, rather than to form unions to give workers better wages and conditions on the job. Or the more recent widespread embrace by white workers of the idea that state aid to workers lacking income is problematic because they believe that such aid goes almost entirely to black persons lacking a work ethic – rather than recognizing that a black–white worker alliance to demand more economic security for all workers would be in white workers' interest. To the extent that a working-class culture develops through unions, working-class media, and other institutions, workers may come together to articulate a counter-hegemony and come to see their interests as actively opposed to the capitalists. But workers are also split by gender, race, and other social fractures so that while workers wage class conflict at some-times, it is misleading to assume that workers possessing a counter-hegemonic class consciousness is the natural state of society.

At any time, class conflict is most likely to be between various class coali-tions. Class conflict takes many forms in contemporary capitalism, between workers and employers, between industrial, financial, and mercantile capital-ists, and between various class coalitions seeking state power. Using historical case studies, this chapter argues that explaining conflict over the terms of the economic relationship between workers and employers, and the role of the state in raising and lowering working-class economic and social security, is critical for understanding the development of US society over the last century. The relative prominence and power of the subsumed classes, especially industrial versus finance and merchants, also shapes class outcomes in important ways.

Class Conflict and the Development of the US Economy Since the Great Depression

The US capitalist class is exceptional – exceptionally powerful and exception-ally opposed to sharing power in the workplace, politics, or society. This is in contrast to typical European nations where powerful working-class movements and political parties forced employer classes into more collaborative relation-ships with workers and the state (McIntyre and Hillard 2013).

Prior to the 1930s, working-class movements often gained momentum only to face legal and military repression by an alliance of employers, courts, and state governments. A powerful working-class movement during the Great Depression galvanized unions and a state more sympathetic to workers during Franklin Roosevelt's "New Deal" presidency. Organized capital was able to limit the New Deal by the 1940s creating the "Little New Deal," which was gnawed away and then eviscerated by organized capitalists and their political allies by the 1980s. Since 1980, financial capitalists have emerged as a powerful group subordinating enterprise managers to the short-term profit targets pre-ferred by Wall Street. Merchant capitalists, such as Walmart, have also increased their power to subordinate small producers and small merchants around the world. Since the crisis of 2008, capitalists and their allies have lost some of their hegemony, and a new wave of class struggles has emerged.

The Great Depression and the New Deal Era

The 1929 economic downturn was precipitated by a multiyear, growing wave of bank failures in Europe and the United States, which saw the US banking system and international trade collapse. Continuing suffering and grassroots radicalism fueled a new, powerful class-conscious labor movement that produced long-lasting class improvements for a majority of American workers, when combined with crucial state interventions during the peak of President Roosevelt's New Deal. Dramatic "sit-down strikes" – factory occupations by workers – and several city-wide general strikes stimulated the "second" New Deal from 1934 to 1938. Union membership grew from 3 to 9 million (rising to 15 million by 1945) as millions of workers forced unionization elections upon recalcitrant employers, led by the new industrial unions of the Congress of Industrial Organizations (CIO) such as the United Auto Workers (UAW). Working class insurgency benefited from the way that big business had been discredited by the Depression and was fueled by Roosevelt's embrace of the labor movement. The result was a brief moment of US social democracy, marked by the passage of financial system regulation (Securities and Exchange and Glass–Steagall Acts), the Wagner Act that legalized union organizing and collective bargaining, a system of income support including unemployment insurance and old age social security, and the Fair Labor Standards Act that gave us the 40-hour work week and minimum wage.

This "Second New Deal" raised the customary standard of living for much of the US working class (with notable gaps, especially southern, largely black, workers) by supporting increases in wages and providing an enhanced social wage through unemployment compensation, social security, and jobs programs. Union contracts, new labor standards, and shop floor militancy combined to lower exploitation by limiting hours and restricting work speed up, the profit-generating nemesis of factory workers. The New Deal regulations that weakened and limited banks also sealed the power of industrial managers over finance, while weakening merchant capitalists by protecting small retailers at the expense of national chains.

The regional character of the New Deal shaped class outcomes in ways that resonate to this day (Katznelson 2013; McIntyre 2013). Congressmen and Senators elected by Northern Democrats came to represent the powerful industrial working-class movement; Northern Republicans represented anti-worker/New Deal capitalists; and overtly white supremacist Southern Democrats were the deciding force. For a time, Southerners allied with Northern Democrats as enthusiastic New Dealers, supporting public infrastructure programs and taking the lead in passing financial regulation against hated northern bankers.

Southerners shaped the mid-1930s' passage of major labor laws to ensure that Black workers were excluded by leaving agricultural and domestic employees uncovered.

When it became apparent that the CIO was successfully organizing southern Black industrial workers, Southern support for the New Deal faded. Southern congressional leaders weakened the 1938 Fair Labor Standards Act so that minimum wage laws effectively didn't apply to southern workers. Industrial employers targeted the new National Labor Relations Board (NLRB), successfully removing its more radical members. In 1938, Democrats lost their Congressional super-majorities while Southern Democrats swung against the New Deal, allying themselves with Republicans on policies affecting class (and race) relations. World War II rehabilitated capitalists' public image as they became central to the war effort, while union leaders limited wartime strikes at the behest of the state and saw their ranks filled with new, culturally conservative workers.

World War II's end saw several reversals for the labor movement. Unions argued for maintaining wartime economic planning favorable to working-class interests but lost this argument. General Motors defeated a radical UAW strike that would have given union leaders some corporate decision-making power. Republicans briefly regained Congressional majorities in 1947, allying with southern Congressional Democrats to pass the anti-labor Taft–Hartley Act. Taft–Hartley restricted union activities, forced Communist unions out of the AFL–CIO, and gave states the right to limit union dues paying requirements, which most Southern states quickly did. In 1951, the Federal Reserve was altered to make possible macroeconomic policies that would engender high unemployment.

Worker victories over capitalists in the mid-1930s changed American capitalism in important ways. However, industrial capital fought back from 1938 on, with increasing success, to roll back the New Deal; by 1948 they had largely succeeded. What was left, the "Little New Deal," certainly was an improvement over pre-1929 conditions, but it hardly matched European social democracies.

The Fool's Golden Age

Radical economists long considered the remainder or the "new Deal Era" (through the 1970s) a "Golden Age" because average working-class living standards doubled between World War II and 1970; union coverage reached historic highs. Together, US global economic domination (which spurred domestic industrial prosperity), Keynesian macroeconomic policy, and progressive taxation narrowed income inequality and kept unemployment low. A large part of the US working class saw its share of the economic pie increase, while law and union contracts reduced working hours and gave many workers a measure of control over the pace of production in combination with an expanding social wage.

But calling this a "Golden Age" is problematic in two ways:

• Black workers and women were largely excluded from the protections and benefits of labor laws and the social wage, including social security, unemployment insurance, unionization, and minimum wage protection (Huret and Vinel 2019).

- Industrial capital used its control over profits to build a counter movement against labor and the New Deal era system of regulation. Capitalist class formation created the foundations for the eventual successful class warfare against workers, anticipating Warren Buffett's later proclamation. With a steady focus on building a counter ideology to the New Deal, capital waged a long ideological and political war against working-class power (McIntyre and Hillard 2013; Phillips-Fein 2009).

Postwar, Northern and "Sunbelt" (southwestern/west coast) industrial capital and southern elites coalesced around an attack on liberalism. Rich, right-wing capitalists' long-term strategy began financing an ideological movement to discredit unions and the New Deal system. By the 1970s, they had built the political power necessary to destroy it.

Targeting New Deal thought and politics – the economic consensus for moderate government intervention in labor and macroeconomic policy, and acceptance of unions – was the first order of business. Capitalists funded a new network of right-wing economic institutes, popular ideologues, and political operatives, who generated a counterpoint ideology under the moniker of "free enterprise." The tenets of free enterprise were:

- The US was formed on the basis of individual liberty.
- Laissez-faire capitalism is the only economic system that delivers both liberty and a "good society."
- Labor unions created new elites that took away individual liberty and promised results that could not be sustainably realized without destroying the fabric of society; they were outside "third parties" that stole from employees, provided no tangible improvement to workers, and sparked gratuitous violent conflict, with workers supposedly caught in the middle.
- The welfare and regulatory state, and unions, threatened the core of American values and way of life.
- Liberalism was a greater existential threat to the United States than communism.

In fact, the New Deal state and the labor movement ended the Great Depression, won World War II, and created a stable, equitable postwar economy. But plucking on the heartstrings of resilient Social Darwinism and upper-class fears, this well-funded ideological drive was rooted in growing segments of the populace from the 1950s to the 1970s. Capital began first by waging an indirect ideological "war of position" to prepare the conditions for the overt class warfare, or "war of maneuver," it would conduct in the 1980s (Jones 2006).

The National Association of Manufacturers (NAM) led the way. NAM became a more focused and mobilized organization promoting the Taft–Hartley Act. It successfully challenged the NLRB, curbing the labor board's powers to protect workers' organizing rights. Its members funded right-wing think tanks and used their control of the workplace to indoctrinate workers.

Key were the new "thought factories" – the Mont Pelerin Society, the American Enterprise Institute, and the Foundation for Economic Education – that leveraged the popular work of Friedrich Von Hayek and other right-wing intellectuals. To Hayek, New Deal liberalism put the United States on the "road" to Soviet communism. Unions and Social Security were totalitarian. This ideology was popularized through national radio programs, the new National Review, and John Birch Society publications. They attacked unions as communist led, dominated by "corrupt union bosses." Daily columnist Westbrook Pegler led the charge in newspapers read by tens of millions, while the 1957 McCarran hearings made Jimmy Hoffa the face of labor corruption. Right wingers funded "right to work" referenda that weakened unions at the state level.

Powered by Sunbelt and Deep South politicians, the war of position gained a new political currency with Arizona Senator Goldwater's 1964 presidential candidacy. Goldwater was a powerful free enterprise advocate. Free enterprise conservativism gained momentum in the late 1960s cultural wars, with Richard Nixon's 1968 "southern strategy" capitalizing on white race fear and white working-class antipathy to antiwar and feminist movements. As free enterprise capitalists became more linked to popular conservative politics, their longer ideological war of position virtually ensured that, over the long run, an emerging 1970s' "values-based" social and religious conservatism would take free enterprise tenets as articles of faith.

Capitalist mobilization accelerated with the formation of Business Roundtable in 1972 – a new association of corporate giants – and the US Chamber of Commerce's dramatic quadrupling in membership to 250,000. Both entities heightened business mobilization on behalf of free enterprise politics. High inflation and unemployment discredited New Deal economic policies, and, fueled by falling profits, helped businesses build a powerful anti-New Deal political alliance, as white middle- and working-class voters broke ranks with the Democratic Party over race, the Vietnam War, gun rights, and abortion. Business poured vast sums into political action committees. With a new, cross-class conservative coalition, Capital's war of position galvanized the winning electoral coalition politics behind "neoliberalism," the idea that an economy based on self-interested behavior, free markets, and limited government would produce a good society. The Carter presidency (1977–1981) initiated the attack on labor by deregulating transportation, a move that decimated airline and trucking unions. Ronald Reagan's 1980 election ushered in a fuller onslaught against the Little New Deal, a war of maneuver that reversed labor's prior gains.

The Age of Capitalist Euphoria

President Reagan enacted significant parts of the free enterprise agenda, ostentatiously busting a large union of federally employed air traffic controllers, cutting taxes on the rich, neutering a host of labor and environmental regulations, and cutting the social wage for the poor and the unemployed.

Class warfare against workers accelerated in the 1980s, permanently lowering wages and benefits, granting greater capitalist control to reshape the workplace, and truncating the social wage. A higher rate of exploitation increased the portion of the social product that took the form of profits, interest, and rents; real wages stagnated. This was accomplished through the attack on unions and job "restructuring," replacing well-paid with lower paid, insecure jobs.

The attack began as Reagan and leading capitalist employers weakened or eradicated existing unions. Similar efforts ensured that new industries – primarily the service sector and retail industries that defined all net employment growth in the post-1980 era – remained union free. Reagan stacked the NLRB with union-busting consultants, minimized what little protection the labor board previously offered organizing workers, and destroyed the 11,000 member Professional Air Traffic Controllers' Union (PATCO), permanently firing its members when they struck. This ended the New Deal norm that unions were legitimate institutions. After a rush of failed defensive strikes in the early 1980s, striking became rare because it was an existential risk (Greenhouse 2019). Unionized employers embraced a "concessions movement." Aided by high unemployment due to recession, deregulation, and import competition, big companies successfully attacked unions. They either forced unions to accept lower wages and benefits and fewer workplace restrictions or destroyed their workers' unions outright.

As a result, union representation for private sector workers went into a tailspin. In 1979, private sector union density – the proportion of nongovernmental workers who belonged to unions – was still over 21 percent. Density fell by half by 1995 to 10.3 percent and is a mere 6 percent today (Michel et al. 2020). Large nonunion firms also cut wages, jobs, and benefits. As a result, employers freely squeezed workers' wages and benefits, and enforced speed up, generating higher profits.

Union busting prevented workers from organizing in growing sectors. Unions were concentrated in domestic "mature industries" like manufacturing, mining, and transportation where employment was contracting. From 1979 to 2009, manufacturing employment fell from 19 million to 11.6 million. while service employment grew from 63 million to 126 million (Harris 2020). The only way union coverage could maintain or even grow was if workers in new growth industries could unionize (Freeman and Medoff 1984); the perfection of union busting in an era with weakened organizing protections ensured that almost none of these new jobs would ever unionize, despite repeated efforts to do so (Ferguson 2008). Two key entities about to explode in employment growth – Walmart and the fast-food industry – pioneered draconian union busting, leaving them free to pay wages at or just above the minimum wage, whose value was constantly eroded by inflation. Benefits once taken for granted – vacations, health insurance coverage, and pensions – disappeared, leaving dead-end jobs for tens of millions. AFL-CIO efforts to restore organizing protections met overwhelming, successful business opposition, going down to defeats in 1978, 1994, and 2009. Thus, for every ten union members lost, unions gained only one in return (Greenhouse 2019).

As the proportion of the working class composed of women and people of color grew dramatically, workers were now locked into a more exploited standard of living, reproducing the longstanding effects of structural racism and patriarchy (Draut 2018).

The dominance of the industrial manager subsumed class peaked during the New Deal Era. A new finance capital revved up post-1970, powered by the rise of retirement and mutual funds, the new ideology of shareholder "primacy," and financial deregulation. Wall Street financial capital became a powerful force, equipped with tools that it applied to undermine managerial independence, restructuring capitalist enterprises to serve new dictates (Lazonick and Shin 2020). After 1980, financial capital deposed the older managerial group and prevented the subsumed class distributions it long favored. By gaining control over top management, financiers turned industrial enterprises into short-term extraction machines that heightened distributions of surplus to asset funds. Merchant capital, following Walmart's template, used new supply chain power to push US-based production to low-wage countries with demands to relocate factories to East Asia, enforced by a willingness to put recalcitrant firms out of business altogether (Lichtenstein 2009; McIntyre and Hillard 2022).

Newly powerful financial and merchant classes implemented a fundamental restructuring of capitalism that targeted well-paid, secure employment. Merchant capital, as noted, led the way in two areas – accelerating the loss of unionized factory jobs through globalization, and by being the leader of the new low road service-sector employment. Financial capital used its new power to insist that corporate CEOs dismantle well-paid employment and, in turn, "fissure." Fissuring meant radical outsourcing, both domestically and globally, systematically replacing well-paid, directly employed workers with low-wage workers in subcontracted firms (McIntyre and Hillard 2022; Weil 2014).

Neoliberal ideology provided the cover for a successful, continuous class warfare by capital against the working class, presented as enhancing freedom by new right-wing media, ideologists in business schools, and economics departments. The victory of merchant and financial subsumed classes over industrial managers proved to be a critical force in the restructuring of the primary class relationship between worker and boss. The other side of heightened worker exploitation has been prolific profit-making and the explosion of financial wealth, found in the astronomical growth of CEO salaries and the disgorging of trillions of dollars through private equity maneuvers, stock buybacks, and huge dividends.

By the 2000s, an increasingly exhausted and indebted working class faced a recomposed capitalist class that had never had it so good. Capitalists were awash in the increasing revenues appropriated from workers whose productivity had risen over the past three decades but whose wages had not. Part of this astounding increase in the economic surplus was lent back – to be paid back with interest – to workers who continued to pursue the American dream of higher living standards but without the increasing wages that had been part of that dream since the 19th century.

Typical of capitalism's history, financial capitalists "forgot" that production must occur somewhere between the laying out of capital and the realization of profits. Merchant capitalists "forgot" that wages must be high enough so that what is produced can be bought. This all came to a crashing halt in 2008 when the US financial markets froze, precipitating a global capitalist crisis (Wolff 2010).

Staving off a depression required the state to "bail out" capitalism through massive Federal Reserve purchases of financial assets, fiscal stimulus, and direct aid to particular capitalist enterprises such as General Motors. Whereas neoliberalism had taught that the state was the problem, it now became the only possible solution. Central bank action protecting banks and investors happened in the United States, Europe, and elsewhere (Tooze 2018). Fiscal stimulus and Fed bond purchases continued right up to the moment of the COVID-19 pandemic when they became even larger.

The transparency of this state action fragmented politics. Graffiti with some version of "where's my f*cking bailout" appeared across cities and towns in the United States and elsewhere. Right-wing groups, reacting already to the election of a Black President and his moderate efforts to expand health care, responded to the bank bailouts with rage. This rage fused with traditional conservatism and heightened animosity to immigrants, providing fertile ground for Trump's racist populism. Left-wing groups supported the Occupy movement in 2011, whose goal was to attack banks' control of Congress, and this coalesced in the Sanders Presidential campaigns of 2016 and 2020, and the rise of Democratic Socialists of America.

Left and right rejected Walmart-style globalization. Free trade Democrats and Republicans alike had ceded remaining well-paid employment to China. When Trump was elected, one of his first acts was to table the so-called Trade Partnership of the Pacific, a trade and investment liberalization pact that had been pushed hard by merchant, financial, and some industrial capitalists.

The COVID pandemic exacerbated these trends. The scale of the bailout of financial institutions in 2020 was truly astounding (Brenner 2020). Unlike 2008, there was significant aid to families and individuals as well. This created the hope among some that a European-style social welfare state might be the silver lining of a pandemic that was so much worse than it had to be, not only because of Presidential mismanagement but also because decades of austerity left the United States without the public health infrastructure it needed.

Capital seems to have lost its control of the narrative about the US economy. This has contributed, in part, to a wave of strikes since 2019, especially in services, warehouses, health care, and education. A new round of uneven and as yet incomplete working-class formation is taking place. At the same time, Capital is increasingly split between financial interests who recognize climate change and radicalization of youth as existential threats, and natural resources–based and proprietary (individual owner/operators) capitalists who do not (McIntyre and Hillard 2022).

The state of class relations is in flux. The struggle between class coalitions in the workplace, in the realm of ideas, and over state power, will continue to drive changes in US society. An empowered, class-conscious working class is an essential tool for an improvement in the quantitative terms of the worker–employer class relationship and working-class life, as the Little New Deal showed. Unchecked capitalist class power has done the reverse.

A new moment of consequential working-class power may just be in the offing, thanks to a resurgence of union popularity, widespread rejection of neoliberalism, revulsion against the debasement of working-class life, and popular animosity toward finance and merchant capital. The authors hope that growing connections between working-*class* activism and climate change, racial and gender justice movements coalesce to wage class struggle that effectively pushes back against 40 years of capitalist class warfare.

References

Brenner, Robert R., Escalating Plunder, *New Left Review*. v. 123, 2020. https://newleftreview.org/issues/ii123/articles/robert-brenner-escalating-plunder

Draut, Tamara, Understanding the Working Class. *Demos*, 2018. https://www.demos.org/research/understanding-working-class

Ferguson, John Paul, The Eye of the Needle: A Sequential Model of Union Organizing, 1999–2004. *Industrial and Labor Relations Review*. v. 62 (1). 3–21, 2008.

Freeman, Richard and James Medoff, *What Do Unions Do?* New York: Basic Books, 1984.

Greenhouse, Steven, *Beaten* Down, *Worked Up*. New York: Alfred A. Knopf, 2019.

Harris, Katelyn, Forty Years of Falling Manufacturing Employment. *Beyond the Numbers: Bureau of Labor Statistics*. v. 9 (16), 2020. https://www.bls.gov/opub/btn/volume-9/forty-years-of-falling-manufacturing-employment.htm

Huret, Romain and Jean-Christian Vinel, From the Labor Question to the Piketty Moment: A Journey Through the New Deal Order. *Beyond the New Deal Order: U.S. Politics from the Great Depression to the Great Recession*. Edited by Gary Gerstle, Nelson Lichtenstein, and Alice O'Connor. Philadelphia: University of Philadelphia Press, 2019. 17–35.

Jones, Steven, *Antonio Gramsci*. New York: Routledge, 2006.

Katznelson, Ira, *Fear Itself*. New York: W.W. Norton, 2013.

Lazonick, William and Jang–Sup Shin, *Predatory Value Extraction*. New York: Oxford University Press, 2020.

Lichtenstein, Nelson, *The Retail Revolution: How Wal–Mart Created a Brave New World of Business*. New York: Henry Holt, 2009.

Marx, Karl, *The 18th Brumaire of Louis Bonaparte*. 1852. https://www.marxists.org/archive/marx/works/1852/18th-brumaire/preface.htm

Marx, Karl, *Capital*, Volume I. New York: Vintage, 1977.

Marx, Karl, *Capital*, Volume II and Volume III. New York: Penguin, 1978 & 1981.

McIntyre and Hillard, Stakeholderism: The Folly of a Kinder and Gentler Capitalism. *New Labor Forum*, 2022.

McIntyre, Richard, Radical Labor and the New Deal: Lessons for Today. *When Government Helped: Learning from the Successes and Failures of the New Deal*. Edited by S. Collins and G.S. Goldberg. New York: Oxford, 2013.

McIntyre, Richard and Michael Hillard, Capitalist Class Agency and the New Deal Order: Against the Notion of a Limited Capital-Labor Accord. *Review of Radical Political Economics*. v. 45 (2), 2013. 129–148.

Michel, Lawrence, Lawrence, Lynn Rhinehart, and Lane Windham, Explaining the Erosion of Private Sector Unions, *Economic Policy Institute*, 2020. https://www.epi.org/unequalpower/publications/private-sector-unions-corporate-legal-erosion/

Munoz de Bustillo, L. and F. Rafael Estella Mura, Social classes in economic analysis. A brief historical account, JRC Working Paper Series on Social Classes in the Digital Age. 2022. https://ideas.repec.org/p/ipt/dclass/202202.html

Phillips-Fein, Kim, *Invisible Hands*. New York: W.W. Norton, 2009.

Piketty, Thomas, *Capital in the 21st Century*. Cambridge: Harvard University Press, 2014.

Resnick, Stephen A. and Richard Wolff, *Knowledge and Class*. Chicago: University of Chicago Press, 1987.

Stein, Ben, *In Class Warfare, Guess Which Class is Winning*. New York Times, 2006.

Thompson, E. P., *The Making of the English Working Class*. London: Vintage, 1963.

Tooze, Adam, *Crashed*. New York: Viking, 2018.

Tucker, Frederick, *The Marx-Engels Reader*, 2nd Edition. New York: W.W. Norton, 1978.

Weil, David, *The Fissured Workplace*. Cambridge: Harvard University Press, 2014.

Wolff, Richard, *Capitalism Hits the Fan*. Northampton, MA: Olive Branch Press, 2010.

Wright, Erik Olin, *Understanding Class*. London: Verso, 2015.

2

IDEOLOGY AND RADICAL POLITICAL ECONOMY

Ann E. Davis

Ideology and Property

In an era of rapid social change, ideas are often in flux (Durkheim 1965; Gramsci 1971; Marx 1978a, 1978b; Davis 2018). There are competing narratives and notions of truth. There is some doubt as to who to believe, and who is the reliable authority. What had been conventional wisdom in one period can become "fake news" in the next. To understand periods like this, this chapter will turn to examples in history of the shifting sources of knowledge and authority, to provide clarification, and to highlight the possibility and urgency of critique and debate, and the formulation of new visions.

One of the long-standing shibboleths, foundations of ancient wisdom that seem to be unassailable, is the notion of property. The common notion is that property is a concrete object, owned by a person. Yet the history of property reveals considerable flux (Banner 2011). So, a layperson can inquire, "How can a concrete object change? How can there be a history of property?" The answer proposed in this chapter is that property is a relation among people, prescribed in law, enforced by the court and the police. That is, the object of interest is protected against trespassing and theft from other people. The owner has a right to exclude non-owners, which sets up a relationship among people. Because property is a social relation documented in language, the "thing" to which it refers can change, whether ideas, land, or financial assets (Poovey 2002; Searle 2010), whether tangible or intangible. What matters in a particular context is the specific law (Pistor 2020), its interpretation and enforcement. Even lawyers can change their minds, in different periods of history, as to which interpretation is correct (Gordon 2017).

DOI: 10.4324/9781003366690-3

Property has served as the foundation of modern industrial societies, with strong constitutional protection, despite its flux in meanings over time. There are well-accepted narratives that explain how property is moral and just, which helps legitimate its use. In a topic as important as property, nonetheless, there have been considerable variations in interpretation. For example, some consider property as synonymous with "freedom." Especially since the French Revolution (Piketty 2020), the fact that a person has property, which she can dispose of as she chooses, is considered the foundation of the freedom for the owner. After World War II, the liberal state based on individual private property became the dominant form, after the defeat of hereditary monarchies and the unraveling of empires. The idea of property was further developed in the post-World War II US as part of the Cold War defense against Communism and Fascism (Arcenas 2022). Economists such as Milton Friedman, who wrote *Capitalism and Freedom*, which was popular in the 1960s, declared that individual private property motivated effort to increase the monetary value of the property, which created wealth in society (Friedman 1962). As a consequence of such property incentives, the whole economy becomes more prosperous. A counterargument offered by C. B. MacPherson pointed out that workers without property must find a job to make a living; this necessity to work for someone else was a form of coercion (Pateman 1988).

As soon as property is associated with the motive for gain and income, class divisions emerge. For example, the owner of financial assets can gain income from interest payments from the borrower. On the other hand, the worker who owns only property in himself must put his body at the direction of his employer during the working day, to keep his job. As a result, the worker must relinquish control over his body and often his mind, at least while at work. These divisions by class are considered expedient by some and necessary for the expansion of total wealth. For others, alternative forms of decision-making, more inclusive and democratic, are important to consider (Bowles and Gintis 1986), even in the workplace.

Ironically, both the advocates and critics of property agree on one key point: the centrality of property. Advocates see property as the foundation of the "free" market economy. Critics see property as the beginning of exclusions and exploitation. For advocates, property must be enshrined in the Constitution, protecting property owners from theft as well as from government expropriation and taxes. For property critics, property "rights" create a monopoly of the means of production (Proudhon 1840), excluding workers from the means of life, forcing participation in the wage labor force, with only contingent exceptions for welfare and unemployment. One key source of disagreement is whether property exists in the "state of nature," according to natural laws that are consonant with God's order, or whether property requires the action of government (Davis 2015). That is, is property eternal or is it the result of the conscious collective action of humans?

When reviewing these debates over the course of several centuries, "ideologies" and their workings can be explored. That is, ideology is the presentation of key terms in an idealized fashion, to gain adherents. In the case of "property," for example, the debates and critiques of both sides are not widely shared, and the inequalities and instabilities are not examined. Or any failures are attributed to not protecting property *enough*, rather than changing definitions and operations of property. But property is not just an ordinary term. According to Piketty (2020), property is "sacralized," and Polanyi mentions the "liberal creed," which amounts to a faith in the free market based on property (Polanyi 1944). Other economists mention "beliefs" which solidify the importance of these ideas. By contrast, the methodology associated with Radical Political Economy would examine the long-term history of a given concept, like property, how it is used, by whom, how it has changed and why, and how it has been operationalized in institutions historically. Such a long-term examination would clarify the debates and downsides, as well as advantages and interests. Such an exploration of the background would make critique possible, as well as formulation of alternatives.

The Foundation of Economics in Property and Money

While the twenty-first century has seemed particularly fraught with partisan diatribes and accusations of falsehoods, there are historic precedents. One reason for the sense of unmooring is the condition of "modernity," when religion and traditional authorities like the aristocracy were overturned. Instead of religious authority, moderns tend to place their faith in science and truth. Yet at the same time, people rely on human constructions like "property" and the "market," while not really understanding their historical evolution and development. One source of presumed authority is the economics profession, which is well established in universities and peer-reviewed publications. Yet there is another side of mainstream economics, which radical political economics (RPE) articulates.

A key foundational concept in mainstream free market economics is individual private property. Typical property "rights" include the right to exclude others, such as trespass laws. Such property rights also include the right to sell, to extract valuable minerals and water, to use exclusively (Ostrom 1990). The earth, when considered parcels of property, allows the owner to use property to increase its market value. Increasing the value of one's own property, whether land, labor, or money, is considered the dominant motive "for gain" (Polanyi 1944; Levy 2021) in market or capitalist economies. The goal is to increase the "wealth of nations" (Smith 1994). When owners obtain and use property solely for their own gain, nonetheless, there are often certain "fallouts" (Searle 2010), or "contradictions" (Harvey 2018).

The moral dimension of property was articulated by John Locke, a seventeenth-century English philosopher (Richardson 2020). Locke's narrative allows a person to gain control over a portion of the commons of the earth, for his own sustenance from his own labor. This parcel can be used to provide for his own needs, as his own property. This use of the earth is endorsed by God, in Locke's view, as necessary for the survival of humans, who are made in his image (Arcenas 2022). In Locke's narrative, the earth can become an individual's own private property, and the product of his own labor, the fruits of his efforts belong to him exclusively. Adam Smith, writing in 1776, also endorsed the idea that property is based on the labor of each person. Compared with feudalism, this is a form of "freedom." Each person owns his own labor and its products. But this person's self-ownership can become a burden when there is no access to land or the means of production. This absence of resources then propels the person to sell his own labor in the labor market to an employer.

Money is a type of property issued by the state, especially after the seventeenth-century "financial revolution" in England and the banking system established in the US to finance the Civil War (Lowenstein 2022). For example, bankers are considered owners of the money that they lend and can claim a rate of return, called interest, as a result. Even though the money was often paper instead of precious metal coins, printed with official imprints, the value of the money was managed by the state. The state-directed financial system would loan money to entrepreneurs who could make more money, and then share the revenue with the state as taxes. This "fiscal military" state could then use the revenues to wage wars against rival nations, increase territory, and provide for military fortifications and weapons. By raising revenue by taxes, the state was able to increase its tools for coercion, if necessary. The state could also issue bonds, or promises to pay in the future, based on expected increases in future tax revenue. This integrated system of property and money then allowed certain "individuals" to increase their wealth, by trading bonds on financial markets.

The notion of the "public" became important, as a source of the authority for taxation. The famous US Revolutionary War phrase, "no taxation without representation," was based on British precedent. One aspect of taxes was the involvement of citizens in deciding how to finance the state expenditures (Knights 2005) and to attain independence from the "Haute Finance" (Polanyi 1944) of the merchant banking families like the Fuggers, Rothschilds, and Medici. The imposition of taxes was decided by Parliament, in the UK, by a representative government. The issue of who would pay, or tax incidence, and how expenditures would be allocated, became an intensely political issue (Thompson 2022). Property owners had representation in the state, as the primary source of wealth, and had to authorize the public budget (Habermas 1962). In contrast, the idea of taxing property owners was even more controversial in the US, where the income tax required a Constitutional Amendment. Property owners viewed themselves as sources of wealth, and victims instead of beneficiaries of the state, especially if property itself were considered a natural law. Workers were at first not eligible for the vote in the UK and the US, but then gradually suffrage was extended to all adult males, and ultimately females as well. Suffrage of immigrants and minorities is still contested, however, as well as disbursements to provide for welfare and unemployment. As a result, property owners were more likely to be enfranchised, and to decide how and what the state would finance, to increase their own wealth rather than aid workers and the poor.

Once money became well-accepted and had gained the confidence of the public in maintaining its value, the motive of gain became dominant. Corporations and landowners became adept at marketing, engaging in various forms of deception to increase the market price, and increase profit (the difference between sales price and the costs of production). The role of advertising and the sales effort is an increasing practice (Akerlof and Shiller 2015), which requires significant portions of corporate expenditure to compete with rivals. Governments may regulate advertising, but increasingly persuasive techniques have been developed to convince the consumer, and status is often acquired by increasing the accumulation of visible possessions. Mass media is largely supported by advertising revenue, with only a minor share supported by the government for the public interest.

Persuasion also operates on financial markets, where consumers can purchase stocks and bonds for future returns. Because the returns to stocks and bonds are in the future, there is uncertainty regarding eventual payment. Periodically, there is a form of "contagion," where the public piles into a specific asset, such as tulips in the Netherlands in the seventeenth century, believing that it will increase in value. That very belief can promote the price increase, at least for a time. Then the increase in price itself is self-fulfilling, providing evidence for others to also buy this particular asset. This phenomenon, called "bubbles," is a feature of "frothy" markets, where "exuberant expectations" are prevalent. The subsequent crash, once the bubble bursts, can be quite damaging to individual investors and to the economy (Ott 2011). Financial bubbles and crashes have been repeated since that time, with respect to housing in the 1920s, corporate stock in the 1930s, oil in the 1970s, Asian currencies in the late 1990s, housing in the 2000s, and crypto currencies in the 2020s.

The government has repeatedly regulated financial markets, while "financial innovation" has evaded these rules, such as "shadow banking" beginning in the late 1990s, financed with short-term "repurchase agreements" of US Treasury bonds. The cat-and-mouse game of regulation and evasion has persisted, with efforts to maintain financial stability globally. The integrity of the financial system requires government oversight, but such regulation is often considered as an interference with "property rights." That is, there is a "politics of property" (Davis 2015), where some believe that property is natural and just, while others observe that property is created and enforced by law and the government, with differential impact of owners vs. non-owners.

Property in Politics

In economics discourse, there is a common phrase, "property rights," which is presumably self-evident. But if property is really a non-human object in the world, like land, then it would not be capable of "rights." It is in fact the human owners of property who have the rights, and who make claims on the polity to respect those "rights," often in legal terms (Pistor 2020) and the platforms of political parties.

With further exploration, it is clearer why "property rights" are so foundational and yet so ambiguous. Property is an example of a concept that is presumably natural, objective, and beyond question, yet it is a social construction (Searle 2010), founded in language. That is, people have designed property to allow for an individual owner to claim the "bundle of rights" that are associated with property (Banner 2011). Property becomes "naturalized" to avoid addressing questions associated with the ownership relation, its operation, institutional foundations, and its political implications. That is, a social relation of property has become "reified" so that it is understood as an object (Davis 2015; 2020), with no possibilities of change.

Reification omits awareness of the notion of "collective intentionality" (Searle 2010), which explores the uniquely human capacity for designing one's own social arrangements. These human capacities reside in language and symbolic communication, by which ideas and insights are retained by means of documentation for use in later generations. That is, culture and knowledge accumulate and provide an ongoing resource for social design. These capacities became more explicitly articulated during the Enlightenment period, when the influence of religion was declining and human reason seemed an alternative source of authority through reflection, observation, and science. Theorists such as Locke, Rousseau, Hume, and Smith felt that human reasoning could discern natural laws for human progress. Ideas such as representation and consent of the governed were articulated during this period (Arcenas 2022). Searle argues that such arrangements must serve the interests of most people, or else change would take place. Although he does not specify the exact mechanisms that would assure serving the public interest, he does give Lenin credit for forming a vanguard party to articulate a new vision (Searle 2010), emphasizing the importance of politics.

A question that can now be asked is: Who is the agent behind property? Who acts to demand, to formulate, and to enforce those "rights"? A general answer is that foundational ideas like property motivate human actors to ally to protect a particular understanding and advocacy for a specific social arrangement. Often human actors form political parties, social movements, revolutions, or religious "awakenings," backed by philosophical or religious ideas, to challenge existing social arrangements and to promote new ones. A cursory review of history provides several examples. During the period of ancient Rome, there were slaves and landowners, with different political rights in the government. In early modern Italy, there were political parties such as the Guelfs vs. Ghibellines, who supported the Pope in Rome or the Holy Roman Emperor in Germany, both forms of religious affiliation that sought to gain control of territory. In seventeenth-century Britain, the Tories vs. Whigs were based on ownership of land vs. merchants (Richardson 2020; Acemoglu and Robinson 2012), who struggled over the formation of the Bank of England. In the early US, the Federalists vs. Anti-Federalists debated the merits of a centralized US Constitution, compared with the Confederacy just after the American Revolution. The Federalists, led by Alexander Hamilton, prevailed, with the stronger central state installed by the Constitutions of 1787. Subsequently, the Republicans vs. Democrats differed on the issue of legalized slavery, a form of property in humans that was outlawed after the Civil War. Political parties express, aggregate, and influence the ideas of their partisans. Protection of particular forms of property has been the central platform of political parties for millennia.

Concept of Property as a Method of Understanding Long-Term History

Ideas and social movements and related political parties, like those mentioned above, can be a method for understanding long-term social change. Widely respected philosophers have drawn upon the concept of property to understand the course of history, as well as social dynamics and class conflict.

For example, Hegel, a nineteenth-century German philosopher, thought that property was essential for personality. He also endorsed a form of the state which empowered property owners. Karl Marx, drawing upon Hegel's work, saw history as driven by conflict between owners of the means of production and workers. For Marx, workers understood history better from their point of view of "proletarians," or non-owners, and could lead a Communist Revolution to share property more widely (Lukacs 1971). Even before Marx, socialists like Robert Owen and Pierre-Joseph Proudhon used ideas of shared property to establish utopian communities and social movements.

For believers in the "free market," like Hayek and Milton Friedman, owners of property were rational in devising methods for increasing the monetary value of their property. This incentive to increase the value of property would increase the "wealth of nations," and improve the standard of living for everyone. Those who contributed most would receive the greatest reward, according to those who see the unfettered market as the best form of distribution of income among owners and workers (Soll 2022). The idealization of the operation of commodity markets was later extended to the financial market, especially after 1980. As a result, investors in any given country were allowed to invest in all other countries, according to the profit motive. In fact, open world trade and investment have led to increasing inequality and loss of democracy.

Ideas of property have been used to justify imperialism, as well. The advanced industrial countries presumably had a more modern concept of property, individual instead of shared (Acemoglu and Robinson 2012). As a result of European competition for colonies, large swaths of the world have experienced domination by another country. This legacy of imperialism has affected the forms of government, as well as national revolutions and decolonization, especially after the 1960s. As a successor to Great Britain, the US became the dominant world power after 1945, promoting free market ideas and supporting governments that would agree to that worldview.

According to Marx, workers would wage a successful revolution to gain control of the state. The revolutionary period in Europe in 1848 seemed to verify his prediction. The consolidated control of the European nations, such as the "Concert of Europe," suppressed the workers' revolution. After the French Revolution and the defeat of Napoleon, there was a concerted backlash against these revolutionary movements. It was only after World War II that the liberal nation-state became the model, allowing for universal suffrage as well as constitutional protection for property, with a "separation of powers" (Polanyi 1944). The leading industrial nations still have this form of government, which is commonly called "democracy."

After the Great Depression of the 1930s, and a wave of labor organization, the New Deal provided social insurance and the rights to organize labor (Ferguson 1989). These advances for labor were progressively undercut, nonetheless, by the "Red Scare" and organizations on the right for defense of property. After the Reagan/Thatcher revolution of the 1980s, free market ideas have gained increasing political influence, based on the ideas of Hayek. Investing in foreign countries was used as a threat to gain compliance from unions. The share of the labor force which is represented by unions has declined since the New Deal, and the share of labor in total income has also declined. Supporters of property rights have increased the "freedom of speech" for corporations and allowed private organizations more flexibility for campaign finance.

After the formation of the Union for Soviet Socialist Republics in 1917, and the Chinese Communist Revolution in 1949, the free-market countries increased military pressure against these alternative economic forms. After World War II, the emergence of the "Cold War" sought to isolate the communist countries and to restrict trade and investment with them. The US sought to lead Europe and other countries to oppose Communism and to defend "property rights." In addition to military repression, the capitalist economy developed ways to avoid reliance on workers, such as automation and outsourcing to countries with less support for human rights and rights to organize. The information technology industry has developed "artificial intelligence" and methods of surveillance that reduce individual autonomy and political empowerment.

Property rights gave owners and corporations the right to organize production and to replace labor with machines, regardless of the impact on workers.

Substitution for human labor by means of hydroelectric power and fossil fuels enabled rapid growth of the industrial economy, although increasingly dependent on imports. The reliance on the Middle Eastern countries for petroleum enabled the formation of a petroleum-exporting cartel, OPEC. These countries, often united by Islam in contrast to Christianity, were able to successfully threaten the industrial economies in the 1970s, for their support of Israel. President Carter recommended the development of alternative fuels and conservation, but the presidencies of Reagan, George H.W. Bush, and George W. Bush sought free market policies and military intervention in the Middle East instead (Jacobs 2016), such as the invasion of Iraq in 2003. The reliance on fossil fuels remains even in the twenty-first century, allowing Vladimir Putin to threaten Europe with a cut-off of natural gas, in cooperation with OPEC, in the context of Russia's invasion of Ukraine in 2022. In this context, the post-Communist countries of Russia and China, along with the Middle East, have allied to oppose the dominance of Western Europe and the US, the advanced industrial countries.

Property and Consciousness

Some theorists believe that types of property influence ideas. Hegel, a German philosopher, postulated that a Geist, or an eternal global spirit, drives history. By contrast, Marx argued that the material conditions and ownership of the means of production generated associated ideas and alliances. Workers as non-owners would have greater insight into the operation of the system of exploitation, in his view. That is, the material "base" determined the political "superstructure." Such an analysis, which suggests that ideas are determined by material relations, provides an important role for property. Other theorists like Karl Polanyi give more credence to the influence of ideas, such as the "liberal creed," and to the role of reformers and citizens, not just workers. Free market proponents, as discussed above, give special importance to the rationality of property owners, with material incentives to make decisions which increase the monetary value of their property.

At stake is the role of the authority: Who should run the system? Who is empowered in market democracies? Who can be relied upon to provide the truth? For Radical Political Economists, the answer is found by observing the respective political positions and the empirical situations of workers and owners. Such factors as employment, wages, unionization, income distribution, and human development become relevant considerations. On the other hand, for those who believe in "free markets," the answer is that "the market will decide." This position removes all political considerations and human agency and provides an automatic answer which is presumably neutral and optimal. Rather than acknowledge that modern institutions are human creations, pro marketers will argue that property and markets are natural and "there is no alternative." That is, Radical Political Economy will make clear the political choices, while mainstream economics will claim that there are none. Whatever the outcome, proponents of both sides will defend their respective positions and seek to attract adherents to their views.

The single thread of property can be used to unravel some of the paradoxes of the market system. For example, modern mainstream economics is based on "the individual" owner, whether owning a specific object or one's own labor. That owner will seek to increase the value of her property in the market. But the market consists of other people, and their utility gained from purchasing that object. Those who are responsible for marketing understand the social dimension, and the desire for status and esteem, which are reflected in the market price. Further, the laws of property are authorized by representatives in government and enforced by the state. The government represents the sovereign nation, a presumed collective. In turn, the national currency, sometimes called the sovereign, can become individual private property. The credit made available to borrowers is managed by the government-regulated financial system, based on public credit. That public credit is based on the productive and tax capacity of the entire population projected into the future. Government bonds, based on that public credit projected into the future, are the "backing" of the financial system, rather than any precious metal like gold.

That is, the ultimate collateral for the modern system of property, money, and finance is the health of the population and the earth. These interlocking institutions are circular and reinforcing, rather than "individual" and "autonomous." Persons who claim the privileges of individual private property owners may inadvertently damage the resilience of the system, like knowingly marketing an asset which is worthless, or refusing to become vaccinated or to wear masks in a pandemic, or polluting a river upon which agricultural production depends. The market system which presumes to rely on the "individual" is social and political. Paradoxically, treating the market as an automatic machine, beyond politics, is a type of politics. The presumably self-regulating market, that Adam Smith called "the invisible hand," is like an alternative reality like "The Matrix," which can only "grow" at the expense of humans and other living things. The "ruling ideas" of property and markets bring freedom for property owners but coercion for everyone else.

Analysis of usage of terms like property enables greater understanding of political struggles. The earliest electoral franchise in eighteenth-century Britain was for white male property owners who represented the "public" (Knights 2005). In the nineteenth century, Polanyi's concept of "Double Movement" considers the actions of public interest groups to protect the public from too intense a focus solely on the profit motive (Polanyi 1944). For Polanyi, reformers understood the dangers of too much emphasis on individualism and competition, and mobilized to protect the collective, or "society." More recently there is a new style of politics, called "populism." The populists often declare a new collectivity worthy of representation, regardless of electoral vote count, whether Marx's "dictatorship of the proletariat" or Trump's "Make America Great Again." The history of populism follows the organizational efforts of those whose types of property have become devalued, such as farmers and small businesspersons in the late nineteenth century and manual workers in the late twentieth.

Property Paradigms and Systemic Fallouts

In previous works, property paradigm has been defined as a set of beliefs which declare that property is individual, the result of natural laws, whereas this chapter argues that laws and human institutions are necessary for the definition and protection of property (Davis 2015). Property can even constitute a worldview, which defends ownership and its rewards as fair and just.

This property paradigm which declares property as individual leads to certain omissions, nonetheless. Treatment of property as a mere object omits insights into the human agency and social relations which are necessary for its operation. Such an omission leaves property as an inert thing, whereas its effect on human personality and social incentives are part of what makes it effective. The treatment of property as an object, like land, also omits the essential ecological relationships which are necessary to make the earth inhabitable.

As Marx noted in *Capital*, Volume I, Chapter 15 (Marx 1967), the true sources of wealth are human efforts and the soil, not money or property (Davis 2022). Marx also noted that property affects social relations. In the essay "On the Jewish Question," Marx noted that property induces humans to see each other as obstacles, instead of sources of recognition and affirmation. The French Revolution declared the rights of man as equality, liberty, security, and property. But when based on property and the rights to exclude others,

> The liberty of man [is] regarded as an isolated monad... Liberty as a right of man is not founded upon the relation between man and man, but rather upon the separation of man from man. It is the right of such separation. The right of the *circumscribed* individual, withdrawn into himself... It is the right of self-interest...It leads every man to see in other men, not the *realization* but rather the *limitation* of his own liberty... The term "equality" ... [allows] that every man is equally regarded as a self-sufficient monad."
>
> *(Marx 1978a)*

The reification of property as an object allows dehumanization of workers and destruction of the environment. There are Systemic Fallouts (Searle 2010), or unexpected outcomes, discussed in more depth in other chapters, such as inequality, instability, climate change, and erosion of democracy.

Problems of Knowledge and Truth

The challenge is to have a reliable basis for knowledge. As the highly regarded historian of science, Thomas Kuhn, noted, even ideas in natural science have social implications (Kuhn 1962). Scientists, as human members of a specific community, have basic ideas in common, that are not always recognized, but which can influence their theories. A prominent example is the shift from Ptolemy to Copernicus, regarding the role of the earth in the universe. Similarly, natural science often presumes that there is a distinction between positive description, as objective, contrasted with normative value judgments. But if language is social, communicating ideas and values, and affecting social relationships, then the strict dichotomy breaks down.

The emerging awareness of the impact of humans on earth systems, called the Anthropocene, is an example of an idea with moral implications. Rather than viewing the earth as an object to be dominated by property owners seeking wealth, it is important to see humans in relation to the earth, with mutual effects and moral implications. That is, instead of private property and free markets, it is important to shift to a new understanding, valuing human development and ecological sustainability. Any other value system risks destabilizing the climate in dangerous ways, reaching a tipping point which alters previously stable systems.

Conclusion

Property is an idea which has been understood as "natural," that is consistent with God's will. On the other hand, property is viewed as a human construction, with contributions by social sciences like philosophy, history, and economics. In periods of intense ideological debate like the present, neither claim to truth is universally accepted. The approach of RPE is to understand the concepts, their history, implicit values, and implications. Speech is not just an individual matter, but has social effects, such as promotion and mobilization of key leaders and ideas, or alternatively demonization, or defamation. It is important to interrogate key concepts for each historic period, rather than accepting conventional wisdom at face value, and to seek an understanding of the moral implications. Political and social stability can seem more certain if basic concepts remain uncontested (Searle 2010), like property and the economy, but in times of change, an enhanced awareness of fault lines can facilitate informed debate and the development of progressive alternatives.

References

Acemoglu, Daron and James A. Robinson, *Why Nations Fail: The Origins of Power, Prosperity, and Poverty*. New York: Crown Publishers, 2012.

Akerlof, George A. and Robert J. Shiller, *Phishing for Phools: The Economics of Manipulation and Deception*. Princeton, N.J: Princeton University Press, 2015.

Arcenas, Claire Rydell, *America's Philosopher: John Locke in American Intellectual Life.* Chicago: University of Chicago Press, 2022.

Banner, Stuart, *American Property: A History of How, Why, and What We Own.* Cambridge, MA: Harvard University Press., 2011.

Bowles, Samuel and Herbert Gintis, *Democracy and Capitalism: Property, Community and the Contradictions of Modern Social Thought.* New York: Basic Books, 1986.

Davis, Ann E., *The Evolution of the Property Relation: Understanding Paradigms, Debates, Prospects.* New York: Palgrave MacMillan, 2015.

Davis, Ann E. *The End of Individualism and the Economy: Emerging Paradigms of Connection and Community.* Routledge. February, 2020.

Davis, Ann E. *Whole Earth: Beyond the Entitlements of the Property Owner.* Springer Nature, 2022.

Davis, Mike, *Old Gods, New Enigmas: Marx's Lost Theory.* London: Verso, 2018.

Durkheim, Emile, *The Elementary Forms of the Religious Life.* New York: The Free Press, 1965 [1915].

Ferguson, Thomas, Industrial Conflict and the Coming of the New Deal: The Triumph of Multinational Liberalism in America, In Steve Fraser and Gary Gerstle (eds.). *The Rise and Fall of the New Deal Order.* Princeton, NJ: Princeton University Press, 1989. 3–31.

Friedman, Milton, *Capitalism and Freedom.* Chicago: University of Chicago Press, 1962.

Gordon, Robert W., *Taming the Past: Essays on Law in History and History in Law.* New York: Cambridge University Press, 2017.

Gramsci, Antonio, *Selections from the Prison Notebooks.* Edited and translated by Quintin Hoare and Geoffrey Nowell Smith. New York: International Publishers, 1971.

Habermas, Jurgen, *The Structural Transformation of the Public Sphere: An Inquiry into a Category of Bourgeois Society.* Cambridge, MA: MIT Press, 1962.

Harvey, David, Marx, *Capital, and the Madness of Economic Reason.* New York: Oxford University Press, 2018.

Jacobs, Meg, *Panic at the Pump: The Energy Crisis and the Transformation of American Politics in the 1970s.* New York: Farrar, Straus, and Giroux, 2016.

Knights, Mark, *Representation and Misrepresentation in Later Stuart Britain: Partisanship and Political Culture.* New York: Oxford University Press, 2005.

Kuhn, Thomas S., *The Structure of Scientific Revolutions.* Chicago: University of Chicago Press, 1962.

Levy, Jonathan. *Ages of American Capitalism: A History of the United States.* New York: Random House, 2021.

Lowenstein, Roger, *Ways and Means: Lincoln and His Cabinet and the Financing of the Civil War.* New York: Penguin Press, 2022.

Lukacs, Georg, *History and Class Consciousness: Studies in Marxist Dialectic.* Cambridge, MA: MIT Press, 1971.

Marx, Karl, *Capital: A Critique of Political Economy.* New York: International Publishers, 1967.

Marx, Karl, On the Jewish Question. Robert G. Tucker (ed.). *The Marx-Engels Reader.* New York: W.W. Norton, 1978a. 26–52.

Marx, Karl, The Communist Manifesto. Robert G. Tucker (ed.). *The Marx-Engels Reader.* New York: W.W. Norton, 1978b. 473–500.

Ostrom, Elinor. *Governing the Commons: The Evolution of Institutions for Collective Action.* New York: Cambridge University Press, 1990.

Ott, Julia C., *When Wall Street Met Main Street: The Quest for an Investors' Democracy*. Cambridge, MA: Harvard University Press, 2011.

Pateman, Carole, *The Sexual Contract*. Oxford: Polity Press, 1988.

Piketty, Thomas, *Capital and Ideology*. Cambridge, MA: Harvard University Press, 2020.

Pistor, Katharina, *The Code of Capital: How the Law Creates Wealth and Inequality*. Princeton, NJ: Princeton University Press, 2020.

Polanyi, Karl, *The Great Transformation*. Boston: Beacon Press, 1944.

Poovey, Mary. "The Liberal Civil Subject and the Social in Eighteenth-Century British Moral Philosophy." *Public Culture*, 2002, Vol. 14, No. 1, 125–145.

Proudhon, Pierre-Joseph, *What is Property: An Inquiry into the Principle of Right and of Government*, 1840.

Richardson, Heather Cox, *How the South Won the Civil War: Oligarchy, Democracy, and the Continuing Fight for the Soul of America*. New York: Oxford University Press, 2020.

Searle, John R., *Making the Social World: The Structure of Human Civilization*. New York: Oxford University Press, 2010.

Smith, Adam, *An Inquiry into the Nature and Causes of The Wealth of Nations*. New York: Modern Library, 1994 [1776].

Soll, Jacob, *Free Market: The History of an Idea*. New York: Basic Books, 2022.

Thompson, Helen, *Disorder: Hard Times in the 21st Century*. Oxford, UK: Oxford University Press, 2022.

3

USING THE THEORY OF INNOVATIVE ENTERPRISE TO ANALYZE US CORPORATE CAPITALISM

William Lazonick

Progressive Value Creation or Predatory Value Extraction?

Large corporations dominate the US economy. In 2019, 540 companies with 20,000 or more employees in the United States were only 0.009% of all US businesses; however, with an average workforce of 58,357, the companies had 23.7% of business-sector employees and 26.1% of business-sector payrolls (US Census Bureau 2022a). What are the policy reforms that can ensure that large business corporations contribute to stable employment opportunity, equitable income distribution, and sustainable productivity growth in the US economy?

We cannot simply assume that big business is bad business. Breaking up the giant corporation into smaller firms, with a view to creating more price competition, would not solve the economic problems that have afflicted the US economy since the late 1970s. Indeed, it is possible that by undermining productivity and creating unemployment, these classic antitrust remedies could make adverse economic conditions worse.

Large dominant businesses may be able and willing to price gouge their customers or suppress their workers' wages. The fundamental big-business problem is not, however, an absence of price competition. Rather, the fundamental problem is resource allocation. *Innovative* business corporations that, through "progressive value creation" (PVC), grow to be large create possibilities for achieving stable and equitable growth that would otherwise not exist in the economy. The financialization of these large business corporations, in the form of "predatory value extraction" (PVE), undermines these possibilities for stable and equitable growth.

PVC refers to the power of those workers whose skills and efforts contribute to the corporation's value creation to extract an equitable share of corporate revenues as the returns to their productive contributions. Many corporations

DOI: 10.4324/9781003366690-4

grow to be large by investing in the productive capabilities of their labor forces, providing superior wages and benefits to their employees, and generating products that are higher quality and lower cost than those that would otherwise be available on the market. Companies that invest in the organizational learning of their workforces, which is the essence of the innovation process, can enable employees to improve their living standards on a sustainable basis.

PVE refers to the power of shareholders to extract from the corporation far more value for themselves than they contribute to the corporation's value creation. America's "big business" problem is not the size of the corporation but rather, as laid out in Section "The Era of (Somewhat) Progressive Value Creation" of this chapter, the transformation of its resource allocation from PVC to PVE. Rather than invest in and reward the productive capabilities of employees through PVC, the financialized corporation seeks to increase the incomes of shareholders who engage in PVE (Lazonick 2023).

As outlined in Section "The Theory of Innovative Enterprise and the Creation-Extraction Relation", the theory of innovative enterprise (TIE) can comprehend the growth of the business corporation through PVC and the subsequent looting of the business corporation through PVE. The generic activities of any firm are strategy, organization, and finance. TIE captures the behavioral content of these three activities in the concepts "strategic control," "organizational integration," and "financial commitment," which, combined, constitute "social conditions of innovative enterprise" (Lazonick 2019a). This chapter contrasts TIE to the neoclassical theory of the optimizing firm, which portrays the business corporation as impotent and the market as omnipotent in the operation and performance of the economy. As an historical process, functioning markets in products, labor, land, and finance are outcomes, not causes, of economic development (Lazonick 2003). The "theory of the market economy" – which is the intellectually appropriate name for neoclassical economic theory – is *a theory of value extraction posing as a theory of value creation* (Lazonick 2022).

As such, the theory of the market economy has provided microfoundations for the real-world application of MSV ideology to legitimize PVE, contributing to unstable employment opportunity, inequitable income distribution, and unsustainable productivity growth at the levels of the firm and the US economy. Section "The Theory of Innovative Enterprise Exposes MSV Ideology" deploys the theory of innovative enterprise to critique the version of agency theory that, building on the theory of the market economy, contends that for the sake of economic efficiency a company should allocate resources in order to MSV. The chapter concludes with reference to a five-part reform agenda, elaborated in a recent book (Lazonick 2023), which can confront PVE and support PVC.

The Era of (Somewhat) Progressive Value Creation

The central issue in the contest between PVC and PVE is the respective contributions to corporate value creation by shareholders and workers in relation to the financial resources that these two types of corporate participants extract from the business corporation. In the post-World War II decades, entering the 1970s, PVC suppressed PVE in the large publicly listed US corporation, although, as both shareholders and employees, white males were a privileged group. Shareholders, who were mainly households as savers (as distinct from institutional shareholders), received a steady stream of dividends, ostensibly paid out of profits, even though their contributions to the value-creation processes of the publicly listed corporations in which they held shares were virtually nil (Lazonick 2018).

At the same time, white-male workers, both blue collar and white collar, experienced stable employment and rising real compensation through their access to the era's "career with one company" (CWOC) employment norm. The funding for their increasing living standards came from the corporate productivity that their skills and efforts helped to generate. Individual and intergenerational upward socioeconomic mobility, rooted in PVC, gave rise to a (seemingly) robust middle class. With these social relations of production, supported by the world's most formidable developmental state, US business corporations attained global leadership in a range of technology-intensive industries (Lazonick 2015a).

My microeconomic explanation for this "shared prosperity" as a macroeconomic outcome is the dominance of PVC, governed by a "retain-and-reinvest" corporate resource-allocation regime. While providing shareholders with a steady stream of dividend income, the typical business corporation of the era retained a substantial portion of its profits and reinvested in the productive capabilities of the labor force (Lazonick 2023). Figure 3.1, which replicates a well-known graph popularized by the Economic Policy Institute, shows that, for all US civilian employment, from the late 1940s to the mid-1970s, rates of increase in real wages kept up with rates of increase in labor productivity.

From the late 1970s, however, the productivity-growth rate began to outstrip the wage-growth rate, and over the ensuing decades, the gap between the two metrics grew wider and wider, as shown in Figure 3.1. For masses of Americans, including white males, the quantity and quality of employment opportunities that could support upward mobility within major business corporations have eroded, while the distribution of income within the companies has grown increasingly unequal (US Census Bureau 2022b). This growing productivity–pay gap is a marked shift in the dominant US corporate resource-allocation regime from retain-and-reinvest to "downsize-and-distribute": the corporation lays off experienced, often more expensive, workers and distributes corporate cash to shareholders (Lazonick 2015b).

For "Old Economy" companies that in the post-World War II decades adhered to the CWOC norm, the transformation from retain-and-reinvest to downsize-and-distribute entailed three structural changes in employment relations, which is summarized as "rationalization," "marketization," and

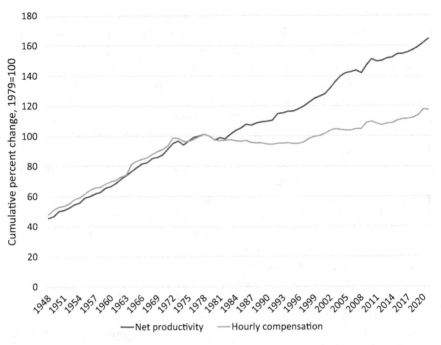

FIGURE 3.1 Index of cumulative annual percentage changes in productivity per hour and real wages per hour (1979 = 100), 1948–2021.

Source: Economic Policy Institute, "The Productivity-Pay Gap," EPI, October 2022.

"globalization" (Lazonick et al. 2021). From the early 1980s, *rationalization*, characterized by plant closings, terminated the jobs of high school-educated blue-collar workers, most of them well-paid union members. From the early 1990s, *marketization*, characterized by the end of the CWOC norm, placed in jeopardy the job security of middle-aged white-collar workers, many of them college-educated. From the early 2000s, *globalization*, characterized by the accelerated movement of even advanced employment opportunities offshore to lower-wage nations, especially China and India, left all members of the US labor force vulnerable to displacement, whatever their educational credentials and work experience.

Initially, structural changes in employment through rationalization, marketization, and globalization were business responses to changes in technologies, markets, and competition. During the onset of the rationalization phase in the early 1980s, plant closings as well as cost-cutting by offshoring component manufacture were reactions to the superior productive capabilities of Japanese competitors in consumer-durable and related capital-goods industries in which US companies employed large numbers of unionized blue-collar workers. During the onset of the marketization phase in the early 1990s, the erosion of the CWOC norm among white-collar workers was a response to the dramatic technological shift from proprietary systems to open systems, integral to the microelectronics revolution, which favored younger workers with the latest computer skills acquired through higher education and transferable across companies over older workers with many years of firm-specific experience. During the onset of the globalization phase in the early 2000s, the sharp acceleration in the offshoring of high-end jobs was a response to the emergence in developing nations such as China and India of large supplies of highly educated but lower-wage workers, who could perform increasingly sophisticated activities that had previously been carried out in the United States.

Once US corporations transformed their employment relations, they often pursued rationalization, marketization, and globalization to cut current costs rather than to reposition their organizations to produce a new generation of innovative products. Corporate profits ceased to provide funds for reinvesting in the growth of the firm and instead became "free cash flow" that could be distributed to shareholders. Defining superior corporate performance as ever-higher quarterly earnings per share, companies turned to massive open-market stock repurchases – aka stock buybacks – to "manage" their own corporations' stock prices (Lazonick 2014, 2015b).

Meanwhile, in the last decades of the century, through retain-and-reinvest, several "New Economy" companies, which were rationalized, marketized, and even globalized from their inception, engaged in retain-and-reinvest to transform from venture-backed startups into highly profitable businesses with employment in the tens of thousands. From the late 1990s, however, these successful New Economy companies also began to do massive stock buybacks. Trillions of dollars that these corporations – both Old and New – could have allocated to investment in productive capabilities have been used instead to buy back corporate shares for the purpose of manipulating their own company's stock price (Lazonick 2014). Increasingly over the past four decades, the US corporate economy turned from PVC based on retain-and-reinvest to PVE based on downsize-and-distribute, contributing significantly to the growing productivity–pay gap displayed in Figure 3.1.

The Theory of Innovative Enterprise and the Creation–Extraction Relation

Nothing is more basic to academic economics than the notion that the price of a product is – or for the sake of economic efficiency should be – determined by the equilibrium of the demand for the product with the supply of the product. As anyone who has taken an introductory course in economics has been taught, the existence of an equilibrium price occurs when a downward-sloping demand curve intersects an upward-sloping supply curve (Figure 3.2). The sensible intuition behind the downward-sloping demand curve is that as a product is offered at lower prices, the population of actual and potential buyers will want to purchase larger quantities of the product. The much less sensible – and possibly nonsensical (Lazonick 2022) – intuition behind the upward-sloping supply curve is that firms that supply the product incur increasing costs as they seek to provide larger quantities of the product to the market.

Underpinning the upward-sloping supply curve is a theory of the firm that seeks to compete by maximizing profit subject to technological and market conditions that its manager takes as *given constraints* on the firm's economic activity. Indeed, the theory assumes that all firms that compete in an industry optimize subject to the same externally determined technological and market constraints. At the level of the individual firm, an upward-sloping marginal-cost curve exists when an increase in average variable cost (AVC) more than outweighs a decrease in average fixed cost (AFC), as depicted in the U-shaped cost curve in Figure 3.3. The upward-sloping marginal-cost curve enables – or, more accurately, constrains – the firm to maximize profit at the point at which marginal revenue equals marginal cost. The aggregation of the identical marginal-cost curves of all the firms in the industry yields the upward-sloping industry supply curve as shown in Figure 3.2.

In contrast to the optimizing firm of neoclassical economic theory, the "theory of innovative enterprise" (TIE) posits that, by transforming the technological and market conditions that it faces for the sake of generating a product that is higher quality and lower cost than that of its competitors, the innovating firm can structure a downward-sloping supply curve (Lazonick 2019a). If

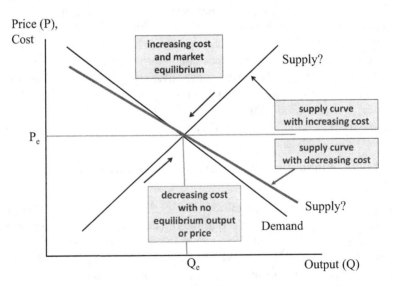

FIGURE 3.2   The slope of the supply curve and alternative theories of the firm.

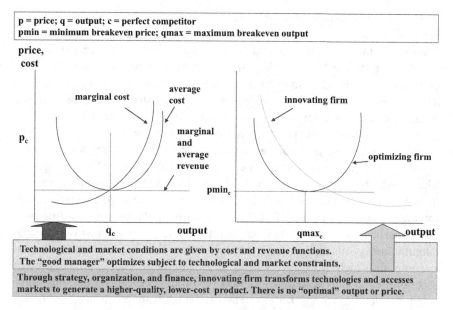

FIGURE 3.3   How the innovating firm can outcompete the optimizing firm.

the innovating firm succeeds in generating a higher-quality, lower-cost product than had previously been available – the economic definition of an innovative outcome – it gains competitive advantage over its less innovative competitors, thus creating a superior standard of economic efficiency than that which had existed previously. Thus, as shown in Figure 3.3, the innovating firm outcompetes the optimizing firm idealized by neoclassical theory.

The upward-sloping supply curve ignores two fundamental and interrelated characteristics of products that determine the cost of transforming inputs into outputs that can be sold on the market. The first characteristic is *product quality*. In most industries, firms seek to compete on a product market by developing products that are higher quality than those of their rivals. The definition of the quality of a product is both subjective and subject to change. For any product, there may be myriad dimensions of quality. In the passenger car industry, for example, "high quality" may mean that a car is safe (high-quality brakes, high-quality tires, seat belts, airbags, injury-proof design, etc.), fuel-efficient, and environmentally friendly – dimensions of quality that are of public concern and are hence often subject to regulation. It may also mean that the car is rust-resistant, air-conditioned, roomy, stylish, comfortable, etc. – dimensions of quality that will be left to consumer choice. It costs money to build quality into cars, and different types of government regulators and car buyers may register very different views about what "high quality" means and how much consumers are willing to pay for it.

The second characteristic is *scale economies*. In most goods-producing industries, firms compete on a product market by spreading the fixed cost of developing, manufacturing, and delivering the product over larger quantities of sold output, thus lowering the unit cost of the product. The high fixed cost of expenditures on plant and equipment makes scale economies of importance in mass-production industries such as automobiles, steel, and semiconductor fabrication. Scale economies are also significant in R&D-intensive industries such as pharmaceuticals, microelectronics, and clean energy.

Even though, for accounting purposes, R&D expenditures are generally treated as current costs (because a company cannot own the "human assets" which embody the organizational learning that R&D spending may enable), from an economic perspective, R&D outlays represent a fixed cost that can be spread out over many units of sold output within and across accounting periods. Firms also invest in human capabilities in activities such as purchasing, manufacturing, marketing, and administration that require organizational learning to which R&D accounting does not apply, but which represent expenditures in one accounting period on productive capabilities that, provided the learning organization remains intact, can be utilized in future accounting periods. These expenditures on the development of human capabilities represent high fixed cost which, by gaining a larger extent of the product market, the innovating firm seeks to transform into low unit cost.

In TIE, product quality and scale economies interact because the generation of a higher-quality product can enable the innovating firm to gain a larger extent of the market than its competitors, and thus, if it can expand output without compromising product quality, transform the high fixed cost of generating the higher-quality product into the low unit cost of its sold output (see the right-hand side of Figure 3.3). Within the firm, "economies of scope" are a type of scale economies that result from utilizing the same fixed-cost investments, including human capabilities, across different products.

The innovation process that can generate a higher-quality, lower-cost product is *uncertain, collective*, and *cumulative*. Hence, a theory of innovative enterprise must comprehend these characteristics of the innovation process.

- **Uncertain**: When investments in transforming technologies and accessing markets are made, the product and financial outcomes cannot be known in advance. If they were, the result would not be innovation. Hence, the need for *strategy*.
- **Collective**: To generate a higher-quality, lower-cost product, the business enterprise must integrate the skills and efforts of large numbers of people with different hierarchical responsibilities and functional capabilities into the learning processes that are the essence of innovation. Hence, the need for *organization*.

- **Cumulative**: Collective learning today enables collective learning tomorrow. These organizational-learning processes must be sustained continuously over time until financial returns can be generated through the sale of innovative products. Hence, the need for *finance*.

Strategy, organization, and finance are generic activities in the operation of any business corporation. But it is the social content of these generic activities, embodied in distinctive social relations, that can transform the interactions of strategy, organization, and finance into innovative performance. Even a relatively small company is a highly complex social organization. The "social conditions of innovative enterprise" framework provides a conceptual guide to empirical company-level investigation of how a business enterprise operates and performs over time.

Specifically, in the implementation of the three generic business activities, strategic control, organizational integration, and financial commitment are social conditions that can enable the corporation to manage the uncertain, collective, and cumulative character of the innovation process.

- **Strategic control**: For innovation to occur in the face of technological, market, and competitive uncertainties, executives who control corporate resource allocation must have the abilities and incentives to make strategic investments in innovation. Their abilities depend on their knowledge of how strategic investments in new productive capabilities can enhance the corporation's existing capabilities. Their incentives depend on the alignment of their personal interests with the corporation's purpose of generating innovative products.
- **Organizational integration**: Implementation of an innovation strategy requires integration of people working in a complex division of labor into collective and cumulative learning processes. Work satisfaction, promotion, remuneration, and benefits are important instruments in a reward system that motivates and empowers employees to engage in collective learning over a sustained time period.
- **Financial commitment**: For collective learning to accumulate over time, the sustained commitment of "patient capital" must keep the learning organization intact. For a young company that, because it is a "start-up," has not yet been able to turn a profit, various forms of "venture capital" can provide financial commitment. For a going concern that has achieved sustained profitability, retained earnings – leveraged, if need be, by debt issues – are the foundation of financial commitment.

The uncertainty of an innovation strategy is embodied in the fixed-cost investments required to develop the productive capabilities that may, if the strategy is successful, result in a higher-quality product. Fixed cost derives from both the size and the duration of the innovation investment strategy. If the size of investment in physical capital tends to increase the fixed cost of an innovation strategy, so too does the duration of investment in human capabilities required to engage in the collective and cumulative – or organizational – learning that, by transforming technologies and accessing markets, can result in innovative products.

An innovation strategy that may eventually enable the enterprise to develop a higher-quality product may place that company at a competitive disadvantage if it only attains low levels of output. The high fixed cost of an innovation strategy creates the company's need to attain a high level of utilization of the productive resources it has developed – that is, scale and scope economies. Given its existing productive capabilities, the innovating firm may experience increasing cost to maintain the productivity of variable inputs it buys as needed on the market to expand production.

To overcome the constraint on its innovation strategy posed by reliance on the market to supply an input that results in increasing cost, the innovating firm integrates the production of the supply of that input into its internal operations. That is, the innovating firm transforms a variable cost into a fixed cost. The development of the productive capability of this newly integrated input, therefore, adds to the fixed cost of the innovation strategy. The innovating firm is now under even more pressure to generate a higher-quality product and expand its sold output to transform high fixed cost into low unit cost.

The company's higher-quality product enables it to access a larger portion of the market than its competitors. The fixed cost of the innovation strategy generally depends, however, on investments in not only transforming technology but also accessing markets. Besides distribution facilities, accessing a larger market share may entail fixed costs for branding, advertising, distribution channels, and a salaried sales force. Learning about what potential buyers want, and convincing potential buyers that the company's product is actually "higher quality," add to the fixed cost of the innovation strategy.

Indeed, in some industries, the fixed cost of accessing a larger market share is greater than the fixed cost of investing in the transformation of product and process technologies. An increase in fixed cost of accessing the market requires an even larger extent of the market to convert high fixed cost into low unit cost. A potent way for an innovating firm to attain a larger extent of the market is for the company to share some of the gains of this cost transformation with its customers in the form of a lower product price. The setting of product price, therefore, can be central to the company's innovation strategy.

Along with investment in plant and equipment, investment in productive resources entails training and retaining employees. When a company enhances an employee's productive capability, through either formal or on-the-job training, the employee's upgraded capability represents an asset that can improve the quality of the innovating firm's product, which in turn can enable the company to attain a larger extent of the market to transform the increased fixed cost of its investment in human resources into low unit cost. When the company succeeds in generating a higher-quality, lower-cost product, innovation drives its growth.

To retain and motivate the employees whom the company has hired and trained, the innovating firm can offer them higher pay, more employment security, superior benefits, and more interesting work, all of which add to the fixed cost of the asset that an employee's labor represents. If these rewards to employees result in innovative products, the gains of employees may represent contributions to value creation that make the company an even more profitable business enterprise. The innovating firm shares the gains of innovation with its employees by making investments in their "collective and cumulative careers" (CCCs).

Individuals develop their own productive capabilities as members of collectivities organized by the corporation (in some cases in collaboration with other business corporations or with government agencies). And the specialized knowledge that enables individuals to become more productive over time cumulates through their ongoing involvement in collective learning processes. Over the course of their careers, individuals may change employers, making it necessary for them to engage in collective and cumulative learning, in a coherent and continuous manner, across a series of business, government, and civil-society organizations.

Career employees, therefore, can become more productive because of their sustained involvement in processes of collective and cumulative learning. In rewarding employees for this engagement, the innovating firm makes its employees better off. It can afford, and indeed profit from, the increased labor expense when the employee's productive capability enables the company to gain a competitive advantage by generating a higher-quality, lower-cost product than had previously been available. Under such circumstances, increases in labor income and increases in labor productivity tend to show a highly positive correlation – as, indeed, was the case in the post-World War II decades (see Figure 3.1), when the CWOC employment norm prevailed.

When the innovating firm is successful, it may come to dominate its industry. The company's output is far larger and its unit cost, and hence potentially its product price, is far lower than would be the case if a large number of small firms with lower-quality products and lesser scale economies populated the industry. The overall gains from innovation depend on the relation between the innovating firm's cost structure and the industry's demand structure, while the distribution of those gains among the company's various stakeholders depends on their relative power to appropriate portions of these gains (Lazonick 1990; 2019a).

It is theoretically possible (although by no means inevitable) for the gains of an innovative enterprise to permit, simultaneously, higher pay, more stable employment, and better work conditions for its employees; a stronger balance sheet for the firm; more secure paper for creditors; higher dividends and stock prices for shareholders; more tax revenues for governments; and higher-quality products at lower prices for consumers. To some extent, what is theoretically possible has been, in certain times and places, historical reality. In the rise of the United States to global industrial leadership during the 20th century, a retain-and-reinvest resource-allocation regime enabled a relatively small number of business enterprises in a wide range of industries to grow to employ tens of thousands, or even hundreds of thousands, of people and attain dominant product-market shares (Lazonick 2004, 2009).

One result was the emergence in the post-World War II decades of an upwardly mobile blue-collar and white-collar middle class, dominated by white males. Indeed, by the 1960s and 1970s, aided by the civil-rights movement, low levels of immigration, and strong demand for blue-collar workers in mass-production industries, significant numbers of Blacks also began to gain access to well-paid and stable unionized employment. From the 1980s, however, with the rise of MSV, upward socioeconomic mobility based on PVC would give way to downward mobility perpetrated by PVE, undermining the employment opportunities available to members of the US labor force with no more than high-school educations (Lazonick 2015a; Lazonick et al. 2021). The neoclassical theory of the optimizing – and hence *uninnovative* – firm, with its agency-theory application, played a central ideological and political role in this reversal of fortune for the US working class.

The Theory of Innovative Enterprise Exposes MSV Ideology

As already discussed, in the post-World War II decades in the United States, there was, in aggregate, a trend toward somewhat greater income equality, rooted in the CWOC employment norm of major US corporations. This norm, which applied especially to white males, was protected at the blue-collar level by the seniority rules of unions and was manifested at the white-collar level by defined-benefit, nonportable pensions based on years of service with the company. Adopting a retain-and-reinvest resource-allocation regime, major US corporations retained a substantial portion of profits and reinvested in the productive capabilities of their employees, sharing with them, in the form of secure employment and rising remuneration, the gains of innovative enterprise that these employees helped to create (Lazonick 2004, 2015a). As a result, in the US macroeconomy (as shown in Figure 3.1), the growth of real wages tracked the growth of productivity, and there was a tendency toward less income inequality.

Since the late 1970s, however, as has also been noted, there has been a growing gap between productivity growth and wage growth, resulting in downward socioeconomic mobility for Americans with no more than high-school educations. Over these decades, US business corporations have transformed from a retain-and-reinvest to a downsize-and-distribute resource-allocation regime (Lazonick 2023). Under the latter, major US corporations downsize their labor forces – at times terminating long-time employees even when the firm is profitable, often in the context of outsourcing and offshoring – and distribute corporate cash to shareholders in the form of cash dividends and stock buybacks.

Stock buybacks are a particularly egregious and potent mode of PVE. In November 1982, the US Securities and Exchange Commission (SEC) adopted Rule 10b-18, which enables publicly listed corporations to do massive open-market shares repurchases, with a safe harbor against charges of manipulating the company's stock price (Lazonick 2018). Whereas dividends provide all common *shareholders* with a yield for holding shares, buybacks done as open-market repurchases provide gains to corporate executives, Wall Street bankers, and hedge-fund managers who, as *sharesellers*, are in the business of timing stock trades. In effect, SEC Rule 10b-18 is a license to loot (Lazonick 2015b; Lazonick et al. 2020).

Coming into the 1980s, buybacks were minimal. For the 216 corporations included in the S&P 500 Index in January 2020 that were publicly listed from 1981 through 2019, from 1981 to 1983 buybacks absorbed only 4.4% of net income, while dividends accounted for 49.7%. From 2017 to 2019, for the same 216 companies, buybacks were *62.2%* of net income and dividends 49.6%. For the decade 2012–2021, 474 corporations that were included in the S&P 500 Index in January 2022 repurchased shares valued at $5.7 trillion, equal to 55% of their net income, while also paying out $4.2 trillion in dividends, another 41% of net income (Lazonick and Tulum 2023).

These distributions to shareholders come at the expense of rewards to employees in the form of higher pay, superior benefits, and more secure jobs as well as corporate investment in the new products and processes that can sustain a company as an innovative enterprise. These distributions to shareholders are a prime cause of the concentration of income among the richest households and the erosion of middle-class employment opportunities (Lazonick 2015a). Massive payouts in the form of buybacks and dividends are also integral to resource-allocation strategies that have caused US corporations to fall behind global competitors in major technology sectors, including ICT, pharmaceuticals, and aviation – sectors in which the United States once possessed world leadership (Lazonick and Tulum 2023; Lazonick and Sakinç 2019; Lazonick and Hopkins 2021; Carpenter and Lazonick 2023).

The rise of MSV ideology in the 1980s legitimized the replacement of retain-and-reinvest by downsize-and-distribute as the dominant regime of corporate resource allocation in the United States (Lazonick and O'Sullivan 2000; Lazonick 2014). The leading academic advocate for MSV was Michael C. Jensen, a Chicago-School "agency theorist," who from 1985 disseminated this ideology as a professor at Harvard Business School. Jensen argued that for the sake of superior economic performance corporations should "disgorge" their "free cash flow" so that financial markets would be able to allocate these financial resources to their most efficient uses (Jensen 1986). The term "disgorge" implies that the funds that a company retains out of profits are ill-gotten when controlled by the corporation rather than distributed to its shareholders, while the term "free" could be applied to cash flow made available by laying off employees, including longstanding personnel who had contributed to the growth of the firm and had held the realistic expectation of a CWOC.

The agency-theory rationale for distributing profits to shareholders in the form of not only cash dividends but also stock buybacks is that shareholders, and shareholders alone, make risky investments in the business corporation, without a guaranteed return, and hence only shareholders have a claim on profits if and when they occur (Lazonick and Shin 2020). The theory assumes that other stakeholders in the corporation, including workers, receive guaranteed prices (i.e., wages) for their productive contributions. Agency theory, however, overstates the risks borne by shareholders in making corporate investments, while ignoring risky investments in productive resources by not only workers but also taxpayers that can enable business corporations to generate revenues and profits.

Public shareholders do not, as a rule, invest directly in the firm. Rather, once a corporation is publicly listed, households, corporations, governments, and civil-society organizations, directly or indirectly through asset managers, become shareholders by purchasing shares outstanding on the stock market. In placing their funds in shares listed on a highly liquid stock market such as the New York Stock Exchange or NASDAQ, public shareholders take little risk; they enjoy limited liability if they hold the shares and, given the liquidity of the stock market, at any instant and at a very low transaction cost, they can sell the shares at the going market price.

Through government investments in human capabilities and physical infrastructure, taxpayers regularly provide productive resources to companies without a guaranteed return. As an important example, but only one of many, the 2023 budget of the US National Institutes of Health (NIH) was $47.5 billion, part of a total NIH investment in life-sciences research spanning 1938–2023 that adds up to almost $1.5 trillion in 2023 dollars (Lazonick 2023). Businesses that make use of NIH-sponsored research benefit from the public knowledge that it generates. As risk-bearers, taxpayers who fund investments in such research, or in physical infrastructure such as roads, have a claim on resulting corporate profits, if they are generated. Through the tax system, governments, representing households as taxpayers, seek to extract this return from corporations that make profitable use of government investment in human capabilities and physical infrastructure.

No matter what corporate tax rate prevails, however, households as taxpayers face the uncertainty that changes in technological, market, and/or competitive conditions may prevent enterprises from generating profits and the related business tax revenues that serve as a return on the taxpayers' investments in human capabilities and physical infrastructure. Moreover, tax rates are politically determined; households as taxpayers face the political uncertainty that predatory value extractors may convince government policymakers that they will not be able to make value-creating investments unless they are given tax cuts or financial subsidies that will permit adequate profits. Households as taxpayers face the risk that politicians may be put in power who accede to these demands for PVE.

Through their skills and efforts, workers regularly make productive contributions to the companies for which they work that are beyond the levels required to lay claim to their current pay. However, they do so without guaranteed returns (Lazonick 2023). Any employer who is seeking to generate a higher-quality, lower-cost product knows the profound difference in the productivity levels of those employees who just punch the clock to get their daily pay and those who are committed to supporting the company's goals of generating products that can compete in terms of quality and cost. An innovative company wants workers who apply their skills and efforts to organizational learning so that they can make enduring productive contributions – including those that will enable the development of the firm's next generation of high-quality, low-cost products.

For their part, in making these productive contributions, employees expect that they will be able to build their careers within the company, putting themselves in positions to reap future benefits at work and in retirement. Yet these potential careers and returns are not guaranteed. In fact, under the downsize-and-distribute resource-allocation regime that MSV ideology legitimizes, these careers and returns are generally undermined.

Workers, therefore, supply their skills and efforts to the process of generating innovative products that, if successful, could create value, but they take the risk that their endeavors could be in vain. Far from reaping expected gains in the form of higher remuneration, more job security, and better working conditions, employees could face cuts in pay and benefits, or even find themselves laid off. Even if the innovation process is successful, workers face the possibility that the institutional environment in which MSV prevails will empower corporate executives to cut some workers' wages and lay off other workers – all so that the value they helped to create can be redirected to shareholders, including the senior executives themselves with their copious stock-based pay as well as hedge-fund managers whose stock-trading strategies count buybacks as money in the bank (Lazonick and Shin 2020). In short, the corporate resource-allocation strategy may transform from retain-and-reinvest to downsize-and-distribute, with devastating impacts on the realized gains that committed employees had expected and deserved.

Proponents of MSV may accept that a company needs to retain some cash flow to maintain the functioning of its physical capital, but, with their economic analysis rooted in the theory of the market economy, they generally view labor as an interchangeable commodity that can be hired and fired as needed on the labor market. In addition, they typically ignore the contributions that households as taxpayers make to business value creation. As a branch of neoclassical economics, agency theory assumes that markets, not organizations, allocate resources to their most efficient uses. But lacking a TIE, agency theory cannot explain how the "most efficient uses" are created and transformed over time (Lazonick 2019a).

The consequences of the colossal intellectual failure of neoclassical economics are not merely academic. Since the mid-1980s, MSV ideology has functioned to legitimize massive open-market issuer repurchases in addition to dividends. In the thrall of MSV, senior corporate executives seek to boost profits by price-gouging buyers, suppressing wages, terminating employees, squeezing suppliers, and avoiding taxes – all for the purpose of creating more "free cash flow" that can be distributed to shareholders – including the senior corporate executives themselves. As documented in a large and growing body of research, the purpose of stock buybacks done as open-market repurchases is to manipulate a company's stock price, concentrating income in the bank accounts of the richest households and making most Americans worse off (Lazonick 2023).

Confronting Predatory Value Extraction and Supporting Progressive Value Creation

Drawing upon my book *Investing in Innovation: Confronting Predatory Value Extraction in the US Corporation*, this concluding section explores a five-part corporate-governance reform agenda for the United States to start the transition from a PVE economy, characterized by extreme inequality, to a PVC economy, characterized by stable and equitable growth. The agenda includes:

- Banning stock buybacks as open-market repurchases by rescinding SEC Rule 10b-18.
- Compensating senior corporate executives for their contributions to value creation, and not for value extraction.
- Reconstituting corporate boards by including directors who are representatives of workers and taxpayers while excluding predatory value extractors.
- Reforming the tax system so that it recognizes and supports businesses and households in enhancing productive capabilities.
- Deploying corporate profits and government tax revenues to launch and sustain collaborations between business corporations and government agencies that support the "collective and cumulative" careers for future and existing members of the US labor force.

Banning Buybacks

TIE argues that the earnings that a company retains from profits represent the financial foundation for ongoing investment in innovation as well as rewarding stakeholders, and especially employees, for their value-creating contributions to prior innovation. The reinvestment in innovation can take place within the legal structure of the existing corporate entity or by spinning off new divisions as distinct legal entities. Buybacks tend to subvert the social conditions of innovative enterprise. They manifest the vesting of strategic control in the hands of executives who prioritize corporate resource allocation for the purpose of stock-price manipulation. By enabling PVE to trump PVC, buybacks undermine organizational integration – the essence of the innovation process. And by distributing profits for the benefit of share-sellers, buybacks reduce financial commitment.

Redesigning Executive Compensation

TIE recognizes that a business corporation must attract, retain, motivate, and reward senior executives who possess the abilities to allocate resources to innovation strategies and oversee their successful implementation through organizational integration. If, through their educational backgrounds and employment experience, senior executives have not acquired these capabilities, they should not be placed in positions of strategic control. Once in those positions, they should expect to be remunerated in ways that are equitable relative to the company's other employees.

In the United States, however, the most important components of executive pay are stock-based – realized gains from the exercise of stock options and the vesting of stock awards – with very strong, and typically explicit, incentives to allocate corporate resources to distributions to shareholders. A company's stock price can be driven by a combination of innovation, speculation, and manipulation, and a senior corporate executive can reap tens of millions of dollars in stock-based gains even in the absence of innovation (Lazonick 2019b). US-style stock-based executive pay incentivizes and rewards value extraction, specifically for stock-price increases that result from the allocation of corporate cash to stock buybacks to manipulate the company's stock price. Armed with the right to do massive buybacks afforded by SEC Rule 10b-18, the explosion of senior executive stock-based pay in the United States since the 1980s has undermined the abilities and incentives of its recipients to invest in innovation (Hopkins and Lazonick 2023).

Reconstituting Corporate Boards

The prime functions of a corporation's board of directors are to appoint senior corporate executives, oversee the ways in which these executives choose to allocate the corporation's resources, and determine their compensation. The vast majority of US-based corporations elect directors (typically nominated by the incumbent CEO) by the proxy votes of common shareholders. Under the business judgment rule (Sharfman 2017), directors have the right, if they so choose, to support and reward corporate executives who engage in retain-and-reinvest, a resource-allocation regime that, through investment in innovation, has enabled many US-based corporations to grow to leadership positions in their industries.

In effect, the growth of these firms can be viewed as the application of TIE – which is not surprising because TIE derives its insights by exploring rather than ignoring the history of industrial development (Lazonick 2002). In the MSV era, however, the appointment of board members to advocate for the interests of workers, taxpayers, consumers, and the community is a necessary condition for shifting the corporate resource-allocation regime from PVE to PVC (Lazonick 2019b). TIE provides the intellectual rationale for this transformation of corporate boards.

Fixing the Corporate Tax System

In 2021, households paid 42.1% of all corporate taxes, while corporations contributed 6.0% (Bunn and Weigel 2023). From the TIE perspective, the investment triad of business corporations, government agencies, and household units invests in the nation's productive capabilities. Household taxes form the financial foundation for government agencies' investments in human capabilities and physical infrastructure, a significant portion of which business corporations operating in the United States use as freely available or subsidized public resources.

We can think of *corporate* taxes as payments to the government for the use of these human and physical resources by business corporations. It is for this reason that TIE argues that, in funding government expenditures, households as taxpayers incur risk concerning corporate performance and hence should have board representation to oversee corporate resource allocation. TIE provides an analytical framework for beginning the national discussion concerning the appropriate size of the corporate tax bill in relation to corporate use of government-funded capabilities and infrastructure.

Supporting Collective and Cumulative Careers

In a world of rapid technological innovation and intense global competition, the value-creating economy depends on the continuous augmentation of the productive capabilities of the labor force. Both higher education and the work experience of the national labor force need constant upgrading as a necessary condition for producing innovative products. Achieving productive outcomes and returning a substantial portion of the profits from the productivity gains to productive workers are fundamental to attaining stable and equitable economic growth. Policies for the upgrading of employment opportunities on a massive scale are essential for a transition from PVE to PVC.

Just as companies need collective and cumulative learning to be innovative, employees need *collective and cumulative careers* (CCCs) to make productive contributions to innovation processes over working lives that now span four decades or more. Increasingly in the decades after World War II, higher education became essential for access to a CCC in what became known as white-collar employment. The collective and cumulative learning that is the essence of innovation relied upon the CWOC employment norm which characterized the Old Economy business model (Lazonick 2009).

With the rise to dominance of the New Economy business model in the 1980s and 1990s, however, the CWOC norm disappeared. Yet the need for collective and cumulative learning remains, which means that members of the US labor force require new interorganizational systems for CCCs, spanning business corporations, government agencies, and civil-society organizations, often operating on a global scale. TIE provides an analytical framework for understanding the transformation of business models (the interactions of strategic control, organizational integration, and financial commitment) and the implications for the sustainability of value-creating employment opportunities available to members of the US labor force over the course of their careers.

References

Bunn, D. and C. P. Weigel, Sources of U.S. Tax Revenue by Tax Type. *Tax Foundation*, 2023.

Carpenter, M. and W. Lazonick, The Pursuit of Shareholder Value: Cisco's Transformation from Innovation to Financialization. *Institute for New Economic Thinking Working Paper* (202), 2023.

Hopkins, M. and W. Lazonick, The Mismeasure of Mammon: Uses and Abuses of Executive Pay Data. *Institute for New Economic Thinking Working Paper*, (49), 2016.

Jensen, M. C., Agency Costs of Free Cash Flow, Corporate Finance, and Takeovers, *American Economic Review*. v. 76 (2), 1986. 323–329.

Lazonick, W., *Competitive Advantage on the Shop Floor*, Harvard University Press, 1990.

Lazonick, W., Innovative Enterprise and Historical Transformation. *Enterprise & Society*, v. 3 (1), 2002. 35–54.

Lazonick, W., The Theory of the Market Economy and the Social Foundations of Innovative Enterprise. *Economic and Industrial Democracy*, v. 24 (1), 2003. 9–44.

Lazonick, W., Corporate Restructuring, in S. Ackroyd, R. Batt, P. Thompson, and P. Tolbert eds., *The Oxford Handbook of Work and Organization*. Oxford University Press, 2004. 577–601.

Lazonick, W., *Sustainable Prosperity in the New Economy? Business Organization and High-Tech Employment in the United States.* Upjohn Institute for Employment Research, 2009.

Lazonick, W., Profits Without Prosperity: Stock Buybacks Manipulate the Market and Leave Most Americans Worse Off. *Harvard Business Review*, September, 2014. 46–55.

Lazonick, W., Labor in the Twenty-First Century: The Top 0.1% and the Disappearing Middle Class, in C. E. Weller ed., *Inequality, Uncertainty, and Opportunity: The Varied and Growing Role of Finance in Labor Relations.* Cornell University Press, 2015a. 143–192.

Lazonick, W., *Stock Buybacks: From Retain-and-Reinvest to Downsize-and-Distribute,* Center for Effective Public Management, Brookings Institution, 2015b.

Lazonick, W., The Functions of the Stock Market and the Fallacies of Shareholder Value, in C. Driver and G. Thompson, eds., *What Next for Corporate Governance?* Oxford University Press, 2018. 117–151.

Lazonick, W., The Theory of Innovative Enterprise: Foundations of Economic Analysis. Thomas Clarke, Justin O'Brien, and Charles R. T. O'Kelley eds., *The Oxford Handbook of the Corporation.* Oxford University Press, 2019a. 490–514.

Lazonick, W., The Value-Extracting CEO: How Executive Stock-Based Pay Undermines Investment in Productive Capabilities. *Structural Change and Economic Dynamics*, v. 48, 2019b. 53–68.

Lazonick, W. "Is the Most Unproductive Firm the Foundation of the Most Efficient Economy?" *International Review of Applied Economics*, v. 36 (2), 2022. 1–32.

Lazonick, W., *Investing in Innovation: Confronting Predatory Value Extraction in the US Corporation*, Cambridge University Press, 2023.

Lazonick, W. and M. Hopkins, Why the CHIPS Are Down: Stock Buybacks and Subsidies in the U.S. Semiconductor Industry. *Institute for New Economic Thinking Working Paper* (165), 2021.

Lazonick, W. and M. O'Sullivan, Maximizing Shareholder Value: A New Ideology for Corporate Governance. *Economy and Society.* v. 29 (1), 2000. 13–35.

Lazonick, W. and M. E. Sakinç, Make Passengers Safer? Boeing Just Made Shareholders Richer. *American Prospect*, 2019.

Lazonick, W. and J.-S. Shin, *Predatory Value Extraction: How the Looting of the Business Corporation Became the US Norm and How Sustainable Prosperity Can Be Restored*, Oxford University Press, 2020.

Lazonick, W. and Ö. Tulum, Sick with 'Shareholder Value': U.S. Pharma's Financialized Business Model during the Pandemic. *Competition & Change*, 2023.

Lazonick, W., P. Moss, and J. Weitz, The Unmaking of the Black Blue-Collar Middle Class, *Institute for New Economic Thinking Working Paper* (159), 2021.

Lazonick, W., M. E. Sakinç, and M. Hopkins, Why Stock Buybacks are Dangerous for the Economy, *Harvard Business Review*, January 7, 2020.

Sharfman, B. S., The Importance of the Business Judgment Rule. *New York University Journal of Law & Business.* v. 14 (1), 2017. 27–69.

US Census Bureau, *2019 SUSB Annual Datasets by Establishment Industry*. Census Bureau, 2022a.

US Census Bureau, *Income Gini Ratio of Families by Race of Householder, All Races [GINIALLRF], FRED*. Federal Reserve Bank of St. Louis, 2022b.

4

FORMS OF CAPITALISM

David M. Kotz

Introduction

Capitalism first became established in the sixteenth century in Europe, replacing the preceding system of feudalism. Over the following five centuries, capitalism has evolved and changed in various ways. Despite the many changes, the system we call "capitalism" has a few core features that have remained through all of the changes.

First, capitalism is a market economy. That is, the goods and services are produced for sale, not for self-use or as part of a larger economic plan. However, that is far from sufficient to define a capitalist economy. People have engaged in market exchange for thousands of years, under feudalism, in slave economies, and in other kinds of economic systems.

Second, the actual production is performed by "free" wage laborers, who sell their ability to work (their "labor-power") to a company whose owners are referred to as "capitalists." The wage earners are free in the sense that they have no obligations that would prevent them from offering to work for an employer of their choice. That condition did not apply to the working population in earlier feudal or slave systems. Third, the aim of production, which leads a company to undertake production and sale, is the expectation of gaining a profit from the process. Fourth, companies must compete with one another to sell their products in the market.

Thus, capitalism is a market economy in which capitalists who own the enterprises hire wage earners to produce products, which they then compete to sell in the market, aiming for a profit from the process. A capitalist system has two main classes, capitalists who own and control the enterprises and workers who do the work. Capitalists and workers have conflicting interests. The higher the

DOI: 10.4324/9781003366690-5

going wage rate, the lower the profit for the capitalist. If workers as a group can push up their wages, they will obtain a greater share of the value of what they produce, while capitalists will be left with a smaller share. The wage must be above a level that would provide bare minimum physical survival for workers, based on the necessary food, shelter, clothing, etc. The wage cannot be higher than the total net value of the output produced by the workers, since that would leave no incentive for the capitalist to hire them.[1] Where the actual wage rate falls between that very low minimum and the unachievable maximum is determined primarily by the relative bargaining power of workers versus capitalists.

Thus, capitalism gives rise to class conflict, between capitalists who have an interest in minimizing labor costs, and workers whose interest is in a wage that provides a reasonable living standard. This conflict involves not just wages but also working conditions, since providing safe and healthy working conditions costs money and reduces profits. Competition among capitalists compels each capitalist to minimize labor costs, since that increases profit, which is the fuel to wage the competitive struggle.

The account of capitalism in general given above is a sparse account of the complex socioeconomic system of society in the capitalist era. That complex socioeconomic system includes various institutions, practices, norms, and class relations that are not specified by the core features of capitalism in general. The specific institutional form of capitalism, which changes over time, has important implications for the way a capitalist system works. To address the many important questions about today's capitalist economy, it is necessary to supplement an understanding of capitalism in general with an understanding of its specific institutional form.

This chapter presents a theory of the changing institutional form of capitalism, known as social structure of accumulation (SSA) theory. SSA theory arose in the late 1970s and early 1980s. Major works on SSA theory include Gordon et al. (1982), Bowles et al. (1983), Kotz et al. (1994), and McDonough et al. (2010). SSA theory draws inspiration from Marxist economics, Keynesian economics, and institutionalist economics. A similar analysis of the changing form of capitalism arose in France in the 1970s, known as Regulation Theory (Aglietta 1979). This chapter presents the SSA theory, which is useful for analyzing many of the problems of contemporary capitalism. SSA theory provides a basis for explaining the periodic severe economic crises that have emerged in capitalism about once every 30–50 years. It also sheds light on the forces that periodically bring about a structural change in the institutional form of capitalism – a process that appears to be underway today.

Social Structure of Accumulation Theory

Since its inception, capitalism has displayed a powerful expansion drive. As capitalists compete to increase their profits, they are driven to invest part of the profit to expand their capital and hence their expected future profit. The process of increasing capital through investment of profits is called accumulation of capital, or just accumulation for short.

However, while capitalism has a powerful accumulation drive, it also presents obstacles to accumulation. Capitalists hope to increase their future profit by accumulating capital and thereby enlarging their productive capacity, but whether that hope will be realized is uncertain. This is not just because unpredictable non-economic events such as wars or natural disasters might occur. Capitalism itself generates problems that increase the uncertainty about the future conditions for profit-making, which tend to discourage accumulation. Specifically, three features of capitalism tend to discourage capital accumulation by the individual capitalists who must make the accumulation decision: (1) class conflict and competition tend to create disorder and uncertainty about the future conditions for profit-making in each sector of the economy and the economy as a whole; (2) the rate of profit in a capitalist economy as a whole has ups and downs, and it might be lower in the future than it is today; (3) expanding the capital makes sense only if a growing volume of output can be sold in the future, which depends on the level of demand in the future, which cannot be known in advance, since that depends on the decisions of all the actors in the economy.

SSA theory notes that capitalism has taken on a series of particular institutional forms over time. Each institutional form of capitalism has promoted vigorous accumulation for one or several decades, followed by a period of subnormal or no accumulation that also lasts for a decade or more. The key claim of SSA theory is that each institutional form of capitalism has a set of economic and political institutions that promotes capital accumulation for a prolonged period of time. Hence, each set of institutions is called a social structure of accumulation. An SSA fosters accumulation by creating relative stability and predictability through regulation of class conflict and competition, by promoting a high rate of profit in the economy, and by fostering growth of total demand over time.

However, an SSA does not remain effective at promoting accumulation forever. Eventually, the very process of one or several decades of expansion undermines the effectiveness of an SSA, which turns from a structure that promotes accumulation into one that obstructs it. There follows a period of subnormal accumulation and economic instability, referred to as a "structural crisis" because it emerges from the institutional structure of capitalism in the period. A structural crisis can be resolved and normal accumulation resumed only with the construction of a new SSA.

SSA theory offers a way to analyze and understand the series of institutional forms of capitalism that have emerged in history. It is also a theory of the periodic severe economic crises that take place around once every 50 years. SSA theory itself does not have a ready-made explanation of how a particular institutional form of capitalism emerges in each period, but it provides a framework for studying and uncovering the particular forces that bring an SSA into existence during a structural crisis. SSA theory itself does not fully explain why each structural crisis happens, but it provides a framework for analyzing the forces in a particular period that turns an SSA from a promoter of accumulation into an obstacle to it.

We defined an SSA as a set of economic and political institutions, but associated with each SSA there has also been a particular form of dominant ideas, or ideology. Ideas and beliefs facilitate the emergence of a new set of economic and political institutions and help stabilize the institutions by protecting them against challenges once they have emerged.

Social Structures of Accumulation since 1900[2]

SSA theory and its uses can be fleshed out by reviewing the sequence of SSAs and their structural crises since 1900. We will examine the past three SSAs in the United States. While each SSA has institutions that regulate the global economy, domestic institutions in each SSA vary somewhat across countries, reflecting features of the political economy, class relations, and history of each country.

Around 1900, the face of capitalism changed significantly (Table 4.1). A giant merger wave in the United States culminating in the late 1890s to early 1900s gave rise to a highly concentrated industrial structure in manufacturing, transportation, and communication. A few major banks, led by J.P. Morgan and Company, played key roles in promoting the mergers and became power centers over the nonfinancial sector. That transformation was favorable for maintaining a high and stable rate of profit, after the previous period characterized by chaotic price wars that drove down profits. New mass production techniques requiring homogeneous, semi-skilled labor drove productivity gains and helped managers control labor at the workplace. The government actively repressed trade unions, promoting a high rate of profit. U.S. imperialist expansion in the Americas and Asia promoted growing markets for the export of goods and capital. The government's new antitrust policies focused on banning destructive forms of competition. A new ideology of corporate liberalism (Weinstein 1968) claimed that all groups in society were now benefiting from a more stable industrial system with some government oversight, replacing the rugged individualist ideology of the previous period.

TABLE 4.1 Early Twentieth-Century Social Structure of Accumulation

1. Concentrated industrial structure.
2. Finance capital (close financial–industrial links with major banks at the center).
3. Homogeneous semi-skilled labor.
4. State repression of trade unions.
5. Imperialist expansion beyond the continental U.S.
6. Antitrust policy.
7. Corporate liberal philosophy.

In 1929, the Great Depression marked the beginning of the structural crisis of the early twentieth-century SSA. The powerful bankers had spawned a growing wave of speculation in the 1920s, leading to overbuilding of many sectors of the economy and bringing the stock market crash of 1929. The mass production method that grouped large numbers of semi-skilled workers in giant workplaces ended up empowering workers to strike and shut down the highly integrated production process, which contributed to the massive strike wave that arose in the mid to late 1930s. The U.S. and global capitalist economies were stuck in stagnation until World War II military spending revived economies. However, after the war ended in 1945, removing the stimulus of massive arms spending, there was widespread fear that the Great Depression would return.

In the late 1940s, a new SSA was constructed called the regulated capitalist SSA, or regulated capitalism (Table 4.2). Regulated capitalism emerged from the actions of both capitalists and workers. An informal capital–labor compromise was achieved, under which most large corporations agreed to recognize and bargain with the trade unions representing their workers.[3] The unions agreed to limit their demands to wages and working conditions, leaving the management of the workplace in the hands of the capitalists. The more radical trade union leaders were expelled from their positions. The role of government in the economy expanded, with strict regulation of the banks, a welfare state, and a high level of government spending for infrastructure and education, funded by a progressive income tax structure.

The government also used fiscal and monetary policy tools, aiming for robust economic growth, a low unemployment rate, and a moderate inflation rate. The new government roles fostered growing demand for output, economic stability, and rising profit rates. The new financial regulatory system compelled the banks to focus on providing funds for productive economic activity and prevented financial panics. Large corporations in concentrated industries

TABLE 4.2 Mid-Twentieth-Century Regulated Capitalist Social Structure of Accumulation

1. Bretton Woods system.
2. Peaceful collective bargaining.
3. Government regulation of finance and basic industries.
4. High level of public investment in infrastructure and education.
5. Fiscal and monetary policies aimed at low unemployment rate and moderate inflation.
6. Government regulation of job safety, consumer product safety, and the environment.
7. Welfare state.
8. Progressive income tax.
9. Co-respective competition among large corporations.
10. Keynesian ideology.

followed a policy of "co-respective competition," under which they avoided destabilizing price wars while still competing over market shares.

A new system of managing the global monetary and financial system arose after World War II, known as the Bretton Woods system. It featured fixed currency exchange rates, a gold-backed U.S. dollar for international transactions, and a moderately open world economy for trade in goods, although tariffs were permitted and governments were allowed to regulate capital flows under certain conditions. The International Monetary Fund and World Bank, both dominated by the United States, ran the new system. The U.S. government together with the seven major oil companies regulated global oil markets aiming for a stable price of oil that was low enough to promote economic expansion while guaranteeing high profits for the oil companies.

A new ideology, often called Keynesianism, became dominant. It held that contemporary capitalism had become a system that shares the benefits of technological progress among employers, workers, and the public. The term "capitalism" largely disappeared from public discourse and replaced by the "mixed economy," which pointed to the large role of government.

The quarter-century after World War II is often called the Golden Age of capitalism, due to the rapid economic growth, absence of financial panics or severe recessions, and rapidly rising real wages alongside high profits. Many analysts believed that regulated capitalism would remain in place forever. However, in the early 1970s, the economy suddenly stopped performing effectively. Regulated capitalism empowered workers, and their bargaining power increased over time. After the mid-1960s, the rate of profit in the United States began to fall, a trend that continued relentlessly through the 1970s (Figure 4.1).[4]

The structural crisis of regulated capitalism in the 1970s was resolved relatively rapidly in the late 1970s to the early 1980s by the rise of the neoliberal SSA (Table 4.3). Unlike the previous regulated capitalist SSA, the neoliberal SSA was imposed on labor by a relatively unified capitalist class. The capitalists and their political representatives sought to restructure capitalism to reverse the long decline in profit rates. Large corporations shifted from a willingness to compromise in collective bargaining to active efforts to expel unions from their workplaces. Trade unions were unable to resist the capitalist offensive, and the share of workers represented by unions in the private sector declined rapidly. Large companies now could impose wages and working conditions on their workers instead of having to compromise with them.

In the political arena, big business organizations were able to push through a set of major changes in government policy. The previously regulated sectors of transportation, communication, and power were largely deregulated. The closed financial regulatory system with its restrictions on interest rates and permitted activities for banks was dismantled. Much of the provision of public goods and services was contracted out to private companies. Antitrust enforcement was weakened, allowing big companies greater freedom to gain monopoly power.

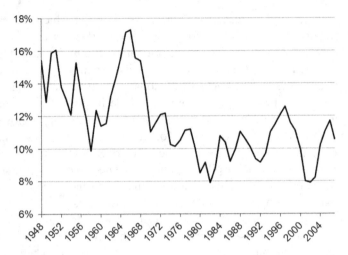

FIGURE 4.1   Rate of Profit of the U.S. Nonfinancial Corporate Business Sector, 1948–2007.

Source: U.S. Bureau of Economic Analysis 2013, Table 1.14, Fixed Assets Table 4.1.

TABLE 4.3 Neoliberal Social Structure of Accumulation

1. Flexible exchange rate system with relatively free movement of goods, services, and capital in the global economy.
2. Employers control wages and working conditions.
3. Deregulation of finance and basic industries.
4. Reduced levels of public investment in infrastructure and education.
5. Fiscal and monetary policies focused on low or no inflation.
6. Cutbacks in government regulation of job safety, consumer product safety, and the environment.
7. Elimination, cutbacks, and privatization of welfare state programs.
8. Cuts in taxes on corporations and the rich.
9. Unrestrained competition among large corporations.
10. Neoliberal (free market) ideology.

Consumer product safety and job safety regulation enforcement were weakened, along with environmental protection. Social welfare programs were cut back or discontinued. Taxes on corporations and the rich were reduced sharply. The government's macroeconomic policies shifted from the pursuit of a balanced goal of low unemployment and moderate inflation to a single-minded focus on low or no inflation without regard to the unemployment rate.

The previous Keynesian ideas were replaced by neoliberal ideas, which held that government efforts to improve economic performance only made performance worse. These ideas called for a "free market" without any significant public regulation. Trade unions were portrayed as monopolists in the sale of labor that violated the right of individual workers to make their own bargains with employers. Taxes were viewed as unfair to companies and individuals who should be allowed to keep what they earn. Neoliberal ideology claimed that freeing businesses from regulation and taxes and from powerful unions would unleash a wave of investment, innovation, and economic growth that would benefit everyone, as suggested by the slogan "A rising tide lifts all boats."

The rapid neoliberal restructuring of capitalism did lead to a recovery of the rate of profit in the United States in the early 1980s. The long decline in the profit rate from the mid-1960s gave way to a rising trend in the early 1980s (Figure 4.1). The average real wage had risen steadily from 1948 through 1973, but after 1979, the average real wage trended downward for several decades, which allowed a growing share of the rising value of output to go to profits (Figure 4.2). There followed 25 years of long economic expansions – from 1982 to 1990, 1991 to 2001, and 2001 to 2007 – punctuated by relatively brief and mild recessions and with little inflation. The incomes of the rich grew rapidly over that period. The ratio of average CEO pay to that of the average worker in a large corporation rose from 30 in 1978 to 331 in 2007 and 366 in 2020 (Bivens and Kandra 2022).

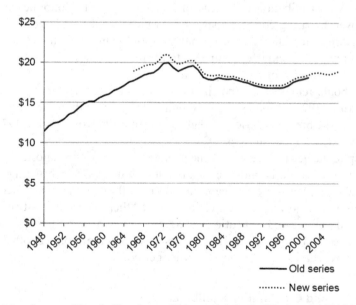

FIGURE 4.2   Average Hourly Earnings of Nonsupervisory Workers in 2011 Dollars, 1948–2007.

Note: The Bureau of Labor Statistics revised the methodology for the series for average hourly earnings in 2004, and, as a result, there is no consistent series available from 1948 to 2007. Figure 4.3 presents the old and new series for the subperiods over which they are available.

Source: Economic Report of the President, 1990, 2003, 2010.

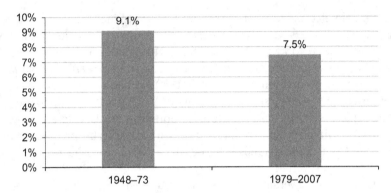

FIGURE 4.3   Investment as a Percentage of Output in the United States.

Note: Average of annual ratios of net private domestic investment to net domestic product.

Source: U.S. Bureau of Economic Analysis 2023, National Income and Product Tables 1.7.5 and 5.2.5.

However, the means by which neoliberal restructuring brought relatively stable economic expansion was different from what had been promised by the advocates of neoliberalism. Instead of rising investment, economic expansion was driven by rising consumer spending, which was driven largely by households taking on growing debt to make up for stagnating wages. Investment performance was lackluster compared to the previous period of regulated capitalism (Figure 4.3). Instead of growth "lifting all boats," the yachts rose while the rowboats remained in the shallows. The rate of GDP growth over the period from 1979 to 2007 was 3.0%, significantly lower than the 4.0% rate of growth of the previous period of regulated capitalism from 1948 to 1973 (U.S. Bureau of Economic Analysis 2023.

Despite the negative results of the neoliberal SSA for the majority, no effective resistance could be mounted against it as long as it was bringing normal accumulation plus impressive gains in wealth for the capitalist class. Neoliberal ideology was a powerful force, claiming that "there is no alternative" to the neoliberal policies and institutions. Leading politicians in both major political parties accepted the neoliberal claims, just as both major political officials had accepted Keynesian policies in the earlier period.

Expansion and Crisis under Neoliberal Capitalism

As for any SSA, the long period of relatively stable accumulation and expansion in the neoliberal SSA contained the seeds of its own destruction. The particular way in which expansion under neoliberalism led to an eventual structural crisis was based on the particular way that neoliberal institutions have operated. Neoliberal institutions brought three developments: (1) rising inequality between workers and capitalists and among households; (2) a series of large asset bubbles in corporate securities and real estate[5]; (3) a shift of the activities of financial institutions toward highly risky (and highly profitable) activities. Those three developments together brought the 25 years of relatively stable expansions – but they fostered long-term trends that were unsustainable and would eventually plunge the economy into a structural crisis.

As the unemployment rate declined during expansions, neoliberal institutions kept workers' bargaining power so weak that there was no risk that wages would rise to squeeze profits. This made possible long expansions without giving rise to either a profit squeeze or rising inflation. However, while profits growing faster than wages created an incentive to invest and expand, it gave rise to a problem of lack of buyers for the rising output. That is, economic expansion under neoliberal capitalism faced a problem of inadequate growth in aggregate demand, given that wages were stagnating or falling and government spending was restrained.

Large asset bubbles provided the solution to the problem of adequate demand growth. Asset bubbles in corporate securities and especially housing provided collateral, which enabled households to borrow to finance consumer spending. A stock market bubble in the 1990s stimulated rising consumption by upper-middle and upper-income households, which brought a very long economic expansion lasting 10 years (Kotz 2003). That expansion ended only when the stock market bubble deflated in 2000. An even larger real estate bubble began in the early 2000s that stimulated rising demand, bringing another expansion through 2007 (Figure 4.4).

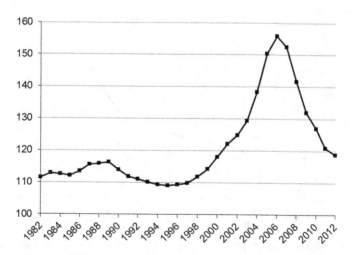

FIGURE 4.4 House Price Index Relative to Homeowner's Equivalent Rent, 1982–2012.

Source: Federal Housing Finance Agency, 2013; U.S. Bureau of Labor Statistics, 2018.

While asset bubbles provided collateral, deregulated financial institutions provided the loans enabling people to spend their growing asset wealth without selling the asset. After 2000, the deregulated financial institutions found ways to make huge profits from making mortgage loans to a broad swath of the population including low-income households. They did this through subprime mortgages, alt-A mortgages, and other new types of mortgages. Any undue risk was transferred by the mortgage issuer onto others through securitization of mortgages, with the help of compliant security rating agencies. Such loans seemed safe as long as housing prices kept rising, since foreclosure would bring the creditor institution an asset that was appreciating in value. As always happens during large-scale asset bubbles, many actors became persuaded that asset prices would continue to rise indefinitely.

Over the whole period of neoliberal capitalism in the United States, the series of long expansions gave rise to unsustainable trends. First, each long expansion further increased the indebtedness of households (Figure 4.5). Household debt as a percentage of household disposable income rose from 59.2% in 1982 to 77.9% in 1990 and 89.5% in 2000, before ballooning to 126.7% in 2007. This trajectory had become unsustainable by the end of the 2001–07 expansion.

A system in which wages are repressed so severely that economic expansion is possible only through growing household debt cannot continue indefinitely. Furthermore, not only did the financial pressure on households increase over time but also the level of fragility of the financial sector grew over time. As financial institutions sought ever higher profits through ever more opaque and risky activities, the threat posed by an asset bubble deflation grew. The debt of the

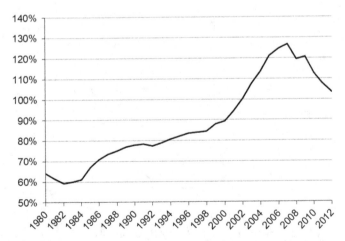

FIGURE 4.5   Household Debt as a Percentage of Disposable Personal Income, 1980–2012.

Source: Board of Governors of the Federal Reserve System 2013, Flow of Funds Accounts, Table B.100; U.S. Bureau of Economic Analysis 2013, NIPA Table 2.1.

financial sector grew even more rapidly than the debt of households, as financial institutions became ever more leveraged to maximize their profits. As trillions of dollars in risky mortgage-related securities spread through the U.S. (and global) financial system in the mid-2000s, the financial system became ever more vulnerable to a deflation of the housing bubble. The housing bubble of the 2000s was massive, and the impact of its eventual deflation would accordingly be huge.

As is the case with all asset bubbles, the housing bubble of the 2000s was bound to deflate at some point. Once the housing bubble began to deflate, all of the foregoing trends would become unsustainable. The deflation of the housing bubble would take down a large number of households who could no longer make payments on their existing loans and could no longer refinance to make their payments manageable. The increasingly fragile financial sector could not survive the deflation of the housing bubble. The deflation of the massive housing bubble, so necessary for the third installment of economic expansion in the 2000s under the neoliberal SSA, brought financial crisis of 2008. The banks survived only on government handouts.

Thus, growing borrowing by households driven by stagnating wages, the rising debt of financial institutions as they pursued highly profitable creation and sale of new financial securities, and the resulting spread of those highly risky securities throughout the banking system eventually brought the massive financial crisis. Those unsustainable trends also brought the most severe recession since the 1930s in 2008, known as the Great Recession.

The financial crisis and the Great Recession of 2008 marked the beginning of the structural crisis of the neoliberal SSA. The ability of that SSA to promote normal capital accumulation reached its end. The mechanism of debt-financed consumer spending could not be recovered. Households with reduced property values could not borrow to finance growing consumer spending and instead began to pay off their debt rather than expand it.

The financial crisis was resolved by a huge taxpayer-funded bailout of the banks plus the Federal Reserve taking a number of radical steps including buying toxic securities from the banks and pumping reserves into the banks. A large fiscal stimulus bill in February 2009 led to a resumption of GDP growth in the summer of 2009. However, the recovery was very sluggish for the next decade, as GDP grew at the rate of only 2.3% per year from 2009 to 2019, a rate that qualifies as "stagnation" (Figure 4.6). Despite a recovery in the rate of profit in the U.S. economy after 2010, investment did not grow very rapidly. One study found that the usual strong effect of a rising rate of profit on the rate of capital accumulation was broken after 2008 (Kotz and Basu 2019). The neoliberal SSA was no longer able to promote normal capital accumulation.

From 2009 to 2019, not just American capitalism but global capitalism was stuck in stagnation, although China was an exception. Then, starting in 2020, the course of the structural crisis was affected by two events, the COVID-19 pandemic that began in early 2020 and then the Ukraine War that started in

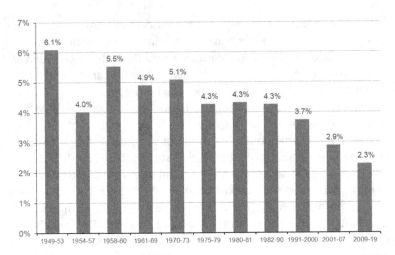

FIGURE 4.6 Annual Growth Rate of GDP from Trough Quarter to the Following Peak Quarter, 1949–2019.

Note: The trough quarter is the last three-month period of a recession, and the peak quarter is the last three-month period of the following expansion.

Source: U.S. Bureau of Economic Analysis 2023, National Income and Product Table 1.1.6.

February 2022. Those events effectively overrode the factors that usually govern the ups and downs of capital accumulation.[6] The COVID-19 pandemic brought a very short and very severe economic downturn in the first half of 2020, followed by an immediate very steep recovery. The pandemic had drastic effects on global supply chains, an effect worsened by the outbreak of the Ukraine war. Those developments caused supply disturbances leading to rising inflation and various distortions of the global economy. When the economic effects of those two developments recede, we can expect a continuation of the stagnation crisis, until that crisis is resolved by another structural change in the system.

A New Social Structure of Accumulation?

SSA theory provides some insight into the possible ways that a particular structural crisis can be resolved. The structural crisis of the neoliberal SSA followed a period of growing inequality, big asset bubbles, and the spread of new highly risky financial assets. There was no long-term fall in the rate of profit prior to 2008. The structural crisis was set off by a financial collapse. It appears that a resolution of the post-2008 structural crisis, that responds to the trends and imbalances that gave rise to the financial crisis, would require a new form of regulated SSA with active state regulation of business and the economy. The construction of a regulated form of capitalism is a more complex process than the dismantling of regulated capitalism that occurred in the late 1970s–early 1980s. The last episode of regulated capitalism after World War II was not consolidated until around 1948, almost 30 years after the beginning of the preceding structural crisis in 1929.

As of this writing, it is now 15 years since the start of the current structural crisis, which has not yet been resolved. However, the conditions of the structural crisis appear to be driving the growing influence of policy ideas that could lead to a new form of regulated capitalism. By 2016, a large section of the population was angry, in the United States and elsewhere, and ready to support a radical departure from the established policies. The political candidates supported by the ruling elite were offering no solution to the festering economic problems. Two policy directions that had been marginalized suddenly have drawn growing support, coming from the political right and the political left.

First, in many countries, authoritarian right-wing nationalist political parties and leaders have recently been elected to government. Second, supporters of left-wing social democracy have gained popularity in some countries.[7] In the United States, the rise of Donald Trump has represented the first trend, while the popularity of Vermont Senator Bernie Sanders indicated a possible shift in the second direction.[8] Both call for greater government management of the economy, although their proposals about the role of trade unions and the rights of workers are diametrically opposed. The 1930s structural crisis, which is similar to that of today in significant respects, previously saw the rise of authoritarian nationalist regimes in several major countries in the form of fascism (Germany, Italy, Spain, and Japan), while social democratic reform took hold in others (the U.S. New Deal and Scandinavian social democracy).

Either policy direction could potentially lead to a new regulated capitalist SSA. A right-wing nationalist regime might pursue state repression of trade unions, which would promote a high profit rate, along with the expansion of government spending for the military and infrastructure, which would bring rising total demand. That combination could promote a long period of normal capital accumulation. As the president, Trump advocated authoritarian nationalist policies although for various reasons there was no consistent implementation of the policies.[9] Also, the absence of any call to regulate the financial sector is a problem for the viability of such a new SSA.

A new wave of social democratic reform could also resolve the crisis. Such a direction might include policies to strengthen trade unions and restore collective bargaining, which could lead to wages again rising together with profits, while a big public investment program to upgrade infrastructure and combat global climate change would bring rising total demand. The policies of the Biden Administration since 2021 surprised many analysts by sharply departing from Biden's past support of neoliberal policies. The Biden Administration has pushed through some mildly social democratic measures on infrastructure and climate change as well as more generous social welfare programs. Despite some labor organizing successes, trade unions remain weak. Also, no steps toward reregulating financial institutions have yet emerged.

Concluding Comment

The account given above of the evolution of the institutional structure of U.S. capitalism shows the usefulness of SSA theory for understanding the long-run ups and downs in macroeconomic performance. It directs our attention to the role of institutions, class relations, class conflicts, and particularly the conflicting interests of capitalists and workers, all of which play important roles in the long-run ups and downs of the economy and the periodic transformations of the institutional structure of capitalism.

Every socioeconomic system before the rise of capitalism eventually passed away and was replaced by a different system. While capitalism has survived challenges in the past, it too may not last forever. Capitalism faces major problems today, including a high level of income inequality, the economic insecurity that results from market competition and its effects, its promotion of inequality based on race/ethnicity/gender, which divides the working class for the benefit of capitalists, and its tendency to lead to conflicts and wars in the global system over control of resources and markets. Perhaps the greatest challenge is the process of global climate change, which threatens humanity's future, a threat that requires prioritizing the public good over the profits of corporations.

Such challenges may eventually lead to a transition from capitalism to its long-time challenger, socialism. Advocates of socialism today argue that only a new democratic socialism can resolve the problems generated by capitalism. SSA theory suggests that such a transition is most likely to occur in a period of structural crisis of capitalism, at a time when socialist movements have sufficient popular support to bring about such a transition. Thus, SSA theory is only partly a theory of the periodic reform of capitalism. It is also a theory relevant for considering a possible transformation that goes beyond capitalism.

Notes

1 The net value of output is the total (gross) value of output less the cost of the non-human goods used up in production, which must also be covered by the revenue received if production is to continue.
2 The following sections draw upon analysis and figures in Kotz (2015).
3 In the 1930s, New Deal legislation had guaranteed the right of collective bargaining for workers. However, the law was widely ignored at first. Only after World War II did peaceful collective bargaining become the norm in most industries. There were still strikes in the postwar decades, but they represented jockeying over the rate of wage increase and were relatively peaceful.
4 A similar trend arose in the major west European economies.
5 An asset bubble is a self-sustaining rise in the market price of an asset driven by the belief that past increases in the price of the asset imply that the price will continue to rise in the future, yielding capital gains for the asset holders. As more funds are drawn into purchasing the asset, the rising demand drives up the price, seeming to confirm the rosy belief. However, an asset bubble must eventually collapse when no additional funds can be drawn into purchasing it.

6 Capitalism tends to generate pandemics and wars at times, which temporarily change the macroeconomic trajectory of the economy. When such events end, the previous economic trajectory is likely to resume unless structural changes have been made to the economy.

7 The term social democracy refers to the form of regulated capitalism that arose in some European countries after World War II, such as Sweden and the U.K. The regulated capitalism in the U.S. after World War II can be considered a weak form of social democracy.

8 While Senator Bernie Sanders states that he is a socialist, he actually advocates reforms in capitalism that are usually called social democratic reforms. He does not call for replacing capitalism with an alternative socialist system.

9 President Trump's frequent calls for big infrastructure investments did not receive an enthusiastic response from the Republicans in Congress.

References

Aglietta, Michel, *A Theory of Capitalist Regulation: The U.S. Experience*. London: Verso, 1979.

Bivens, Josh, and Jori Kandra, CEO Pay Has Skyrocketed 1460% since 1978. *Economic Policy Institute report*, 2022. Available at https://www.epi.org/publication/ceo-pay-in-2021/

Board of Governors of the Federal Reserve System, 2013. http://www.federalreserve.gov

Bowles, Samuel, David M. Gordon, and Thomas E. Weisskopf, *Beyond the Wasteland: A Democratic Alternative to Economic Decline*. Garden City, NY: Anchor Press/Doubleday, 1983.

Economic Report of the President, 1990 Washington, DC: U.S. Government Printing Office, various years. Available at http://www.gpo.gov/fdsys/browse/collection.action?collectionCode=ERP

Federal Housing Finance Agency, House Price Indexes, 2013. https://www.fhfa.gov/

Gordon, David M., Richard Edwards, and Michael Reich, *Segmented Work, Divide Workers. The Historical Transformation of Labor in the United States*. Cambridge: Cambridge University Press, 1982.

Kotz, David M., Neoliberalism and the U.S. Economic Expansion of the 1990s. *Monthly Review* 54:11, 2003. 15–33.

Kotz, David M., *The Rise and Fall of Neoliberal Capitalism*. Cambridge: Harvard University Press, 2015.

Kotz, David M., and Deepankar Basu, Stagnation and Institutional Structures. *Review of Radical Political Economics* 51:1, 2019. 5–30.

Kotz, David M., Terrence McDonough, and Michael Reich (eds.), *Social Structures of Accumulation: The Political Economy of Growth and Crisis*. Cambridge: Cambridge University Press, 1994.

McDonough, T., and Michael Reich, and David M. Kotz, *Contemporary Capitalism and Its Crises*, Cambridge: Cambridge University Press, 2010.

U.S. Bureau of Economic Analysis, 2023 various years. https://www.bea.gov/

U.S. Bureau of Labor Statistics, 2018. various years. https://www.bls.gov/

Weinstein, James, *The Corporate Ideal in the Liberal State. 1900-1918*. Boston: Beacon Press, 1968.

5

FINANCIALIZATION

Ramaa Vasudevan

Introduction

An important dimension of the structural transformation of contemporary capitalism, specifically since 1980s, involves what has been termed financialization. Associated with the neoliberal policies of liberalization and globalization that were widely adopted in this period, this transformation reflects a fundamental reshaping of social relations.

While recent research has pointed to the ambiguous and non-linear relationships between the level and pace of financial deepening and financial development on the one hand and growth and stability on the other (Sahay et al. 2015), mainstream neoclassical economics, which remains focused on the impact of financial markets on incentives and market outcomes, is inadequately equipped to theorize financialization. Radical political economy, however, provides an analytical framework that is better placed to identify and comprehend this phenomenon.

The term itself has been defined in a variety of ways across literature. Two widely cited definitions of financialization define it as:

1. "a pattern of accumulation in which profit making occurs increasingly through financial channels rather than through trade and commodity production" (Krippner 2012).
2. "the increasing importance of financial markets, financial motives, financial institutions, and financial elites in the operation of the economy and its governing institutions, both at the national and international levels" (Epstein 2005).

DOI: 10.4324/9781003366690-6

While conceptual proliferation around the term has rightly led to a call for caution (Christophers 2015), the focus on financialization, however vague, imprecise or chaotic its definition, does capture a defining characteristic of contemporary capitalism that needs analysis (Mader et al. 2020).

Capitalism is viewed as a fundamentally financial system in both Marxian and Post-Keynesian analytical frameworks. The mechanisms of production, growth and accumulation are embedded in the financial system. A secular tendency of the expansion of the scale and scope of finance driven by financial innovation can also be discerned (Vercelli 2013). Overlaid on this long-run trend are recurrent phases of financial dominance. These are characterized by a systemic transformation in the patterns and structure of accumulation. The historical perspective in Arrighi (1994) points to three prior periods when finance came to be dominant, with each of these periods marking the autumnal phase of a long wave of capital accumulation. If we focus more specifically on the two phases after the Industrial Revolution, parallels can be drawn between the current phase of financialization and the period from the last quarter of the nineteenth century till the First World War which can be viewed as the first era of financial ascendancy of industrial capitalism.

This chapter will briefly delineate the features or tendencies that characterize the contemporary phase of financialization before surveying how financialization has been analyzed within Post-Keynesian, and Marxian approaches, specifically. It will also draw out the implications of these approaches to comprehending what is distinctive about contemporary neoliberal financialization.

Characterizing Financialization

Financialization is characterized by the expansion and proliferation of financial markets and the acceleration of financial innovations alongside the deregulation of finance since the 1980s. Securitization – the process by which certain types of risky and illiquid financial assets are pooled and repackaged by the US-dominated banking system into new, more liquid interest-bearing securities with a higher credit rating – has been key to the spectacular growth of finance in recent decades. Multiple loans, like mortgages, are bundled together, then "sliced and diced" into novel kinds of instruments to take on a parallel existence that bears an extremely complex and opaque relationship to the original loans. Beyond straightforward loans and deposits, the financial system has come to be dominated by more complex market-based intermediation between borrowers and lenders, the so-called shadow-banking system (Mehrling 2010; Pozsar et al. 2010).

This expansion in the scale and scope of finance has been entwined is a structural transformation that consolidated the power and dominance of finance over industry. This manifests in the growth of the financial sector's share of profits in the US and the increasing implication of non-financial firms in financial markets both as a source of funding and as a source of earnings (Krippner 2012; Palley 2013; Lapavitsas 2013). The management of financial portfolios has become a key component of investment strategies with the rise of the ideology of shareholder value that privileges financial returns, share buybacks and dividend distribution overgrowth (Lazonick and O'Sullivan 2000). Mergers and acquisitions, and the corporate mantra of "downsize and distribute," has also weakened the bargaining power of workers, making employment more precarious.

At the same time, as neoliberal policies have eroded the welfare state and cutback social provisioning, finance has become more pervasive not just in the economy but in the social and economic reproduction of households – mortgages, health and student debt on the one hand, and market-based pension plans on the other (Lapavitsas 2009). Debt and financial markets have become integral to material provisioning of working-class households. Households have also become implicated in financial markets on the asset side, through their involvement in pension-funds and mutual funds.

The role of the state has also transformed. The embrace of liberalization and deregulation in the 1980s facilitated the growth of finance (Krippner 2012; Epstein 2005). The growing scale and scope of operation of financial markets, however, rests on the critical role of central banks in managing and providing a backstop to financial markets. Inflation-targeting and central bank independence were adopted as the pillars of monetary policy, and central bank interventions in the market for US Treasuries emerged as the anchor of the financial markets (Mehrling 2010; Lapavitsas 2013). The development of the capacity of central banks, the US Federal Reserve in particular, to intervene more widely and extend its safety net in times of financial meltdowns provided a powerful impetus to the growth of finance (Crotty 2009; Tooze 2018).

While much of the above description is focused on the US and advanced capitalist economies, financialization is deeply enmeshed in the process of globalization, the rise and spread of neoliberalism across the globe, and the uneven, asymmetric integration of countries around the world into international financial markets (Karwowski et al. 2017; Karwowski and Stockhammer 2017; Alami et al. 2022; Bonizzi et al. 2020).

Marxist Approaches to Financialization

Marxian analysis of financialization draws on his theorization of money and credit and on the implications of the pervasive spread of the corporation as a form of organizing accumulation. Marx had spelled out the contradictory role of finance as a driver of capitalist accumulation and technological progress on one hand and of inequality and instability on the other (Marx 1981). Marxian analysis of the financial system is rooted and derived from the more abstract analysis of money and its functions. The development of finance receives an impetus and evolves alongside the accumulation of capital and the development of capitalism.

A key analytical insight of Marx is the qualitative distinction between "monied" and "industrial" capitalists and the specificity of the social relations between the two, where the former represents capital in its role as property while the latter represents capital in its role as function facilitating the process of extraction of surplus value in production. By lending to the functioning capitalist who invests in building productive capacity, "monied capital" is in effect selling a special commodity – interest-bearing capital – on the condition that the amount is repaid with interest. Interest constitutes a claim on surplus value produced by the expansion of productive capacity by the borrower, so that the surplus value extracted in production gets divided into the categories of interest and profit of enterprise giving rise to the illusion that money has an intrinsic capacity to yield interest. While the term "monied" capitalist suggests a coupon-clipping rentier who owns money, the development of banking led to the development of a financial system where the loaned money was itself borrowed from others, and money that would have otherwise remained idle is centralized and mobilized toward capital accumulation or the generation of financial returns. Beyond passively mobilizing savings and idle hoards, the financial system also actively creates and deals in tradeable titles to future streams of revenue. The valuation of these titles and claims is based on discounting the expected flows of future income and revenue, forming what Marx characterized as fictitious capital. The value of these financial claims is fictitious in the sense that their value fluctuates relatively independently of the original outlay on productive capital as it continues to be traded after the initial purchase.

The circulation of these financial assets multiplied and lengthened channels of credit beyond the capital directly owned or held by financial institutions. A simple loan is transformed into fictitious capital in the form of marketable bonds. The future earnings of corporations are transformed into shares that are bought and sold on the stock exchange. The organizational form of joint stock companies, the precursor to modern corporations, is, thus, embedded in the development of the financial system where the stocks are traded. The division between shareholders and the managers embodied in the corporate form is another manifestation of the distinction of capital as property and capital as function.

The relation between financial and non-financial corporate capital has become deeper and more complex in recent decades. The significance of qualitatively distinct role of finance since the 1980s was first highlighted by the Monthly Review School (Magdoff and Sweezy 1987; Sweezy 1994, 1997). The rise of the modern corporation, in what is characterized as a stage of monopoly capitalism, generated a tendency for rising economic surpluses by squeezing wages. As these rising economic surpluses outpaced the growth of investment opportunities, a tendency toward stagnation was engendered. Consequently, the growing volumes of surpluses found profitable outlets in the sphere of finance, leading to a shift in the center of gravity of economic activity from industrial production (and even from much of the service sector) to finance in what was later conceptualized as a stage of monopoly-finance capital caught in the trap of the twin tendencies of stagnation and financialization (Foster 2007; Foster and McChesney 2009).

Duménil and Lévy (2004, 2013) see financialization as an outcome of the coup of finance after the US Federal Reserve hiked interest rate in 1979. The focus here is not so much on finance as an investment opportunity but rather on the pivotal role of the administrators of interest-bearing capital and the modes of financing capital accumulation in the quest for higher returns in shaping social relations. The assertion of power by finance – defined as the upper fraction of capitalist class and their financial institutions and its alliance with the managerial class – imposed a new discipline on labor. The expansion of financial mechanisms was not simply parasitic but paved the way for restructuring the balance of power and restoring profitability after the profitability crisis of the 1970s. This development blurred the lines between financial and non-financial corporations. It also reflected a hierarchical relation and the hegemony of finance, while stoking macro-disequilibria in the form of rising domestic and external debt in the US.

A link can be drawn between both these approaches and Hilferding's analysis of the period of financial ascendancy at the beginning of the nineteenth century in terms of the emergence and consolidation of finance capital and the specific institutional forms in which finance and industry were linked together through interlocking holdings, directorships and control. The pervasive spread of the corporation as a mode of organizing both financial and non-financial capital paved the path for the emergence of new mechanisms of control and coordination through the evolving financial markets. Unlike the bank-centered formulation of finance capital by Hilferding, capital markets have become key to forging the synthesis of industrial and financial capital and imposing the power of finance (and the ideology of shareholder value) on the organization of production and accumulation in contemporary financialization.

Lapavitsas (2009; 2011; 2013) draws on Marx's monetary theory of credit, and the contradictory relation between finance and capital accumulation as the financial system evolves and develops endogenously from the real circuits of capital accumulation. Financialization is conceptualized as a systematic transformation of the social organization of capitalism, emerging from the spontaneous interactions between non-financial corporations, banks and households as they become implicated more deeply in financial markets. (Lapavitsas 2013). Focusing on the molecular processes of accumulation and the increasing importance of financial transactions in the interrelationships and activities of non-financial enterprises, banks and workers, Lapavitsas (2011, 2013) high-lights three tendencies. First, banks and financial institutions have reoriented toward trading in capital markets and lending to households rather than to non-financial enterprises. Second, households have become more deeply imbricated in the financial system through both growing indebtedness and the mobilization of their savings through pension funds and mutual funds. Finally, non-financial enterprises rely less on bank loans and more on financial markets for funding and are more involved in financial activities.

These transformed behaviors and inter-relations led to the transformed and expanded role of financial profits in the accumulation process. Apart from being derived from the redistribution of surplus value between different segments of the capitalist class in the form of interest, dividends and capital gains, financial profits are also being extracted from increasingly indebted working-class households. While predatory forms of usury predate capitalism, financial expropriation plays a distinct role in the accumulation processes of contemporary "financialized" capitalism as a source of financial profits (Lapavitsas 2009; 2013).

In contrast to this approach that locates financialization as arising endogenously from the interactions of the key economic actors/classes, another path to theorizing financialization begins from the expanding scale and widening scope of the incorporation of interest-bearing capital (and fictitious capital) in the overarching process of capital accumulation with the rise and spread of neoliberalism (Fine 2010, 2013). This entails both the deeper penetration of finance and the more concrete, hybrid forms of interest-bearing capital in the accumulation processes, and its entry into new sites of both economic and social reproduction. Financialization is not simply the expansion of finance but the generalized subordination of economic interactions and inter-relations to the abstract logic of interest-bearing capital that has fundamentally restructured the way economic activities are organized (Fine 2013).

Post-Keynesian Approaches

Post-Keynesian approaches to financialization draw on Keynes' theorization, Kalecki's remarkably analogous macroeconomic analysis of demand and distribution drawing on Marx and Minsky's exploration of Keynes ideas of capitalism as an inherently unstable financial system.

Keynes, like Marx, put forward a monetary theory of production in his critique of classical political economy. His approach, however, was based on the role of fundamental uncertainty in conditioning the demand for money as a secure and liquid financial claim – his theory of liquidity preference (Keynes 1964). Instead of equilibrating savings and investment, Keynes formulated a liquidity theory of interest rates where the determination of interest rates took place in money and capital markets. Alongside this monetary analysis, Keynes elaborated his theory of the role of effective demand and constraints on full employment. He identified the rentier – "the functionless investor" – as exploiting the scarcity of capital to earn higher returns on accumulated wealth-holdings. While the entrepreneur earns from the yield of assets used in production, rentier earnings arise from speculating on the changing price of financial assets. The redistribution of income toward the rentier as interest rates rise (and as deflationary policies are adopted) squeezes investment and employment, impoverishing workers at the expense of rentier wealth-holders. The role of the rentier is thus embedded in the theory of distribution and demand.

Minsky (2008) developed Keynes' theory of liquidity preference and its role in the pricing of financial assets and explored how financial innovations driven by profit-seeking activities of financial institutions were integral to capitalist development. Building on Keynes' insight into the role of monetary mechanisms in financing investment, Minsky turned his lens to the significance of the structure of liabilities that funded market activities and positions. Economic actors are subject to a binding survival constraint and must balance the pattern of inflows of cash with that of outflows. The only viable way to alleviate the constraint for the economy as whole is by expanding productive capacity through debt-financed investment such that cash inflows are greater than the commitments of cash in the initial investment. But expansionary periods create incentives conducive for speculative investors who are willing to pursue more risky ventures and take on higher levels of debt and reduce their holdings of safe liquid assets in pursuit of higher profits. This erosion of the margins of safety leads to increasing difficulties in repaying debt and refinancing positions foster financial fragility. As the level of risk rises with the growing complexity and scale of the capitalist enterprises, speculative aspects become dominant. Unlike Keynes, Minsky drew a less sharp distinction between speculative rentiers and productive entrepreneurs, while underscoring how financial markets not only transform the market power of firms into capital gains but also induce rising indebtedness (Minsky 1986).

Minsky's focus on the financing of accumulation has parallels to Marx's conception. Minsky developed a formulation of investment as being driven by the difference between expected valuation of assets and purchase price of investment output, with the prices of assets (in contrast to current investment output) being determined in the market based on expected flows of earnings, the state of aggregate demand and market power (Minsky 1986; 2008). Minsky also underscored how the validation of financial innovations after financial meltdowns through central bank interventions underpinned the resilience and growth of the financial system even though it could not contain the inherent instability of finance (Minsky 1983, 1990, 1992, 2008).

An important strand of post-Keynesian analysis conceptualizes contemporary financialization as the resurgence of the social strata of the parasitical rentier and its domination over productive enterprise. The embrace of deregulation and liberalization since the 1980s dismantled the structure of regulatory constraints that sought to contain finance, giving the rentier free rein. As a consequence of the flawed institutions and practices of the neoliberal policy regime, the growth of financial markets accelerated, outpacing that of the non-financial economy (Crotty 2009). Profits in the financial sector rose rapidly as a result of greater concentration, increased risk-taking and financial innovations that fed the growing demand for financial products (Crotty 2008). Financial products became more complex, opaque and illiquid, engendering fragility.

This strand of post-Keynesian analysis of financialization or finance-dominated capitalism draws on Keynes' arguments about the implications of the rise of the rentier for demand and distribution, to explore the macroeconomic implications of finance-dominated accumulation regimes (Hein 2010; Taylor 2011). The phenomenon has involved on the one hand an increasing recourse to debt in order to finance consumption, and on the other rising claims of shareholders on the profits of corporations and re-orientation of corporate strategies toward financial returns. Financialization is also a driver of declining wage shares and a redistribution of income away from workers toward rentiers (Jayadev and Epstein 2019; Dünhaupt 2017). Thus, the dominance of finance reconfigures the macroeconomy through three broad channels: investment, consumption and a redistribution of income away from workers (Hein and Van Treeck 2010a).

The shareholder revolution through this period reoriented management incentives toward maximizing shareholder value and shorter time horizons of decision-making. The increased opportunities for financial profits, and the changing incentives of managers affected through remuneration schemes based on financial market performance, led to funds being siphoned away from real investment. At the same time, the increasing burden of financial payments including higher debt and dividend obligations reduced financing from equity issues and squeezed the funds available for expansion of productive capacity (Crotty 2003; Stockhammer 2004; Orhangazi 2008; Hein and Van Treeck 2010b). This explains the perverse paradox at the heart of the financialized economy – the slowdown in investment despite the recovery of profitability as rising profits are channeled to financial accumulation rather than investment in productive capacity. Fiebiger (2016), however, points to the global expansion of corporate activity to argue that growth objectives were not entirely abandoned but pursued in the context of globalized production.

Apart from the impact on investment, this literature also investigates the impact of rising household debt and asset-holdings on consumption demand. The relaxation of lending norms and the potential offered by securitization to offload risk expanded the availability of credit to low-income households enabling consumption norms to grow faster than the growth wages. But while consumer debt and the wealth effects of the housing and stock market booms stimulate consumption demand, growing debt obligations and the collapse of asset bubble eventually undermine this stimulus (Bhaduri et al. 2006; Dutt 2005).

The third channel explored in this literature is how the redistribution of income from workers to rentiers and capital affects demand (Hein 2012a; 2012b). The shift in the sectoral composition of the economy, the rise in managerial salaries and the claims of rentiers and the erosion of trade unions and worker bargaining power squeezed the income share of workers under finance-dominated capitalism (Hein 2015). Given the lower propensity to consume among rentiers, the impact on demand hinges on whether the rise in their income shares at the expense of workers compensates for the reduction in consumption demand among workers. The operation of these three channels by which finance impacts demand and distribution points to the possibility of either stagnation or unstable finance-led growth (Skott and Ryoo 2008; Hein and Van Treeck 2010a; Vasudevan 2017).

A second strand of this literature – the Money View and Critical Macro-Finance perspectives – draws more explicitly on Minsky's analysis of the structure of interlocking balance sheets of financial institutions and the institutional determinants of liquidity and credit-creation that constitute the hierarchy of monetary claims (Mehrling 2017; Gabor 2020). The spotlight is on the nuts and bolts of the financial plumbing that undergirds economic interactions, concentrating on how liabilities are being managed to meet the survival constraint. Of particular importance are the processes of clearing and settlement of gross flows constituted by these interlocking balance sheets, and of the pricing of the outstanding claims in financial markets. Beyond functional analysis that comprehends financial markets as instrumental to rentier's exercise of dominance over the economy, the focus is on uncovering how the mechanisms of payment and market-making shape the financialized economy (Dutta et al. 2020).

Far from the euthanasia of the rentier, the permissive, low-interest regime launched in the 1990s has, perversely, fueled the proliferation of finance by easing market conditions and regulatory oversight. The driving force of financialization in this framework is rooted in the continuous flow of financial innovations, that make the survival constraint more elastic and flexible, even as negative externalities including increasing instability are generated at the macroeconomic level (Vercelli 2013). Key here is the evolution of the shadow-banking system – the money-market funding of capital-market lending (Mehrling et al. 2013; Pozsar et al. 2010). Instead of managing liquidity and profitability through the management of assets, banks turned to the active management of liabilities (Minsky 1990). The pursuit of returns by money managers, including both institutional investors and asset management funds, drove the market for securitized assets in a symbiotic relation (Minsky 1990, 1992).

Shadow banking draws on pension funds and money-market funds flush with inflows from wealthy individuals and corporate cash-pools seeking safety, while deploying these funds to engineer financial products to meet demand by investors with a high appetite of risk and yield through securitization. Underpinning this growth of financial trading and market-based finance are new private mechanisms of liquidity creation – what is called shadow money (Pozsar et al. 2010; Gabor and Vestergaard 2016). This includes the widespread use of "repos" – repurchase agreements involving a sale of a security with a commitment to repurchase the security at a later date – a practice that greatly enhances liquidity. The underlying security is tradeable collateral, which the repo lender can reuse, so that the ability to trade the underlying collateral at par becomes critical to the mechanisms of liquidity governing the survival constraints of the system. Liquidity becomes tied to increasing leverage and debt in market-based finance and monetary mechanisms, fueling fragility while the growth of finance gets increasingly delinked from the sphere of production, and further concentrates wealth (Caverzasi et al. 2019). In addition to the pivotal role of the state in fostering the growth of finance with the adoption of liberalization and regulation policies, the state also takes on a new role in absorbing risk and providing a safety net as private finance takes on riskier bets (Gabor 2020).

Financialized Capitalism: A Distinct Stage?

From this brief overview, it is clear that both Marxian and Post-Keynesian traditions see capitalism as inherently financial. Finance is essential to technological innovation and the dynamic possibilities of capital accumulation. At the same time, finance is unproductive in the sense of being incapable of producing surplus value within the Marxian approach, while Minsky has argued that the valuation of financial asset is bounded by the capacity of the real economy to generate cash flows necessary to sustain the asset inflation. In both approaches, the dominance of finance is seen to have engineered a fundamental transformation of the economy – marking an epochal shift. This transformation goes beyond demand and distribution stressed in post-Keynesian analysis, to the restructuring of the organizations and conditions of both work and life underscored in Marxian approaches.

But if capitalism is inherently financial, what is distinct or novel about the present phase of "financialized" capitalism? What are the underlying drivers that explain its emergence and spread?

Post-Keynesian explanations of the emergence of financialized, finance-dominated capitalism ascribe this transformation to the role of the state and the institutional and policy changes embedded in neoliberalism, including liberalization and globalization. Within Marxian analysis seeking structural reasons for the recent ascendancy of finance, financialization is seen as a consequence of the rise of corporate monopoly and its search for outlets for investible surplus on the one hand, and as corporate capital's response to the crisis of profitability of the 1970s on the other. Distinct from structural explanations of financialization as an escape from stagnation and declining profitability are approaches that comprehend financialization as the logical outcome of the inner tendencies of capitalism, and the contradictions inherent in finance's separation and growing relative autonomy from the realm of production and commerce. There are some echoes of this insight in Minsky's approach to the historical development. He identified financialized capitalism as the stage of money-manager capitalism where corporations are more deeply embedded in money and financial markets so that "the main business in financial markets became far removed from the financing of the capital development of the country" (Minsky 1992). The very success of the post-war period of paternalist, managerial capitalism paved the way for this evolution (Wray 2009).

Finally, what distinguishes contemporary financialization from the preceding period of financialization before the First World War is the pivotal role of US-led finance and dollar hegemony in the growing web of global finance. Sterling, which was the anchor of the international financial system in the earlier period, has been supplanted by the dollar, the monetary liability of the US state in the contemporary period. Instead of being backed by bullion, like sterling in the preceding phase of financial ascendancy, the dollar is backed by the authority and structural power of the US state. The US Federal Reserve is at the critical hub of this global network of finance and the proliferating private monetary mechanisms that have spurred financialization globally, backed by the US state and US-led financial institutions (Lapavitsas 2013; Vasudevan 2021; Gabor 2020). Contemporary financialization is also distinct in that global integration is not restricted to trade and financial flows but involves more fundamentally the internationalization of production and the establishment of global production networks under the control of global corporations (Powell 2019).

Marxian approaches investigating the systemic reorganization of production relations and structure of accumulation, post-Keynesian analysis of the impact of the rise to dominance of finance on demand and distribution and investigations of the implications of evolving modes of liquidity on power and performance drawing on Minsky – together provide critical insights that help us comprehend contemporary financialization. Financialization can be theorized as the outcome of inner tendencies and logic of capitalist development, but it is also necessary to address how it is historically entrenched in the specificities of dollar-hegemony and the corporate-controlled global re-organization of production and accumulation that emerged in the recent decades.

References

Alami, Ilias, Carolina Alves, Bruno Bonizzi, et al., International Financial Subordination: A Critical Research Agenda. *Review of International Political Economy*. 2022. 1–27. https://doi.org/10.1080/09692290.2022.2098359

Arrighi, Giovanni, *The Long Twentieth Century: Money, Power, and the Origins of Our Times*. London: New York, NY: Verso, 1994.

Bhaduri, Amit, Kazimierz Laski, and Martin Riese, A Model of Interaction Between the Virtual and the Real Economy. *Metroeconomica*. v. 57 (3), 2006. 412–27. https://doi.org/10.1111/j.1467-999X.2006.00247.x

Bonizzi, Bruno, Annina Kaltenbrunner, and Jeff Powell, Subordinate Financialization in Emerging Capitalist Economies. In *The Routledge International Handbook of Financialization*, edited by Philip Mader, Daniel Mertens, and Natascha van der Zwan, 1st ed., 2020. 177–87. Routledge. https://doi.org/10.4324/9781315142876-15

Caverzasi, Eugenio, Alberto Botta, and Clara Capelli, Shadow Banking and the Financial Side of Financialisation. *Cambridge Journal of Economics*. 2019. 20. https://doi.org/10.1093/cje/bez020

Christophers, Brett, The Limits to Financialization. *Dialogues in Human Geography*. v. 5 (2), 2015. 183–200. https://doi.org/10.1177/2043820615588153

Crotty, James, The Neoliberal Paradox: The Impact of Destructive Product Market Competition and Impatient Finance on Nonfinancial Corporations in the Neoliberal Era. *Review of Radical Political Economics*. v. 35 (3), 2003. 271–79. https://doi.org/10.1177/0486613403255533

Crotty, James, If Financial Market Competition Is Intense, Why Are Financial Firm Profits So High? Reflections on the Current 'Golden Age' of Finance. *Competition & Change*. v. 12 (2), 2008. 167–83. https://doi.org/10.1179/102452908X289811

Crotty, James, Structural Causes of the Global Financial Crisis: A Critical Assessment of the 'New Financial Architecture.' *Cambridge Journal of Economics*. v. 33 (4), 2009. 563–80. https://doi.org/10.1093/cje/bep023

Duménil, Gérard, *The Crisis of Neoliberalism*. 1. Harvard Univ. Press paperback ed. Cambridge, MA: Harvard Univ. Press, 2013.

Duménil, Gérard, and Dominique Lévy, *Capital Resurgent: Roots of the Neoliberal Revolution*. Cambridge: Harvard University Press, 2004.

Dünhaupt, Petra, Determinants of Labour's Income Share in the Era of Financialisation. *Cambridge Journal of Economics*. v. 41 (1), 2017. 283–306. https://doi.org/10.1093/cje/bew023

Dutt, Amitava Krishna. Conspicuous Consumption, Consumer Debt and Economic Growth. In *Interactions in Analytical Political Economy*, edited by Mark Setterfield. New York: Routledge, 2005.

Dutt, Amitava Krishna, Maturity, Stagnation and Consumer Debt: A Steindlian Approach. *Metroeconomica*. v. 57 (3), 2006. 339–64. https://doi.org/10.1111/j.1467-999X.2006.00246.x

Dutta, Sahil Jai, Ruben Kremers, Fabian Pape, and Johannes Petry, Critical Macro-Finance: An Introduction. *Finance and Society*. v. 6 (1), 2020. 34–44. https://doi.org/10.2218/finsoc.v6i1.4407

Epstein, Gerald A., *Financialization and the World Economy*. Edward Elgar Publishing, 2005.

Fiebiger, Brett, Rethinking the Financialisation of Non-Financial Corporations: A Reappraisal of US Empirical Data. *Review of Political Economy*. v. 28 (3), 2016. 354–79. https://doi.org/10.1080/09538259.2016.1147734

Fine, Ben, Locating Financialisation. *Historical Materialism*. v. 18 (2), 2010. 97–116. https://doi.org/10.1163/156920610X512453

Fine, Ben, Financialization from a Marxist Perspective. *International Journal of Political Economy*. v. 42 (4), 2013. 47–66. https://doi.org/10.2753/IJP0891-1916420403

Foster, John Bellamy, The Financialization of Capitalism. *Monthly Review*. v. 58 (11), 2007. 1–12.

Foster, John Bellamy, and Robert W. McChesney, Monopoly-Finance Capital and the Paradox of Accumulation. *Monthly Review.* v. 61 (5), 2009. https://doi.org/10.14452/MR-061-05-2009-09_1

Gabor, Daniela, Critical Macro-Finance: A Theoretical Lens. *Finance and Society.* v. 6 (1), 2020. 45–55. https://doi.org/10.2218/finsoc.v6i1.4408

Gabor, Daniela, and Jakob Vestergaard, Towards a Theory of Shadow Money. *Institute for New Economic Thinking.* 2016.

Hein, Eckhard, A Keynesian Perspective on 'Financialisation'. In *21st Century Keynesian Economics*, edited by Philip Arestis and Malcolm Sawyer. International Papers in Political Economy Series. London: Palgrave Macmillan UK, 2010. 120–61. https://doi.org/10.1057/9780230285415_4

Hein, Eckhard, Finance-Dominated Capitalism, Re-Distribution, Household Debt and Financial Fragility in a Kaleckian Distribution and Growth Model. *PSL Quarterly Review.* v. 65 (260), 2012a. https://doi.org/10.13133/2037-3643/9937

Hein, Eckhard, *The Macroeconomics of Finance-Dominated Capitalism and Its Crisis.* Cheltenham; Northampton, MA: Edward Elgar, 2012b.

Hein, Eckhard, Finance-Dominated Capitalism and Re-Distribution of Income: A Kaleckian Perspective. *Cambridge Journal of Economics.* v. 39 (3), 2015. 907–34. https://doi.org/10.1093/cje/bet038

Hein, Eckhard, and Till Van Treeck, 'Financialisation' in Post-Keynesian Models of Distribution and Growth: A Systematic Review. In *Handbook of Alternative Theories of Economic Growth*, edited by Mark Setterfield, 12814. Edward Elgar Publishing, 2010a. https://doi.org/10.4337/9781849805582.00022

Hein, Eckhard, and Till Van Treeck, Financialisation and Rising Shareholder Power in Kaleckian/Post-Kaleckian Models of Distribution and Growth. *Review of Political Economy.* v. 22 (2), 2010b. 205–33. https://doi.org/10.1080/09538251003665628

Jayadev, Arjun, and Gerald Epstein, The Rise of Rentier Incomes in OECD Countries: Financialization, Central Bank Policy and Labor Solidarity. In *The Political Economy of Central Banking*, edited by Philip Arestis and Malcolm C. Sawyer, Edward Elga. Cheltenham, UK: Edward Elgar Publishing, 2019. 350–78. https://ideas.repec.org/h/elg/eechap/18820_13.html

Karwowski, Ewa, Mimoza Shabani, and Engelbert Stockhammer, Financialization: Dimensions and Determinants. A Cross-Country Study. Economics Discussion Paper 2017-1. School of Economics, Kingston University London, 2017. https://econpapers.repec.org/paper/riskngedp/2017_5f001.htm

Karwowski, Ewa, and Engelbert Stockhammer, Financialisation in Emerging Economies: A Systematic Overview and Comparison with Anglo-Saxon Economies. *Economic and Political Studies.* v. 5 (1), 2017. 60–86. https://doi.org/10.1080/20954816.2016.1274520

Keynes, John Maynard, *The General Theory of Employment, Interest, and Money.* 1st Harvest/HBJ ed. San Diego: Harcourt, Brace, Jovanovich, 1964.

Krippner, Greta R, *Capitalizing on Crisis: The Political Origins of the Rise of Finance.* 1. Harvard Univ. Press paperback ed. Cambridge: Harvard Univ. Press, 2012.

Lapavitsas, Costas, Theorizing Financialization. *Work, Employment and Society.* v. 25 (4), 2011. 611–26. https://doi.org/10.1177/0950017011419708

Lapavitsas, Costas, *Profiting without Producing: How Finance Exploits Us All.* London: New York: Verso, 2013.

Lapavitsas, Costas, Financialised Capitalism: Crisis and Financial Expropriation. *Historical Materialism.* v. 17 (2), 2009. 114–48. https://doi.org/10.1163/156920609X436153

Lazonick, William, and Mary O'Sullivan, Maximizing Shareholder Value: A New Ideology for Corporate Governance. *Economy and Society*. v. 29 (1), 2000. 13–35. https://doi.org/10.1080/030851400360541

Mader, Philip, Daniel Mertens, and Natascha van der Zwan, Financialization: An Introduction. In *The Routledge International Handbook of Financialization*, edited by Mader, P., Mertens, D, and van der Zwan, N. New York: Routledge, 2020, 1–24.

Magdoff, Harry, and Paul M. Sweezy, *Stagnation and the Financial Explosion*. New York: Monthly Review Press, 1987.

Marx, Karl, *Capital*. London: Penguin Books, v. 3, 1981.

Mehrling, Perry, *The New Lombard Street: How the Fed Became the Dealer of Last Resort*. Princeton University Press, 2010.

Mehrling, Perry, Zoltan Pozsar, James Sweeney, and Daniel H. Neilson, Bagehot Was a Shadow Banker: Shadow Banking, Central Banking, and the Future of Global Finance. *Central Banking, and the Future of Global Finance*, 2013.

Mehrling, Perry. Financialization and Its Discontents. *Finance and Society*, v. 3 (1), 2017. 1–10.

Minsky, Hyman, Money and Crisis in Schumpeter and Keynes. Paper 334. Hyman P. Minsky Archive, 1983.

Minsky, Hyman, Schumpeter: Finance and Evolution. In *Evolving Technology and Market Structure: Studies in Schumpeterian Economics*, edited by Arnold Heertje and Mark Perlman. AN Arbor: The University of Michigan Press, 1990. 51–74. https://digitalcommons.bard.edu/hm_archive/314

Minsky, Hyman, Schumpeter and Finance. In *Market and Institutions in Economic Development: Essays in Honour of Paulo Sylos Labini*, edited by Salvatore Biasco, Alessandro Roncaglia, and Michele Salvati. New York: MacMillan, 1992. 103–15. http://digitalcommons.bard.edu/hm_archive/280

Minsky, Hyman, *Stabilizing an Unstable Economy*. Neuaufl. New York: McGraw-Hill, 2008.

Minsky, Hyman P, The Evolution of Financial Institutions and the Performance of the Economy. *Journal of Economic Issues*. v. 20 (2), 1986. 345–53. https://doi.org/10.1080/00213624.1986.11504505

Orhangazi, Özgür, Financialisation and Capital Accumulation in the Non-Financial Corporate Sector: A Theoretical and Empirical Investigation on the US Economy: 1973–2003. *Cambridge Journal of Economics*. v. 32 (6), 2008. 863–86. https://doi.org/10.1093/cje/ben009

Palley, Thomas I., *Financialization: The Economics of Finance Capital Domination*. Basingstoke, Hampshire: Palgrave Macmillan, 2013.

Powell, Jeff, Towards a Marxist Theory of Financialized Capitalism. In *The Oxford Handbook of Karl Marx*, edited by Jeff Powell. Oxford University Press, 2019. 628–50. https://doi.org/10.1093/oxfordhb/9780190695545.013.37

Pozsar, Zoltan, Tobias Adrian, Adam Ashcraft, and Hayley Boesky, Shadow Banking. *New York* v. 458 (458), 2010. 3–9.

Sahay, Ratna, Martin Cihak, Papa N'Diaye, Adolfo Barajas, Diana Ayala Pena, Dayala, Ran Bi, et al., Rethinking Financial Deepening: Stability and Growth in Emerging Markets. *Staff Discussion Notes*. v. 15 (8), 2015. 1. https://doi.org/10.5089/9781498312615.006

Skott, P., and S. Ryoo, Macroeconomic Implications of Financialisation. *Cambridge Journal of Economics*. v. 32 (6), 2008. 827–62. https://doi.org/10.1093/cje/ben012

Stockhammer, E., Financialisation and the Slowdown of Accumulation. *Cambridge Journal of Economics*. v. 28 (5), 2004. 719–41. https://doi.org/10.1093/cje/beh032

Sweezy, Paul M., The Triumph of Financial Capital. *Monthly Review*. v. 46 (2), 1994. https://monthlyreview.org/1994/06/01/the-triumph-of-financial-capital/

Sweezy, Paul M., More (or Less) on Globalization. *Monthly Review*. v. 49 (4), 1997. 1–5. https://doi.org/10.14452/MR-049-04-1997-08_1

Taylor, Lance, *Maynard's Revenge: The Collapse of Free-Market Economics*. Cambridge, Massachussetts: Harvard University Press, 2011. https://www.hup.harvard.edu/catalog.php?isbn=9780674050464

Tooze, J. Adam. *Crashed: How a Decade of Financial Crises Changed the World*. New York: Allen Lane, 2018.

Vasudevan, Ramaa, Finance and Distribution. *Review of Keynesian Economics*. v. 5 (1), 2017. 78–93. https://doi.org/10.4337/roke.2017.01.06

Vasudevan, Ramaa, Dollar Standard and Imperialism. In *The Palgrave Encyclopedia of Imperialism and Anti-Imperialism*, edited by Immanuel Ness and Zak Cope. Cham: Springer International Publishing, 2021. 602–13. https://doi.org/10.1007/978-3-030-29901-9_203

Vercelli, Alessandro, Financialization in a Long-Run Perspective: An Evolutionary Approach. *International Journal of Political Economy*. v. 42 (4), 2013. 19–46. https://doi.org/10.2753/IJP0891-1916420402

Wray, L. R., The Rise and Fall of Money Manager Capitalism: A Minskian Approach. *Cambridge Journal of Economics*. v. 33 (4), 2009. 807–28. https://doi.org/10.1093/cje/bep024

6

FEMINIST RADICAL POLITICAL ECONOMY

Smita Ramnarain

Introduction

The first recorded strike by women in the United States was held in Dover, New Hampshire in 1828, when about 400 women working in cotton factories marched through town in protest, much to the bafflement of the town and factory-owners. The *Dover Enquirer's* reportage on the matter called the march "one of the most disgusting scenes ever witnessed." While the early women's strikes – such as the match girls' strike in London in 1888, the Chicago garment workers' strike in 1910, the transport women's strike of 1918, and the Woolworths' strike in 1937 – protested workplace inequities such as unsafe working conditions, unequal employment opportunities, or low pay, later demonstrations grappled with the deep connection between the home and the workplace for women. Iceland's Long Friday strike in 1975 – where 90 percent of its female population refused to perform household or paid work – and the Global Women's Strike in 1999 engaged with issues surrounding not only paid work but also unpaid domestic and care work, violence against women, reproductive justice, childcare provisions and payments, and the rights of sex workers. The most recent A Day Without a Woman strike in 2017 went a step further to include violence against immigrants and broader gender oppressions such as discriminatory policies against lesbian, trans, or queer women in their call for solidarity and equality.

This brief history of protest recapitulated above is, in some ways, a reflection of the broad contours of the evolution of feminist radical political economic thought. Feminist radical political economy (FRPE) takes women's work and reproductive labor as the starting point of its inquiry. At its core, FRPE raises the following questions. Even as workers produce things for

DOI: 10.4324/9781003366690-7

society, why does the labor that produces (and reproduces) *workers* in society remain invisible or undervalued? In what ways does this labor interact with capitalist development and accumulation processes? And how do power and privilege, structured into social relations under capitalism, allocate these forms of invisibilized work to specific groups in society? If, as Aristotle put it, the end of labor is to gain leisure, FRPE raises the counter-questions, whose labor, whose leisure, and to what end?

This chapter describes the emergence of FRPE from classical and Marxian political economy, its contributions in highlighting the integral role played by domestic and reproductive work under capitalism, to its current resurgence as social reproduction feminism. While the initial sections largely focus on theoretical developments in the Minority World/Global North, insights from the Majority World/Global South that complicate and extend FRPE are taken up in the last section.

Class Struggle and the Woman Question

FRPE's roots lie in classical political economy explorations of the status of women in class societies. The classical political economists – namely, Adam Smith, David Ricardo, Thomas Malthus, John Stuart Mill, and Karl Marx, among others – were focused on explaining how emerging capitalist societies produced, divided up, and consumed their wealth. In doing so, however, they largely neglected gender and excluded women from their theories of the economy. Work done in markets was privileged, while the work performed at home – in service of the market economy's participants – did not have much analytical significance. For instance, self-interest and rational thought, the precepts that Adam Smith is most remembered for, did not extend to or apply to women (Bodkin 1999). Ricardo, whose labor theory of value designated labor as the most important input of production, failed to consider how this labor came to be (Folbre 2009). Malthus's theory of population never considered the plausibility of a connection between women's economic well-being, socio-political agency, and reproduction (Folbre 2009; Horrell, Humphries, and Weisdorf 2020).[1]

What of Marx? A famous and funny meme has a picture of Karl Marx along with the statement "I don't always criticize, but when I do, it is a ruthless criticism of all that exists." Marxian analyses centered concepts such as *exploitation, accumulation,* and *primitive accumulation,* to interrogate the sources of *surplus,* and of eventual capitalist expansion.[2] In Marx's ruthless critique of capitalism, however, women were incidental to the analysis. To be sure, he was cognizant of women's roles as secondary workers facing unequal pay or in the latent "reserve army." He commented on the "cheapening of labor-power" and the transformation of the members of the family into wage-slaves as capitalist industrial production increasingly drew women and children into the workforce – under poor conditions of work – as substitutes to male labor (Marx 1977). In other places, Marx and Engels (1998, 52) found the family to be the fount of "unequal distribution, both quantitative and qualitative, of labor and its products." And although the process by which labor becomes commodified, i.e., the process by which labor power appears for sale in the market, and how capital–labor relations are (re)produced under capitalism were central to Marx's analysis, he never explored how *labor power and the worker* came to be (re)produced in the first place (and women's role in this process).

Marx's contemporaries, August Bebel and Friedrich Engels, attempted to address this – the woman question – in their own works. They were not the first to do so: Flora Tristan, a socialist writer, had long maintained that women's inclusion in unions was critical to the emancipation of the working class in her essays in 1844 (see Ferguson 2020). Bebel and Engels took these ideas further. Bebel's work *Women and Socialism* was published in 1879, while Engels' treatise *The Origin of the Family, Private Property and the State* was published in 1884 (a year after Marx's death). Acknowledging the double disadvantage of women in capitalist society – social subservience to men and economic subservience to capital – Bebel argued that even as women were entitled to the same rights as men, legal equality alleviated this condition of dependence, but did not resolve it. Full emancipation could only result from the complete dissolution of the capitalist economic system. Women were thus exhorted to participate in the class struggle for their own sakes as much as in support of working-class men.

Engels applied the historical materialism lens developed by Marx to the woman question. Using anthropological studies, he ascribed the root of women's oppression to the emergence of private property (and consequently, monogamy) in a class society. The emergence of private property necessitated "children of undisputed paternity; such paternity is demanded because these children are later to come into their father's property as his natural heirs" (Engels 1942, 33). Prior to this development, Engels argued that despite a gender division of labor, women's work was not regarded as inferior. The emergence of class societies, and the consequent necessity of surveilling women's reproduction and sexuality closely, led to this devaluation where "the woman was degraded and reduced to servitude ... a mere instrument for the production of children" (Engels 1942, 30). Engels' work made two key contributions: first, it demonstrated that there was nothing self-evident or natural about women's oppression. Second, it connected women to class struggle. Since class oppression and women's oppression had the same material genesis, the implication was that the dismantling of capitalism and private property was central to the liberation of women.

These works – by two stalwart figures in the socialist movement of the late 1800s – played a significant role in galvanizing women's participation in class struggle and in catalyzing further feminist explorations on the role played by domestic and reproductive labor in women's oppression under capitalism. They were also the subject of critique. For instance, in exhorting women to become "useful member(s) of human society" (Bebel 1879, 4), Bebel took for granted that women's reproductive work was not useful. In his turn, Engels was critiqued for an inadequate explanation of the processes by which men attained supremacy in the transition to a class society, for the simplistic ascription of a common root to patriarchy and capitalism, and for his reductionist optimism that the dissolution of class will end patriarchy. These discussions and critiques took shape in subsequent Marxist-feminist scholarship.

Marxist-Feminism, Domestic Labor, and Dual Systems

Marxist-feminists took Marx and Engels' historically materialist work – and its omissions – as the starting point for their explorations into the status of women and the role of women's work in capitalism, branching off into multiple, but interconnected, strands of thought. One strand saw Marxist-feminists examine the role of housework and domestic labor in reproducing capitalist systems. For Marx, domestic labor produced use-values but not exchange-value and was thus deemed "unproductive"; only that labor which produced surplus-value was regarded as central to the workings of capitalism. Marxist-feminists – Mariarosa Dalla Costa, Silvia Federici, and Selma James among others – contested the notion that domestic labor was marginal to capitalism and evaluated its integral role in upholding and reproducing capitalism. The Wages for Housework (WFH) campaign was started by these scholar-activists in 1972, with calls for a "general strike" in Italy in 1974. WFH feminists argued that it is through women's unwaged housework – cooking, cleaning, and sexual services – that the commodity labor power is able to be produced. And only when this labor power is sold to capitalists does it produce value. The production of labor power is therefore the precondition to value being produced. In Federici's (1975, 82) words, "housework is already money for capital." The WFH campaign sought to locate women's oppression in the deep socialization processes that assign this work to women, transform it into a natural attribute, and thereby ordain it to be unwaged. The payment of wages, therefore, would provide social recognition of women as workers, and ameliorate the conditions of women's exploitation and dependence on men.

The focus on women's uniquely dual oppressions – within the family and in capitalist production processes – led to the famous "domestic labor debates" in the 1970s, where participants explored the extent to which Marxist terms and concepts could be applied to studying domestic labor. On the one end of the debate was the claim that domestic labor *was* indeed productive because it produced the commodity labor power and was capable of producing surplus-value that is expropriated within the household (Benston 1969; Dalla Costa and James 1973).[3] Some scholars also insisted that women were a distinct social class due to the nature of their exploitation (Delphy 1980). On the opposite end, scholars pointed out that although domestic labor contributes to the accumulation of capital, it is not productive in the strict Marxian sense of being labor that produces capital and surplus-value, and that which is paid for directly (Fee 1976). Wally Seccombe (1974) argued that even though housework reproduced the ability to work and the family reproduced the culture and ideology necessary to uphold the social order, housework was not directly related to capital and is "unproductive" or indirectly productive at the very least. For Jean Gardiner (1975), domestic labor contributed to subsidizing the value of labor power and only indirectly, to surplus-value. A further difficulty was the impossibility of knowing how much of the surplus-value was domestic labor's contribution. In a rebuttal of the notion that all women constituted a distinct social class, Maxine Molyneux (1979) pointed to the privileges some women derived from their husbands' wealth. Notwithstanding these robust debates, in an era where the overwhelming emphasis was on women's equal access to wage work and employment, WFH was also rejected by the overall feminist movement for potentially reifying women's roles as housewives (Toupin 2018) and for its limited imagination in designating wages as women's succor from domestic drudgery (Davis 1983).

A second strand of this early Marxist-feminist literature took up Engels' implication that the solution to women's oppression would be the dissolution of the class system. Countering this proposition, Juliet Mitchell (1966) noted that various socialist movements and regimes had left women's socio-economic situation unchanged. A closer examination of whether it was possible for exploitation to occur within the household led this group of Marxist-feminists to posit two separate but interlinked systems of oppression – capitalism *and* patriarchy – which, while distinct modes, nevertheless interacted with one another. Christine Delphy (1980), for instance, reasoned that these two modes of production co-existed in modern society: an industrial mode of production characterized by capitalist exploitation and also a patriarchal mode whereby women are exploited by the beneficiaries of free housework, their husbands. Heidi Hartmann (1979, 7) further argued that subsuming women's struggles under the struggle against capitalism obscured the labor process within the family, the ordering of power in society through gendered roles, and the "material interest in women's continued oppression." Connecting housework and intra-family processes to inferior labor market outcomes for women, Hartmann claimed that women's designation as secondary earners, gendered pay disparities, and occupational segregation of women into low-paying jobs were all means of maintaining their dependence on men and ensuring the provision of reproductive labor. Patriarchy, in other words, "has shaped the course of capitalist development" (Hartmann 1979, 14).

The "dual-systems" postulation of a symbiotic relationship between capitalism and patriarchy through notions of patriarchal capitalism or capitalist patriarchy had its share of critics. Although this approach highlighted the productivism of Marxist theories to the neglect of reproduction, the postulation of production and reproduction as separate modes of production tended to move the analysis away from being materialist in the Marxian sense. Patriarchy also tends to take different forms across different societies, and so dual-systems theorists were hard-pressed to find an overarching, singular explanation of the connection between women's oppression and capitalist exploitation. Finally, dual-systems raised new difficulties for organizing struggle: while feminism required uniting women of all classes to unite against patriarchy and the structures of power upheld by men, Marxist struggle seeks to unify all workers in the struggle against capitalism.

These strands of Marxist-feminist thinking arose around the time of second-wave feminism and shared its problems. The emphasis on housework and WFH, for instance, assumed a default white housewife as the protagonist of this struggle, to the exclusion of Black women who – in their post-slavery roles as maids, cleaners, cooks, and nannies – had always performed housework for a wage, but were nevertheless exploited with low wages, degraded, and subjected to poor working conditions and violence. Indeed, this experience of Black women in the paid labor force contradicted the notion that paid work was the route to women's emancipation. Way back in 1949, activist Claudia Jones (1949) had already pointed out that Black women were "still confined to the lowest paying jobs" and that the domestic worker was the "victim of exclusion from all labor and social legislation" (11). Many of the concepts developed by second-wave Marxist feminism did not apply to the lives of Black women. For instance, the notion of "dependency" did not make much sense when applied to the lives of Black women, many of whom were the prime earners and heads of their household (Carby 1982). Angela Davis (1983) took Jones' ideas further to insist that housework was only one element of the social relations involved in reproduction and that a race-blind analysis elided the violent role racism plays – in conjunction with gender and class oppression – in economic exploitation under capitalism.

Similarly, feminist scholars focusing on the Majority World – Maria Mies, Lourdes Beneria, Gita Sen, Carmen Diana Deere among others – were critical of the binary between gender and class that Marxist-feminism upheld. For Beneria and Sen (1982) and Mies (1980), the productive and reproductive spheres were closely intertwined in the lives of women in the Majority World. For instance, Beneria and Sen (1982, 161) argue that women's work in gathering fuel, food, water, and other raw materials used in home-based production, the hours spent on production at home alongside reproductive activities, and women's participation in industries are all part of the same continuum of production and reproduction in an "inherently hierarchical and contradictory structure of production and accumulation" that places women and their work at the bottom. Marxist-feminism largely did not heed these insightful criticisms until later.

Marxist Feminist Theories of Social Reproduction

Alongside the two strands of Marxist-feminism discussed above, some scholars sought to provide an integrated analysis of capitalist political economy and what they term 'social reproduction.' Social reproduction is differentiated from Marx's own use of the term. For Marx, social reproduction denoted the gamut of social, political, and cultural processes that reproduced the capitalist mode of production and the relations between capital and labor. Marxist-feminists, however, redirect the term 'social reproduction' to describe the maintenance and reproduction of life at the daily or generational level, within the framework of class relations (Arruzza 2016). Thus, an amalgamated definition of the labor of social reproduction (LSR) – "at the heart of creating or reproducing society as a whole" (Bhattacharya 2017, 2) – might include the spatially and historically contextual biological and sexual work of physically reproducing children; the work undertaken in caring for the young, the old, the sick, and others; the production or processing of food, clothing, shelter and other goods and services needed for the maintenance of life; and the labor expended in the emotional, cultural, and ideological practices required to reproduce and maintain a compliant labor force (Laslett and Brenner 1989; Bhattacharya 2017). This reframing centers capitalism's inexorable need for reproductive labor for its own existence, rather than discussing such labor only in relation to productive labor.

Marxist-feminist theories of social reproduction (henceforth, the social reproduction framework, SRF) arose from the desire to unify questions of production and reproduction, rather than the parallel structures of oppression espoused by dual-systems theorists. Rather than attribute women's oppression narrowly to unpaid housework, SRF focuses on the significance of the LSR for the reproduction of capitalism itself, i.e. as the "coercive underbelly of capitalist value creation" (Ferguson 2020, 121). Thus, while the family might have been the primary site of the appropriation of this labor historically, it need not be its only site. The community, market, and state also feature in how this labor is distributed (Laslett and Brenner 1989), as also concrete institutions such as prisons, orphanages, hospitals, labor camps, schools, and universities (Vogel 1981, 1983). Similarly, slavery or immigration are also ways in which this labor emerges, in addition to childbirth in kin-based households (Bhattacharya 2017).

SRF highlights the ways in which capital is always seeking to offload the costs of this labor – essential for its own survival – on to marginalized, gendered and racialized 'others'. Thus, the question of who performs the LSR becomes simultaneously less *and* more critical. While the housewife's labor was a historically specific way by which capital obtained the LSR it required (Mies 1980), other marginalized groups within the working class – the poor, imprisoned populations, immigrants, those in the so-called 'lower' castes, indigenous peoples etc. – were all just as easily be brought into such appropriation because it is, in fact, logically and historically *necessary* for capitalism to obtain unlimited supplies of labor to reproduce itself (Manning 2015). In Bhattacharya's (2017, 14; italics mine) words, therefore, "categories of oppression (such as gender, race and ableism) are *coproduced* in simultaneity with the production of surplus value." So, even as the analysis is extended beyond the domain of the family (and women specifically) to the commodification and sexualization of this labor through practices, policies, and institutions, the processes by which this labor is racialized, and by which ever-newer vulnerable groups are recruited to lower the costs of this labor, also come to the fore in this framework. That is, SRF seeks to unify an understanding of the inequalities – class exploitation, racism, heterosexism, casteism, ableism, transphobia etc. – formed and embedded in the capitalist order, and the ways in which these are deployed in capitalism – by hierarchical institutions such as the family, the market, or the state – to organize both the unwaged *and* waged labors of social reproduction.

The dependency of capitalist accumulation on labor power – a fundamental insight of earlier Marxist-feminist theory – is retained by SRF, noting, however, that the process by which labor power is actually produced (i.e. how life itself may be produced) and reproduced (from day-to-day through cooking, cleaning, caring) lies outside the immediate supervision of capital. Even as capital might circumscribe how, where, and when this labor might be carried out – after work hours, at homes, schools, communities, hospitals etc. – capital is unable to directly exercise full control over it. A relatively small proportion of this labor may itself be waged, and even when it is waged, it may choose to prioritize life-needs as opposed to the needs of capital (Fraser 2017; Ferguson 2020). This structure presents a fundamental contradiction for capital: the logic of accumulation drives capitalists to keep wages and other costs of social reproduction as low as possible, but these low wages impede the very reproduction of the labor power that capital categorically requires. Nancy Fraser (2017, 24) notes that this dilemma paves the way for the recognition of another crisis tendency in capitalism, where "capital's accumulation dynamic effectively eats its own tail." The chronic undersupply of care – the 'care crisis' – is a mere symptom of a *systemic* crisis of social reproduction, due to capital's perpetual tendency to undermine and destabilize social reproduction in its quest for ever-higher profit (Fraser 2017). Crises of social reproduction are therefore features, not bugs, under capitalism and only resolved through a complete overhaul of the social order.

By recognizing the intersectional *and* systemic nature of social oppressions and processes of marginalization beyond the household that are implicit in the system's reproduction, SRF scholars argue that it provides greater political possibility in unifying diverse and multiple groups – coalitions along the axes of class, gender, race, sexuality; groups both within and outside the reach of capital; workplace crusades and other anti-oppression movements – in anti-capitalist struggle (Bhattacharya 2017; Fraser 2017; Ferguson 2020). SRF does not, of course, resolve all debates within FRPE and Marxist-feminism. A central concern is whether the definition of social reproduction is too broad, since in the ultimate analysis everything can be connected to life-making. The notion that social reproduction is everywhere and nowhere at once also creates quandaries around how diverse groups might be organized in anti-capitalist struggle (Katz 2001). Some others are more optimistic about its unifying capacity on questions of livelihoods, social provisioning, and welfare in non-capitalocentric ways (Weeks 2011; Arruzza et al. 2019). Such interrogations of the SRF framework, its applicability to global issues, and its ability to bring about social transformation or visualize alternative futures, have been promising areas of discussion.

FRPE Contributions to Global Political Economy

Scholars focusing on the Majority World and the interlinkages between the Majority and Minority Worlds have critiqued and extended FRPE in global and transnational directions. Herein the chapter briefly discusses three areas where FRPE's fundamental insight on the intimate connection between accumulation and reproductive labor has been invaluable to a deeper understanding of neoliberal globalization. Limitations of space do not permit a more exhaustive recapitulation of FRPE's contributions. It is hoped, however, that these examples serve as illustrations of the possibilities FRPE presents in terms of expanding theoretical and political avenues in radical political economy.

Radical political economists have always been deeply concerned by the role of both internal and transnational migrant labor in striating the working class, reinforcing racism and precarity, and providing the virtually unlimited supply of low-wage workers to the industrial, agricultural, and care sectors of the Minority and Majority Worlds. While mainstream theories focus on migration's role in modernization processes and ascribe it to innocuously termed "push/pull factors" that are eventually an outcome of individual choice, radical political economy draws attention to the unequal international division of labor, legacies of colonialism and imperialism, and the undercurrents of precarity that propel migratory processes (Rajan and Neetha 2019; Hanieh 2019; Ferguson and McNally 2015; Rao 2021). Following the intersectional path first laid out by Black feminists, FRPE points to the gendered and racialized migrant labor that capital has historically used to replenish its labor within national boundaries, to allocate low-paid domestic, sex and care-work, and thereby, to lower the costs of its own reproduction (Bhattacharya 2017; Hopkins 2017). Early literature on global "care chains" and the global division of reproductive and domestic labor (Hochshild 2000; Parreñas 2000) is extended by FRPE to complicate the distinction between productive and reproductive work in the globalization-migration-social reproduction nexus

(Arat-Koç 2006; Kofman and Raghuram 2015; Nassif 2022). FRPE also discusses the role of state agencies in institutionalizing various forms of oppression that keep migrant labor cheap and precarious, through visa restrictions, threats of deportation, and exclusion from various forms of social citizenship (Herrera 2012; Kofman and Raghuram 2015; Rajan and Neetha 2019).

A second key area of FRPE contribution has been toward understanding women's work in factory production and in global value chains (GVCs) and the blurred lines between production and reproduction in these settings. In the export-oriented production of newly industrializing countries, Mies (1980) detailed how processes of "housewifization" – where women's lace-making work done at home for export markets is designated a pastime or simply an extension of their home-making duties and therefore, as "non-work" – conceal women's substantive contributions to family and national incomes. Similarly, Elson and Pearson (1981) highlighted the ways in which capitalist cost-cutting operations benefit directly from hiring women as cheaper workers. Race and gender intersect in this exploitation, with factory owners' descriptions of women's "natural differentiation" (92) and "the manual dexterity of the oriental female" (93). Capital can easily ignore the costs behind the social reproduction of these putative "nimble fingers" – the training and socialization of women by "their mothers and other female kin since early infancy" – since these are subsumed under "tasks appropriate to women's role" (93). Other work has interrogated discourses on women workers such as their supposed passivity, obedience, manageability, and as supplementary earners (Fernández-Kelly 1983; Ong 1987). In the late 1980s and 1990s, studies from Latin America, Asia, and Africa discussed the fallout from structural adjustment policies where women's labor – paid and unpaid – was a bastion against the shrinkages in social services, public goods, public-sector job, and public assistance (see Elson 1989; Sparr 1994). In the late 1990s and early 2000s, as globalization and financialization continued, the focus of FRPE shifted from cheap labor to flexible and "disposable" labor in increasingly complex GVCs and to the gender division of labor underwriting flexibilization in specific ways (Standing 1989; Wright 2006; Beneria et al. 2016). FRPE continues to uncover ever newer strategies of capital accumulation – new forms of home-based work through industrial subcontracting and putting-out processes, new kinds of labor control and disciplining regimes, and the role of extra-economic discourses – that exacerbate the crises of social reproduction (Carr et al. 2000; Mezzadri 2016).

A third front of FRPE exploration has been the informal economy. Contrary to the expectations of modernist development theory, the informal economy – production and employment that remains unregulated, unmonitored, and untaxed, and frequently without labor protections – constitutes a significant proportion of economic activity, especially in the Majority World. It is estimated that around 93 percent of India's workforce and 74 percent of the workforce in sub-Saharan Africa is informally employed (i.e., employed in informal jobs, working for informal enterprises, or self-employed) (ILO 2018). The informal economy is a key axis of recent debate on social reproduction in FRPE. In response to some scholars' perspective of social reproduction as unproductive labor compared to directly value-producing labor (Bhattacharya 2017; Ferguson 2020), critics focusing on the Majority World respond that this distinction elides the complex intersections of production and reproduction, since only a small proportion of workers have access to formal employment globally in the first place (Kunz 2010; Bhattacharya and Kesar 2020; Rao 2021; Mezzadri 2020). For many informal economy workers in the Majority World, especially women, the workplace *is* the home, the employer *is* the family, non-commodified household resources *are* employed in commodity production to lower costs, and discourses of the housewife *are* employed to seamlessly extract both productive and reproductive labor. As non-standard work arrangements spread around the world – informal employment and contingent work – FRPE insights from the Majority World add complexity to simplistic notions of the boundaries between capitalist and non-capitalist spheres, expand the understanding of work and work conditions beyond standard formal employment, and allow us to think about labor and classes of labor that do not fit into the Western model of advanced capitalism.

Conclusion

This chapter presented the evolution of FRPE and its key contributions to radical political economy. In sum, FRPE turns the question of social reproduction on its head: rather than subsuming reproduction within production, it underscores the indispensability of LSR for the reproduction of the capitalist social system. In her article, Cohen (2018) persuasively argues that it is feminist political economy – its systemic holism in the integration of productive and reproductive spheres, and its focus on the hidden processes of appropriation and marginalization under capitalism – that, in fact, constitutes the "radical" in radical economics. And yet, perhaps as a reflection of the obscured role of reproductive labor in capitalism, questions of social reproduction and the manner in which it is gendered or racialized remain sidelined in radical political economy.

If the aim of radical political economy, through its scrutiny of capitalism, neoliberalism, financialization, and inequality, is ultimately to ensure sustainable social reproduction, FRPE has provided singular insights that expand the theoretical frontiers of radical political economy in critical directions. FRPE has traced the convoluted entanglements between waged and unwaged work, between production and social reproduction, the ways in which social divisions may be transmuted and recruited in service of capitalism, as well as spaces outside of, or only tenuously within, capital's reach. As women's protests through the ages and across the globe have indicated, FRPE has drawn attention to the gendered and racialized impacts of global capitalism across national boundaries, spaces, and contexts. It has sharpened the focus on the fundamental (and intensifying) incompatibility of life-making and profit-making under contemporary capitalism, to highlight the urgency of the need for alternatives, and to articulate new spaces for resistance or new avenues of solidarity. And while debates continue about the specific paths forward, the unification of production and social reproduction that is FRPE's critical contribution remains pivotal to understanding the profound and multifaceted consequences of global capitalism.

Notes

1 The one exception in this pantheon with regard to recognizing women as a constituency, the existence of patriarchal control, and its consequences, was Mill (Folbre 2009).
2 In the interest of space, these concepts are not detailed further here.
3 Benston (1969) regards domestic labor as simply producing use-values; for Dalla Costa and James, both use-value *and* exchange-value are produced (Fee 1976).

References

Arat-Koç, Sedef, Whose Social Reproduction? Transnational Motherhood and Challenges to Feminist Political Economy. In *Social Reproduction: Feminist Political Economy Challenges Neo-Liberalism*, edited by Meg Luxton and Kate Bezanson, Montreal: McGill-Queen's University Press, 2006. 75–92.

Arruzza, Cinzia, Functionalist, Determinist, Reductionist: Social Reproduction Feminism and its Critics. *Science & Society*. v. 80 (1), 2016. 9–30.

Arruzza, Cinzia, Tithi Bhattacharya, and Nancy Fraser, *Feminism for the 99%*. London: Verso, 2019.

Bebel, August, *Women and Socialism*, 1901. Socialist Literature Company, 1879.

Benería, Lourdes, Günseli Berik, and Maria Floro, *Gender, Development and Globalization: Economics as if All People Mattered*. New York and Abingdon: Routledge, 2016.

Beneria, Lourdes, and Gita Sen, Class and Gender Inequalities and Women's Role in Economic Development: Theoretical and Practical Implications. *Feminist Studies* v. 8 (1), 1982. 157–176.

Benston, Margaret, The Political Economy of Women's Liberation. *Monthly Review*. v. 21 (4), 1969. 31–44.

Bhattacharya, Snehashish, and Surbhi Kesar, Precarity and Development: Production and Labor Processes in the Informal Economy in India. *Review of Radical Political Economics*. v. 52, (3), 2020. 387–408.

Bhattacharya, Tithi, *Social Reproduction Theory: Remapping Class, Recentering Oppression*, London: Pluto Press, 2017.

Bodkin, Ronald, Women's Agency in Classical Economic Thought: Adam Smith, Harriet Taylor Mill, and JS Mill. *Feminist Economics*. v. 5 (1), 1999. 45–60.

Carby, Hazel, White women listen! Black feminism and the limits of sisterhood. In *The Empire Strikes Back: Race and Racism In 70's Britain*, edited by Gilroy, Paul. London: Routledge, 1982. 183–211.

Carr, Marilyn, Martha Alter Chen, and Jane Tate, Globalization and Home-Based Workers. *Feminist Economics*. v. 6 (3), 2000. 123–142.

Cohen, Jennifer, What's 'Radical' About [Feminist] Radical Political Economy? *Review of Radical Political Economics* v. 50 (4), 2018. 716–726.

Dalla Costa, M. and S. James, *The Power of Women and the Subversion of the Community*. Bristol, England: Falling Wall Press, 1973.

Davis, Angela, *Women, Race, and Class*. New York: Vintage, 1983.

Delphy, Christine, The Main Enemy. *Feminist Issues*. v. 1 (1), 1980. 23–40.

Elson, Diane, How is Structural Adjustment Affecting Women? *Development*. v. 1 (68), 1989. 67–74.

Elson, Diane, and Ruth Pearson, 'Nimble Fingers Make Cheap Workers': An Analysis of Women's Employment in Third World Export Manufacturing. *Feminist Review*. v. 7 (1), 1981. 87–107.

Engels, Friedrich, *The Origin of the Family, Private Property and the State*. 1942. Downloaded from https://www.marxists.org/archive/marx/works/1884/origin-family/.

Federici, Silvia, *Wages Against Housework*, Bristol: Falling Wall Press, 1975.

Fee, Terry, Domestic labor: An Analysis of Housework and its Relation to the Production Process. *Review of Radical Political Economics*. v. 8 (1), 1976. 1–8.

Ferguson, Susan, *Women and Work: Feminism, Labour, and Social Reproduction*, London: Pluto Press, 2020.

Ferguson, Susan, and David McNally, Precarious Migrants: Gender, Race and the Social Reproduction of a Global Working Class. *Socialist Register*. v. 51, 2015. 1–23.

Fernández-Kelly, Maria Patricia, *For We Are Sold, I and My People: Women and Industry in Mexico's Frontier*. Albany: SUNY Press, 1983.

Folbre, Nancy, *Greed, Lust and Gender: A History of Economic Ideas*. Oxford: OUP, 2009.

Fraser, Nancy, Crisis of Care? On the Social-Reproductive Contradictions of Contemporary Capitalism. In Tithi Bhattacharya (ed.) *Social reproduction theory: Remapping class, recentering oppression*, London: Pluto Press, 2017. 21–36.

Gardiner, Jean, Women's Domestic Labor. *New Left Review*. v. 89, 1975. 47–58.

Hanieh, Adam, The Contradictions of Global Migration. *Socialist Register*. v. 55, 2019. 50–78.

Hartmann, Heidi, The Unhappy Marriage of Marxism and Feminism: Towards a More Progressive Union. *Capital & Class*. v. 3 (2), 1979. 1–33.

Herrera, Gioconda, States, Work, and Social Reproduction Through the Lens of Migrant Experience: Ecuadorian Domestic Workers in Madrid. In Isabella Bakker and Rachel Silvey (eds.) *Beyond States and Markets: The Challenges of Social Reproduction*, London: Routledge, 2012. 93–107.

Hochschild, Arlie Russell, Global Care Chains and Emotional Surplus Value. In Will Hutton and Anthony Giddens (eds.) *On the Edge: Living with Global Capitalism*, London: Jonathan Cape, 2000. 130–46.

Hopkins, Carmen Teeple, Mostly Work, Little Play: Social Reproduction, Migration, and Paid Domestic Work in Montreal. In T. Bhattacharya (ed.) *Social reproduction theory: Remapping class, recentering oppression*, London: Pluto Press, 2017. 131–147.

Horrell, Sara, Jane Humphries, and Jacob Weisdorf, Malthus's Missing Women and Children: Demography and Wages in Historical Perspective, England. *European Economic Review*. v. 129 (103534), 2020. 1280–1850.

International Labor Organization (ILO), *Women and Men in the Informal Economy: A Statistical Picture (3rd Edition)*. Geneva: ILO, 2018.

Jones, Claudia, *An End to the Neglect of the Problems of the Negro Woman!* New York: Political Affairs, 1949.

Katz, Cindi, Vagabond Capitalism and the Necessity of Social Reproduction. *Antipode.* v. 33 (4), 2001. 709–728.

Kofman, Eleonore and Parvati Raghuram, *Gendered Migrations and Global Social Reproduction*. London: Palgrave Macmillan, 2015.

Kunz, Rahel, The Crisis of Social Reproduction in Rural Mexico: Challenging The 'Re-Privatization of Social Reproduction' Thesis. *Review of International Political Economy*. v. 17 (5), 2010. 913–945.

Laslett, Barbara and Johanna Brenner, Gender and Social Reproduction: Historical Perspectives. *Annual Review of Sociology*. v. 15 (1), 1989. 381–404.

Manning, FTC, Gender and Capitalism: Debating Cinzia Arruzza's Remarks on Gender. *Viewpoint Magazine*, 2015.

Marx, Karl, *Capital, Volume* (1867). New York: Vintage Books, 1977.

Marx, Karl and Friedrich Engels, *The German Ideology* (1845). Amherst, New York: Prometheus Books.

Mezzadri, Alessandra, *The Sweatshop Regime: Labouring Bodies, Exploitation, and Garments Made in India*. Cambridge University Press, 2016.

Mezzadri, Alessandra, The Informal Labours of Social Reproduction. *Global Labour Journal*. v. 11 (2), 2020. 156–163.

Mies, Maria, *Housewives Produce for the World Market: The Lace Makers of Narsapur*. Geneva: International Labour Organization, 1980.

Mitchell, Juliet, The Longest Revolution. *New Left Review*. v. 40, 1966. 11–37.

Molyneux, Maxine, Beyond the Domestic Labour Debate. *New Left Review*. v. 116 (3), 1979. 27.

Nassif, Gabriella, If We Don't Do It, Who Will? Strategies of social reproduction at the margins. *Gender, Work & Organization*, 2022. https://doi.org/10.1111/gwao.12897

Ong, Aihwa, *Spirits of Resistance and Capitalist Discipline: Factory Women in Malaysia*. Albany, New York: SUNY Press, 1987.

Parreñas, Rhacel Salazar, Migrant Filipina Domestic Workers and The International Division of Reproductive Labor. *Gender & society*. v. 14 (4), 2000. 560–581.

Rajan, S. Irudaya and Neetha (eds.), *Migration, Gender and Care Economy*. South Asia: Routledge, 2019.

Rao, Smriti, Labor and Social Reproduction. In Akram-Lodhi, Haroon, Kristina Dietz, Bettina Engels, and Ben McKay (eds.), *Handbook of Critical Agrarian Studies*, Northampton: Edward Elgar, 2021. 99–108.

Seccombe, Wally, "The Housewife and Her Labour Under Capitalism. *New Left Review*. v. 83 (1), 1974. 3–24.

Sparr, Pamela, (ed.) *Mortgaging Women's Lives: Feminist Critiques of Structural Adjustment*. London and New Jersey: Zed Books, 1994.

Standing, Guy, Global Feminization Through Flexible Labor. *World development*. v. 17 (7), 1989. 1077–1095.

Toupin, Sophie. *Wages for Housework*. London: Pluto Press, 2018.

Vogel, Lise, *Beyond Domestic Labor: Women's Oppression and The Reproduction of Labor Power*. Waltham: Brandeis University, 1981.

Vogel, Lise, *Marxism and The Oppression of Women: Toward a Unitary Theory*. Massachusetts: Brill, 1983.

Weeks, Kathi, *The Problem with Work*. Duke University Press, 2011.

Wright, Melissa, *Disposable Women and Other Myths of Global Capitalism*. London: Routledge, 2006.

7

THE ECONOMICS OF IMPERIALISM

Markets, Primary Commodities, and the Periphery

Prabhat Patnaik

Introduction

"Mainstream" economics analyzes capitalism as a closed self-contained system which *may* have interactions with an "outside" world but is not compelled to do so. This perception, however, is both logically untenable and historically false: capitalism must not only interact with its surrounding pre-capitalist environment but must actually dominate it – a domination we call "imperialism".

The Need for External Markets

Imperialism necessarily follows from the fact that capitalism is a money-using economy. It uses money not just as a medium of circulation but also as a form of wealth-holding. Indeed, the medium-of-circulation role of money implies that it must also be a form of wealth-holding, for even as a medium of circulation, money is held as wealth though only for a certain period between transactions: when commodities are exchanged for money, which in turn is exchanged for commodities after a time-lag, there is this time-lag during which wealth is held in money-form.[1] There is no reason why money would not be held for a longer period under certain circumstances, in which case it is being held as an independent wealth-form and means of accumulation. To argue that money is only a medium of circulation and not a form of wealth-holding therefore is logically untenable.

The fact that money Is held as a wealth-form opens up the possibility of *ex ante* generalized overproduction at full employment (or full capacity use), or what Keynes calls "involuntary unemployment". This is because to have *ex ante* generalized overproduction of produced goods and services at full

DOI: 10.4324/9781003366690-8

employment, there must, as a logical necessity, be an *ex ante* excess demand for some non-produced goods. Money is such a non-produced good; but there can be an *ex ante* excess demand for money when production is at full employment (or full capacity) only if there is a wealth demand for money, not if the demand for money arises only as a medium of circulation, for only then would Say's Law not hold.

If there is involuntary unemployment in any period, then investment decisions get scaled down, so that investment gets curtailed in the subsequent period, which further lowers aggregate demand, and so on. The possibility of generalized overproduction therefore has the effect of making the system demand-constrained in general, which has important implications.

In a demand-constrained system, if there are only endogenous stimuli for growth, that is, if the growth of the system is predicated only upon the fact that it has been growing in the past, then there will be no sustained positive growth. Just as growth in the past by generating expectations of growth in the future will stimulate investment that actually drives the system forward, a cessation of growth for whatever reason will push it toward stagnation from which it will be unable to extricate itself. Indeed, as Kalecki has shown, the only stable trend that a demand-constrained system can experience on the basis of endogenous stimuli alone is a zero trend (Kalecki 1962); this means that sustained growth can be explained only on the basis of exogenous stimuli, which ensure that there is some investment that regularly occurs quite independent of the past growth rate of the economy.

Kalecki had believed that innovations that involve the introduction of new processes and products, constituted such an exogenous stimulus, that they gave rise to some additional investment over and above what the expected growth of markets alone would bring forth, because they enabled the firms introducing them to steal a march over their rivals and enlarge markets at the latter's expense. This claim, however, does not stand scrutiny: innovations are not a genuinely exogenous stimulus because when the firms are large and have staying power, to the point of engaging in a price-war if necessary, even the innovating firms would find it difficult to increase their market-share by the sheer fact of innovations. Innovations, in short, can affect the *form* of investment, embodying the new processes that become available, but not the *magnitude* of investment. This is also borne out by the fact that capitalists are reluctant to introduce innovations in a period when demand is stagnant, as was evident during the Great Depression when a large number of inventions were not put into effect in the form of innovations.

Thus the money-using nature of a capitalist economy means that, left to itself, the system would be unable to experience expanded reproduction on a sustained basis; it would settle down at a state of stagnation. What enables it to break out of such a state of stagnation and experience sustained growth is the existence of exogenous stimuli, of which two are important: encroachments on the surrounding pre-capitalist economics that Rosa Luxemburg had correctly and presciently underscored (Luxemburg 1963), and state expenditure whose role as a promoter of aggregate demand, however, is of recent origin. Rosa Luxemburg had visualized the *entire* surplus value of the capitalist sector being realized through sales to the pre-capitalist sector at the expense of local producers there, and this process of destruction of pre-capitalist production being simultaneously a process of *assimilation* of the pre-capitalist sector into the capitalist one; both these conclusions, however, are neither theoretically warranted nor historically valid. An exogenous stimulus does not have to realize the entire surplus value of the capitalist sector; and the degraded remnants of the pre-capitalist sector providing such a stimulus can linger on as a permanent adjunct to the capitalist sector without getting assimilated into it, as has happened historically.

Tropical Agricultural Commodities

The need for the capitalist sector to encroach upon its surrounding pre-capitalist sector arises for an *additional* reason as well. The capitalist sector requires a whole range of commodities for current inputs and for the consumption of both the workers and capitalists, which it cannot either produce, or produce in adequate quantities, or produce all the year around. These include not only a key commodity like oil, the bulk of whose reserves lie outside the geographical boundaries of metropolitan capitalism, but also tropical agricultural commodities. It is noteworthy that the Industrial Revolution, with which capitalism came into its own, occurred in cotton textiles in a country that could produce no cotton at all!

It needs to obtain these commodities from these outside regions and to do so without experiencing any inflationary pressures, for that would undermine the value of money which a money-using economy like capitalism can ill afford. In the case of mineral resources, this is typically ensured by simply acquiring control over the sources of such materials; in the case of the tropical and sub-tropical agricultural commodities, however, which are produced by millions of peasants, the problem is far more complex. Since the case of control over minerals has been widely discussed in the literature, this chapter shall concentrate on tropical and sub-tropical agricultural commodities.

The peasants producing them are not even engaged in commodity production to start with. A hallmark of commodity production is that the product constitutes for the producers *only* pure exchange value, just a sum of money, and not a use-value at all, while for the buyers, it is both a use-value and an exchange value (Kautsky 1903). Commodity production in this sense did not exist in the case of the tropical and sub-tropical agricultural products earlier even when these products were marketed and exchanged for money, because in most cases, it was the surplus over and above the peasants' own subsistence that was at best being sold; a significant part of production was undertaken for family consumption or exchange within a small village community under the *jajmani* system. To make the peasants produce in accordance with the dictates of metropolitan demand, that is, to introduce commodity production to serve the interests of the metropolis by breaking the self-sufficiency of the village was the first requirement of capitalism. In addition, it was also necessary to ensure that supplies were made available in adequate quantities.

Since the land mass producing such commodities is more or less fully used up, and since "land augmenting" practices that raise productivity per unit of net sown area, such as irrigation, require substantial state investment in these outlying regions which capitalism in the metropolis typically frowns upon, obtaining them in adequate quantities for metropolitan use, invariably entails a squeeze on their local absorption; sometimes there has to be a squeeze on the local absorption of other crops from which land can be diverted toward the ones the metropolis demands. Hence, the imposition of demand compression on the periphery becomes necessary for the metropolis even after it has dragged the former into the ambit of commodity production (Patnaik and Patnaik 2016).

This demand compression could take the form of imposing a profit inflation on the periphery, that is, a rise in the local price of the crop relative to local money wages, so that supplies are squeezed out for metropolitan use; and if the exchange rate of the local currency relative to the metropolitan currency depreciates *pari passu*, as it would in a situation of inflation if there is some degree of convertibility between currencies, then the metropolis can get its supplies without any increase in their price in terms of its own currency, that is, without any threat to the stability of the value of its own currency.

Profit inflation, however, has the potential for causing a precipitous decline in the value of the currency of the *periphery* and hence threatening to upset the entire supply arrangement, which is why the metropolis prefers an alternative route of imposing a demand compression on the periphery. This alternative is to reduce the incomes of the consumers (who would include the producers of the commodities as well). Within the stylized framework of a pure capitalist economy, the effects of a profit inflation can be exactly mimicked by a wage deflation; likewise, even in a peripheral economy, the compression of local demand that a profit inflation achieves can be brought about by a squeeze on incomes of classes who are the main consumers of the locally grown crops. Imperialism invariably incorporates a mechanism for imposing such an income squeeze.

Colonialism at the Service of Capitalism

Imperialism is not just the arbitrary use of force; it is an arrangement for subordination. The nature of this arrangement has differed in different epochs of capitalism. Colonialism in its various forms that included semi-colonialism and dependency was one such arrangement. It served both the purposes mentioned above quite admirably for capitalism. Encroachments into the colonial and semi-colonial markets leading to the displacement of local artisans provided the exogenous stimulus required by capitalism to keep its growth process going;

the long boom of the "long twentieth century", stretching right until the First World War, was the outcome of this encroachment. The consequent deindustrialization of these economics that swelled the ranks of the unemployed and the underemployed automatically imposed an income compression on the working people, which released supplies of primary commodities for the metropolis.

Additionally, the colonial taxation mechanism was used to introduce a specific form of commodity production and to ensure that adequate supplies were made available to the metropolis through compressing local absorption. In what follows, the chapter uses the Indian case to illustrate the point. For paying taxes to the colonial state in time (otherwise they would forfeit whatever rights they had on the land they cultivated), the peasants were forced to take advances from merchants who dictated to them what crops to produce and bought these crops at pre-contracted prices (Chaudhuri 1964). These merchants, in fact, were responding exclusively to market signals. Thus, the closed nature of production for family consumption or for local exchange (other than what was given to the pre-colonial overlord) was broken, though not by any voluntary choice on the part of the peasants.

The taxation system did not just open up peasant agriculture to metropolitan demands; it served *ipso facto* to compress demand in the local economy. And what is more, the tax proceeds were simply siphoned off to the metropolitan colonizing countries in the commodity-form of primary products, without any quid pro quo. This siphoning off constituted what the Indian nationalist writers had called a "drain of surplus" from the colony to the metropolis, against which, since the balance of payments always had to balance, there were a whole range of concocted or unwarranted items (such as military expenditure imposed on India by Britain for fighting its wars for global imperial expansion, costs of maintaining British embassies in many foreign countries, and "gifts" that India was forced to make to Britain that no Indian knew anything about). Thus, the metropolis used the taxation system to obtain its required commodities, in the required *form* (of use-values), and in the quantity required (through compressing local demand); moreover, it obtained them virtually gratis. (This last point, though of great historical importance, is not however a necessary characteristic of imperialism.)

The market role of the tropical and sub-tropical colonies got exhausted, as it had to be sooner or later, by the First World War. Capitalism now needed an alternative exogenous stimulus, which could only be provided by state expenditure in the metropolis financed through a fiscal deficit or a tax on the capitalists who typically save a part of their profits. But this could be institutionalized only in the post-Second World War period when the existential crisis of capitalism in the face of much greater working-class assertiveness within the metropolis and of a greatly expanded socialist bloc of countries, forced metropolitan capitalists to accept such state intervention. They had been opposed to such intervention in the pre-war years notwithstanding Keynes' advocacy of it, for any such intervention that *directly* involves the state in the determination of the level of activity and employment under capitalism, undermines the social legitimacy of the system; however, in the post-war period, they had little choice.

In fact, the Great Depression can be seen *inter alia* as an interregnum when capitalism lacked such an exogenous stimulus, with the colonial and semi-colonial markets having exhausted their potential and with state intervention not yet being acceptable to metropolitan capital; its depth and long duration can be explained by this peculiar circumstance. The fact that the Depression led to the postponement of the introduction of a whole range of inventions that were utilized only after the war and also the truncation of the automobile boom in the United States, which resumed only in the post-Second World War era (Baran and Sweezy 1966) shows that innovations do not constitute an authentic exogenous stimulus as is commonly supposed. Innovations cannot be a substitute for either the external markets or state intervention in demand management.

Even as colonial and semi-colonial markets got exhausted, the role of these regions as suppliers of primary commodities largely *gratis* continued to remain crucial. In fact, this role was sharply accentuated during the Second World War when the metropolitan powers extracted huge amounts of surplus from their colonial possessions for fighting the war. What was taken as *gratis* through taxation could hardly suffice for the purpose; it had to be supplemented by huge amounts of fiscal deficit. These deficits extracted forced loans from the colonies and semi-colonies through a profit inflation that squeezed out "forced savings" from their working people.

In Asia, for instance, it was not just Japan that ruthlessly squeezed its newly acquired colonies for financing the war, but Britain as well. The British colonial government in India resorted to massive fiscal deficits, in addition to its tax measures, both for financing its own "contribution" to the war effort (as it made India join the war without consulting Indian opinion) and for giving loans to Britain for financing the British war effort on the eastern front. These massive deficits caused a "profit inflation" whose impact on the people of Bengal was so severe that an estimated 3 million people died in the ensuing famine (Patnaik and Patnaik 2021). India's loans to the British government which were denominated in pound sterling were substantially negated by the 1949 devaluation of that currency and also by the worldwide rise in prices after the war. This meant that the "forced savings" extracted from the people did not even leave behind any significant assets for the newly independent country.

International Monetary System

Apart from the decline in the role of the periphery in providing an external market, there are two basic differences between the colonial period and the present neo-liberal one: first, while in the colonial period, a large part of the supply of primary commodities from the colonies and semi-colonies came to the metropolis *gratis*, such unrequited transfer has not been the case later. There are no doubt various forms in which surplus is still siphoned off from the colonies and semi-colonies, such as through unequal exchange and through payments for intellectual property rights; but their scale is less than the unrequited transfers of the colonial period through the taxation system (or the "drain of wealth" to the metropolis as Indian nationalist writers called it). Second, the means of imposition of income compression on the working people of the periphery today are different from those of the earlier period. In today's world of independent states, such income compression, that releases supplies of primary commodities for metropolitan use, is imposed through the *modus operandi* of the neo-liberal regime.

This "drain" had been historically crucial for sustaining the Gold Standard, a fact generally ignored by "mainstream" economists. Any international economic system requires for its durability that the leading capitalist country of the time must accommodate the ambitions of its rival emerging powers by keeping its own economy open for their goods and services without demanding reciprocity; if it does not do so then the rival emerging powers would abandon the international economic system of which the leading country is the leader. Britain was the leading country under the Gold Standard and its markets could be freely accessed by the emerging economic powers of that time like the United States and Germany even though they themselves were heavily protected economics. Simultaneously, Britain made capital exports to Continental Europe and the United States; indeed, Britain had vis-à-vis these emerging rivals, taken together, not only a current account deficit but also a capital account deficit. Nonetheless, Britain could balance its payments because of what it earned from its colonies and semi-colonies through imposing deindustrialization upon them (i.e., by selling its industrial goods at the expense of their local producers) and what it obtained from them by way of the "drain". In India's case, this "drain" amounted to its entire commodity export surplus (merchandise plus commodity gold) which was simply diverted to Britain and was offset by miscellaneous concocted or unwarranted items on the debit side (Patnaik and Patnaik 2021).

India's key role in sustaining the British balance of payments, and hence the Gold Standard, during the long Victorian and Edwardian boom, is brought out by economic historian S. B. Saul (1960). Of the total resources required by Britain to finance its balance of payments deficits (current account plus gold) vis-à-vis Continental Europe and the United States, more than one-third came from its current account surplus vis-à-vis India in 1880; this was contributed to by both the deindustrialization-causing exports to India and the "drain of surplus" from India against the unwarranted items on India's debit side.

Since India had a commodity export surplus (taking merchandise and gold together) vis-à-vis the rest of the world other than Britain and since this entire amount was impounded by Britain and kept in London and the rupee equivalent of it was handed to Indian exporters out of the tax revenues raised within India, this entire amount represented a "drain of surplus"; the offsetting unwarranted items, which figured in both the government budget and in the balance of payments, were always suitably adjusted to ensure that this entire export surplus was "drained away".

By 1910, Britain's current account surplus vis-à-vis India (consisting of both deindustrializing exports to India and the "drain of surplus") financed over 60 percent of its total payments deficit vis-à-vis Continental Europe and the United States. In short, Britain absorbed the goods from these regions which were the newly emerging economics of that time on the basis largely of its earnings including the "drain" from its empire and even made substantial capital exports to them. Had these earnings not been there it would have been forced to protect itself; not only would the Gold Standard have collapsed but the immense diffusion of capitalism of the long nineteenth century would have been impossible (Bagchi 1972).

This should also clear up a common misconception. It is often claimed that the argument that capitalism required colonial possessions is refuted by the experience of the newly emerging economics of the nineteenth century. Neither Germany nor the United States, not to mention the Scandinavian countries, possessed any significant colonies; and yet they emerged as major capitalist powers, which shows that colonial possessions were not necessary for the growth of capitalism. What this argument misses, however, is that these newly emerging powers were indirect beneficiaries of Britain's colonial possessions, since Britain kept its own market open to their goods while itself seeking refuge in colonial and semi-colonial markets, what Hobsbawm calls "a steady flight from the modern, resistant and competitive markets into the undeveloped" (Hobsbawm 1969).

When the leadership role of the capitalist world was assumed by the United States after the war, it could neither benefit from the existence of colonial markets, nor, unlike Britain, have access to resources obtained through "drain" from the colonies. State intervention in demand management, the new "external stimulus" that took the place of colonial markets earlier, which underlay the post-war boom, entailed above all significant fiscal deficits by the United States, which meant printing of dollars that were declared to be "as good as gold" under the Bretton Woods system and that poured into metropolitan banks. American investment in Europe taking the form of purchase of European enterprises was also financed by such printed dollars. And later, when the United States started having a current account deficit on its balance of payments, it was also settled by exporting dollars to the surplus countries.

For all these reasons, there was a substantial dollar build-up with metropolitan banks, which they were keen to deploy in profitable avenues all over the globe. The enormous superstructure of finance that got built up under post-war capitalism, as well as the pressure to dismantle capital controls that existed under the Bretton Woods system and to usher in a neo-liberal regime globally that allows free mobility of capital, including above all finance, across country borders, was thus a direct result of the post-colonial setting. The "drain" from the colonies that the earlier leader of the capitalist world had access to was replaced now with massive borrowings by the new leader of the capitalist world, the United States. The dollar build-up with metropolitan banks was a component of this massive borrowing.

The end of colonialism has thus contributed in no small measure to the current phenomenon of "financialization". But "financialization" has led to the imposition of a neo-liberal regime worldwide, which also provides a new mechanism through which contemporary capitalism imposes an income squeeze, and hence demand compression, on the tropical and sub-tropical regions of the world to ensure adequate supplies of their commodities for the metropolis.

It may be thought that since the value of the primary commodities from tropical and sub-tropical regions imported into the metropolis relative to the value of the output in the metropolis into which they enter directly or indirectly (including as labor-feeding inputs) is very small, their importance is being grossly exaggerated, and, hence, any explanation of imperialism in terms of the need to acquire raw materials in adequate quantities, is wholly unwarranted. But the relative smallness of the value of imported tropical and sub-tropical goods into the metropolis reflects the valuation process, not of their importance. They remain critical to the metropolis as *use-values* (Magdoff 1969), and hence ensuring the supply of such commodities, which requires income compression in the periphery, continues to be crucial.

The Neo-liberal Arrangement

The post-colonial *dirigiste* regimes in the periphery had introduced "land augmenting" measures to raise tropical and sub-tropical crop output, so that demand compression became not only impossible to impose by metropolitan countries in the new circumstances but also unnecessary. The absence of any mechanism for doing so therefore did not inconvenience the metropolis in any way. Things, however, changed in the early 1970s when there was an upsurge in primary commodity prices and metropolitan capitalism felt the need for re-fashioning a mechanism of demand compression, that is, for tightening once again metropolitan control over the periphery. The neo-liberal order that emerged from controlling inflation in the metropolis provided such a mechanism.

There are two clear ways that international institutions dominated by metropolitan capital now influence land-use in the countries of the periphery with the objective of making adequate supplies of primary commodities available to the metropolis. One is through the *restoration* of commodity production. In the colonial period, commodity production had been established in the periphery not through inducing the peasantry to treat what they produce exclusively as exchange value, but by forcing the peasantry to take loans from merchants for paying the revenue demands of the colonial state, and making the merchants respond to market signals and get peasants to produce accordingly.

After independence, even this refracted form of commodity production was attenuated by restrictions imposed by the post-colonial state, restrictions that generally encouraged foodgrain production, promoted national food self-sufficiency, and introduced a system of procurement of foodgrains at pre-announced prices, both to provide price support to peasants and to obtain supplies for the public distribution system. Even in the case of commercial crops, a regime of support prices was established, which, together with trade protection, came in the way of peasants responding "freely to the market forces", as required by authentic commodity production.

The WTO, in its current garb in which it has replaced GATT, has taken upon itself to eliminate state intervention in the operation of markets, including those of agricultural primary commodities. Hence, even though advanced countries give billions of dollars of direct cash subsidies to their farmers without incurring the wrath of WTO, input price subsidies and output price-support given by the countries of the periphery are frowned upon. The idea is to introduce authentic commodity production, discourage efforts toward food self-sufficiency, and ensure that output decisions in the periphery are taken in response to the pull of the greater purchasing power of the metropolitan economics.

Since in today's world, the advanced capitalist economics require not food-grains, of which they have a surplus, and which they would like, if anything, to sell in the periphery, but a range of commercial crops, their interest lies in shifting land use in the periphery from foodgrains to these commercial crops; and for this, the removal of government intervention and restoration of commodity production is a first step.

The WTO seeks to achieve this. African countries have been "persuaded" to abandon efforts at foodgrain self-sufficiency, leading to frequent famines and food scarcity. Their precarious state in the wake of the Ukraine war is a result of this. The Indian government has already removed price-support, and protection to a large extent, for commercial crops in accordance with WTO demands, but has not been able to withdraw price-support for foodgrains. Its efforts to remove this price-support regime were so strongly opposed by farmers in 2021–22 that it was forced to backtrack.

If the introduction of commodity production by removing government intervention in the market is one plank of an imperialist agenda with regard to primary commodities, the other is to introduce a mechanism of demand compression in the periphery so that the requisite quantities of the crops demanded by the metropolis are made available to it. The rise in the demand for such crops in the face of relatively inelastic supplies causes inflation in the periphery. As long as the exchange rate remains unchanged, the prices of such crops rise in the metropolis as well, though given their low weight, the overall inflation they cause in the metropolis, unlike in the periphery, may not always assume a significant form.

In the periphery, however, matters are different. The rise in the inflation rate has socially destabilizing consequences there. It also creates expectations of exchange rate depreciation and triggers a flight of finance out of the peripheral economy, which causes an actual depreciation of the exchange rate, further exacerbating inflation through a rise in the cost of essential imported inputs like oil. If the peripheral economy approaches the International Monetary Fund (IMF) (or the World Bank) for support at this point, then the "conditionality" imposed upon it necessarily takes the form of raising interest rates, curtailing the level of aggregate demand, and thereby generating larger unemployment, which is but a means of imposing income compression. Besides, the very form that the primary curtailment of aggregate demand takes is fiscal austerity that entails a rise in tax revenue at the expense of the working people and a cutback in government expenditure by reducing the social wage, and salaries and pensions of government employees; all these instruments directly compress the incomes of the working people and the salariat.

Even when the peripheral economy does not approach the IMF, the IMF recipe is by now so internalized by the ruling echelons in the economy, comprising large numbers of ex-employees of the Fund and the Bank, that they spontaneously adopt the same recipe even without any conditionality being imposed upon them. This amounts to resolving inflation at the expense of the working people by compressing their incomes and hence demands; in particular, it results in a reduction in the demand for those crops which the metropolis requires. Such crops in short are made available to the metropolis in requisite quantities even when the overall output of agricultural primary commodities does not increase owing to the absence of land augmentation.

In other words, the same process, of extracting growing amounts of tropical and sub-tropical products, that the metropolis had effected through colonialism, is now carried out in a different manner despite decolonization. The only difference, as noted earlier, is that under colonialism the metropolis paid nothing in return for a large chunk of such products (since they were the commodity form of the "drain"), but now the metropolis has to pay in return (though an element of "drain" is not altogether absent).

The Crisis of Neo-liberalism

The neo-liberal arrangement therefore is in some ways reminiscent of the colonial arrangement, but it has to have some internal social support within the peripheral society that can substitute for the use of external force by the metropolis. This support has come not just from the corporate–financial oligarchy within the periphery that is now globalized and hence integrated with globalized capital but also from an upper middle class that benefits both from the possibility of migration to the metropolis and from the outsourcing of certain activities from the metropolis to the periphery where its skills and training are much in demand.

Neo-liberal capitalism therefore creates a deep cleavage within the peripheral society. The anti-imperialist struggles of the twentieth century that had resulted in decolonization had united virtually the whole of society against the domination of the metropolis (except a segment of the landed interests and comprador bourgeoisie). This unity continued more or less through the *dirigiste* economic regime after decolonization. Neo-liberalism, however, has broken this unity: the division now is no longer between the nation and the metropolis but *within* the nation itself. At an economic level, there is on the one hand an income compression imposed on the working people, that is, the peasantry, other petty producers, and the rural and urban workers, to squeeze out supplies of tropical and sub-tropical goods to meet metropolitan demand from a relatively stagnant agricultural output that results from the adoption of neo-liberal policies; on the other hand, there is an immense increase in the share of surplus in the economy which swells not only the profits of the big capitalists but also the incomes of the urban upper-middle class consisting of service sector professionals and managerial and technical personnel.

This neo-liberal arrangement, however, is coming unstuck. Owing to greater global mobility of capital, not just finance but, more pertinent here, of productive capital, the real wages in the metropolis have become tethered to those in the periphery since capital can relocate to the latter in the event of a widening wage gap. In the periphery, on the other hand, despite such relocation and the resultant higher growth of the gross domestic product, at least in certain regions, real wages scarcely increase. This is because the labor reserves, created initially by colonial deindustrialization, do not get exhausted despite such relocation, as increased competition arising from greater trade openness raises greatly the rates of labor productivity growth.

The vector of real wages across nations therefore remains relatively stagnant even as the vector of labor productivities increases, causing a rise in the share of surplus in output, both for the capitalist world as a whole and also for individual countries. Since the propensity to consume from the surplus is lower than from the income received by the working people, this causes an *ex ante* over-production crisis.

Such an *ex ante* over-production crisis cannot be offset by state expenditure, since, for this to happen, such expenditure has to be financed either through larger taxes on capitalists and other surplus earners (who save a part of their incomes) or through a larger fiscal deficit, both of which are anathema for globalized finance capital: if state expenditure is financed through taxes on the working people who consume the bulk of their incomes anyway, then there is little net addition to aggregate demand. As globalized finance capital confronts nation-states in the neo-liberal era, its preference becomes decisive, for fear that otherwise its "confidence" in the country in question would get undermined and there might be a capital flight.

States therefore lack the capacity for overcoming the *ex ante* over-production crisis. Barring the transient effects of asset-price bubbles in the United States in keeping up world aggregate demand, the neo-liberal economy moves into an over-production crisis and hence stagnation. This has happened since 2008 when the last of the US bubbles collapsed with nothing comparable emerging subsequently (Patnaik and Patnaik 2021).

Neo-liberal capitalism and the imperial arrangement it had worked out has thus reached a dead-end. What will replace it depends on the outcome of class struggles that the period will generate. Meanwhile, neo-liberal capitalism is forming alliances with neo-fascist elements to buttress its position, since neo-fascism seeks to divide the working people within each country, to create hatred against the "other", typically some minority group, and to change socio-political discourse away from issues of material life. The struggle of the working people against the neo-liberal order and the domestic corporate–financial oligarchy integrated with it thus gets directly linked to the struggle for the defense of democracy and political freedom.

Note

1 It is worth noting that there is no reason why money should be reconverted to commodities automatically after a *fixed* time-lag as would be *logically* implied if money was taken to be *only* a medium of circulation (as is captured in the constant k of the Cambridge Quantity Equation or the constant v in Irving Fisher's version of it).

References

Bagchi, A. K., Some International Foundations of Capitalist Growth and Under-development, *Economic and Political Weekly*, v. 7, 1972. 31–33.

Baran, P. A. and P. M. Sweezy, *Monopoly Capital*. New York: Monthly Review Press, 1966.

Chaudhuri, B. B., *The Growth of Commercial Agriculture in Bengal 1757–1900*. Kolkata: Quality Printers, 1964.

Hobsbawm, E. J., *Industry and Empire: From 1750 to the Present Day*. Harmondsworth: Penguin, 1969.

Kalecki, M., Observations on the Theory of Growth. *Economic Journal*. v. 72 (285), 1962. 134–154.

Kautsky, K., *Economic Doctrines of Karl Marx*. 1903. Retrieved from, www.marxists.org

Luxemburg, R., *The Accumulation of Capital*. London: Routledge Paperback, 1963.

Magdoff, H., *The Age of Imperialism: The Economics of U.S. Foreign Policy*. New York: Monthly Review Press, 1969.

Patnaik, U. and P. Patnaik, *A Theory of Imperialism*. New York: Columbia University Press, 2016.

Patnaik, U. and P. Patnaik, *Capital and Imperialism: Theory, History and the Present*. New York: Monthly Review Press, 2021.

Saul, S. B., *Studies in British Overseas Trade*. Liverpool: Liverpool University Press, 1960.

PART II

Issues and Debates in Radical Political Economics

8

CRISES AND CYCLES IN CAPITALISM

Michael Roberts

"The awareness that economic development does not proceed smoothly is as old as economics itself. Speculation manias, crop failures, political troubles, natural catastrophes and other events wrought havoc well before the capitalism".[1]

Panics, Crises and Cycles

But it is only since the capitalist mode of production (i.e., production for profit for the private owners of the means of production) became dominant, first in the major economies of what we now like to call the "global north" and eventually everywhere that regular and recurring (cyclical) crises of production, investment and employment emerged.

The budding new "science" of economics, or political economy as it was called in the early 19th century, did not ignore crises and cycles of boom and slump in economies. As early as 1810, William Huskisson talked of expansions leading to excessive financial speculations, which would eventually prove unsustainable and bring "generalized ruin and distress".[2] Indeed, Huskisson emphasized that these crises or slumps were man-made and endemic to the economic system of production and finance – not exogenous shocks like events of nature or wars.

As a series of what were then called "panics" materialized in the 19th century, starting with the first global one in 1825, the term "crisis" started to be used in English. Occasionally for the events of 1836 and 1837, and again more frequently in 1847 and 1857. The term "cycle" also became more frequently used from the 1820s to describe "an interval of time during which a characteristic, often regularly repeated event or sequence of events occurs".[3]

DOI: 10.4324/9781003366690-10

The length of these cycles of boom and slump seemed to be around ten years or so (in Britain in 1815, 1825, 1836–39, 1847, 1857, 1866, 1878). As Gerolamo Boccardo observed in 1879, "such a regularity leads in all probability (I was about to write certainty) to conjecture the existence of a law. The caprices of randomness are not suited to explain this order of [economic] disorders".[4]

The liberal economist John Stuart Mill noted the same. He concluded that commercial slumps "are not occasional but tend to recur" and advanced an explanation of the phenomenon that "such revulsions are almost periodical" and was "a consequence of the very tendency of profits which we are considering". Moreover, Mill pointed out that these slumps prepared conditions for a future recovery and boom.

> Does not this demonstrate how speedily profit would be at the minimum, and the stationary condition of capital would be attained, if these accumulations went on without any counteracting principle? But the diminished scale of all safe gains inclines persons to give a ready ear to any projects which hold out...to produce a temporary rise of interest and profit, make room for fresh accumulations and the same round is recommenced.[5]

Mills' explanation for cycles of boom and slump paralleled that of Marx, as we shall see.

Indeed, socialists too noted the unique boom and slump nature of capitalist production for profit. In 1827, William Thompson introduced his *Labour Rewarded* by pointing out that "as long as the present principle of action remains, crisis will succeed to crisis, at intervals more or less distant". He also insisted that "Periods of crisis, recurring at irregular intervals, inseparable from the present principle of action, strike every vulgar eye".[6]

But it was the young Marx and Engels who really expanded the theory of regular and recurring crises in capitalism. Engels, as was often the case, was before Marx on this. As early as 1843, in his *Umrisse* (Outline of a Critique of Political Economy), Engels attacked the view of mainstream economics (unchanged over 180 years later) that slumps or crises in production were exogenous to the capitalist profit-driven economy.

> The economist comes along with his lovely theory of demand and supply, proves to you that 'one can never produce too much,' and practice replies with trade crises, which reappear as regularly as the comets, and of which we have now on the average one every five to seven years.[7]

Engels took his estimates of the cycle length from John Wade who had previously analyzed the crises of 1763, 1773, 1793, 1811, 1815–16, and 1825–26, which he described as "commercial vicissitudes, which, like a plague or a pestilence, visit the country at regular intervals of five, seven or nine years" (Engels 1844) and provide an "indubitable proof of the existence of radical defects in

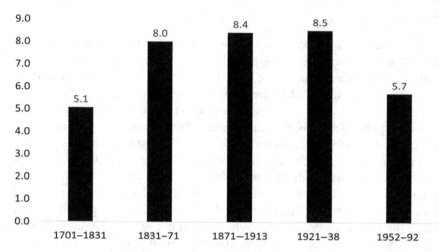

FIGURE 8.1   Average Length of Cycles of Boom and Slump from 1701, Bank of England* Author's calculation from NBER data.

the principles and practice of mercantile transactions".[8] Modern research supports the observations of Wade and Engels. The Bank of England found the gaps between major peaks and troughs during the 19th century were about 6–8 years and a little longer in the 20th century. In the 21st century, we can record 2001, 2008–9, 2020 so far, or cycles of about 10 years.[9]

But the leading economists of the 19th century with few exceptions denied that crises were endemic to capitalist production or there was anything that could be called "business cycles". They generally considered crises to be mostly isolated events limited to particular markets. They subscribed to the idea of Jean-Baptiste Say, who denied that a "glut," that is, overproduction, could be general affecting the "free market" economy.[10] Marx called this "vulgar economics" which looked only at the surface appearance of economies and failed to consider the underlying contradictions.[11]

In contrast, Marx's view was that capitalism expanded through a succession of periods of accumulation of capital separated by crises, in an alternating process that he called the "industrial cycle", or "crisis cycle". With

...sudden immense leaps, necessarily give rise to the following cycle: feverish production, a consequent glut of the market, then a contraction of the market, which causes production to be crippled. The life of industry becomes a series of periods of moderate activity, prosperity, over-production, crisis and stagnation. The uncertainty and instability to which machinery subjects the employment, and consequently the conditions of existence, of the operatives becomes a normal state of affairs, owing to these periodic turns of the industrial cycle.[12]

The Great Recession

Modern mainstream economics has not really altered its view of crises under capitalism. Mainstream economists still ignore the idea of any cycles of boom and slump. For them, slumps are caused by "shocks" to an otherwise harmonious market economy. When there are slumps in production or collapses in prices of financial assets, these "shocks" are put down to financial greed, bad economic policy decisions, wars and or other "unknown unknowns" as former US Defense Secretary Donald Rumsfeld famously called such events.[13]

Take the debate over the causes of the Great Recession of 2008–9, the largest collapse in global production and investment since the 1930s, until the pandemic slump of 2020. When the UK's Queen of England visited the London School of Economics in the depth of the Great Recession, she immediately asked the assembled professors: "Why did you not see this coming?" It took them three days to come up with an answer: "there was a failure of the collective imagination of many bright people"![14]

Former Fed chairman Alan Greenspan said the Great Recession was a chance event that was caused by "massive natural forces constituting a perfect storm".[15] Nobel Prize winner, Eugene Fama, stated, "We don't know what causes recession. We've never known... Economics isn't very good at explaining swings in economic activity".[16] On the global financial crash causing a deep slump in investment and production, Fama said: "If I could have predicted the crisis, I would have. I did not see it. I'd love to know more what causes business cycles".

Looking back at the Great Recession in 2011, Greg Mankiw, the author of the main textbook used in economics departments of US universities, wrote: "the area where I have devoted most of my energy and attention, namely the ups and down of the business cycle, is where I find myself most often confronting important questions without obvious answers."[17]

And it was not just the mainstream so-called neoclassical economists who were non-plussed. So were the Keynesian economists. For them, it was due to a collapse in "effective demand". Consumers stopped spending and capitalists stopped investing. But why did they stop? To this question, there was no clear answer. Paul Krugman, the doyen of Keynesian economics, said it was due to a "technical malfunction" in capitalist production.[18] Even those of more radical bent in the so-called post-Keynesian school could not provide an answer to that question, except to say that "instability is an inherent and inescapable flaw of capitalism" (Hyman Minsky).[19]

Profitability and Crises

What was missing from all these various explanations was the role of profit – and yet capitalist production only takes place if profits are made by the owners of capital (money and means of production). For Marx, crises that arise under

capitalism are the result of changes in the profitability of investment and production. This brings us to Marx's law of the tendency of the rate of profit to
fall. In Marx's view, this was "most important law of political economy".

> The declining profit rate is in every respect the most important law of mod-
> ern political economy, and the most essential for understanding the most
> difficult relations.... Beyond a certain point, the development of the powers
> of production [productivity of labor M.R] become a barrier for capital [the
> decreased production of surplus value M.R]; hence the capital relation
> becomes a barrier for the development of the productive powers of labour.[20]

Marx's measure of profitability of capital is denoted in the simple formula:
$s/(C+v)$, where (s) is the surplus value (or profit) appropriated from the value
in production created by the labor force; C is the stock of assets and raw materials advanced by the capitalist to be used by the workforce, called constant
capital by Marx; and (v) is the wages paid to the labor force called variable
capital by Marx. The stock of assets is called constant because machinery and
raw materials do not add any new value in production but merely consume the
value already embodied in their previous production. And it's variable capital,
because only labor power creates new value in production and it is part of this
new value that capitalists appropriate as surplus value (surplus over that paid
in wages to workers), S, when realized in the sale of the commodities or services produced.

There are two drivers of the rate of profit. The first is rising investment in
constant capital relative to investment in more labor. So, C/v, called the organic
composition of capital by Marx, rises as a tendency. Typically, productivity is
raised through new technologies, which are productivity-increasing, but also
labor-shedding. Given that only the exertion of labor power creates value, if
labor declines relatively in each unit of production, the new value of that unit
falls. When new technologies are brought into the production process to
increase efficiency, as a rule, assets replace labor. This raises the ratio of the
capital invested in the means of production (technology, equipment and structures) relative to the investment in the employment of labor power. As that
ratio rises, so the rate of profit falls, ceteris paribus. Marx recognized that there
could be occasions when new technologies would cheapen constant capital sufficiently to raise profitability – but such results would be exceptions and not
long lasting. The central tendency was for a rising ratio of constant capital to
labor – and the historical evidence confirms that.

There is another factor that can counteract the effect of the rising organic
composition. This is a rising rate of surplus value or exploitation, i.e., s/v. If
C/v rises faster than s/v, then the rate of profit will fall – and vice versa. It is
Marx's argument that C/v will rise faster than s/v over time. That's because
there is a limit to a rise in the rate of surplus value (s/v) both physically (there

FIGURE 8.2 Global Annual Rate of Profit.

Source: World profitability dashboard, https://dbasu.shinyapps.io/World-Profitability/ Data for the profitability analysis reported on this dashboard comes from the Extended Penn World Table and the World Input-Output Database. This dashboard has been created and is maintained by Evan Wasner (ewasner@umass.edu), Jesus Lara Jauregui (jlarajauregu@umass.edu), Julio Huato (jhuato@sfc.edu) and Deepankar Basu (dbasu@econs.umass.edu).

are only 24 hours in a day and workers cannot live on air) and socially, with laws on limiting hours, improving conditions at work and workers organization for higher wages. But there is no limit to the rise in the organic composition of capital.

That's the theory or law. Do the facts bear this theory out? Indeed, they do. Here is a measure of the rate of profit on fixed assets in the major economies of the world since 1950.

As the graph in Figure 8.2 shows, the rate of profit falls over time, but not in a straight line. There are periods when the counteracting factors described above are stronger than the tendency, as in the so-called neoliberal period of the last two decades of the 20th century. The first two decades of the 21st century have seen a resumption of the decline in average profitability.

How does Marx's law take the form of cycles of boom and slump? As the rate of profit falls, it is perfectly possible, indeed likely, that the mass of profit will rise. This can keep investment and production rising. But a persistently falling rate of profit must eventually slow and reverse the rise in the mass of profit. When the rate of profit falls to the point where the mass of profit falls, Marx called this point "absolute over-accumulation", the tipping point for crises. As Marx put it:

the so-called plethora (overaccumulation) of capital always applies to a plethora of capital for which the fall in the rate of profit is not compensated by the mass of profit... and so "overproduction of commodities is simply overaccumulation of capital.[21]

In short, Marx's law of profitability goes as follows: as capitalism develops, new labor-saving, but productivity-increasing, new technologies replace the old ones, and the amount of constant capital rises in relation to variable capital. Because labor power hired with variable capital is the only part of capital that produces value and thus surplus value, the amount of value (and ceteris paribus of surplus value) falls relative to total capital invested and this depresses the rate of profit – unless there is a faster increase in the rate of surplus value, among other countertendencies. But Marx contends that the law will assert itself sooner or later.[22] If profitability falls in the productive sectors, less surplus value can be appropriated by the financial sectors. These sectors, by lending less, see their profits fall. The crisis is born in the productive spheres and extends itself into the unproductive ones. When the speculative bubble explodes, financial firms go bust and the crisis moves from the financial and speculative sectors back to the productive ones. Thus, the financial crisis is a catalyst of the crisis of profitability, but the origin of the crisis is not in finance and speculation.

The countertendencies introduce cyclical trends in the long-term trend of the downward rate of profit. The operation of these countertendencies transforms the breakdown into a temporary crisis, so that the accumulation process is not something continuous but takes the form of periodic cycles. A crisis or slump in production is necessary to correct and reverse the fall in the rate and eventually any fall in the mass of profit. But the downward profitability cycle generates from within the crisis an upward cycle. Accumulation and growth accelerate. The upswing, in its turn, generates from within the next downward profitability cycle. In short, the crisis is expressed in the fall in the average rate of profit and the concomitant bankruptcy of the weakest capitals and thus reduced production. The recovery and boom is the opposite: it is expressed in rising profitability and expanded production. We can call this a profit cycle.

Crises and Credit

While the underlying cause of crises is to be found in the law of tendency of the rate of profit to fall, the actuality of crises can "only be deduced from the real movement of capitalist production, competition and crises".[23] Marx recognized that the possibility of breakdown in the circulation of capital was inherent in commodity production. The possibility of crises existed in the separation of sale and purchase in commodity circulation and in the role of money as

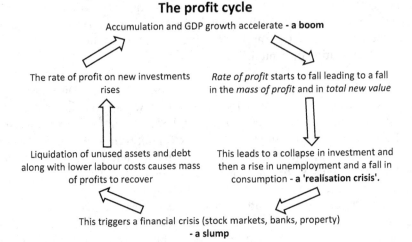

The profit cycle

Accumulation and GDP growth accelerate - **a boom**

The rate of profit on new investments rises

Rate of profit starts to fall leading to a fall in the *mass of profit* and in *total new value*

Liquidation of unused assets and debt along with lower labour costs causes mass of profits to recover

This leads to a collapse in investment and then a rise in unemployment and a fall in consumption - **a 'realisation crisis'**.

This triggers a financial crisis (stock markets, banks, property)
- **a slump**

FIGURE 8.3 The Profit Cycle – Tendencies, Triggers, and Tulips.

means of payment. But this only raised the possibility of crises not their regular cause. That was the barrier set up by "capitalist profit, which was the basis of modern overproduction".[24]

That does not mean the financial sector (and particularly the size and movement of credit) does not play any role in capitalist crises. On the contrary, Marx argues that the growth of credit and speculative investment in stocks, bonds and other forms of money assets (Marx called this fictitious capital) appears to function as a compensating mechanism for the downward pressure on profitability in the accumulation of real capital. A fall in the rate of profit inevitably promotes speculation. If capitalists cannot make enough profit producing commodities, they will try making money betting on the stock exchange or buying various other financial instruments. Capitalists experience the falling rate of profit almost simultaneously, so they start to buy these stocks and assets at the same time, driving prices up. When stock and other financial asset prices are rising everybody wants to buy them – this is the beginning of a "bubble". Such credit bubbles have been part and parcel of speculative investment, going back as far as the very beginning of capital markets – since the infamous Tulip crisis of 1637.[25]

If, for example, the speculation takes place in housing, this creates an option for workers to borrow (mortgages) and spend more than they earn (more than the capitalists have laid out as variable capital), and in this way, the "realization problem" (sufficient money to buy all the goods produced) is solved. But sooner or later, such bubbles burst when investors find that the assets (mortgage bonds) are not worth what they are paying for them. Because fictitious capital is unproductive (i.e., it does not create any new value), fictitious profits are actually a deduction from real profits, which becomes clear when they are cashed in. Then the compensating mechanism of speculation fails, and the result is even greater overproduction than was avoided before by the credit boom.

Indeed, the

> so-called plethora of capital is always basically reducible to a plethora of that capital for which the fall in the profit rate is not outweighed by its mass or to the plethora in which these capitals are available to the leaders of the great branches of production in the form of credit.[26]

Credit takes the accumulation of capital to its limit: "if the credit system appears as the principal lever of overproduction and excessive speculation in commerce, this is simply because the reproduction process, which is elastic by nature, is now forced to its most extreme limit".[27] Thus, "a crisis must evidently break out if credit is suddenly withdrawn and only cash payment is accepted.... at first glance the entire crisis presents itself as simply a credit and monetary crisis".[28]

Each crisis of capitalism does have its own characteristics. The trigger in 2008 was the huge expansion of "fictitious capital" that eventually collapsed when real value expansion could no longer sustain it, as the ratio of house prices to household income reached extremes. But such triggers are not causes. Behind them is a general cause of crisis: the law of the tendency of the rate of profit to fall.

Cycles of Boom and Slump

Marx was continually searching for scientific explanations and evidence of this cyclical process. "All of you know that, from reasons I have not now to explain, capitalistic production moves through certain periodical cycles".[29] Marx commented that "Once the cycle begins, it is regularly repeated. Effects, in their turn, become causes, and the varying accidents of the whole process, which always reproduces its own conditions, take on the form of periodicity".[30] He wrote to Engels at the end of May 1873 about "a problem which I have been wrestling with in private for a long time". He had been examining

> 'tables which give prices, discount rate, etc. etc.'.... I have tried several times – for the analysis of crises – to calculate these ups and downs as irregular curves and thought (I still think that it is possible with enough tangible material) that I could determine the main laws of crises mathematically.

Marx saw the immobility of fixed capital as a part of the explanation of the periodicity of the cycle. He thought that the duration of the accumulation cycle (boom and slump) was about 5–7 years, a view which he revised when the expected crisis did not strike in 1852 in favor of 10 years. In the course of his research, Marx developed the idea that the cycle was connected with the replacement of fixed capital. On this basis, he argued,

> there can be no doubt at all that the cycle through which industry has been passing in plus ou moins[or less] ten-year periods since the large-scale development of fixed capital, is linked with the total reproduction phase of capital determined in this way. We shall find other determining factors too, but this is one of them.[31]

Although the rise of information technology (both hardware-like computers and software-like programs) has reduced the period of replacement of fixed assets in these areas; in others as in infrastructure and energy investment, the replacement period has risen. Marx considered that "So far the period of these cycles has been ten or twelve years, but there is no reason to consider this a constant figure". Indeed, he thought that the cycle of replacement of capital would shorten. However, later Engels began to argue that

> the acute form of the periodic process, with its former ten-year cycle, appears to have given way to a more chronic, long drawn out, alternation between a relatively short and slight business improvement and a relatively long, indecisive depression – taking place in the various industrial countries at different times.[32]

The key point for Marx was that

> the cycle of related turnovers, extending over a number of years, within which the capital is confined by its fixed component, is one of the material foundations for the periodic cycle [crisis] ... But a crisis is always the starting point of a large volume of new investment. It is also, therefore, if we consider society as a whole, more or less a new material basis for the next turnover cycle.

So, Marx connected his theory of crisis to cycles of turnover of capital. The accumulation of capital, including fixed assets, under capitalism depends on its profitability for the owners of capital. From that fundamental premise, if there is a replacement cycle of some duration in any capitalist economy, there is likely to be a cycle of profitability.

We can link the cycle of profitability to another cycle: the movement of share prices. The prices of the shares of US capitalist companies in aggregate also appear to move in cycles, with up and down waves of about sixteen years, very similar to the profit cycle. Investment analysts call the up-wave in stock market prices, a bull market and the down-wave, a bear market. These are very long periods for broadly one direction for stock prices to go. These phases are called secular bull or bear markets.

The US stock market cycle follows a similar pattern to the profit cycle. That close relationship can be established by measuring the market capitalization of companies in an economy against the accumulated assets. Tobin's Q takes the "market capitalization" of the companies in the stock market (in this case the top 500 companies in what is called the S&P500 index) and divides that by the replacement value of tangible assets accumulated by those companies. On this measure, there was a bull market from 1948 to 1968, followed by a bear market until 1981 and then another bull market until 1999. The US stock market cycle appears pretty much the same as the US profit cycle, although slightly different in its turning points. Indeed, the stock market seems to peak in value a couple of years after the rate of profit does. This is really what we would expect, because the stock market is closely connected to the profitability of companies, much more than bank loans or bonds. When the rate of profit enters its down-wave, the stock market soon follows, if with a short lag.

Some Marxists deny the role of Marx's law of profitability in his theory of crises. Instead, they look to theories of disproportionality between accumulation and consumption (due to the anarchy of capitalist production); or the gap between the expansion of capitalist production and the "limits of the market"; or to the lack of purchasing power for workers (a "wage-led" crisis of "realization").

Marx recognized the problem of "realization". The anarchy within capitalist production and accumulation permanently excludes the realization of a part of the produced surplus value, so that the realized surplus value is always different from that produced. Whether commodities are over- or underproduced relative to the market can only be discovered after their production. The value and surplus value contained in unsaleable commodities is lost and cannot be capitalized. When the production oriented toward expansion reaches a point that puts its valorization in jeopardy, it ceases to expand and thereby produces an unsaleable mass of commodities whose value cannot be realized by accumulation and so cannot be realized at all.

What the theorists of disproportional crises forget is that Marx shows the necessity of crises, of over-production of capital, even assuming proportionality between departments of accumulation and consumption. While disturbances and disproportionalities are a continual feature of the capitalist system of production, they are only partial in their effect, and since they are always present, they cannot be the explanation of the crisis cycle. For Marx, it is the discrepancy between material and value production that leads to difficulties in the accumulation process. The crisis is an overproduction of capital in relation to profitability or, what amounts to the same thing, an underproduction of surplus value in relation to the growing mass of total capital. "An overproduction of capital, not of individual commodities, signifies therefore an over accumulation of capital-although the overproduction of capital always includes the over-production of commodities" (1867).

Marx reminded his readers of this when discussing the 1857 panic:

> What are the social circumstances reproducing, almost regularly, these seasons of general self-delusion, of over-speculation and fictitious credit? If they were once traced out, we should arrive at a very plain alternative. Either they may be controlled by society, or they are inherent in the present system of production. In the first case, society may avert crises; in the second, so long as the system lasts, they must be borne with, like the natural changes of the seasons.[33]

As Marx puts it,

> over-speculation and fictitious credit arise from regular crises in the capitalist system of production. They cannot be eradicated by social action unless the mode of production is replaced. It is not possible to separate crises in the financial sector from what is happening in the production sector. "That is to say, crises are possible without credit.[34]

None of the alternatives to Marx's law as the underlying cause of crises seems convincing. Marx's law shows that the capitalist system does not just suffer from a "technical malfunction" in its financial sector but has inherent contradictions in the production sector, namely, the barrier to growth caused by capital itself. What flows from this is that the capitalist system cannot be repaired to achieve sustained economic growth without booms and slumps – it must be replaced.

Longer Cycles?

Can we talk about even longer cycles in capitalist production? In the 1880s, Engels observed that the 'business cycles' were getting longer in duration. In the preface to the first English edition of Capital Volume One (1886), Engels elaborated: "The decennial cycle of stagnation, prosperity, over-production and crisis, ever recurrent from 1825 to 1867, seems indeed to have run its course; but only to land us in the slough of despond of a permanent and chronic depression". Engels tentatively concluded that

> perhaps it is only a matter of a prolongation of the duration of the cycle. In the early years of world commerce, 1815–47, it can be shown that these cycles lasted about five years; from 1847–67 the cycle is clearly ten years; is it possible that we are now in the preparatory stage of a new world crash of unparalleled vehemence?

Just as the capitalist profit cycle appears to be spread over approximately 32–36 years from trough to trough and so does the stock market cycle, there also appears to be a cycle in prices that is about double that size, or around 64–72 years. Such a cycle was first identified by Nicolai Kondratiev, a Russian leftist economist, in the 1920s. He argued that there appeared to be a period when prices and interest rates moved up for about a couple of decades or so and then a period when the opposite occurred. Kondratiev followed Marx in reckoning these long-duration cycles were based on the gestation period of large capital projects that could not be completed in the normal business cycle and so these investments would take place in a series of waves. He rejected criticism that any long cycles were caused by exogenous factors.

The existence of longer-duration K-cycles is debated continually among economists interested in cycles and crises, not just Marxists. There is some empirical support for endogenous Kondratiev cycles. Theoretical and empirical backing has been developed for Kondratiev's suggestion that long cycles are the result of clusters of innovation or long duration capital projects. Ernest Mandel attempted to link long cycles to movements in profitability, although he claimed, rather oddly, that the down phase in such cycles was endogenous to capitalist production but the up phase was exogenous. Anwar Shaikh also connected these longer waves to crises:

> The general economic crisis that was unleashed across the world in 2008 is a Great Depression. It was triggered by a financial crisis in the United States, but that was not its cause. This crisis is an absolutely normal phase of a long-standing recurrent pattern of capitalist accumulation in which long booms eventually give way to long downturns.[35]

There are three more cycles of motion that operate under modern capitalism: the cycle in real estate prices and construction, the cycle of economic boom and slump (the so-called business cycle that was first referred to above), and the inventory cycle. There appears to be a cycle of about 18 years based on the movement of real estate prices. The US economist Simon Kuznets discovered the existence of this cycle back in the 1930s.

Clément Juglar was the first mainstream economist to notice a business cycle of about 10 years. This cycle of economic growth and recession now seems to be about 9–10 years. That is the average time between troughs of each recession in the recent period. Finally, there is an even shorter business cycle of about four to five years. Kitchin discovered this in the 1930s. This cycle seems to be the product of even more short-term decisions by capitalists on how much stock inventory to keep to sell. It seems that capitalists cannot see further ahead than about two to four years. They expand production and maximize the utilization of existing production capacity. In the struggle to compete, capitalist producers end up with more stock than they can sell. So production is slowed until stocks are run down.

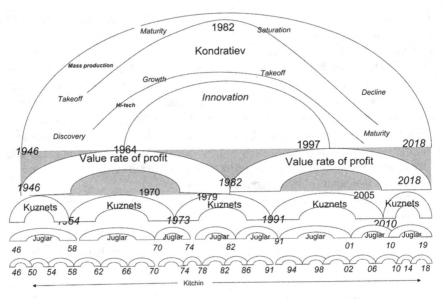

FIGURE 8.4 Cycles in Capitalism.

These cycles can be integrated. In other words, the long Kondratiev cycle of 54–72 years can be divided all the way down to the short Kitchin cycle of 4–5 years. Thus, there are 2 profit cycles in the Kondratiev cycle, 4 Kuznets cycles, 8 Juglar cycles, and 18 Kitchin cycles.

The graph in Figure 8.4 also depicts the so-called innovation cycle that Joseph Schumpeter identified.[36] In this cycle, a scientific discovery is made. Eventually, this leads to the development or growth of a new technology in capitalist production. Later this technology takes off and is applied across sectors or in newly expanding sectors. Then it reaches a period of maturity, where its added value consolidates. Then it enters a period of saturation when it has run out of profitable expansion. Eventually, this technology goes into decline and disappears.

Schumpeter, among others, identified different technology revolutions connected to each long wave. The first wave of innovation under capitalism was through waterpower and iron foundries at the start of the "Industrial Revolution" from the 1780s to the 1830s; the second wave from the 1830s to the 1890s was based on steam power, leading to steel production and railways. The third wave from the 1890s to the 1940s came through the application of electricity, chemical discoveries, and internal combustion vehicles. And the fourth wave from the 1950s to now saw the application of aviation, electronics (including computers) and energy. These latter innovations have now matured and become "saturated". As we begin this decade, a new cluster of innovations is emerging, based on robots, artificial intelligence, biotechnology and non-fossil fuel energy.

Can this latest cluster of innovations lay the basis for a new lease of life for capitalist accumulation, as in previous waves? Is the fifth wave with us? That depends on the trend in profitability. These new innovations will only be applied sufficiently to raise the productivity of labor and launch a new long-term boom if average profitability in the major economies rises enough to make it worthwhile for capitalists to invest. Up to now, average profitability has remained at all-time lows and productivity growth is weak.

According to Marx's theory of crises, what is needed is a sufficiently deep destruction of existing capital values to raise profitability, i.e., a large fall in the denominator (C+v) in Marx's profit formula. This is what Schumpeter called "creative destruction". That can happen if there is a slump or a series of slumps that reduce capital values – as in the depression of the late 19th century; or in the physical destruction of capital during WWII. Either way, a new lease for capital will be at the expense of labor.

Notes

1 Daniele Besomi, editor, Crises and Cycles in Economic Dictionaries and Encyclopaedias: 130 (Routledge Studies in the History of Economics) Hardcover – Illustrated, 18 Aug. 2011.
2 Alexander Brady, William Huskisson and Liberal Reform: An Essay on the Changes in Economic Policy in the Twenties of the Nineteenth Century, Routledge.
3 Besomi, Crises and Cycles in Economic Dictionaries and Encyclopaedias: 130
4 D Besomi, The preriodicity of crises, a survey of the literature before 1850, https://www.cambridge.org/core/journals/journal-of-the-history-of-economic-thought.
5 Mill, J.S., 1848, Book IV, Ch. iv, x 5, Principles of Political Economy, in Robson ed., The Collected Works of John Stuart Mill, University of Toronto Press, 1963.
6 William Thompson, 1827, Labor rewarded. The claims of labor and capital conciliated; or, How to secure to labor the whole products of its exertions London, Hunt and Clarke.
7 Friedrich Engels, Umrisse, outline of a critique of political economy, October 1843.
8 John Wade's early endogenous dynamic model: 'Commercial cycle' and theories of crises, in European Journal of the History of Economic Thought 15(4):611–639 by Daniele Besomi.
9 There is evidence to suggest that there would have been a slump in 2020 even without the COVID-19 pandemic and so there is the likelihood of a new slump by 2024, in effect a delay from 2019.
10 Say, Jean-Baptiste (1803). A Treatise on Political Economy. pp. 138–139. https://cruel.org/econthought/essays/classic/glut.html.
11 Karl Marx, Capital Volume One, preface to 2nd edition.
12 Marx Capital Volume One, Chapter 15.
13 Known and Unknown: A Memoir by Donald Rumsfeld (2011-02-08).
14 https://www.theguardian.com/uk/2009/jul/26/monarchy-credit-crunch.
15 Alan Greenspan, testimony to Congress, October 23, 2008, http://www.ft.com/cms/s/0/aee9e3a2-a11f-11dd-82fd-000077b07658.html?siteedi-.
16 John Cassidy, "Interview with Eugene Fama," *New Yorker*, January 13, 2010, http://www.newyorker.com/news/john-cassidy/inter-view-with-eugene-fama.
17 Ryan Grim, "How the Federal Reserve Bought the Economics Profession," *Huffington Post*, October 23, 2009.

18 Paul Krugman, *End This Depression Now!* (New York: Norton, 2013), chapter 2.
19 Hyman Minsky, "The Financial Instability Hypothesis," Levy Economics Institute Working Paper 74, 1992.
20 Karl Marx, Grundrisse, 1968, p748.
21 Marx Capital Volume 3, Chapter 13.
22 For a fuller analysis of Marx's law and a defence of the critical arguments against it, see G. Carchedi and M. Roberts, "Old and New Misconceptions of Marx's Law," *Critique: Journal of Socialist Theory* 41 (2014), 571–94.
23 Marx Grundrisse p512.
24 Marx Collected Works 32, 157-8.
25 https://en.wikipedia.org/wiki/Tulip_mania.
26 Capital Volume 3 p359.
27 Capital Volume 3 p572.
28 Capital Volume 3 p621.
29 Karl Marx Value, Price and Profit (1864, London Wildside Press 2008), chapter 12.
30 Karl Marx to Friedrich Engels, 1865 CI, 633.
31 Marx Collected Works, CW29, 105.
32 K Marx Collected Works, MECW 40, 278, March 1858.
33 Dispatches for the New York Tribune, Penguin p201.
34 Marx, Grundrisse, p282.
35 Anwar Shaikh, "The Falling Rate of Profit as the Cause of Long Waves," in New Findings in Long Wave Research, edited by A. Kleinknecht, Ernest Mandel, and Immanuel Wallerstein (London: Macmillan, 1992), pp. 174–95, http://gesd.free.fr/shaikh92w.pdf.
36 Joseph Schumpeter, Business Cycles: A Theoretical, Historical and Statistical Analysis of the Capitalist Process (New York: McGraw-Hill, 1939).

References

Besomi, Daniele, The Periodicity of Crises: A Survey of the Literature Before 1850. *Journal of the History of Economic Thought*. v. 32 (1), 2010. https://www.cambridge.org/core/journals/journal-of-the-history-of-economic-thought

Besomi, Daniele, Crises and Cycles in Economic Dictionaries and Encyclopedias. *Routledge Studies in the History of Economies*, 2011.

Besomi, Daniele, John Wade's Early Endogenous Dynamic Model: 'Commercial Cycle' and Theories of Crises. *The European Journal of the History of Economic Thought*. v. 15 (4), 2008. 611–639.

Brady, Alexander, *William Huskisson and Liberal Reform: An Essay on the Changes in Economic Policy in the Twenties of the Nineteenth Century*. Routledge, 1967.

Carchedi, Guglielmo and Michael Roberts, Old and New Misconceptions of Marx's Law, Critique. *Journal of Socialist Theory*. v. 41, 2014. 571–594.

Engels, Friedrich, Outlines of a Critique of Political Economy. *Deuth-Franzosische Jahrbucher*, 1844.

Krugman, Paul, *End This Depression Now!* New York: W. W. Norton & Company, 2012.

Marx, Karl, *Capital: A Critique of Political Economy*. Progress Publishers, v. 1 & 3, 1867.

Marx, Karl, *Grundrisse: Foundations of the Critique of Political Economy*. Foreign Language Publishers, 1968. 748.

Marx, Karl, *Price and Profit*. International Co. Inc, 1969.

Marx, Karl, *Dispatches for New York Tribune: Selected Journalism of Karl Marx*. Penguin Classics, 2008. 201.

Mill, J. S. *Principles of Political Economy: With Some of Their Applications to Social Philosophy*. Hackett Publishing Company, INC: Indianapolis/Cambridge, 2004. 32–65.

Minsky, Hyman, The Financial Instability Hypothesis. Levy Economics Institute, *Working Paper (74)*, 1992.

Rumsfeld, Donald, *Known and Unknown: A Memoir*. Sentinel, 2011.

Say, Jean-Baptiste, *A Treatise on Political Economy*. Philadelphia: Claxton, Remsen & Haffelfinger, 1821.

Schumpeter, Joseph, *Business Cycles: A Theoretical, Historical and Statistical Analysis of the Capitalist Process*. New York: McGraw-Hill, 1939.

Shaikh, Anwar, The Falling Rate of Profit as the Cause of Long Waves: Theory and Empirical Evidence. Edited by A. Kleinknecht, *Ernest Mandel, and Immanuel Wallerstein*. London: Macmillan Press, 1992. 174–202.

Stewart, Heather, This is How We Let the Credit Crunch Happen, Ma'am.... *The Observer*, 2009.

Thompson, William, Labor Rewarded: The Claims of Labor and Capital Conciliated; or, How to Secure to Labor the Whole Products of its Exertion. *Hunt and Clarke*, 1827. 75–88.

Wikipedia, Tulip Mania. *Wikipedia*, 2023.

9

A MARXIST-FEMINIST-CAPABILITY PERSPECTIVE ON MOTHERHOOD

Elaine Tontoh

Introduction

Can women who experience motherhood[1] achieve equal human capabilities? A human capability is defined as the ability of each human being to be and to do what they have reason to value (Nussbaum 2000, 2011; Sen 1992; Robeyns 2003). From a human capability standpoint, the first question explains the suppression of women's capabilities after becoming engaged in reproductive labor[2] through motherhood. For Martha Nussbaum, the absence of what she refers to as central human capabilities, such as the capability of life, bodily health, bodily integrity, emotions, affiliation, and play for women, should be at the core of any analysis of gender inequality and gender justice. Thus, the inability of many women to reach their full capability potential due to undertaking the reproductive labor of childbearing and childrearing is a problem of gender and social justice. It is this situation that is referred to as maternal capability suppression.

Throughout the COVID-19 pandemic, women and mothers who engaged in reproductive labor saw an expansion of their time spent on childcare and other housework responsibilities. This expansion was due to lockdown measures that led to school shutdowns, at-home learning, and reduced commercial services related to healthcare for minor illnesses, cooking, laundry, and recreation. At the same time, women and mothers engaged in wage labor as essential workers within the healthcare industry also saw an expansion of their working hours in response to the high rate of infections from the COVID-19 virus. A 2021 Pan American Health Organization (2021) report indicated that the disproportionate impact of COVID-19 on women led to gender inequality in health and threatened the development and well-being of women. The report showed that

DOI: 10.4324/9781003366690-11

female healthcare workers, who were also often responsible for 80% of chores at home, suffered the physical and emotional costs of working long hospital shifts. Compared to their male counterparts, they were more likely to suffer from anxiety and depression, insomnia, or burnout. The dual role of women and mothers as caregivers in the home and hospitals is a classic triple-day problem example. It shows how the time spent away from self-care and other valuable human flourishing activities – self-reproducing activities – exacerbates the problem of gender inequality in the achievement of human capabilities.

Second, should capitalist societies compensate mothers for the monetary and non-monetary costs of undertaking reproductive labor? From a Marxist-feminist standpoint, the second question explains how oppression within motherhood is ignored due to the invisibility of reproductive labor within capitalist commodity production. It emphasizes the capability advantages of compensating mothers for their reproductive labor costs. To put the invisible nature of women's work in capitalist society into perspective, Silvia Federici (2012) explains:

> Beginning with ourselves as women, we know that the working day for capital does not necessarily produce a paycheck and does not begin and end at the factory gates. And we rediscover, first, the nature and extent of housework itself. For as soon as we raise our heads from the socks we mend and the meals we cook and look at the totality of our working day, we see clearly that while it does not result in a wage for ourselves, we nevertheless produce the most precious product to appear on the capitalist market: labor power. Housework, in fact, is much more than house cleaning. It is servicing the wage earner physically, emotionally, sexually, getting him ready to work day after day. It is taking care of our children – the future workers – assisting them from birth through their school years, ensuring that they too perform in the ways expected of them under capitalism. This means that behind every factory, behind every school, behind every office or mine, there is the hidden work of millions of women who have consumed their life, their labor power, in producing the labor power that works in those factories, schools, offices, or mines.

Using Federici's terminology, the consumption of life represents both the "usefulness" of women's reproductive labor for the benefit of capitalist society and the detrimental "trade-offs and opportunity costs" experienced by women from undertaking reproductive labor. One such cost is the depletion of women's human capabilities by spending less time undertaking self-reproductive labor. Thus, if the reproductive labor of childbearing and childrearing is the "useful" labor that generationally replaces children as wage laborers for economic production, it sustains capitalist economies. The lack of compensation for the costs of reproductive labor is a problem of gender and economic justice. This chapter defines this as maternal economic oppression.

Beyond the problems of capability suppression and economic oppression, it is imperative to acknowledge that generally parenthood, "being a parent," and parenting, "what parents do in terms of raising, supporting and socializing children throughout their lives," comes also with joys and rewards (Nomaguchi and Milkie 2020). Nomaguchi and Milkie (2020) explain rewards as the "aspects of parenting that facilitate achievement of parenting goals or stimulate personal growth and a positive self-concept." Nomaguchi and Milkie further explain that although parents dedicate a long stretch of their lives to parenting, having children provides parents "with a sense of purpose and meaning in life," which contributes to parental well-being. While the triple-day thesis embraces the rewards perspective of parenthood, it emphasizes the suppressive–oppressive perspective due to the gendered and time-demanding nature of parenting that affects mothers' capability achievement.

Where and how do these two motivating questions intersect to help resolve the triple-day problem? The concept of the triple day of motherhood divides a mother's typical 24-hour time into three competing days. There is the single day in which a mother spends time reproducing children. Activities within a single day can range from nursing an infant and brushing a toddler's teeth to supervising homework from school. The double day (Hochschild 2003) represents a typical working mother who spends time in the labor market reproducing capitalist profit. The triple day represents either a single-day or double-day mother who makes time to self-reproduce. For the purposes of this chapter, self-reproduction is defined as the activities a mother undertakes to replenish herself physically, medically, emotionally, intellectually, socially, psychologically, or other forms of replenishment that are primarily beneficial to her non-economic well-being (Tontoh 2021) and secondarily beneficial to her economic well-being.

In contrast to Tontoh's emphasis on self-reproduction to pursue human flourishing for women and mothers, Nussbaum (2000, 2011) emphasizes the attainment of central human capabilities. In drawing a relation between Tontoh and Nussbaum's view on the pursuit of human flourishing, the triple-day thesis maintains that the five forms of self-reproduction, which are recreation, friendships, healthy living practices, me-time, and schooling, are necessary for the achievement of Nussbaum's central human capabilities such as the capability of play, affiliation, bodily health, and practical reason. The triple-day problem is described as the lack of time to self-reproduce due to activities within the single and double days: a lack of self-reproduction results in capability failures.

The point of intersection for the two preceding questions on whether women who experience motherhood can achieve equal human capabilities and whether capitalist societies should compensate mothers for the costs of undertaking reproductive labor emanates from the fact that the problems of maternal capability suppression and maternal economic oppression arise from the same premise: reproductive labor. Whereas maternal capability suppression describes the limitation of mothers' potential capabilities and current capabilities to be and to do what they value in life due to undertaking the "reproductive labor" of childbearing and childrearing, maternal economic oppression describes the undervaluation of "reproductive labor" performed in the home because it is unpaid.

To resolve the triple-day problem, the explanations in response to the two motivating questions on mothers' equal capability achievement and compensation for reproductive labor costs point toward a combined strategy. In this strategy, mothers can be empowered with "monetary resources" through compensation for reproductive labor to effectively "bargain for time" to undertake self-reproductive labor within a 24-hour day. Direct economic compensation for reproductive labor that resolves maternal economic oppression could enable mothers to buy the real-time needed to engage in capability-creating and capability-enhancing self-reproducing activities: the resolution of maternal capability suppression.

The following section will explain the theory of maternal capability suppression. After that, the chapter will explain the theory of maternal economic oppression using Foley's Marxist model of social labor time and will be used as a broader framework to address maternal capability suppression.

A Theory of Maternal Capability Suppression

Human capability is each person's ability to be and do what they have reason to value. The emphasis of the capabilities approach on each person's capability is valuable to study the triple-day problem and the questions it seeks to investigate.

Do women who experience motherhood also experience capability suppression? Capability suppression is conceptualized as features of a person's present capability that are likely to limit other current or potential capabilities of that person to function, while those same features simultaneously play a fertile role in promoting the capabilities of others (Tontoh 2021). Within the context of motherhood, capability suppression explains the limitation of a mother's capabilities to function in critical areas of her life due to undertaking the reproductive labor of childbearing and childrearing, which simultaneously develops the capabilities of her children.

Against this explication, the capabilities approach responds to the question of capability suppression by saying that by definition of human capability, if mothers fail to achieve specific central human capabilities, then it is a failure of basic justice (Nussbaum 2011).

Within the triple-day thesis, the theory of maternal capability suppression is grounded in the central elements of the capabilities approach (Nussbaum 2011). The theory first treats motherhood as an "end," a desirable outcome in and of itself for a woman. In this way, motherhood can be understood beyond its dominant character as "caring labor" to include an equally important characterization as a "central human capability." Folbre (1995) uses the term caring labor "to denote a caring motive: labor undertaken out of affection or a sense of responsibility for other people, with no expectation of immediate pecuniary reward." Such activities include caring for children, caring for the elderly, caring for the sick, and teaching. Folbre asserts a distinction between the motives of caring and caring effects. That is, providing care for a child or the sick may not necessarily result in that child or sick person having the feeling or the outcome of being cared for. From a triple-day perspective, it is evident that the gap between caring motives and caring effects is that of capabilities. If teaching others in an educational institution requires a person to "become" a trained teacher, as providing professional medical care requires a person to "become" a trained doctor or a nurse, then mothering or parenting in general also requires a person to "become" a mother or parent or to have the capability of motherhood or parenthood. As a capability, motherhood, according to Tontoh (2021), offers women the opportunity to achieve their maternal aspirations of having and raising children.

Second, the theory of maternal capability suppression treats each person who "becomes" a mother as an "end" in and of herself. By this, the theory does not treat mothers only as the "means" to the capability advancement of their children through providing caring labor but rather as individuals within their families who also require opportunities, choices, and autonomy for their capability achievement. In so doing, the theory avoids the pitfall of promoting a false sense of total family well-being which makes invisible capability failures among the women and mothers in the family on whom the childcare burden most often disproportionately falls.

To identify these hidden capability failures, the theory of maternal capability suppression requires confronting the tensions between achieving the capability of motherhood, "becoming a mother," and the current and potential capabilities of a mother that depend on her ability to self-reproduce. These unresolved tensions engender inequalities because they limit the choices and freedoms each mother ought to have to take advantage of human flourishing self-reproducing opportunities. One such important freedom critical to the theory of maternal capability suppression is that of time. The theory further stipulates that those invisible forms of gender inequality arising from time deficiency or insufficiency would require public and private interventions through policy programs where the role of policy is to set enabling conditions to encourage maternal self-reproductive work.

Maternal Self-Reproduction

Self-reproducing or self-realizable activities can take various forms. Below includes a non-exhaustive core list of self-reproducing activities (Tontoh 2021).

(i) **Recreation**: Recreation can involve time for travel, playing outdoor and indoor games, listening and dancing to music, or simply uninterruptedly watching a series of movies.

(ii) **Healthy Living Practices**: Healthy living practices can involve taking time for routine medical check-ups at a women's clinic; taking time off to heal from an illness, injury, miscarriage, or postpartum depression; taking time for relaxation and good sleep; undergoing emotional and mental health counseling; actively exercising indoors or outdoors; enrolling in a weight loss and wellness program; and making time to eat a healthy balanced diet.

(iii) **Forming Friendships**: Self-reproduction also takes the form of friendships. That is, having time for friends, forming new friendships, and joining associations within the community, such as women's self-help groups, awareness groups, and reading groups.

(iv) **"Me Time"**: Another aspect of self-reproduction is having the "me time" to promote basic personal hygienic practices such as taking regular showers or engaging in self-grooming activities such as visiting a hair or nail salon and having a body or facial massage. "Me time" can also involve having a quiet time to pray, reflect on life, and plan one's life.

(v) **Schooling**: Schooling is the more intellectual form of self-reproduction. Schooling involves spending time pursuing academic work. Undertaking academic work at a high or higher level of education informs us of a person's desire to learn and acquire knowledge beyond basic literacy and numeracy for everyday living, political participation, community engagement, and self-transform into a marketable "intellectual commodity" for waged work.

Although activities within each item on the self-reproduction list would require varying amounts of time for their fulfillment, all activities on the list provide opportunities for capability creation and improvement. The list of self-reproducing activities can provide opportunities to achieve items on Nussbaum's 10 central capabilities list, which she prescribes as required for women to flourish. Nussbaum's list includes the capability of life; bodily integrity; bodily health; emotions; play; affiliation; practical reason; senses, imagination, and thought; concern for other species; and control over one's material and political environment (Nussbaum 2003, 2011). Nussbaum further explains that these central capabilities can set the stage for real choices in important areas of women's lives (Nussbaum 2000) and should be the goal of public policy.

Maternal Self-Reproduction, Maternal Capability, Suppression, and the Triple-Day Problem

Self-reproducing activities take place within the triple day. The labor used to undertake self-reproducing activities within the triple day is self-reproductive labor. Therefore, this self-reproductive labor would necessarily compete with the reproductive labor of childbearing and childrearing in a single day, as well as wage labor if a mother is employed. Also, due to the excessive time demand from reproductive labor, sometimes intensified by unequal gender relations in child-care and housework distribution, this self-reproductive labor is often suppressed – maternal capability suppression – and leads to the triple-day problem.

A Theory of Maternal Economic Oppression: Understanding the Value and Costs of Motherhood Labor

Traditionally, motherhood labor is non-wage labor. In other words, the labor of motherhood is considered outside of labor market work and not rewarded with a wage when women undertake childbearing and childrearing at home. In this sense, women who undertake motherhood labor do not receive compensation for the monetary costs of their reproductive work. On the contrary, in the labor market, compensation for the monetary costs of labor, which includes professional childcare services, is wages.

Traditionally, women who engage in the reproductive labor of childrearing and childbearing outside the labor market do not also receive compensation for the non-monetary costs of non-wage labor. These non-monetary costs are evident in what has already been described within maternal capability suppression as the triple-day problem – the lack of self-reproduction in health, recreation, schooling, community engagement, and self-grooming, among others. On the contrary, in the labor market, compensation for the non-monetary costs of formalized wage labor is visible in employee benefits. These benefits cover the cost of healthcare; tuition to pursue a higher educational degree; emotional, mental, and financial counseling; and sometimes the provision of employee discounts for recreational activities. Therefore, it appears that a lessening of the triple-day burden occurs for a woman who chooses wage labor over motherhood labor.

Do women who experience motherhood face exploitation and oppression within capitalist society due to the lack of compensation for the monetary and non-monetary costs of reproductive labor? To develop a theory of maternal economic oppression within capitalist commodity production, a response to the question requires a discussion of the value of motherhood labor (i) within Marx's explication of use value and exchange value in conjunction with Nancy Folbre's explication of the undervaluation of caring labor, and (ii) within Foley's Marxian model of socially necessary non-wage-labor time.

Motherhood Labor as Use Value, Exchange Value, or Both?

Being a mother in a capitalist society embodies two central social relations. The first relation of motherhood is the direct relation of family production, where mothers engage in the reproductive labor of childbearing and childrearing at home. These activities constitute the motherhood substructure on which capitalist society exists. From a Marxian perspective, childbearing and childrearing activities are unproductive activities that constitute private labor. Private because motherhood labor is not commodity-producing. From Marx's perspective in Volume I of *Capital* (Marx et al. 1976), the value of motherhood labor as a "commodity" is realized in its usefulness or consumption – the use-value character of motherhood labor. Motherhood labor is not commodity-producing because it is not exchanged in the labor market for the production of commodities. Thus, it commands no value in exchange (Foley 1986) – that is, no exchange value.

The second relation of motherhood in capitalist society is the indirect relation of commodity production. Although motherhood labor is not commodity-producing, the reproductive labor of motherhood is responsible for the generational replacement of wage laborers for commodity production: wage laborers are the products of motherhood labor. From a Marxist perspective, the activities performed within commodity production by wage laborers are productive activities that constitute social labor. Social labor because wage labor as a "useful" commodity embodies the kind of value-producing labor power that can be exchanged for wages in the labor market to produce other useful commodities: the exchange value character of wage labor. In his explication of exchange values, Marx et al. (1976) asserts that once the useful character of the products of labor disappears, then "the useful character of the kinds of labor embodied in them also disappears." Where motherhood labor only represents useful labor in the reproduction of wage labor, we can interpret Marx's assertion as this: once wage labor is exchanged for the production of commodities, its useful character disappears along with the usefulness of motherhood labor embodied in it. By implication, motherhood labor would vanish overall in Marx's explanation of value creation. This implication is an unfair judgment of the role of motherhood labor within capitalist commodity production.

On the contrary, motherhood labor remains the only necessary precondition that begins the human processes that generationally create and replace wage labor, which produces exchangeable value. Motherhood labor as a useful commodity does not "disappear" or "vanish." However, it remains "hidden" in the exchangeability of its finished "human product," who are not only future and current wage laborers but also future and current taxpayers that benefit society as a whole.

The Undervaluation of Motherhood Labor

From a feminist perspective, this unfair judgment could be interpreted as the undervaluation of motherhood labor. However, whether the term undervaluation makes little or more sense in explaining the value of motherhood labor depends, according to Folbre (1995), on the economic approach to theorizing undervaluation. For example, within traditional neoclassical economics, two theories are worth mentioning: the theory of utility maximization and the theory of externalities. In the former, a mother is perceived to be a utility-maximizing individual who chooses to engage in the kinds of reproductive labor that offers no monetary return but is just as happy because she is rewarded through deriving greater satisfaction or utility from caring for her children. In the presence of choice and greater satisfaction, then, for this approach, the problem of undervaluation would be non-existent. In the latter theory of externalities, mothers are conceived as care laborers who "enjoy positive externalities or receive 'psychic income'" from providing childcare (Folbre 1995) and, by so doing, unintendedly lower or devalue the market wage for professional childcare workers by increasing the overall supply of unpaid childcare labor. The triple-day thesis would defer from these two theoretical conclusions because while a mother as an individual makes maternal choices that may reward her with "happiness" or "psychic income," there could occur at the same a minimization of her utility and a devaluation of her life through capability suppression.

Folbre (1994, 1995) distinguishes her approach by redirecting attention toward the value derived from children. Children are seen as public goods, positive externalities that benefit society. In her children as public goods argument, Folbre (1995) explains that although taxation of the future generation socializes the benefits of caring for children to all citizens, the costs of caring for children are not equally socialized: where within the triple-day framework, the non-monetary costs are capability failures. Undervaluation is evident in the free-riding behavior of citizens, capitalist and non-capitalist alike, who contribute relatively little to no time and energy resources in raising children while benefiting immensely from the performance of such labor. In this instance, the path to achieving equality between the socialization of the costs and benefits of motherhood labor requires both private and government-funded programs directed toward minimizing the cost burden of raising children to reduce or eliminate the free-riding problem.

A Formal Marxism Model for Socially Necessary Motherhood Labor: Defining Maternal Economic Oppression

In modern capitalist societies, women and mothers who undertake the reproductive labor of motherhood, in Marx's terminology (Marx et al. 1976), would constitute the "material bearers of wealth." Whereas the term "bearers" partly connotes the very essence of motherhood labor, the term "wealth" represents the actual value created by wage labor – wages and profits – within capitalist commodity production.

I adopt Foley's (1986) social labor time model (Figure 9.1), which describes the value of labor power – wages and profits – within capitalist commodity production in terms of both socially necessary "wage labor" time and socially necessary "non-wage labor" time. Foley's model helps advance a theory of maternal economic oppression because it correctly situates motherhood labor into capitalist commodity production and shows a clear path to identifying the source of exploitation and oppression.

In Figure 9.1, Foley (1986) describes capitalist commodity production as social labor time. In this model, the value of labor power, the total value added to capitalist commodity production, is divided between wages and profit. The division represents Marx's working day or capitalist labor time (Foley 1986) and introduces us to the first kind of labor in Foley's model, wage labor. Wage labor time consists of paid and unpaid wage labor time. Paid wage labor time in Figure 9.1 is socially necessary labor rewarded with a wage in capitalist commodity production. Unpaid wage labor is surplus labor expended beyond what is socially necessary for capitalist commodity production. Unpaid wage labor creates surplus value appropriated as profit by capitalists – owners of capital.

Foley introduces the second kind of labor into his model in addition to wage labor for understanding value creation in capitalist commodity production: non-wage labor. Non-wage labor, like paid wage labor, is socially necessary labor. Motherhood labor enters the social labor time model as shown in Figure 9.1 as socially necessary non-wage labor. Motherhood labor is socially necessary because, like paid wage labor, motherhood labor is within the boundaries of what is considered needed for capitalist commodity production. Non-wage labor because motherhood labor is unpaid. Additionally, because motherhood labor as socially necessary non-wage labor is wholly unpaid, it could be expressed as a positive externality that benefits capitalist society because the costs of capitalist commodity production do not account for it.

Is this free-riding relation, the relation between motherhood labor and capitalist commodity production, exploitative and oppressive? As Figure 9.1

Non-wage-labor	Wage-Labor		
	Paid Labor Time	Unpaid Labor Time	Working Day
	Wages (Variable Capital)	Profits (Surplus Value)	Value Added
	Necessary Labor	Surplus Labor	Reproductive Labor
	Value of Labor Power		

FIGURE 9.1 Social Labor Time.

Source: Foley (1986).

illustrates, motherhood labor as socially necessary non-wage labor is excluded from the distribution of the value of labor power, wages, and profits and remains unpaid. This outcome is exploitation. In this model, women who expend time and energy undertaking socially necessary motherhood labor also suffer a non-monetary cost: the triple-day problem through maternal capability suppression. The lack of compensation for such non-monetary costs is oppressive. Therefore, this chapter formally defines maternal economic oppression as the exploitation of the labor of motherhood as socially necessary non-wage labor through zero payment for monetary costs and a lack of compensation for the non-monetary costs of performing such labor.

Patriarchal Forms of Maternal Economic Oppression

Beyond economic oppression, it is essential to acknowledge the existence of patriarchal relations of oppression within the family. Hartmann (1979) explains how women can experience oppression through subordination where husbands, fathers, and men within the household require all the domestic work and their self-care to be taken care of by their wives, mothers, and daughters while they, as men, spend their time and energy pursuing better opportunities within the labor market. By imposing time and energy limitations on mothers, patriarchal relations of oppression also result in the triple-day problem.

Resolution of Maternal Economic Oppression and the Triple-Day Problem

How can the dual problems of maternal economic oppression and maternal capability suppression be resolved? Motherhood labor is socially necessary non-wage labor. Oppression, therefore, begins with the wage-less condition of motherhood labor. Drawing then, from the central political perspective of the Wages for Housework (WFH) campaign of the 1970s (Federici 2012; 1975; Dalla Costa and James 2017), which is demanding a wage for housework, a proposed solution to maternal economic oppression is monetary compensation for the socially necessary labor of motherhood from capitalist profit. Within this political perspective (Federici 2012; 1975), paying a wage for housework, which includes reproductive labor, should be understood beyond its immediate character of remuneration to understanding it as capital, which gives mothers the social power to command their own labor. For the triple-day thesis, commanding one's own labor power also means commanding one's own time and energy since the performance of any work would require the simultaneous use of time and effort. Economic compensation for motherhood labor will not only resolve capitalist exploitation but also give mothers the social power to effectively bargain for the time needed to command self-reproductive labor: the kind of labor that resolves capability failures.

What about patriarchal relations of oppression within the family? Does paying a wage or monetarily compensating women and mothers for domestic work in the home resolve such forms of oppression and the triple-day problem? To the extent that economic compensation for reproductive labor could provide mothers with a guaranteed status of economic independence from their male spouses or male relatives within the home, it could weaken male domination that causes subordination by giving mothers the power to refuse to assume some or all of the responsibilities of childrearing and man-rearing: man-rearing meaning the daily maintenance of adult men including husbands and fathers for their survival. However, breaking the patriarchal institution of domestic work as feminine work and the resulting practice of subordinating women to perform such work requires more than providing economic options through monetary compensation. First, it will require a cultural shift from socializing girls from birth to become "female house workers" and "mothers" to socializing boys too to do housework in the home. Second, it will require public and private initiatives such as (paid) parental leave programs and more flexible working options for both fathers and mothers. This will create an enabling environment for fathers to share the burden of childcare with mothers in the home. An example of this shared childcare model is Australia's Dad and Partner Pay under its parental leave program.[3] Within this program, working dads can take up to 12 months of unpaid leave in the first year after the birth of a child and can also get up to 2 weeks of government-funded parental leave pay at the national minimum wage. This shared childcare model has been a practical and effective tool used by countries such as Australia to socialize their public and private institutions to develop mother- and father-friendly policies and practices. The triple-day thesis maintains that strategies for combating patriarchal oppression through reorganizing the division of labor further highlight the policy relevance of targeting men as husbands, fathers, and sons in promoting the positive socio-economic outcomes of women (Farre 2013).

Is a universal pre-k program a sufficient solution to the triple-day problem? The goal of free or subsidized public kindergarten such as universal pre-kindergarten programs in countries like Germany, Chile, Denmark, Canada, and the United States, such as New York City's Universal Pre-Kindergarten (UPK) program,[4] is to boost women's participation in paid employment and yield long-term academic benefits for children (Eden 2021). A third but often undermined outcome of universal pre-k programs is its potential to boost women's participation in self-reproductive work. The triple-day problem of motherhood is a problem of the "lack of time" to self-reproduce due to the time spent raising children and time spent in the labor market if a mother is employed. Therefore, by freeing up time away from childcare, the reorganization of childcare outside the home is necessary to resolve the triple-day problem. However, one potential drawback of a public kindergarten program for mothers would be the conflict or competition between the desired outcomes of female labor force participation and self-reproduction since the former remains one of its main focuses. For example, in assessing the effects of the US child-care subsidy system on parental and child well-being using nationally representative surveys, Herbst and Tekin (2014) found that childcare subsidies that aimed at increasing the employment of low-skilled mothers had adverse effects on mothers' physical and mental health. Subsidized low-income single mothers, in particular, were found to exhibit anxiety, depression, parental stress, and more psychological and physical aggression toward their children. Providing universal pre-k programs as a work-based economic option for mothers will be a sufficient solution if it also enables mothers to improve their non-economic well-being through self-reproduction. Therefore, the triple-day thesis maintains that the sufficiency of such programs requires an intentional effort to rethink overall policy goals to include a strategy to boost women's participation in self-reproductive work due to its capability advantage for women and mothers' human flourishing.

The Relevance of an Integrated Marxist-Feminist-Capability Framework for Mothers: Emancipation, Equality, and Maternal Well-Being

The integrated Marxist-feminist-capability framework on motherhood brings a new perspective to developing a motherhood theory that challenges policymakers' and researchers' approaches to addressing women's emancipation, unequal capability achievement, and well-being. Emancipation within motherhood from a capability perspective is one in which women and mothers are free from capability suppression. Emancipation within motherhood from a Marxist–feminist perspective is one in which women and mothers are free from oppression. With the primary focus of the integrated framework on mothers, the triple-day thesis calls for disaggregated data on women caregivers to elicit a more inclusive response toward achieving within-gender equality. The integrated framework also can potentially redirect policy attention from traditionally addressing gender inequality from the perspective of income poverty to addressing gender inequality from the perspective of time poverty and capability poverty. Thus, the emphasis on the time limitations of self-reproductive labor, which is the basis of the triple-day thesis, sheds new light on the missing link for feminist researchers and policymakers alike to make progress in achieving gender equality and positive maternal well-being.

Notes

1 The essay focuses on mothers, so the terminology, motherhood rather than parenthood, will be used often. The term motherhood is also used to depict the gendered division of parental labor. The essay, however, acknowledges the role of men as fathers in raising children.

2 Throughout the essay, the terms reproductive labor, reproductive labor of motherhood, motherhood labor, and the reproductive labor of childbearing and childrearing will be used interchangeably.

3 Government of Australia Fair Work Ombudsman, *Parental Leave*, April 5, 2023, https://www.fairwork.gov.au/tools-and-resources/best-practice-guides/parental-leave.

4 New York City Department of Education, Program Universal Pre-Kindergarten, April 5, 2023, https://www.nyconnects.ny.gov/services/universal-pre-kindergarten-142#:~:text=CEO's%20Universal%20Pre%2DKindergarten%20(UPK,the%20needs%20of%20each%20child).

References

Dalla Costa, Mariarosa, and Selma James, The Power of Women and The Subversion of the Community. In *Class: The Anthology*, edited by S. Aronowitz. John Wiley & Sons, Incorporated, 2017. https://www.wiley.com/en-us/Class%3A+The+Anthology-p-9780631224990#download-product-flyer

Eden, Max, *The Drawbacks of Universal Pre-K: A Review of the Evidence*. Manhattan Institute, 2021. https://www.manhattan-institute.org/drawbacks-universal-pre-k-review-evidence

Farré, Lídia, The Role of Men in the Economic and Social Development of Women: Implications for Gender Equality. *The World Bank Research Observer*. v. 28 (1), 2013. 22–51. http://www.jstor.org/stable/24582371

Federici, Silvia, *Wages Against Housework*. Bristol: Falling Wall Press Ltd, 1975.

Federici, Silvia, *Revolution at Point Zero: Housework, Reproduction, and Feminist Struggle*. PM Press. ProQuest Ebook Central, 2012.

Folbre, Nancy, Children as Public Goods. *The American Economic Review*. v. 84 (2), 1994. 86–90. http://www.jstor.org/stable/2117807

Folbre, Nancy, Holding Hands at Midnight: The Paradox of Caring Labor. *Feminist Economics*. v. 1 (1), 1995. 73–92. https://doi.org/10.1080/714042215

Foley, Duncan K., *Understanding Capital*. Cambridge, MA, and London: Harvard University Press, 1986. 41.

Hartmann, Heidi I., The Unhappy Marriage of Marxism and Feminism: Towards a More Progressive Union. *Capital & Class*. v. 3 (2), 1979. 1–33. https://doi.org/10.1177/030981687900800102

Herbst, Chris M., and Erdal Tekin, Child Care Subsidies, Maternal Health, and Child-Parent Interactions: Evidence from Three Nationally Representative Datasets. *Health Economics*. v. 23, no. 8, 2014. 894–916. https://doi.org/10.1002/hec.2964

Hochschild, Arlie, *The Second Shift: Working Families and the Revolution at Home*. New York: Penguin Books, 2003.

Marx, Karl, Ben Fowkes, and Ernest Mandel, *Capital Volume I: A Critique of Political Economy*. New York: Penguin Classics, 1976.

Nomaguchi, Kei, and Melissa A. Milkie, Parenthood and Well-Being: A Decade in Review. *Journal of Marriage and Family*. v. 82 (1), 2020. 198–223. https://doi.org/10.1111/jomf.12646

Nussbaum, Martha, *Women and Human Development: The Capabilities Approach*. Cambridge: Cambridge University Press, 2000.

Nussbaum, Martha, Capabilities as Fundamental Entitlements: Sen and Social Justice. *Feminist Economics*. v. 9 (2–3), 2003. 33–59. https://doi.org/10.1080/13545700 22000077926

Nussbaum, Martha, *Creating Capabilities: The Human Development Approach.* Cambridge, MA: Harvard University Press, 2011.

Pan American Health Organization, *A Gendered Health Analysis: Covid-19 in the Americas.* PAHO/EGC/COVID-19/21-0006, 2021. https://iris.paho.org/handle/10665.2/55432

Robeyns, Ingrid, Sen's Capability Approach and Gender Inequality: Selecting Relevant Capabilities. *Feminist Economics.* v. 9 (2–3), 2003. 61–92. https://doi.org/10.1080/1354570022000078024

Sen, Amartya, *Inequality Reexamined.* Oxford: Oxford University Press, 1992.

Tontoh, Elaine, The Triple Day Thesis: Theorizing Motherhood as a Capability and a Capability Suppressor Within Martha Nussbaum's Feminist Philosophical Capability Theory. *Journal of Human Development and Capabilities*, 2021. https://doi.org/10.1080/19452829.2021.2014425

10

SOCIAL PROTECTION IN POLITICAL STRUGGLE

Barry Herman

Why This, Why Now?

In recent years, governments around the world introduced or expanded their spending on a cluster of economic policies called "social protection." These are government-led programs that can include maternal – and more recently paternal – and child benefits, access to essential health care, assistance to people with disabilities, pensions for the elderly, and support for involuntarily unemployed workers, as well as special programs to respond to specific catastrophes. The programs can be self-financing in which beneficiaries and employers fund the programs ("social insurance"), or they can rely on government budgets to pay for the programs ("social assistance"). The programs can be generous or measly or not at all. Increasingly, political leaders seem to accept that "not at all" is no longer a politically sustainable option.

Social protection, notably in the rich countries, grew out of centuries of social and political struggle that continues today, if in muted forms. In developing countries, it has had not only indigenous but also colonial roots. In today's integrated global economy, the salience of social protection is everywhere and is now part of inter-governmentally encouraged efforts to eradicate world poverty and attain "sustainable development" (United Nations 2015).

Most recently, the COVID-19 pandemic and environmental catastrophes have raised the political imperative of social protection to a new level. Governments survive on the willingness of the governed and that has limits. This reality encourages social movements to mobilize for more social protection. This may only file down the sharp edges of unjust economic systems, but the struggles will save lives and may help build solidarity for more comprehensive movements.

DOI: 10.4324/9781003366690-12

This chapter seeks to introduce readers to the what, why, and how of social protection, where the concept came from, and the economic reasons why only governments can be responsible for its provision. It's not charity.

How Social Protection Entered the Current Political Agenda

Our story starts with the global financial and economic crisis of 2008–2009. It unraveled normal financial relationships among countries and was on its way to plunging the world economy into deep depression, possibly like the 1930s. That was prevented when the government leaders of the 20 largest economies met as the Group of 20 (G20) in November 2008 and agreed to stimulate their economies, increase global financial support, and stiffen the regulation of their financial systems (G20 2008).

Meanwhile, a parallel track of intergovernmental discussion took place at the United Nations (UN). While also advocating reforms to the global financial system, the UN drew attention to the human toll of the crisis. A major intergovernmental conference in 2009 thus called for "necessary flexibility" on the part of the International Monetary Fund (IMF) and other official creditors, which as usual were requiring spending cutbacks as conditions for receiving the crisis-recovery loans that the G20 had expanded (United Nations 2009). Governments were thus encouraged to balance social imperatives against austerity.

Despite the shock of 2008–2009, corporate interests and their allies in governments continued to proclaim that the unrestrained market with few regulations, small governments, and low taxes would be the most effective way to deliver a decent and affluent society. But they were less and less convincing. One aspect of the critique of market fundamentalism that they could not dismiss was the call for better *social* protection. The market did not and would not do this by itself.

This appreciation that there was – or should be – a *social* responsibility for the wellbeing of people was first codified in the Universal Declaration of Human Rights (UN 1948). Minimum standards for social security systems per se were internationally elaborated in 1952 when the representatives of workers, employers, and governments at the International Labor Organization (ILO) adopted Convention 102 (ILO 1952), which 63 countries have thus far ratified. More recently, agreement was reached in 2012 at the ILO on the desired content of "social protection floors," their grounding in human rights, and that "social partners" in labor and business should participate in their design and implementation in individual countries (ILO 2012).

Alas, governments act imperfectly even on the social responsibilities on which they agree. The universalist challenge of the social protection floors recommendation, coming as a response to the global financial crisis, has been unevenly met. Instead, rich-country governments and the international financial institutions they control continue to promote more limited "social safety nets" that extend assistance only to those people somehow identified as sufficiently poor to be considered "deserving." Frequently additional conditions for receiving assistance are required, such as sending the children of beneficiaries to school (Dodlova 2020).

In any event, when governments do wish to increase social protection spending, they need to face its fiscal consequences, requiring either a reallocation of government expenditure or additional tax revenue. The IMF as the lead agency for overall oversight of fiscal and monetary policy in developing countries – actually for all countries but only the developing countries need to pay attention – responded to interest in expanding social protection (or protecting it during austerity drives) by adopting a new "institutional view" that encourages countries to have "adequate, efficient and sustainable" systems of social spending (IMF 2019).

Before the IMF could filter its new policy down to its country missions, the COVID-19 pandemic hit. Suddenly, governments everywhere had to substantially boost their social protection outlays to combat the economic fallout from the crisis, let alone introduce new public health measures. Developed countries paid for their increased spending by borrowing in their capital markets. Developing countries did some of the same but primarily borrowed from international public institutions like the IMF and the international development banks, raising already high public debt to dangerous levels in many cases. The G20 offered to temporarily postpone interest and principal repayments during 2020 and 2021 on their outstanding loans to 72 of the poorest countries (G20 2020a), and when the extent of the crisis became more apparent the G20 offered to negotiate a permanently reduced set of repayment obligations for any of those countries that asked (G20 2020b). In fact, no creditor offer is without complication and thus only 48 countries took up the G20's first offer and only four countries sought the second (as of this writing in September 2023, no debt reduction has taken place).

Developing countries, especially the poorest among them, were hard pressed to increase public spending to combat the crisis, even with the new international support measures. Figure 10.1 shows just how sharp the financial constraint was. From January 2020 to September 2021, covering the first 18 months of the crisis (dating from March 2020), "advanced" economy governments increased their crisis-related spending by 23% of the total value of all spending in their economies, as measured by their gross domestic product (GDP); "emerging" (middle-income) countries managed to increase their spending by only 10% of GDP, and "low-income" countries by only 4%.

The increases in advanced country anti-pandemic social expenditures were meaningful, notably in the United States, where new and additional child benefits were estimated to have helped to reduce child poverty from 14.2% of all US children in 2018 to less than 5.6% of children in 2021. Without the

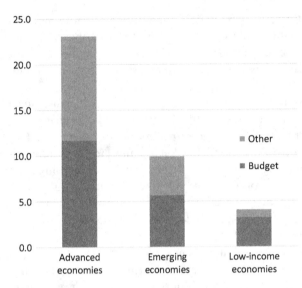

FIGURE 10.1 Fiscal response to the pandemic in groups of countries. Amount of added expenditure as percentage of gross domestic product, January 2020–September 27, 2021.

Note: Data include measures announced or taken by 21 advanced, 29 emerging, and 14 low-income countries; "budget" measures include additional discretionary spending and foregone revenues; "other" measures include loans, equity, and guarantees that do not immediately or necessarily impact budgets.

Source: IMF, Database of fiscal policy responses to COVID-19.

anti-pandemic support, it was estimated that almost one-third of US children would have been living in poverty in 2021 (Wise and Chamberlin 2022).

In the developing world, the number of children and other people living in poverty grew. While definitions and data in this area of economic statistics are subject to controversy, the IMF, working with World Bank data, estimated that the number of people living in extreme poverty (defined as living on income equivalent to less than $1.90 per day) could have risen by about 85 million in 2020 and another 70 million in 2021, or more (IMF 2022).

Even so, there was one encouraging aspect of the anti-crisis spending, namely the extent to which new or expanded social protection programs provided support to people in 2020–2021. The largest category has been cash transfers (in contrast to food aid or public shelter, tax relief or subsidizing continued employment). According to data collected by the World Bank (2022), 90 countries expanded payments to existing beneficiaries of cash transfer programs, but 192 countries increased the number of people covered through new or existing programs.

However, the additional spending was often temporary. The United States, for example, ended its special child benefits at the end of 2021. Many emerging and low-income countries were intending to reduce their fiscal outlays by 2023, assuming a diminished pandemic and renewed economic growth. Surely, political struggles could be expected to try to "ringfence" as much of the increased social spending as possible. However, 2022 was another crisis year owing to the global impact on food and fuel import prices of the war in Ukraine, let alone the unrelenting pandemic.

Moreover, it should be appreciated that most of the world's population does not yet enjoy any social protection. The ILO estimated in 2021 that 47% of all the people in the world benefited from at least one social protection benefit; that left about 4.1 billion people without any coverage (ILO 2021). As might be expected, people in the higher-income countries were more likely to be covered by social protection programs than people in lower-income countries (Figure 10.2). For the most part, those who were covered are in the "formal" economy, employed or operating registered businesses and trades, or included in social service schemes that reach out to target populations. Indeed, a major policy concern in many countries is how best to extend benefits to the people in the "informal" economy, often in distant rural districts but also invisible to the formal economy in cities and towns.

In these times of crisis, one may expect to see increased political struggles to maintain and increase social protection spending. The inevitable question almost everywhere will be how to pay for the social programs, and the answer almost everywhere will be to increase taxes on affluent residents and successful companies. With increased income inequality in most countries over recent decades, this should not be a difficult case to make analytically. Politically, of course, it's a different story. People get the social protection and social services for which the affluent are made to pay.

In sum, there is increasing recognition today, even among governing elites, that some effective system of social protection is needed in every country, if for no other reason than to keep demonstrators off the streets without having to shoot them. At the same time, organized labor where it has influence, churches, community organizations, and other civil society actors campaign for stronger systems of social protection. Expect struggle.

Origins of a Concept

It has been appreciated at least since the writing of the Old Testament of the Bible that economic forces left to themselves tend to unequal levels of income and wealth, that the inequality could undermine community solidarity, and thus that the degree of inequality should be periodically reset in what was called a "Jubilee" year, when slaves would be freed and debts forgiven (Veerkamp 2007). While it does not seem the Jubilee year was ever institutionalized, the Prophet Nehemiah did issue a "Babylonian style clean slate" edict when the governor of Judea (Graeber 2011). While the concept of Jubilee may

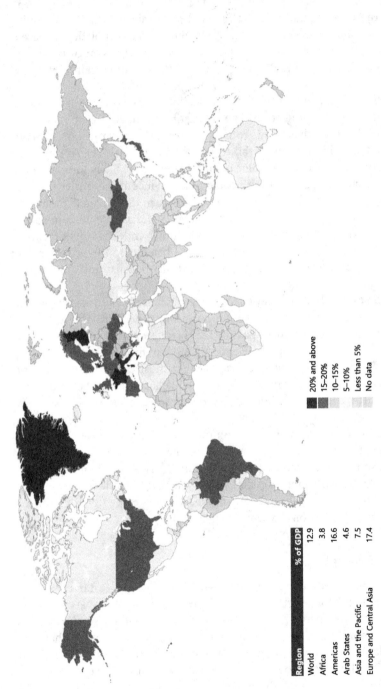

Region	% of GDP
World	12.9
Africa	3.8
Americas	16.6
Arab States	4.6
Asia and the Pacific	7.5
Europe and Central Asia	17.4

20% and above
15–20%
10–15%
5–10%
Less than 5%
No data

FIGURE 10.2 Social protection expenditure around the world. Expenditure (excluding health) as percentage of gross domestic product, 2020 or the latest available year.

Note: Global and regional estimates are weighted by GDP.

Source: ILO (2021).

thus have sought to address a societal failure, aiding the poor is more usually seen as charity, as helping individuals who failed to thrive for one reason or another. In the Middle Ages, Christian churches, which became the main social institutions of Europe, took on some responsibility for charity. The monasteries first provided poor relief in the countryside, as churches came to do in the growing cities and towns (Stolleis 2013).

In time, as secular authority grew, "poor relief" came to be seen as a function of the state. In 1601, Queen Elizabeth proclaimed the English Poor Laws to codify the responsibilities of the State toward its people, in particular those classified as vagrants, involuntarily unemployed, and the helpless, and for local authorities to pay for poor relief through taxation (Hansan 2011). In 1795, the "Speenhamland Law" expanded the concept so as to assure a minimum income, wherein funds collected for poor relief could now be used to top up wages that were below a minimum (based on the price of bread), an initiative that was rescinded in 1834 for undermining Britain's emerging capitalist labor market (Polanyi 1944). As readers of the novels of Charles Dickens know well, Britain's social service system of the mid-1800s did not work out well for the poor.

It should not be surprising that systems of private voluntary cooperation arose in parallel with the concept of poor relief, albeit not for the same populations. Even before the middle-ages, self-help groups formed among workers in dangerous occupations, like miners and seamen, some of which formed "coffers" or joint funds to which the members contributed and out of which they paid benefits to needy members (Stolleis 2013). In a similar manner, guilds arose in Europe in the middle-ages, primarily to promote and regulate their trades or businesses, but often also to offer financial help to members in need, such as for burial, sickness, old age, and widowhood (Van Leeuven 2012).

The main drawback of this attack on social need is its limited coverage. While access to the social benefits of joining a union or fraternal organization may be one factor that can be useful in organizing membership drives, *social* protection works best when it is available to all who qualify within a political entity, both for reasons of justice and the cost-effectiveness of economies of scale. This point was understood at least 225 years ago, as it featured in a proposal by Thomas Paine, revered Enlightenment radical, to establish national social security systems (Paine 1797).

Paine asserted that "the earth in its natural, uncultivated state was…the common property of the human race," but in the process of economic development, which importantly provided the benefits of science, technology, and civilization, some people came to own more property and others less or none at all. Development increased the overall value of property above that of the initial common property, but the winners never compensated the losers when they took other people's shares of the common property. He did not think of the rich as personally evil: "The fault is in the system."

Paine proposed a cash transfer by the rich, funded through a tax on inherited property. As property was income earning, he thought it would be just to tax some of that income and collect it in a fund for redistribution. He thus proposed,

> To create a national fund, out of which there shall be paid to every person, when arrived at the age of twenty-one years, the sum of fifteen pounds sterling, as a compensation in part, for the loss of his or her natural inheritance by the introduction of the system of landed property. And also, the sum of ten pounds per annum, during life, to every person now living of the age of fifty years, and to all others as they shall arrive at that age.
>
> *(Paine 1797)*

Paine proposed that the tax be collected at the time of inheritance, in order not to interfere with other parts of public finance. He also believed that there is no natural "right" to inheritance, and thus no problem in taking a piece of it for social justice. It will not be a surprise that Paine's proposal was not adopted in the England of landed aristocracy and emerging capitalists.

A third strain of social protection also emerged in Europe, this time in order to ease the sudden economic distress of a deserving beneficiary. This third strain was introduced by King Charles III of Spain in 1761 as a formal state pension for the families of dead military officers, in amounts tied to their wages and funded by the monarchy (albeit with some previous contributions by the officers). This *Monte Pío Militar* established the idea of "public protection as an acquired right" (i.e., not charity) and served in Spain as a precedent for subsequent social policy (Ortega-del-Cerro 2019).

Over time, Europe saw additional reforms and proposals, their numbers intensifying as the nineteenth century progressed, and as revolutionary and reform socialist movements contested the evolving capitalist system. By the 1880s, a set of ideas on social insurance coalesced into policies that were adopted in Germany by Chancellor Otto von Bismarck. Seen as a way to ameliorate difficult working conditions and life's risks, the policies were also expected to counter worker attraction to social democratic movements and strengthen worker loyalty to the pro-business German regime. By 1891, the adopted policies came to include health insurance, accident insurance, and a disability and old-age pension scheme; unemployment insurance would be added in 1927 (Scheubel 2013).

The German pension scheme introduced an essential feature of social protection in mandating broad-based worker contributions, first for industrial workers, later adding white-collar workers. Covered workers and their employers were required to pay into a state pension fund, with regional insurance agencies autonomously deciding contribution rates and pension access. Withdrawals began either owing to the onset of disability after 5 years of contribution or on reaching the age of 70 after 30 years of contribution (average life span for a child born when the legislation was being debated was 42 years). The amount of the pension depended on how many and how large the contributions had been (verified by how many self-adhesive stamps workers had accumulated in receipt books over time). However, continued employment was anticipated, as neither pension covered the full cost of living.

While the German innovations thus offered only modest improvements in living conditions, they introduced the very important "contributory" model for state-organized social support that spread far and wide. In fact, multiple European ideas spread around the world, including that the *state* had some responsibility for ameliorating the conditions of the very poor and that it owed support to families of loyal militaries, as well as that contributory social insurance schemes could address the minimum social needs of the working class. These ideas spread not only to new regions of European settlement but also to the European colonies, albeit with different emphases. Thus, the Spanish colonies and independent successor states adopted versions of the *Monte Pío* as basic pensions for public employee retirees and survivors. France adopted limited social security programs for its colonies following their expansion in France, while Britain was more decentralized, expecting the colonies to raise whatever revenue they might need for whatever social protection system they might introduce, thus favoring the more affluent territories (Schmitt 2015).

There were also, however, indigenous ideas about social protection. For example, the imperial Chinese government provided a measure of famine relief after disasters, as well as ongoing relief for "widowers, widows, orphans, elderly without children, and the infirm;" in the early 1900s, the government also introduced vagrant workhouses (Hu 2021). Chinese social protection evolved during the succeeding Chinese Republican and then Communist regimes, where it reflected a more collectivist rather than individualistic notion of social policy, and "a deep-rooted tradition of Confucianism as well as Western imperialism" (Hu 2021).

The spread of social protection around the world as a concept and as a policy has also been the result of intergovernmental cooperation. In particular, after the First World War, the newly created ILO aided countries to expand social protection coverage, at first mainly by promoting the German model (Seekings 2008). During the Second World War, however, ILO broadened its approach; it now sought to extend social security so as to "provide a basic income to all in need of such protection and comprehensive medical care," provide for child welfare and maternity protection, adequate nutrition and more (ILO 1944). This would become a focus after the war of the new United Nations and its operational agencies and programs, eventually becoming a concern as well of the World Bank and the regional development banks established for Africa, Asia, and Latin America.

Different agencies and governments promoted different approaches to social policy in different political contexts. For example, the German model was attractive in countries where there was opposition to any form of state sponsorship, as well as because it would be self-financing after a transition period. It was not an accident that it was the basis for the social security pension and disability system that the United States adopted in 1935, although the United States had a different precedent it could have broadened, as it had modest budget-funded pensions for disabled veterans, widows, and orphans of Union soldiers that had died in the Civil War (Skocpol 1992). In Western Europe, in contrast, social protection shifted to comprehensive universal systems in country after country after the Second World War, responding to political movements and the Communist challenge in the eastern half of the continent (Schmitt 2015).

In sum, today, most countries of the South as well as the North not only have some form of social protection, sometimes limited to pensions for government workers but also often contributory social insurance for the formal sector and some form of budgetary social assistance, usually targeted on the extremely poor. Direct involvement of governments is not just a feature of these programs. It is essential.

The Difference between Private Insurance and Social Protection

It is not an accident that social protection is a set of government-led programs. The private sector can protect individuals and limited groups of people using insurance policies that people and/or their employers undertake, such as to protect workers when harmful events occur (health insurance, injury at work) or assure an income in one's declining years (pensions). These are at best, however, a complement to social protection, not the thing itself, which needs to be both broad-based and mandatory.

In voluntary insurance contracts, individuals make periodic payments, called premiums, into a fund into which many others also pay. An insurance company can figure out more or less how many claims of a specific type it can expect to pay out over a period and thus judge how much it would need to collect in premiums from all of its customers so as to be able to meet its obligations to those who qualify and leave a profit. Typically, such market-based premiums are more than the average worker can afford.

Today, in places where social protection is underprovided, enterprises may contract with an insurance company to offer health insurance or pensions to their employees. The cost per employee in such group plans is usually less than comparable individually purchased insurance, as it is more efficient to administer a group than a set of individual policies (and the employer takes oversight responsibility). In many cases, the employer pays some or all of the employee premiums, which makes voluntary employee participation more attractive and discourages the worker from seeking another employer.

In the case of private pension plans, insurance companies offer pension contracts to individuals or to companies in group plans for their employees. In either case, prospective beneficiaries (and/or their employers) pay a premium each year on a specified schedule until reaching the contracted age of retirement. At that point, the insured receives back the sum of their contributions and their share of how much money the pension fund earned over the years by investing their contributions. Called a "defined contribution plan," the retirees then usually convert what they accumulated to an "annuity" which promises to pay a fixed periodic amount until death (Barr and Diamond 2006).

Readers may appreciate that holders of defined contribution pension plans bear considerable risk (but possibly reward), depending on the state of financial markets during their working life and at the time of retirement. A different pension contract, known as a "defined benefit" plan, shifts the risk to the pension provider. It pays a pension based on the worker's employment history up to retirement, for example, half of average earnings during the last 5 working years, after working for 25 years. While the pension fund invests the annual premiums as in the defined contribution case, it needs to be confident that it can meet its obligations to retirees. Not surprisingly, defined benefit plans are often provided to public sector workers, with the pension fund able to tap the public budget in case of need. However, even that is not risk free as governments can fall into debt crises. Indeed, a major issue in resolving Puerto Rico's recent insolvency was how much to protect the pensions of its teachers and other public sector workers (Molinari 2022).

Since bankruptcy of a company selling pensions, health insurance, or other socially important protections would dampen trust in the industry overall, let alone harm the beneficiaries, insurance companies are virtually everywhere regulated by the government. In addition to prudential regulations that prohibit the insurance firms from making excessively risky investments, governments may (and should) also take responsibility as part of consumer protection policies to require the companies to charge reasonable premiums for their policies and transparently serve their clients' needs.

Regulation, however, is not enough to prevent all insurance company insolvencies. Unexpected events can create investment portfolio losses that impede meeting claims, as during the global financial crisis of 2008 (Marović et al. 2010). Or claims can be much higher than expected, owing to some natural disaster. Insurance companies can protect themselves from such difficulties by insuring themselves with large "re-insurance" companies. However, private re-insurance is expensive and the failure of unprotected insurance providers in a crisis can be politically fraught. Governments may thus set up their own mandatory re-insurance fund, collecting annual fees from each of the covered (and regulated) insurance companies in the country.

The point is that some of the risks that insurance companies face are not easily reduced to the actuarial tables of probabilities that the insurance companies use to set their customer premiums. How the policyholders fair in such situations depends on the ability and willingness of the government to intervene, as by creating public re-insurance funds or ad hoc action to prop up the insurance industry, such as the Bank of England undertook in October 2022 to save British pension funds from bankruptcy (Partington 2022).

Insurance customers have come to appreciate this vulnerability. Indeed, the financial shock from the 2008 crisis was one stimulus for a shift back from private pension accounts to public social security systems in a number of Latin American and Eastern European economies (Ortiz et al. 2018).

Readers may thus see that the market by itself cannot reliably provide protection against the standard risks of the life course even to the limited segments of the population that can access it. Government regulatory oversight of the insurance industry is essential, as is government provision of supplementary funds when unexpected risks occur in order to bail out the insurance companies or their customers. And this approach does not protect everyone. As Bismarck and Tom Paine understood, the social insurance and social assistance models offer superior approaches when the goal is social protection.

The Social Protection "Staircase"

As social protection requires active government engagement, it is a matter of political battle over policy design, operation, and oversight. Programs can entail budgeted social assistance in the form of cash transfers (as for maternal benefits or food stamps), or contributory systems of social insurance (as for social security pensions or unemployment insurance). It can even involve private insurance companies being subsidized by the government to expand coverage beyond what the market provides (as for health insurance). Each country's social protection system will reflect the relative political power of the private sector, organized labor, and civil society (Ząbkowicz 2023).

Considered together, these social programs may be thought of as a staircase of social protection (Figure 10.3). The first priority should be the social protection "floor." It would include a number of "social assistance" programs, including a "social pension" for the poor who are outside the contributory system. Social security benefits through the mandatory contribution system typically provide benefits above the floor level (and thus cover the floor requirement for participants). Finally, voluntary insurance policies to address life risks that are sold to individuals or companies for their employees, as discussed earlier, may be thought of as sitting on top of the social protection staircase, topping up benefits for those so protected.

All the people in a country ought to be covered by one program or another for each of life's major risks, at least at the level of the social protection floor. Contributory approaches should mandate universal participation of all eligible participants, while social assistance payments through the budget should

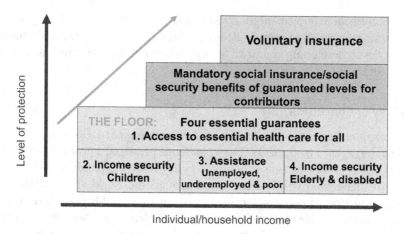

FIGURE 10.3 The social protection staircase.

Source: ILO (2016).

have the status of "entitlements" in that all who meet the qualifications and come forward should receive the benefit.

In normal times, governments should be able to cover their obligations to each component of their social protection system. However, if one views contributory pension schemes as a transfer from the working population to retirees, one sees challenges to sustainability in countries with an aging workforce and a slowly growing population. Postponing the retirement age or reducing promised benefits are typical ways to address this within the standard model (Amaglobeli 2020). Supplementing social security benefits with social assistance expenditures or adding contributory taxation from non-wage income sources are potential, if politically contested, responses.

There are also important challenges to the mobilization of adequate general tax revenues. Suffice it to say here that desirable tax systems should tax the more affluent relatively more heavily (called a "progressive" tax system), be efficient and reliable in collecting the tax revenue (not tolerating tax cheats, plugging loopholes), not taking away with one hand (taxes) what the government gives to the target population with the other hand (social protection) and should collect a fair tax on the share of multinational corporation profits earned in each country's jurisdiction (Herman 2018).

Governments also face the risk that unforeseen events may require a larger than planned expenditure, and this requires an ability to borrow or receive grant assistance to meet obligations. International assistance to developing countries for social protection during crises is a work in progress. At least it may be said that the pandemic stimulated discussion of new forms of international assistance and debt relief to meet the social challenges of crises, some of which are nearer implementation than others (Herman 2022). There are also important proposals to transfer dedicated funds for social protection from rich countries to developing countries facing severe poverty problems (Cichon and Lanz 2022).

By Way of Conclusion

This chapter has sought to describe a politically salient area of social policy. While the urgency of the COVID-19 pandemic provoked a positive response in many, many countries, that stimulus to policy reform is receding and calls for austerity have increasingly been heard around the world. To make matters worse, unfortunate populist sentiments are again or still being heard in some countries that undermine social solidarity, misshaped as they are by racism, misogyny, xenophobia, and narrowmindedness. Working class anger at being in vulnerable economic situations gets dissipated rather than mobilized for progressive change.

Social protection programs were often introduced in times of crisis and political struggle, if not revolution or the threat of revolution. The benefits of each program are palpable. Their absence hurts. Bismarck saw that and used it. Advocacy for social protection can help make people's lives easier and help build solidarity. It should be part of any comprehensive struggle for progressive economic change.

References

Amaglobeli, David, Era Dabla-Norris and Vitor Gaspar, Getting Older but not Poorer, *Finance and Development*, March, 2020. 30–34

Barr, Nicholas and Peter Diamond, The Economics of Pensions. *Oxford Review of Economic Policy*, v. 22 (1), 2006. 15–39.

Cichon, Michael and Hajo Lanz, Creating Fiscal and Policy Space: A Pragmatic Two-Pronged Global Implementation Strategy for Universal Social Protection. *Friedrich Ebert Stiftung Perspective*, February, 2022.

Dodlova, Marina, International Donors and Social Policy Diffusion in the Global South. In Carina Schmitt, ed., *From Colonialism to International Aid: External Actors and Social Protection in the Global South*, London: Palgrave MacMillan, 2020. 189–220.

Graeber, David, *Debt: The First 5,000 Years*, Brooklyn: Melville House, 2011.

Group of 20, Declaration of the Summit on Financial Markets and the World Economy, Washington, D.C., 2008.

Group of 20, Communiqué, Virtual Meeting of the G20 Finance Ministers and Central Bank Governors, Riyadh, Saudi Arabia, 2020a.

Group of 20, Common Framework for Debt Treatment Beyond the DSSI, 2020b.

Hansan, J.E., English Poor Laws: Historical Precedents of Tax-supported Relief for the Poor. *Social Welfare History Project*, 2011.

Herman, Barry, Sustainably Financing Social Protection Floors, *Brot für die Welt Discussion Paper*, Analysis 81, 2018.

Herman, Barry, International Assistance in Catastrophes Need Not Bankrupt Countries. In Daniel Bradlow and Magalie Masamba, eds., *COVID-19 and Sovereign Debt: The Case of SADC*. Pretoria: Pretoria University Law Press, 2022. 22–62.

Hu, Aiqun, The Early Rise of Social Security in China: Ideas and Reforms, 1911–1949. In Lutz Leisering, ed., *One Hundred Years of Social Protection: The Changing Social Question in Brazil, India, China, and South Africa*, London: Palgrave Macmillan, 2021. 55–90.

International Labor Organization, Declaration of Philadelphia, Authentic Text, 1944.

International Labor Organization, C102 – Social Security (Minimum Standards) Convention, 1952 (102), Geneva, 1952.

International Labor Organization, R202 – Social Protection Floors Recommendation, (202), Geneva, 2012.

International Labor Organization, *Social Protection Assessment-Based National Dialogue: A Global Guide*, 2016.

International Labor Organization. *World Social Protection Report 2020-2022: Social Protection at the Crossroads – in Pursuit of a Better Future*. 2021.

International Monetary Fund, A Strategy for IMF Engagement on Social Spending, IMF Executive Board endorsement, Washington, D.C., 2019.

International Monetary Fund, Online Annex 1.1. Poverty Projections using Growth Forecasts. In *Fiscal Monitor: Fiscal Policy from Pandemic to War*, Washington, D.C., 2022.

Molinari, Sarah, New Puerto Rico Debt Plan Is a False 'Solution' Crafted to Benefit Capitalists, *Truthout*, 2022.

Morović, Boris, Vladimir Njegomir and Rado Maksimović, The Implications of the Financial Crisis to the Insurance Industry – Global and Regional Perspective, *Economic Research-Ekonomska Istraživanja*, v. 23 (2), 2010. 127–141.

Ortega-del-Cerro, Pablo, The Spanish Monte Pío Militar: Institutional Protection for the Widows and Other Relatives of Naval Officers, 1730–1900, *Social Science History*, v. 43 (4), 2019. 813–833.

Ortiz, Isabel, Fabio Durán-Valverde, Stefan Urban and Veronika Wodsak, *Reversing Pension Privatizations*, Geneva: ILO, 2018.

Paine, Thomas, *Agrarian Justice*, Philadelphia, 1797.

Partington, Richard, Bank confirms pension funds almost collapsed amid market meltdown. *The Guardian*, 2022.

Polanyi, Karl, *The Great Transformation*, Boston: Beacon Press, 1944.

Scheubel, Beatrice, *Bismarck's Institutions: A Historical Perspective on the Social Security Hypothesis*. Tuebingen: Mohr Siebeck, 2013.

Schmitt, Carina, Social Security Development and the Colonial Legacy, *World Development*. v. 70, 2015. 332–342.

Seekings, Jeremy, The ILO and Social Protection in the Global South, 1919–2005, Center for Social Science Research Working Paper (238), Cape Town, 2008.

Skocpol, Theda, *Protecting Soldiers and Mothers: The Political Origins of Social Policy in the U.S.*, Cambridge, MA: Harvard University Press, 1992.

Stolleis, Michael, Origins of the German Welfare State: Social Policy in Germany to 1945. In M. Stolleis, ed., *Origins of the German Welfare State: Social Policy in Germany to 1945*, Berlin: Springer-Verlag, 2013. 23–176.

United Nations, Universal Declaration of Human Rights. General Assembly resolution 217A, 1948.

United Nations, Outcome of the Conference on the World Financial and Economic Crisis and its Impact on Development. Endorsed by General Assembly resolution 63/303, 2009.

United Nations, Transforming our World: the 2030 Agenda for Sustainable Development, General Assembly resolution 70/1, 2015.

Van Leeuven, Marco H.D., Guilds and Middle-Class Welfare, 1550–1800: Provisions for Burial, Sickness, Old Age, and Widowhood, *Economic History Review*. v. 65 (1), 2012. 61–90.

Veerkamp, Ton, Judeo-Christian Tradition on Debt: Political, Not Just Ethical. In Christian Barry, Barry Herman and Lydia Tomitova, eds., *Dearly Fairly with Developing Country Debt.*, Oxford: Blackwell, 2007. 167–188.

Wise, Paul H. and Lisa S. Chamberlin, Adversity and Opportunity – The Pandemic's Paradoxical Effect on Child Health and Well-being, *JAMA Pediatrics*, 2022.

World Bank, Social Protection and Jobs Responses to COVID-19: A Real-Time Review of Country Measures, *Living Paper*, v. 16, 2022, 907.

Ząbkowicz, Anna, Four Sides of the Coin: The Interplay of Interests in German and Polish Pension Industries, *Review of Radical Political Economics*, v. 55 (2), 2023. 269–289.

11

MIGRATION

Differentiated Mobility Under Capitalism

Smriti Rao

Introduction

Full disclosure, this chapter is written from the perspective of a migrant. Even fuller disclosure, this migration is one of the privilege rather than trauma, beginning from the very first migrations of the author's great-great-great-great grandparents from one kingdom in pre-colonial India to another, and then from cities in Southern India to those in other parts of the country. These migrations over four centuries were in bureaucratic service to pre-colonial kings, then British colonial bureaucrats, then the post-colonial Indian state, and eventually India's increasingly powerful corporations. The author's own migration has followed that trajectory of empire and power, as they moved from India to the United States soon after the end of the Cold War. This personal experience facilitates thought about migration as shaped by structures of power in ways that often serve to strengthen and intensify structural inequalities of class, place, race, gender, and caste rather than, as so much mainstream economic analysis of migration expects, ameliorating those inequalities.

Radical political economy places power at the center of its analysis. Radical political economists identify capitalism as a specific and particular system of power creation and propagation, with the drive to accumulate profit being the "front story" of this system of power: shaping not just the economic but also the political and cultural (Fraser 2017). Radical political economists thus tend to see migration as shaped by structures of power in ways that often serve to strengthen and intensify structural inequalities of class, place, race, gender, and caste rather than, as so much mainstream economic analysis of migration expects, ameliorating those inequalities. This chapter reviews how radical political economists

DOI: 10.4324/9781003366690-13

have thought about, and argued about, the role of capitalism – and capital's drive to accumulate – in shaping and being shaped by migration.

In the twenty-first century, migration within countries – "internal" migration – is estimated to be almost three times larger than international or cross-border migration (UNDESA 2013). South–South international migration is larger than South–North migration, even though it gets far less attention from scholars (World Bank 2016); and finally, temporary or circular forms of migration are larger than permanent forms of migration (Piper and Withers 2018, Triandafyllidou 2022). Thus, rather than moving once and for all, and making a new home in a new village/city/country, the majority of migrants today are "footloose labour" (Breman 2009), leaving, returning, and leaving again, whether from village to city, city to city, or country to country. The vast majority of this migration is undocumented. In fact, upon closer examination, what official sources try to separate out as trafficking or forced migration is better understood as lying along a continuum of migration practices, so many of which involve the abuse and exploitation of migrants, even for those who are "documented" migrants (Anderson et al. 2009). In fact, radical political economy places the specific abuses suffered by migrants within "wider landscapes of exploitation and dispossession" (McGrath et al. 2022)

There is a small group of migrants, often from relatively elite backgrounds, who are able to easily access documented forms of migration that smooth the journey to a better life. But the majority of migration today takes amorphous and precarious forms that are hard to fully see if you are a non-migrant located in the Global North, or even in the North within the South (e.g., a high-income neighborhood in a developing country city). And yet, these add up to enormous flows of labor that are vital to capitalist accumulation, even as they sometimes serve to undermine and challenge it. These flows constitute what Doreen Massey (1994) refers to as the "power geometry" of human mobility, with inequalities of race/class/gender and space shaping who can move where and for what reason, and what they can make of their lives after.

Non-radical or mainstream economic approaches to migration are largely derived from agency-based utility maximization models, where migrants move because the benefits of doing so are greater than the costs (Massey et al. 1993). These models have contributed to mainstream economists' sense of optimism about the win–win character of migration. But these models fail to fully explain the strength of South–South migration and migrations within poor areas more generally or repeated circular and temporary migration by the same individuals and families, or the lack of convergence between the lives of migrants and non-migrants in so many cases where migrants remain ghettoized (Portes 2007; Mezzadra 2016).

The mainstream approach to migration also tends to locate the "cause" of migration in the migrant's origin household/village/country, thus allowing migration to be seen as external to the destination city or country (Munck et al. 2020). You may have noticed the presentation of destinations such as the United States or France or Britain as being "flooded" by migrants from "there" and then forced to decide whether or not to "accept" them. In these presentations, the United States or France or Britain have nothing to do with the generation of these migrant flows and are just trying to manage them. Mainstream economic approaches to migration unfortunately fail to challenge this presentation, even when they argue that the benefits of migration eventually outweigh the costs for destination countries.

The radical political economic view of migration sees migration as part of a global system of capitalist accumulation (Castells 1975; Sassen-Koob 1981). This view of migration emphasizes the role of capitalist dispossession and exploitation in generating flows of migrants and refugees. This approach presumes a deep power asymmetry between labor and capital and sees migration as part of the larger set of processes by which the capitalist labor force is produced and reproduced. The vulnerability and precariousness experienced by so many migrants both during their journeys, but also as they attempt to build lives and livelihoods at their destinations, has thus been part of how radical political economists have understood migration since Marx (Munck et al. 2020).

A radical political economic approach traces how particular migrant flows then affect surplus extraction at the destination and origin and serve to strengthen or weaken labor's capacity to resist capital at both destination and origin. Given that those forms of dispossession and exploitation often originate from, and serve to enrich, places that eventually become migrant destinations (e.g., countries in the global North, or cities more generally in both North and South), radical political economy internalizes migration, challenging the separation between the "there" of migrant origin and the "here" of the destination (Massey 1994).

However, like much of the mainstream economics literature, the radical political economy literature has tended to focus more on South–North migration, and the influence of colonialism and imperialism in shaping those flows. As a result, this literature has tended to neglect South–South migration despite its size and significance (Hujo and Piper 2007). This neglect of South–South migration indicates a need to decolonize the production of knowledge about migration, including the knowledge produced by radical political economists (Fiddian-Qasmiyeh 2020). As discussed elsewhere in this book, political economists are still grappling with the intersectionality of caste, gender, ethnicity along with class. This is true of migration studies as well, with particularly inadequate attention having been paid to understanding how migration is gendered. Finally, radical political economy has sometimes struggled to go beyond a nationalist framework, and beyond treating migrants as victims, to construct a truly "no borders" project of global solidarity (Anderson et al. 2009).

Some Terminology

The role of multiple governments and international organizations in the regulation of migration has inevitably led to a range of terms that are deployed to define and measure migration. Most commonly, migrants are defined as those who move for at least a year, whether that be for work, for study, for tourism, because they are displaced by conflict and dispossession, or due to religious/political/social persecution. This chapter will also address the large and understudied stream of marriage migration that occurs because women are expected to move to their husband's home in many parts of the world (Piper and Lee 2016; Rao and Vakulabharanam 2018). These movements could be within the borders of a nation-state (internal migration) or across borders (international migration). Permanent migrants are those who move and do not ever return, while temporary migrants are those who may move, but eventually return, either because they want to or because they are compelled to by the state, economic necessity, or other life circumstances. As noted earlier, the journeys and lives of temporary and permanent migrants often involve the kinds of abuse and exploitation that place trafficking and migration on a continuum rather than as categories that are separate from one another (Piper and Withers 2018).

The emergence of institutionalized border-policing by nation-states in the twentieth century has added another category to the current understanding of migration. Until the mid-twentieth century almost all migration, whether permanent or temporary, was "undocumented". States invented processes of documentation and enforcement that produced a new hierarchy between "documented" and "undocumented" migrants (Massey et al. 1993). Notably, documented temporary migration has expanded as a category since then, as guest worker programs, temporary worker visa programs, or student workers programs have proliferated across Asia, Europe, and North America (Triandafyllidou 2022). And it is known that there is a large category of global undocumented migration, more often temporary rather than permanent because of the precarious nature of such migration, including the massive flows of undocumented internal migrations in countries such as China and India, which are estimated to dwarf international migration (Chan 2013; Breman 2020).

Finally, if literature considers migration as encompassing undocumented movement, including due to conflict and displacement, South–South migration is much larger than South–North migration. Some of this is not only because of labor migration to high-income areas within the Global South such as the Middle East or Singapore but also because 85% of the world's refugees live in countries in the Global South such as Turkey, Uganda, Pakistan, or Bangladesh (World Bank 2016). Paying attention to South–South migration suggests the usefulness of analyzing migration as a regional rather than national phenomenon, where it is particular regions, rather than countries, that are sending and receiving. These regions sometimes span countries – such as the Middle East – or constitute particular sub-parts of countries, such as the mining towns of South Africa. As a result, the nature and impact of migration vary sharply even within countries. Such a framework helps us see with more clarity the spatially unequal development of capitalism and the impact of both external colonization (by far away powers) and internal colonization (e.g., of an upper caste group over indigenous/tribal peoples in an area within the same country) (Hujo and Piper 2007). As discussed further below, such a regional focus helps us move away from the "methodological nationalism" of so much of the current understanding of migration (Wimmer and Schiller 2002).

Migration and Capitalist Accumulation

Radical theories of capitalism have identified different forms of surplus extraction that contribute to capitalist accumulation. This is a short chapter, and so it will focus on the links between migration and three forms of surplus extraction in particular: dispossession, exploitation, and the subsidies that capital is able to extract from the unpaid/underpaid labors of reproduction.

Dispossession and Migration

The history of early capitalism is impossible to understand without understanding the vast global flows of people generated by what Marx so eloquently called "primitive accumulation". The dispossession and genocide of millions of indigenous peoples in North and South America, Australia, and New Zealand was the necessary condition for the vast flows of migration *from* Europe *to* the "New World", even as the immense subsidies generated by the unequal exchange of primary commodities ranging from silver to tea to rubber flowed in the opposite direction (Sassen-Koob 1981). And then there were the millions of indentured laborers generated by debt-driven dispossession in South Asia, who worked in the plantations of South-East Asia and the Caribbean and whom might today be considered victims of trafficking. Together with the devastations wrought by the slave trade, these early dislocations provided the world with its first glimpse of how capital accumulation in high gear had the capacity to uproot and move millions of people (Portes 2007; Mezzadra 2016). And while these millions did include adventure seekers and risk takers and many fleeing social, political, or economic persecution, when Marx describes capital as coming into the world *"dripping from head to toe, from every pore, with blood and dirt"* (*Marx* 1976), this is the kind of violence and trauma of dispossession and dislocation he is referring to.

Within Europe, new waves of *internal* migration were generated by enclosure movements as ideas about private property became encoded into law. Peasants were pushed off agricultural land, and, if they did not join the debt prisoners or soldiers who were shipped out to the "New World", they ended up in Europe's cities and factories as part of the newly emergent European proletariat. Dispossession thus did, and continues to, generate flows of "internal" migrants (Sassen 2016).

Contemporary examples of the link between dispossession and migration abound. Thus, take the many examples of large dams built across rivers in China and India, that have displaced and dispossessed thousands of the residents of the now flooded banks of those rivers; or the sprawling sites of extractive capitalism – oil fields, mines for coal, and precious metals (O'Laughlin 2002; Li 2010); or the creation of special economic zones across the developing world, where domestic and multinational corporations receive tax breaks and "relief" from labor and environmental regulations (Levien 2018). Rarely do those who used to reside on that land have a choice in the matter. They may be provided nominal compensation by the state but have little voice in the decision. It is even rarer for them to be the ones to receive jobs in these new economic zones or benefit from the power produced by the dams. Instead, many of the displaced join the ranks of internal, temporary migrants, traveling to different cities each year to seek their livelihoods (Sassen 2016).

Notably, migration itself can create the conditions for dispossession, as when migrants from towns come into, for example, a newly developed special economic zone in a rural area, settle there and begin to displace earlier residents, as has happened across the south-eastern coast of China (Chan 2013). Gentrification at the level of city neighborhoods is a well-documented case of such a dynamic, as are of course the violence unleashed by sixteenth- and seventeenth-century migrations of European settlers to the "new world", as discussed above (Mezzadra 2016).

The profits generated from the state subsidized generation of hydropower by dams, or the state-subsidized reduction in costs within the special economic zones of course accrue to the owners of the corporations, often located in the very city or country in which those who are displaced seek to rebuild their lives. And of course, some displaced families do succeed in building better lives postmigration. But the data suggests that the vast majority of those who are displaced remain trapped in precarious livelihoods built on undocumented and precarious forms of migration; and that the greater the disadvantages of race/class/gender before the dispossession, the less likely they are to escape these traps. Thus, dispossession-fueled migration serves to reinforce rather than undermine inequalities of class, race, and gender (Li 2010; Levien 2018). The connections to climate change are impossible to miss. These are the very dispossessions that have simultaneously placed pressures on resources ranging from water to fuel and unleashed the forms of pollution that accelerate climate change. And now climate change in turn generates dispossession and flows of climate refugees (Sassen 2016).

There is a debate here between radical political economy and more mainstream economics, which tends to see large dams or special economic zones as net contributors to economic development and growth. Indeed, a central assumption of early development economists was that the dispossession of agricultural workers from their land and their (permanent) migration to the city was a condition of successful economic development.

In many developing countries, there has been some observed economic growth, although highly variable in quality and quantity, but rather than a well-provisioned, rooted, and stable "formal sector" proletariat emerging in its wake, cities have large urban slums and a persistent and growing divide between a small minority of formal workers and the vast majority of informal workers whose ranks grow and shrink with waves of temporary migration. And rather than a convergence across place that reduces any desire to migrate from the global South to the global North, that imperative has remained strong. These aspects of the world around us fit much better with a radical political economic view of migration as part and parcel of the drive to accumulate and thus embedded in persistent rather than ameliorating global inequalities. The unequal impacts of man-made climate change have only further intensified these inequalities.

There is also a debate here within the ranks of radical political economists. It is difficult to miss the fact that the dispossession caused by large dams or mines or special economic zones tends to be especially concentrated among those whose race or caste or ethnicity is already marginalized (Li 2010). Thus, it is lower castes, indigenous peoples, and ethnic minorities in the United States or India or Indonesia or Myanmar or Mexico who are most intensely affected by these dispossessions. Indeed, the significance of race/caste/ethnicity is hard to miss even if only because mobilizations against migrants are almost always framed around their "other-ness" in terms of these non-class identities. And it is often not just class but also race and caste markers of privilege that identify those who benefit most from these. Thus, there are multiple markers of power beyond class alone, that shape the size and extent and outcomes of migration (Massey 1994). For radical political economists, this means thinking of these other markers of power as co-equal with class, not as dividing the working class and thus as distractions from an anti-capitalist political project but as necessary conditions for that project. As I discuss later, for precisely this reason, the impact of migration on working class solidarity has always been a thorny issue for radical political economy.

Migration and Exploitation

One of Marx's goals was to better understand capitalist extraction of surplus from wage laborers, a process he termed exploitation, and which he saw as a distinct characteristic of capitalism. Understanding the link between migration and exploitation might, however, require us to consider a further distinction that Marx made between the "real" subsumption of labor to capital and "formal" subsumption of labor to capital (Banaji 2010). The classic form of wage labor per Marx – "real subsumption" – occurs when workers are directly employed by a capitalist and paid a daily or monthly wage. Thanks to the labor struggles of the early twentieth century, until a few decades ago a small group of such wage workers in the United States and Europe also enjoyed the protections of various kinds of labor law and welfare provisions such as access to retirement funds or unemployment insurance. But it was always the case that the majority of "real subsumption" wage workers did not enjoy these additional protections and benefits (Munck et al. 2020).

Meanwhile, most workers in the world experienced and continue to experience various kinds of "formal subsumption" to capital. They may appear to be working as independent producers but are part of long subcontracting chains linking them to capitalists; or they may appear to be independent farmers but be so indebted to the capitalist who supplies them with inputs that production decisions are effectively subsumed to the capitalist (Das 2012). The capitalist has little legal responsibility toward such a worker as he or she is not directly their employee. And yet, the production process, and any surplus that is generated, is almost entirely controlled by the capitalist. Gig workers in the advanced capitalist economy, including Uber or Lyft drivers, could also be understood as formally subsumed to capital in this sense.

As noted above, development economists posited that internal and international migration from rural to urban, and from agriculture to industry would be necessary to create a new class of wage workers who would generate capitalist development, and thus could be win–win. In a context of declining population growth, migration can be a way of replenishing the supply of labor. But today's flows of undocumented and temporary migration are driven by the dominance of formal subsumption of labor, where the relationship between particular capitalists and particular workers is "is increasingly mediated and takes forms that are more and more difficult to reconstruct, both analytically and politically" (Mezzadra 2016).

Thus, workers arrive at a city construction site and are paid by (or are using their labor to pay off their debt to) intermediary labor contractors who are formally independent of the builder. The builder bears no responsibility for the worker's safety or welfare, and when necessary – as observed during COVID – the workers can be summarily fired at any time. The contingent nature of work generates contingent, temporary forms of migration, which translate into temporary forms of housing on streets and in slums, little ability to guarantee children a consistent schooling and little to no access to any government services. At least in theory, these workers may still have some land in their village that is in their name, and thus they may not be *de jure* property-less, even if *de facto* that property means little (O' Laughlin 2002). On a global scale, this is the nature of most undocumented migration, which is similarly mediated by intermediary labor contractors/traffickers, with a similar lack of commitment on the part of contractor, capitalist, or state to the migrants' well-being (Mezzadra 2016; Deshingkar 2019).

Of course, the very vulnerability of these workers makes it possible to pay them lower wages and have them work more intensely for longer hours, increasing both the absolute and relative surplus extracted from them. As noted earlier, gender, race, caste, ethnicity, and even language intertwine with class to determine the degree of the migrant workers' vulnerability and thus "exploitability" in this sense.

Migration and Reproductive Labor

If a majority of migration today is temporary and contingent in the ways described above, neither state nor capitalist takes much responsibility for the survival of the worker, and even less so for that of the workers' loved ones. If the post-Reagan and Thatcher periods in the United States and Europe were understood as attempts to have the state shed some of the responsibilities it had taken on for the well-being of at least its formal sector workforce (more white than non-white and more men than women), then the intensification of temporary, precarious migration has served to further separate production from reproduction, and further divest capital and state of the responsibility to ensure the reproduction of workers (Rao and Vakulabharanam 2018; Breman 2020).

Think about the situation of an undocumented woman migrant from Guatemala to the United States. It is the labor of her Guatemalan family that has sustained and "produced" this worker. In the United States, neither her employer nor the state takes responsibility for her reproduction. She likely earns less than the minimum wage in the United States thus forcing her to live in ways that would be considered below subsistence by other workers in the United States. If she falls ill, is injured at work, and/or is fired, there is no one other than her Guatemalan family who is responsible for ensuring her survival. If she has children, they are likely taken care of by that family back home, which she tries to help with by sending money back if she can. Thus, their reproductive labor – which keeps this worker in the workforce producing surplus – is a profound subsidy to capital, and it is her undocumented status, together with the fact that she is a brown woman from the working class of a poorer country, that allows this subsidy to be maximized. The irony is of course that she herself is likely to be working as a nanny or a cleaning lady, helping to bridge the conflict between production and reproduction in her employers' life, even as it intensifies in her own.

Feminist political economists who examine migration today have noted the relatively high share of internal and international migrants across the world who are women (earlier made invisible by scholars who treated them as mere "followers" of male migrants), and who thus contribute to their destination economies through both paid and unpaid labor (Kofman and Raghuram 2010). In a literature that is still very much nascent, they are beginning to understand how marriage migration may fit into a framework of (unpaid) labor migration, and/or respond to and reshape inequalities of class, caste, race, and place (Sen 2016). They have also noted the significance of migrants who provide reproductive labor, in particular, in the global North as well as the North within the South (Piper and Lee 2016). Think about sex workers, janitors and cleaners, farm workers, child-care workers, caregivers to the elderly, and Uber or cab drivers. Waves of brown and black migrants, often women, fill these occupations, allowing their customers/employers to ensure that the daily and generational needs of life-making are fulfilled.

These are certainly not the white male factory workers who were assumed to be the working class in so much of the global North. They may be informalized rather than formal workers, they may work at multiple sites rather than a single factory. They may do things like work at strip clubs, change diapers, or coo at babies rather than work with tools and machines. They may be brown or black and not always speak the same language. To be honest, at least some conventional trade union organizing was quite explicitly designed to exclude these folk from being acknowledged as workers and sharing in social welfare and social insurance programs (Fraser 2017). Even at the realm of radical political economy theory, feminist political economists are still struggling for a full acknowledgment of the role of unpaid and paid reproductive labor in surplus generation, so it is not surprising, although deeply tragic, that there has been a failure to recognize and organize this immense workforce. And all of this is compounded by the long-standing problem that the figure of the migrant worker has posed for labor movements still organized around the concept of the nation-state.

Migration and the Struggle Against Capital

The figure of the migrant worker poses a range of problems for anti-capitalist struggles. They may be difficult to organize for very practical reasons of language, or access to the ghetto-ized neighborhoods in which they live, or their justified fear of being deported if they cause trouble, and/or an equally justified lack of trust in outsiders as a result. There is also their own ambiguous class position – they may have families with some property back home and may see themselves as not quite working class, as only temporarily occupying this position because of the circumstances they find themselves in (Stierl 2018).

And then there is the racism, sexism, or casteism to which radical political economists are hardly immune, making it difficult for them to acknowledge the significance, centrality, or even humanity of certain kinds of internal or international migrants, particularly when they are clustered in reproductive labor, or the agricultural sector, or other sectors assumed to be of secondary importance to twentieth-century capitalism.

The problem that is most prominent in the writings of radical political economists from Marx onwards is the problem that the figure of the migrant workers poses for worker solidarity. The "otherness" of migrant workers in terms of race, caste, language, or ethnicity has always been easy fodder for right-wing movements that feed into racism/casteism/sexism and other forms of prejudice, making the project of solidarity building among workers that much harder. Migrants, often paid less than "native" workers, are quite explicitly used by capitalists to undermine non-migrant workers' wages. Non-migrants may sometimes be replaced by migrant workers and even if that does not actually happen, the threat feels real. Restricting migration might then be seen by labor movements as one way to reduce that threat (Castells 1975).

But capitalism is clearly a global project, and since the 1970s, capital has become almost entirely mobile, not just freed of capital controls or other restrictions against mobility, but with explicit guarantees from most nation-states to safeguard returns from this mobility. Labor, on the other hand, has been forced to be more mobile despite those fetters remaining and even intensifying in the last decade, thus causing a precarious "forced transnationalism" of labor as compared to the legal protections offered to mobile capital (Portes 2007). This is an asymmetry that has contributed greatly to this particular age of increasing inequality.

Despite Marx and Engel's own call for workers of the world to unite, both the theory and practice of radical political economy are too often characterized by a "methodological nationalism" in which theory and politics are situated at the level of the nation-state, not least because information, including quantitative data, is most often available organized at that level (Wimmer and Schiller 2002). Labor has to necessarily respond to the policy shifts of the nation-state, reinforcing this tendency.

One response may be to try to immobilize capital as well. This may work as a tactic, as it did to some extent in the post-World War period, but it goes against the grain of radical political economy's fundamental acknowledgment of capitalism as a system with a global reach, even its manifestations may differ across space. That is, radical political economy sees capitalism as a "no borders" project, so the question is whether labor's resistance under capitalism is equally a "no borders" project.

Anderson et al. (2009) argue that it is not, at least not yet. Transnational labor organizations are still rare, and in political economy analyses of capitalism, migration (too often understood narrowly as permanent, documented, international migration) is still mentioned as an exception rather than as an integral part of the way labor processes are organized today. And migrants are too often cast as victims (McGrath et al. 2022). Yet the history of labor struggle is full of examples of migrant-led resistance (Castells 1975; Mezzadra 2016; Stierl 2018) – Marx himself was a notoriously troublemaking migrant/ refugee. The act of migrating is itself often an act of resistance to local oppressions (O'Laughlin 2002). Efforts to organize international domestic workers may be showing us the way, with worker's rights organizations needing analysis and practice across the home and destination countries of their largely migrant workers to address their vulnerabilities (Kofman and Raghuram 2010). Even if it was required to deploy a tactical nationalism from time and time to deal with the nation-state as it confronts us, the "no borders" approach urges us to consider a methodological de-nationalism as the way to build radical political economy praxis (Anderson 2019).

Conclusion

This chapter argues for an expanded radical political economy view of migration as including internal and international migration, as well as documented and undocumented migration, and recognizing the size and significance of South–South and temporary migration – the dominance of which helps us understand the ways in which migration is central to the specific capitalist forms of surplus extraction at work today. Radical political economy approaches already help us see migration not as an exception but as woven into the fabric of capitalism, and as creating spaces of exclusion and of radical possibility and resistance. Migration is yet another site where radical political economy has to grapple with the role of caste, race, ethnicity, and gender alongside class, but it may be an especially conducive site from which to work toward a "no-borders" project of global solidarity.

References

Anderson, Bridget, New Directions in Migration Studies: Towards Methodological De-Nationalism. *Comparative Migration Studies*. v. 7 (1), 2019. 1–13.

Anderson, Bridget, Nandita Sharma, and Cynthia Wright, Why No Borders? *Refuge*, v. 26 (2), 2009. 5–18.

Banaji, Jairus, Modes of Production: A Synthesis. *Theory as History*. Brill, 2010. 349–360.

Breman, Jan, The Great Transformation in the Setting of Asia. *Public lecture to accept honorary doctorate*. International Institute of Social Studies, 2009. (https://www.wiego.org/sites/default/files/migrated/publications/files/Breman_Transformation.Asia_.pdf).

Breman, Jan, The Pandemic in India and its Impact on Footloose Labour. *The Indian Journal of Labour Economics*. v. 63, 2020. 901–919.

Castells, M., Immigrant Workers and Class Struggles in Advanced Capitalism: The Western European Experience. *Politics & Society*. v. 5 (1), 1975. 33–66.

Chan, Kam Wing, China: Internal Migration. *The Encyclopedia of Global Human Migration*. 2013.

Das, Raju J., Reconceptualizing Capitalism: Forms of Subsumption of Labor, Class Struggle, and Uneven Development. *Review of Radical Political Economics.* v. 44 (2), 2012. 178–200.

Deshingkar, Priya, The Making and Unmaking of Precarious, Ideal Subjects–Migration Brokerage in the Global South. *Journal of Ethnic and Migration Studies.* v. 45 (14), 2019. 2638–2654.

Fiddian-Qasmiyeh, Elena, Introduction: Recentering the South in Studies of Migration. *Migration and Society.* v. 3 (1), 2020. 1–18.

Fraser, Nancy, Behind Marx's Hidden Abode: For an Expanded Conception of Capitalism. *Critical Theory in Critical Times.* Columbia University Press, 2017. 141–159.

Hujo, Katja, and Nicola Piper, South–South Migration: Challenges for Development and Social Policy. *Development.* v. 50 (4), 2007. 19–25.

Kofman, Eleonore, and Parvati Raghuram, *The Implications of Migration for Gender and Care Regimes in the South.* Palgrave Macmillan UK, 2010.

Levien, Michael, 2018. *Dispossession without Development: Land grabs in Neoliberal India.* New York: Oxford University Press.

Li, Tania Murray, To Make Live or Let Die? Rural Dispossession and the Protection of Surplus Populations. *The Point is to Change it: Geographies of Hope and Survival in an Age of Crisis.* 2010. 66–93.

Marx, Karl, *Capital Vol. 1* (B. Fowkes, Trans.) Penguin, 1976 [1867].

Massey, Doreen, *Space, Place, and Gender.* NED-New edition. University of Minnesota Press, 1994.

Massey, Douglas S., Joaquin Arango, Graeme Hugo, Ali Kouaouci, Adela Pellegrino, and J. Edward Taylor, Theories of International Migration: A Review and Appraisal. *Population and Development Review.* 1993. 431–466.

McGrath, Siobhán, Ben Rogaly, and Louise Waite, Unfreedom in Labour Relations: From a Politics of Rescue to a Politics of Solidarity? *Globalizations.* v. 19 (6), 2022. 911–921.

Mezzadra, Sandro, MLC 2015 Keynote: What's at Stake in the Mobility of Labour? Borders, Migration, Contemporary Capitalism. *Migration, Mobility, & Displacement.* v. 2 (1), 2016. 31–43.

Munck, Ronaldo, Lucia Pradella, and Tamar Diana Wilson, Introduction: Special Issue on Precarious and Informal Work. *Review of Radical Political Economics.* v. 52 (3), 2020. 361–370.

O'Laughlin, Bridget, Proletarianisation, Agency and Changing Rural Livelihoods: Forced Labour and Resistance in Colonial Mozambique. *Journal of Southern African Studies.* v. 28 (3), 2002. 511–530.

Piper, Nicola, and Sohoon Lee, Marriage Migration, Migrant Precarity, and Social Reproduction in Asia: An Overview. *Critical Asian Studies.* v. 48 (4), 2016. 473–493.

Piper, Nicola, and Matt Withers, Forced Transnationalism and Temporary Labour Migration: Implications for Understanding Migrant Rights. *Identities.* v. 25 (5), 2018. 558–575.

Portes, Alejandro, Migration, Development, and Segmented Assimilation: A Conceptual Review of the Evidence. *The ANNALS of the American Academy of Political and Social Science.* v. 610 (1), 2007. 73–97.

Rao, Smriti, and Vamsi Vakulabharanam, Migration, Crises and Social Transformation in India Since the 1990s. *Oxford Handbook of Migration Crises.* 2018. 261–278.

Sassen, Saskia, A Massive Loss of Habitat: New Drivers for Migration. *Sociology of Development*. v. 2 (2), 2016. 204–233.

Sassen-Koob, Saskia, Towards a Conceptualization of Immigrant Labor. *Social Problems*. v. 29 (1), 1981. 65–85.

Sen, Samita, Impossible Immobility: Marriage, Migration and Trafficking in Bengal. *Economic and Political Weekly*. v. 51 (44–45), 2016. 46–54.

Stierl, Maurice, *Migrant Resistance in Contemporary Europe*. Routledge, 2018.

Triandafyllidou, Anna, Temporary Migration: Category of Analysis or Category of Practice? *Journal of Ethnic and Migration Studies*. v. 48 (16), 2022. 3847–3859.

United Nations (UNDESA), Cross-National Comparisons of Internal Migration: An Update on Global Patterns and Trends. *Technical Paper. (1)*, 2013. (http://www.un.org/en/development/desa/population/publications/pdf/technical/TP2013-1.pdf).

Wimmer, Andreas, and Nina Glick Schiller, Methodological Nationalism and Beyond: Nation–State Building, Migration and the Social Sciences. *Global Networks*. v. 2 (4), 2002. 301–334.

World Bank. Migration and Remittances Factbook. 2016. (https://openknowledge.worldbank.org/bitstream/handle/10986/23743/9781464803192.pdf).

12

DEVELOPMENT ASSISTANCE AS INTERNATIONALIZATION

Farwa Sial

Introduction

Development assistance is a complex set of economic, social, and, increasingly, financial relations between donors and recipients. Encompassing a large part of the sub-discipline of Development Economics, development assistance has often been framed as a key instrument in the transformation of "underdevelopment". Mainstream discussions have overwhelmingly focused on evaluating the efficacy of aid in relation to its impact on economic growth in developing countries. Such approaches analyze aid as a technical flow of grants and loans, eliciting the use of econometric methods to evaluate socio-economic progress in developing countries. On the whole, mainstream economics has largely been concerned with what development does, as opposed to what development assistance is.

In contrast, various streams in heterodox scholarship have sought to combine analysis on the nature and impact of development assistance. Going beyond a linear representation of aid as a simple transfer of funds from developed to developing countries, heterodox views have analyzed the potential of aid to initiate aspects of structural transformation in recipient countries while simultaneously highlighting that aid is also a tool which perpetuates the dependency of developing countries on developed countries.

Contemporary Landscape of International Development Assistance

As an artifact of a post-colonial global order implemented by developed Western countries and Bretton Woods institutions, development assistance has undergone a series of structural transformations. The most visible of these is

DOI: 10.4324/9781003366690-14

the recent shift in the definition of Official Development Assistance (ODA) as established by the Development Assistance Committee (DAC) of the OECD.

Before 2018, the ODA was defined as capital flows from DAC members and multilateral institutions to recipient countries, in which each transaction is

> administered with the promotion of the economic development and welfare of developing countries as its main objective; and ... is concessional in character and conveys a grant element of at least 25 per cent (calculated at a rate of discount of 10 per cent).
>
> *(OECD Website)*[1]

The DAC had initiated an ODA modernization process since 2012 and the traditional definition of aid was gradually broadened to play a catalyzing role for the private sector investment in international development. Broadening the scope of ODA entailed the inclusion of other concessional flows, a grant equivalent system for foreign loans, statistical reforms, and the implementation of the so-called Private Sector Instruments (PSIs) in 2018. PSIs can be defined as

> financing instruments that ODA providers can use to make direct investments in private enterprises or in "PSI vehicles" – such as development finance institutions (DFIs), investment funds, or other special purpose vehicles – which in turn invest in private entities (e.g. enterprises or investment funds) in developing countries. They consist of loans to private sector entities, equity investments, mezzanine finance instruments (such as subordinated loans, preferred equity, and convertible debt/equity) and guarantees.
>
> *(Caio and Craviotto 2021)*

The inclusion of PSI in ODA effectively removes the concessional character of development assistance and places the focus on "development additionality" of private investments. This move has been contested by civil society for distorting the definition of aid, encouraging tied aid, and boosting the donor country's domestic private sector at the expense of international development (Craviotto 2022). The definitional transformation of development assistance by DAC is unfolding in the current period of a global crisis and geopolitical upheaval in the aftermath of the Russian invasion of Ukraine as well as the Israeli invasion of Palestine. The inadequacy of bilateral and multilateral development assistance to address the crisis of the COVID-19 pandemic, austerity, and the impact of climate change in developing countries has been enhanced by vaccine apartheid and the failure of debt cancellation by a few Global North countries in the Global South (Saldhana 2022). The DAC's technical categorization of grants and loans and statistical reconfiguration to redefine the boundaries of what counts as development assistance is also challenged by the non-traditional aid models of China and emerging donors from other

BRICS countries and the Middle East (Bräutigam 2011; Carmody and Murphy 2022). The variegated nature of capital transfers, technical assistance, and crisis support which determine aid and the underlying relationships between multi-laterals and states therefore necessitates an alternative understanding of development assistance which goes beyond technical and statistical measures. The definition of development assistance as a process, which is commensurate with the changing development landscape and the diverse modes of provision, simplifies the complexity of approaches: "Development assistance is a name covering many different relations between suppliers and recipients" (Wood 1986).

Giving primacy to the "relations" between recipients and donors ensures that the analysis starts from an understanding of what development aid *is* and then focuses on the impact of what development *does* through the different modes and instruments of capital and technical transfer. Taking this view forward, the following discussion provides a brief summary of different hetero-dox political economy analyses on development assistance. The summation of these perspectives in three broad categories accounts for their heterogeneity while illustrating their inclination to grasp the origins of aid as a social and historical construct with the potential of structural transformation. Building on perspectives and extracting some key insights from their analyses, the final section expands on the role of development assistance as a tool for internationalization, which can be simultaneously conducive to capitalist accumulation as well as extractive or imperial in nature.

From Structuralism to Dependency and World Systems Theory

The origins of aid can be traced to the aftermath of World War II with the launch of the Marshal Plan in 1947 through which the US donated around $12.4 billion to Western Europe over a four-year period. The plan was originally designed for the reconstruction of war-torn Europe but soon afterward it expanded as a model for poverty reduction in the Third World (Kozul-Wright 2011). Economists advocating for development aid for Third World countries can be broadly categorized as structuralists. Their approach to aid primarily focused on the conceptualization of development as the universal outcome of industrialization. Developing countries were considered to suffer from structural obstacles, which could be addressed through state-led investment in infrastructure and technology; aid helped ameliorate the impact of fiscal deficits and increased liquidity which could help diversify funds. On the domestic front, developing countries faced obstacles such as low savings, and, on the international front, a lack of technological investment, import dependence, and foreign exchange restraints were considered crucial impediments to economic growth. In this context, the role of aid provided a necessary "push" (Nurkse 1953; Rosenstein-Rodan 1943) for capital formation and large-scale investment (Lewis 1955; Solow 1956).

A common thematic understanding that emerges in these economic perspectives is a vision of late industrialization owing to an inherent structural gap. One way of addressing this structural gap was conceived on the basis of achieving "balanced growth" through simultaneous investments in a number of sectors. Another strategy was to enhance savings for foreign investment and increase foreign exchange to finance imports (Chenery and Bruno 1962). In addition, the provision of financial support to developing governments was considered beneficial to supplement their limited capacity in raising domestic revenues for investment (Bacha 1990). On the other hand, Hirschman (1958) perceived late industrialization as an inherently "unbalanced growth" process which could not be initiated with one big push but necessarily favored some sectors over others. According to this analysis, governments should accept that the uneven pattern of growth would create supply bottlenecks in key industries, which induce backward linkages[2] (private investment in upstream industries) and forward linkages (private investments in downstream industries). To these ends, aid was advocated as a requirement for import-intensive growth in developing countries, rather than a contribution to the savings gap.

The extent, precision, and levels of aid required to enable the big push, initiate growth, and supplement the savings gap and the domestic revenue gap, and "the amount" of foreign exchange "required" were context based and largely undefined. The key message of the structuralist approach was that aid is only viable when recipient countries pursue active industrial policies, i.e., invest in infrastructure and technology and experience trade deficits as a direct result of such extensive investment. As Fischer (2009) has shown, most developing countries were in fact forced to run trade surpluses, without an effective industrial policy and the impact of aid on growth was determined through simplified prescriptions of increasing incentives for growth, without taking global structural conditions into account (see Mkandawire on the impact of World Bank's structural adjustment policies). Similarly, Latin American countries pursued trade surpluses despite import dependence and foreign exchange constraints and were unable to expand export bases in the face of export liberalization. This stood in stark contrast to the long history of the US trade deficit.[3] Most importantly, aid impacts have been measured in developing economies in the aftermath of the oil price rises of 1973 and 1979–80 and subsequent debt crises in 1982. These were the years when developing countries experienced negative growth rates as a direct result of the oil shocks and debt crises. The correlation between aid and growth in Africa, undergoing depression from the 1980s onward, does not relate to the prescriptions of the structuralist approach; in fact, it reaffirmed the structural impediments to economic growth (Nyong'o 1992). The failure to account for the political and structural impediments faced by developing countries in relation to the global political economy undermined the viability of the structuralist account.

A number of structuralist theorists associated with the United Nations Economic Commission for Latin America (ECLA) attempted to address these missing political and structural impediments. The primary analysis of the UN ECLA theorists lay in Latin America's historical marginalization as a result of unequal commercial relations with developed countries such as the United States and Britain. This approach was further diversified to include Marxist and neo-Marxist critiques of imperialism. The ECLA and the Dependencia School theorized dependency as a historical condition, perpetuated by global inequalities and rooted in the internationalization of capital.[4] The structure of the global economy was defined by the hegemonic relation between the core and the periphery. These hegemonic relations were based on unequal exchange at the expense of growth in the periphery, operationalized through multinational corporations, commodity markets, and foreign investments (Prebisch 1950).

Baran (1957) argued that the core was able to maintain the traditional system of surplus extraction by distributing rents to the peripheral elites. Any interaction of the core with the periphery therefore led to the process of the "development of underdevelopment" (Frank 1972), which led these theorists to claim that periods of depression and world war in the core were an opportunity for the periphery to grow since they experienced very limited external influence, in their economies. World System Theory extrapolated the central tenets of dependency theory and extended dependency theory's core–periphery units to include a semi-periphery (Wallerstein 1974), which served as an intermediary for the expansion of capital and strengthening exploitation. Wallerstein's analysis of development was limited to the economic sphere:

> In a formal sense, what we mean by development is first of all increase of the overall productivity of an economy to increase the surplus, and secondly expansion of its capital base, presumably by foregoing a certain amount of immediate consumption of this surplus in favor of investment.
>
> *(Wallerstein 1974)*

However, at the same time, Wallerstein sought to derive the political ends of development from this economic base by arguing that the essential problem of development lay in trying to instill a regime, which could transform the social structure to raise productivity and maintain a national economy, resistant to external and internal power struggles (Wallerstein 1974). This instrumental view of the political serving the economy was also associated with the practice of aid by economists and theorists in the WST tradition. Bornschier, Christopher, and Rubinson (1978) in their analysis of the empirical relationship between foreign investment, aid, and economic growth in the period 1950–1970 concluded that the level of inequalities induced by aid and investment is higher in richer recipients of aid than poorer ones.[5] They attributed the degree of involvement of a recipient country with the world economy as the cause of the exacerbated inequality brought about by aid and speculated that the impacts of aid induced inequalities could be contingent on whether the world economy was in a period of relative expansion or contraction (Chase-Dunn and Grimes 1995).

Aid Regime Theory: Between International Regime Theory and WST

Inspired by the WST/Dependency tradition, Wood's (1986) "aid regime" is one of the few academic studies which addressed the role of development assistance in regulating the conditions of global capitalism and transforming the nature of national capitalism. Wood (1986) identified the main limitation of these theories in their overly holistic analysis of the international system and the inability to address the specificities of relations arising within the evolving role of multilateral institutions, bilateral aid, and concessional lending. Instead, his aid regime analysis identified mechanisms, procedures, and norms as the "operating assumptions" which structured the world system of the aid regime and transformed development choices on a national level (Wood 1986). In a fusion of dependency and international regime theory, Wood's aid regime does not merely conform to the liberal tradition of regime theory or the structural roots of dependency theory but offers a historical exposition of aid as a feature of internationalization since the initiation of the Marshall Plan until the 1980s.

Moreover, his framework of aid regime identified the necessity of development assistance through the establishment of norms, for example, the complementary role of aid in supporting the debt servicing regime of Third World countries and the use of "strategic non-lending" by donors to recipients as an early form of conditionalities (Wood 1986). The strength of Wood's aid regime lies in articulating the consolidation of the internationalizing role of aid from a global and national perspective. Aid regime theory identified the necessity of concessional finance and development assistance in easing the introduction of private capital and inducing a particular kind of growth trajectory in developing countries.

A critique of Wood's work has been offered by Haggard and Simmons (1987) who noted that the concept of regimes was not central to Wood's analysis but in fact summarized state behavior. The aid regime theory offers an interstate analysis of development assistance and accounts for the internationalizing role of aid in transforming national economies and the dynamics of capitalist growth, but it does not address the nature of imperial relations inherent to this process. While Wood affirmed the existence of a "donor-imposed regime" (Wood 1986) and the hierarchy between donors and recipients as "one heavily weighted in favor of the donors", the operating assumptions underpinning the social relations between recipients and donors nonetheless are not themselves concerned with the institutionalization of imperialism.

Aid and Imperialism

A diverse group of theorists associated with academia, activism, and policy-making have identified the necessity of development assistance for the subordination of recipient states to donor states. Notably, Hayter (1971)[6] considered any contributions of development assistance to the Third World as "incidental to its main purposes" (Hayter 1971) of capital accumulation and cautioned that this contribution "must be balanced against its generally negative affect" (Hayter 1971). Hayter's account therefore primarily emphasizes aid as a conduit of imperialist exploitation:

> Aid can be regarded as a concession by the imperialist powers to enable them to continue their exploitation of the semi colonial countries; it is similar in its effects to reforms within capitalist countries, in the sense that the exploiting classes relinquish the minimum necessary in order to retain their essential interests.
>
> *(Hayter 1971)*

Imperial accounts of aid generally emphasize the ways in which development programs serve the role of "projected points" allowing the entry of foreign capital (mainly the United States) in developing countries (O'Conner 1969) and advancing US interests in shaping local policymaking (Alavi and Khusro 1970; Payer 1982; Rodney 1972). However, if development assistance which leads to capitalist accumulation in developing countries is considered "incidental" to the norm of extraction and exploitation, the analysis falls short of explaining the role of aid in driving capitalist accumulation as well as transforming the existent nature of capitalist development in developing countries.

Theories of New Imperialism have sought to go beyond the role of aid as an agent of mere imperialism by focusing on its internationalizing role. A defining feature of New Imperialism can be understood as its attempt to move away from a narrow analysis of state and capitalism to engage in universal accounts of capitalism (Wood 1986). The literature on New Imperialism covers heterogeneous aspects such as the nature of international development (Bond and Garcia 2015; Veltmeyer and Petras 2014), finance, and emerging powers and also finds a common voice in literature on sub-imperialism.

The role of development assistance largely complements the 1970s literature of imperialist theories of aid; Bond (2004) emphasizes the nature of new regional development platforms such as New Partnership for Africa's Development (NEPAD) as an example of new multilateral platforms combining emerging and traditional actors in setting the ground for neoliberal imperialism (Bond and Garcia 2015). Similarly, Boyce and Ndikumana (2008) declared Africa as a net creditor to the world, in their analysis of the "revolving door" relationship between (concessional) loans and capital flight in Africa.

At the extreme, Veltmeyer (2005) identified New Imperialism as marked by "war rather than local development or the projection of political power (aid, trade, investment, globalization)" (Veltmeyer 2005). As with imperialist theories of aid in the 1970s and 1980s, theories of New Imperialism give due emphasis to the extractive mechanisms of the imperial relations of development assistance but fail to theorize the very important legacy of development assistance in internationalizing the nature of capital relations and supporting Imperial wars, notably in Korea's active support for postwar rehabilitation in Afghanistan and Iraq after the US invasions (Ku et al. 2011; Lee 2006).

Aid as Capitalist Internationalization

Complementing the work of theorists on imperialism, social theorists draw attention to the hierarchy of relations which underpin donors and aid recipient nation-states through a focus on the act of "giving" as a social relation. Drawing from the works of Marshal Sahlins and Pierre Bourdieu, Hattori (2001) determines the existence of development assistance as a voluntary act based on unmediated and un-institutional social relations. Donors are at a higher position than recipients in the social hierarchy and their financial assistance to the latter affirms that the effects of what "foreign aid does in a policy sense is secondary to a more basic role of naturalizing the social relation in which it arises" (Hattori 2001). This naturalization of hierarchy also predetermines the nature of the impact that aid can have on recipient countries in that it limits any possibility of a radical or alternative route to economic growth. Aid-induced development is path dependent and produces a homogenizing effect across countries. The act of giving is therefore a rationalization of the existent economic order and aimed at normalization of interstate relations. Hattori stresses this relational aspect in defining aid as a "symbolic domination or a practice that signals and euphemizes social hierarchies" (Hattori 2001).[7]

The naturalization of hierarchy between recipients and donors and the construction of reciprocity in aid recipient countries enables the path for development assistance to restructure or transform existing capital relations. Development assistance can therefore be both accumulative or extractive and the duality of the internationalizing process in restructuring social relations in the donor, as well as the recipient, country. An element of internationalization, which is important in relation to the role of development assistance, is the question of mobility. The state of being internationalized is not determined by national or international mobility per se; rather internationalization is determined by the exposure to and influence of the conditions of accumulation. Bryan (1995) describes this as:

> In addition to cross-national movements of capital in each of its forms, all processes of accumulation subject to international mobility must themselves

be conceived as internationalised, even where capital movement may remain within the nation. Hence, the criterion for the internationality of commodity capital is not that commodities are exported or imported, but that they are exportable or importable. This signals the dominance of international conditions of accumulation even within national limits – that exportables not actually exported are realised nationally because "local" realisation is consistent within international criteria of profitability. Internationalization is defined with reference to the space in which capital is free to circulate; it is not a characteristic attributed ex poste to an individual commodity.

(Bryan 1995)

The ability to be internationalized is therefore not limited to the tangible, physical, or financial speculative movement of goods or capital such as Foreign Direct Investment (FDI) or portfolio investments from one space to another but plays upon the potentiality of transformation. Development assistance also induces such conditions of accumulation through the introduction of norms and conditions, which result in the appropriation of the social sphere by the economy. Technical assistance, concessional finance projects such as microfinance, and conditional cash transfers increasingly transform social and public realms through the introduction of norms and practices which follow an economic rational approach, imposing capitalist discipline and constantly creating markets in a way in which "the economic is not a firmly outlined and delineated area of human existence, but essentially includes all forms of human action and behaviour" (Lemke 2001).

This form of the usurpation of the social by the economic through development assistance can result in extremely extractive relations as shown by Boyce and Ndikumana (2008) and Bracking (2009) especially in the case of Africa but it can equally lead to a process of intertwined accumulation, as evident in the case of Japanese aid to East Asia and the United States aid to Korea and Taiwan. These cases show that aid was not simply incidental to the bigger purpose of imperialism but a necessary form of imperial internationalization, contingent on the introduction of capitalist dynamics in these economies.

Japanese development assistance to East Asia is exemplary and worth elaborating upon. In 1989, Japan was the world's largest bilateral donor and, in 1998, approximately 62% of Japan's bilateral aid went to Asia; the majority of aid given to Asia was in the form of loans (91%) (Söderberg 2002). Five East Asian countries, Indonesia, Thailand, China, Philippines, and Vietnam, were the top recipients of Japanese aid in 1999 and with the exception of China, all countries can be characterized as low-income countries. A complete absence of basic infrastructure and industrial development in low-income countries like Cambodia and Laos was not conducive to the realization of Japanese capital. The policy of using aid to develop industrialization to the end of absorbing Japanese exports helped alleviate Japan's economic problems. Aid also helped to determine and strengthen Japan's leadership role in economic organizations such as ASEAN and regional development banks like ADB in which Japan holds the majority of shares (Dent 2008).[8] For recipient countries in East Asia, Japanese investment and aid not only offered much needed capital for economic growth thus enabling some form of domestic savings but also paved the way for a certain kind of path toward development which integrated East Asian countries with the global economy. The economic growth of low-income East Asian countries after the collapse of the Soviet Union took place in the particular context of neoliberalism. In giving aid, Japan also pursued policies which favored the removal of barriers considered unnecessary for the movement of capital, especially through its funding of the private sector. To these ends Japan offered finance to foreign private companies in joint ventures with Japanese firms and, at times offered its public funds to developing countries in support of private investment which exceeded the amount given in aid for sectors under the direct control of the government (for example, mining).[9] Japan's prominent position in the World Bank and ADB and its membership of OECD also complemented neoliberal policies and, after 2000, Japan's focus on lending for large projects such as infrastructure and industrial lending was gradually reduced and replaced with a new emphasis on soft lending (Söderberg 2002) and a move toward sectors which focused on poverty alleviation.

Another feature of internationalization through development assistance is the reciprocity of the transformation experienced by the donor and the recipient country. The causality which determines development assistance is usually described as a one-way relation, mainly concerned with determining the impact on recipient countries. Theorists who have addressed the internal dynamics of the aid regime have relied on political settlements, negotiating, and bargaining power between actors (Lancastor 2006; Arase 2006). A more critical approach, embedded in the dynamics of the global political economy, has been taken by Essex (2013) in his analysis of USAID. Following Glassman and Samatar (1997), Essex employed the "triple identity" of the state as "a site for strategies, generator of strategies and a product of strategies" to show the ways in which USAID takes part in the production and maintenance of neoliberalism by strengthening the connection between development and security (Essex 2013). Outside, the framework of the development assistance, Susan George (1991) described the impact of Third World debt on creditor countries as a "debt boomerang". She described six major debt connections: environmental destruction, drugs, costs to taxpayers, lost jobs and markets, immigration pressures, and heightened conflict and war which enmesh the populations of the creditor countries in a situation of shared disadvantage with their counterparts in the debtor countries. Her emphasis is not on establishing direct causal relations but showing the ways in which the condition of capital accumulation in one part of the world, particularly to a few classes, reproduces conditions of uneven development on a global scale.

Rarely in human affairs can one show a linear, one-to-one causal link between events; the consequences of the debt crisis are no exception... Thus we stress feedbacks more than linear connections and tend to see debts and its multiple consequences as mutually reinforcing.

(George 1991)

Studies which have addressed the transformative experience of states using the lens of imperialism emphasize the reciprocity with which transformations in the colony are simultaneously reverberated in the metropole. The view that the empire and colony are interrelated concepts (James 1938) was explored by Catherine Hall (2002) in her study, which analyzed the ways in which the British town of Kettering was transformed in its relationship with the British colonial territory of Jamaica. The book demonstrated how the British Empire created and reinforced racial differences and cultural norms within Britain. In its conquest of faraway lands, Britain also underwent a distorted transformation, which created new fault lines against race and class. This understanding can also be applied to relations underpinning development assistance. The internationalizing role of aid also configures the dynamics of social relations simultaneously in donor and recipient countries, manufacturing new concepts of civil society and restructuring the realms of public and private spaces and their interaction with each other. The internationalizing role of aid is therefore multifaceted in transforming conditions of accumulation in different spaces, restructuring the form of capitalism in tandem with the global conditions of accumulation.

Conclusion

Heterodox political economy approaches to development assistance transcend the limitations of analyzing aid as a purely technical tool. This chapter discussed some of these approaches including the structuralist emphasis on development assistance as a tool for socio-economic transformation, the aid regime theory's focus on social relations and the *"dependencia's"* focus on aid as a tool for curtailing the socio-economic progress in developing countries through imperial subordination. Building on these analyses, this chapter proposed the concept of aid as internationalization, which synthesizes the role of aid as a market creation as well as imperial investment simultaneously. A contextual overview of case studies across the world shows that while aid has the potential to accelerate the developmental trajectory of developing countries, these cases are in fact limited. On the contrary, development assistance as a combination of capital flows and technical expertise has overwhelmingly perpetuated conditions of underdevelopment. The inclusion of the private sector in international development is exacerbating this extractive role. A steady reduction in aid figures since the 2008 financial crisis, financialization of development assistance, and the rise of PSIs not only detract from the very purpose of "grants" and concessionally, but are also representative of the crisis of the post Bretton Woods Development Assistance paradigm. Moving beyond development assistance requires concerted efforts to enhance domestic resource mobilization in developing countries including emphasis on enhanced taxation, curtailing illicit flows and capital transfer from the Global South to the Global North, strengthening public finances and public services, and de-financialized solutions toward transformative private investment in developing countries.

Notes

1 OECD Website. Official development assistance – definition and coverage. https:// www.oecd.org/dac/financing-sustainable-development/development-finance-standards/officialdevelopmentassistancedefinitionandcoverage.htm.
2 A forward linkage is created when investment in a particular project encourages investment in subsequent stages of production. A backward linkage is created when a project encourages investment in facilities that enable the project to succeed.
3 The exception to this rule is China, which has managed to operate without a trade deficit.
4 Notable dependency theorists include Raul Prebisch, Paul Singer, Celso Furtado, Osvaldo Sunkel, and Gunder Frank.
5 Their analysis is not limited to a particular region or specific geographical localizations.
6 Also see Hayter and Watson, 1985.
7 Hattori (2001:545) also perceives "loans masquerading as gifts".
8 The ADB's shareholding structure has been changing since the 2000s. In 2022, while the largest non-borrowing shareholders were Japan (15.6%) and the United States (15.6%), the largest non-borrowing shareholder was China (6.4%), followed by India (6.3%).
9 In 1980, Japan gave $770.4 million in public funds to support private investment, well over twice the amount of ODA Japan provided for industry, mining, and construction projects.

References

Alavi, Hamza & Khusro, Amir, 'Pakistan: The Burden of US Aid,' *New University Thought*, Vol. 2, No. 4 (Autumn 1962) reprinted in R. I. Rhodes (ed) Imperialism and Underdevelopment, 1970.

Arase, David, *Japan's Foreign Aid: Old Continuities and New Directions*. Routledge & CRC Press, 2006.

Bacha, Edmar A., Three-gap Model of Foreign Transfers and the GDP Growth Rate in Developing Countries. *Journal of Development Economics*, v. 32, 1990.279–296.

Baran, Paul A. *The Political Economy of Growth*. New York: Monthly Review Press, 1957.

Bond, P., Garcia, A., *BRICS An Anti-Capitalist Critique*. London: Pluto Press, 2015.

Bond, Patrick, African Development and Government: Is Nepal Already Passé. *Journal of Peacebuilding & Development*, v. 2(1), 2004. 68–73. https://doi.org/10.1080/15423 166.2004.565742170784

Bornschier, V., Christopher C.D., and Rubinson R. Cross-National Evidence of the Effects of Foreign Investment and Aid on Economic Growth and Inequality:

A Survey of Findings and a Reanalysis. *American Journal of Sociology*, v. 84 (3), 1978. 651–683.

Boyce, J.K. and Ndikumana L., *Africa's Odious Debts*. Zed Books, 2008.

Bracking, Sarah, *Money and Power: The Great Predators in the Political Economy of Development*. 2009.

Bräutigam, D., Aid 'With Chinese Characteristics': Chinese Foreign Aid and Development Finance Meet the OECD-DAC Aid Regime. *Journal of International Development*, 2011. 752–764. https://doi.org/10.1002/jid.1798

Bryan, Dick, The Internationalisation of Capital and Marxian Value Theory. *Cambridge Journal of Economics*, v. 19 (3), 1995. 421–440.

Caio, C. and Craviotto N., *Time for Action: How Private Sector Instruments are Undermining Aid Budgets*. Belgium: Eurodad, 2021. https://www.eurodad.org/time_for_action

Carmody, P. and Murphy J, Chinese neoglobalization in East Africa: logics, couplings and impacts. *Space and Polity*. 2022. 20–43. https://doi.org/10.1080/13562576.2022.2104631

Chase-Dunn, C. and Grimes P., World-Systems Analysis. *Annual Review of Sociology*, v. 21, 1995. 387–417.

Chenery, H.B. and Bruno M., Development Alternatives in an Open Economy: The case of Israel. *Economic Journal*, v. 72, 1962. 79–103.

Craviotto, Nerea, *Under pressure How private sector instruments are threatening the untying of aid*. Belgium: Eurodad, 2022. https://assets.nationbuilder.com/eurodad/pages/2892/attachments/original/1649245060/tied-aid-2022.pdf?1649245060

Dent, Christopher M., The Asian Development Bank and Developmental Regionalism in East Asia. *Third World Quarterly*, v. 29 (4), 2008. 767–786. https://www.jstor.org/stable/20455071

Essex J., *Development, Security, and Aid: Geopolitics and Geoeconomics at the U. S. Agency for International Development*. Athens: University of Georgia Press, 2013.

Fischer, A.M., Putting aid in its place: Insights from early structuralists on aid and balance of payments and lesson for contemporary aid debates. *Journal of International Development*, v. 21, 2009. 856–867.

Frank, A. D., Lumpenbourgeoisie: Lumpendevelopment. In *Dependence, Class and Politics in Latin America*, New York: Monthly Review Press, 1972.

George, Susan, *The Debt Boomerang: How Third World Debt Harms Us All*. London: Transnational Institute. Pluto Press, 1991.

Glassman, J. and Samatar A., Development Geography and the Third-World State. *Progress in Human Geography*, v. 21 (2), 1997. 164–198. https://doi.org/10.1191/030913297667309393

Haggard, S., and Simmons, B., Theories of International Regimes. *International Organization*, v. 41 (3), 1987. 491–517. https://doi.org/10.1017/S0020818300027569

Hall, Catherine, *Civilising Subjects: Metropole and Colony in the English Imagination*. Chicago: The University of Chicago Press, 2002.

Hattori, T, Reconceptualizing Foreign Aid. *Review of International Political Economy*. v. 8 (4), 2001. 633–660. https://www.jstor.org/stable/4177404

Hayter, T., *Aid as Imperialism*. Harmondsworth, England: Penguin Books Ltd., 1971.

Hayter, Teresa and Catherine Watson, *Aid: rhetoric and reality*. London: Pluto Press, 1985.

Hirschman, A.O., *The Strategy of Economic Development*. New Haven, Conn.: Yale University Press, 1958.

James, C.L.R., *The Black Jacobins: Toussaint Louverture and the San Domingo Revolution*, New York: Vintage, 1938.

Kozul-Wright, R., Post-conflict Recovery: Lessons from the Marshall Plan for the 21st Century, in Kozul-Wright, R. and Fortunato, P. (eds), *Securing Peace: Statebuilding and Economic Development in Post-Conflict Countries*. London: Bloomsbury Academic, 2011.

Ku, Jae H., Drew Thompson, and Daniel Wertz, The U.S.-Republic of Korea Alliance and Afghanistan. *Northeast Asia in Afghanistan: Whose Silk Road?* US-Korea Institute at SAIS, 2011. https://www.jstor.org/stable/resrep11156.7

Lancastor, Carol, *Foreign Aid Diplomacy, Development, Domestic Politics*. London: The University of Chicago Press, 2006.

Lee, Gerald, South Korea's Faustian Attitude: The Republic of Korea's Decision to Send Troops to Iraq Revisited. *Cambridge Review of International Affairs*, 2006. https://www.tandfonline.com/doi/abs/10.1080/09557570600869523

Lemke, Thomas, The Birth of Bio-Politics': Michel Foucault's Lecture at the Collège de France on Neo-Liberal Governmentality. *Economy and Society*, 2001. 190–207. https://doi.org/10.1080/03085140120042271

Lewis, W.A., *The Theory of Economic Growth*. Homewood: Richard D. Irwin, 1955.

Mkandawire, Thandika, *Adjustment, Political Conditionality and Democratisation in Africa*. SpringerLink, 1994. https://link.springer.com/chapter/10.1007/978-1-349-23596-4_8

Nurkse, R., *Problems of Capital Formation in Underdeveloped Countries*. Oxford: Oxford University Press, 1953.

Nyong'o, Peter A., *30 Years of Independence in Africa: The Lost Decades?* Kenya: Academy Science Publishers. ed., 1992.

O'Conner, James, *The Meaning of Economic Imperialism*. Radical Education Project, 1969.

Payer, C., *The World Bank: A Critical Analysis*. New York: Monthly Press Review, 1982.

Prebisch, R., *The Economic Development Of Latin America And Its Principal Problems, Naciones Unidas Comisión Económica para América Latina y el Caribe (CEPAL)*. United Nations, 1950. https://repositorio.cepal.org/handle/11362/29973

Rosenstein-Rodan, P. N., Problems of Industrialisation of Eastern and South-Eastern Europe. *The Economic Journal*. v. 53, (210/211), 1943. 202–211.

Saldhana, Jean, *The Year of Uncertainty*. European Network for Debt and Development Belgium: Eurodad, 2022. https://www.eurodad.org/2022_the_year_of_uncertainty

Söderberg, Marie, Japan's ODA Policy in Northeast Asia. *EIJS Working Paper Series*. v. 158, Stockholm School of Economics, The European Institute of Japanese Studies, 2002.

Solow, R. M., A Contribution to the Theory of Economic Growth. *Quarterly Journal of Economics*, v. 70, 1956. 65–94.

Veltmeyer, Henry, Development and Globalization as Imperialism. *Canadian Journal of Development Studies*, 2005. 89–106. https://doi.org/10.1080/02255189.2005.9669027

Veltmeyer, Henry and James Petras, (eds). *The New Extractivism: A Post-Neoliberal Development Model or Imperialism of the Twenty-First Century?* Zed Books, 2014.

Wallerstein, I., The Rise and Future Demise of the World Capitalist System: Concepts for Comparative Analysis. *Comparative Studies in Society and History*, v. 16 (4), 1974. 387–415. https://www.jstor.org/stable/178015

Rodney, Walter, *How Europe Underdeveloped Africa*. Verso Books, 1972.

Wood, Robert E. *From Marshall Plan to Debt Crisis: Foreign Aid and Development Choices in the World Economy*. Berkeley, CA: University of California Press, 1986.

13

CONTEMPORARY TRAJECTORIES OF STATE CAPITALISM

Ilias Alami

Introduction

The state under capitalism works in curious ways. At times, it appears to protect citizens from the excesses of capitalist market forces. It regulates relations between workers and employers and competition between firms. It defines environmental standards and the modalities according to which economic actors can access natural resources. In some countries, working class and popular struggles have pushed the state to redistribute some of the wealth produced by funding public education, healthcare, infrastructure, social protection, and welfare programs. As it performs these tasks, the state presents itself as the guarantor of public interest formally separated from the economy and civil society, and standing above them, as if it were a sort of benevolent arbiter of the conflictual relations between capitalist firms, markets, workers, and nonhuman natures (Clarke 1991).

Yet the state does many other things that complicate this simplistic picture. For instance, the activities conducted by its repressive arm, which includes the police, prisons, courts, and the military, reveal that the state is generally committed to defending private property, repressing protests that disturb the social order, and securing the political hegemony of the owners of capital. This, of course, comes at the expense of working classes, everyday people, and the (often racialized) poor (Gilmore 2022). Other policies also put a dent into the image of the state as a neutral arbiter and pacifier of social relations, insofar as they directly render visible its class and raced character. Advanced capitalist states currently invest more in border militarization than in decarbonization, green energy, and climate mitigation (Akkerman 2021). Financial bailouts largely benefit the owners of assets and capital, while cuts in public spending

DOI: 10.4324/9781003366690-15

and austerity policies disproportionately affect workers. The costs of capitalist crises are thus shifted to labor.

The state, then, is simultaneously a regulative agency of capitalist social relations and is deeply implicated in the perpetuation of such relations and attendant inequalities. Radical political economy does not see this ambivalence simply in terms of policy incoherence, or as evidence that state managers and policymakers are bad at their job. Rather, this is seen as reflecting the contradictions and conflicts within capitalist societies (Marx 2005). Indeed, the state is not external to capitalism, but immersed in it. As such, it reflects the antagonistic character of the complex web of capitalist social relations. State activities are therefore not only prone to failure and inconsistencies but are also structurally subordinated to the social imperatives of capitalism, such as profit maximization, capital accumulation, and economic growth. They are also the object and outcome of a range of sociopolitical conflicts, such as those between classes, between sections of capital, and between competing states.

Conceiving of the state in such way has direct implications for progressive politics. It forces economists to ask difficult questions: can the state, or at least some of its apparatuses and agencies, be considered an ally in the struggle for more democratic, egalitarian, and sustainable futures? Must economists work to construct such futures through the institutions of the state, or at a distance from it? Radical political economists argue that progressive politics are effective when they operate on multiple levels, with various degrees of engagement with the state. There is a need for political strategies which aim to build working class power and various collective forms of self-organization beyond the state and in autonomy from it. Equally important are strategies that specifically target (and aim at transforming) state activities and institutions. This includes formulating clear demands in order to force states away from ecocidal and socially destructive activities and to push them to intervene toward more progressive ends.

Now, devising effective strategies and tactics of political engagement with (and against) the state requires the development of a solid understanding of contemporary patterns of state intervention: how and why do states currently intervene in the economy and society? Concretely, what policy instruments and vehicles do they use? These questions are decisive because the changing nature of state interventionism can reveal important insights about ongoing transformations in global capitalism, as well as potential tensions, fault lines, and openings. Indeed, as this chapter will address, when states intervene – whether it is to enable capital accumulation or to mitigate crises – they occasionally (and inadvertently) open up realms of possibilities for progressive social change. In short, state interventionism sometimes contains the seeds of progressive future societal transformations. The chapter will now look at some of the most significant developments in state interventionism over the past couple of decades.

Contemporary Landscapes of State Intervention

The world economy witnessed since the turn of the millennium a historic arc in the trajectories of state intervention. Contrary to what mainstream economic theory and neoliberals had predicted in the 1980s and 1990s, the world saw a multiplication of a wide range of state-owned and state-controlled corporate entities. There are at least three types here. First, sovereign wealth funds. These are investment funds which are owned by states and which invest pools of money in financial assets (bonds, stocks, and other financial securities) and across a wide range of economic sectors, from real estate and infrastructure to manufacturing, retail, and media (Babić 2021). As of 2024, there were 179 sovereign funds globally, which is a more than sevenfold increase since 2000 (Sovereign Funds Institute 2024). They control vast amounts of money and capital (worth more than $12.4 trillion) and have become major actors in global financial markets. Second, state enterprises – firms which are wholly or partially owned by a government – have expanded in the world economy in sectors as diverse as transport, engineering, construction, mining, agro-chemicals, utilities, communications, aluminum, steel, aerospace, and semiconductors. Some of them have become highly competitive transnational economic entities, often performing as well, if not better, than comparable privately owned corporations. The International Monetary Fund estimates that state enterprises now account for 20 percent of the world's 2000 largest firms, which is twice as many as twenty years ago (International Monetary Fund 2020). Third, there has been a multiplication of national development and policy banks – that is, banks which are owned or controlled by governments. According to a recent estimate, there are now more than 1115 around the world, controlling assets worth $91 trillion (Marois 2021).

This resurgence of various state-owned corporate entities (sovereign funds, state enterprises, development, and policy banks) has been accompanied by a proliferation of other forms of state activism, notably in the realms of industrial policy, national development strategies, trade defense measures (such as tariffs), and restrictions on foreign investment, particularly from 2015 onward (Schindler et al. 2023). These policies signal a general turn toward more muscular forms of state interventionism, where states attempt to leverage their positions in the global economy to favor themselves over others. These trends do not indicate a backlash against (neo)liberal globalization, or the end of free markets. Rather, they are best understood as "new modes of geo-capitalist engagement," where state power is increasingly mobilized in the political management of economic competition and geoeconomic relations (Jayasuriya 2023). In sum, there have been rapid transformations in modalities of state intervention, characterized by an expansion of state-controlled capital and the concomitant development of muscular forms of statism. How to explain these changing forms of state interventionism?

A Variety of State Capitalism Coming from the East?

These emerging modalities of state intervention have been debated within a lively and pluri-disciplinary field of scholarly inquiry called "new state capitalism" (Alami and Dixon 2020). This notion refers to configurations of capitalism where the state plays a particularly strong role as promoter, supervisor, and owner of capital. In the past, the notion of state capitalism has been applied to a range of things, from state-led capitalist development in Western Europe between the 1930s and 1970s to the classical East Asian developmental state and the Soviet mode of production (Sperber 2019). Over the past decade, scholars and political commentators have re-deployed the notion of state capitalism (and added the qualifier "new") in order to explain the emerging modalities of state interventionism earlier discussed. One of the most influential arguments in this literature is the following: the expansion of state-owned corporate entities and the development of muscular forms of statism can be explained by the rise of a new variety of state-centric capitalism, which comes from developing and emerging economies (such as China, Russia, Brazil, Turkey, and Indonesia), and which is increasingly competing with the neoliberal varieties of capitalism that (allegedly) predominate in the West (Bremmer 2010).

This argument might have been plausible in the mid-2000s. Back then, state intervention indeed appeared to be more visible in rapidly growing developing and emerging economies. But consider what has happened since: the 2007/2008 global financial crisis required massive government and central bank interventions to bail out the private sector and maintain financial markets on life support; trade wars have escalated; purportedly free-market capitalist economies like the United States and the European Union have deployed aggressive forms of techno-industrial policy (think about, for instance, the recently passed US CHIPS and Science Act); and the COVID-19 pandemic has arguably deepened and accelerated all these trends. In short, the narrative according to which state-centric models of capitalism coming from the east/South are increasingly rivaling Western free-market economies is increasingly less convincing. In fact, a closer look at the state-owned corporate entities described earlier (sovereign funds, state enterprises, development, and policy banks) suggests that this narrative was always limited, even in the early 2000s. These entities have not only proliferated in developing and emerging economies. They have prospered in countries across the income spectrum and in diverse types of political regimes, in both the global North and the global South. More generally, arguments locating state capitalism outside of the liberal market economies tend to underappreciate the fundamental, if not always visible, the role of the state in ostensibly neoliberal economies.

If this argument is insufficient to explain the historic arc in the global trajectories of state intervention currently taking place, then what can? Recall that, according to the radical political economy approach outlined earlier, the state is immersed in capitalist social relations and its activities are conditioned by the dynamics of global capital accumulation. Consequently, the root causes of changing forms of state interventionism must not be sought after in the institutional specificities of emerging economies. Rather, economists must ask: What material transformations in global capitalism may have triggered changing forms of state interventionism?

World Capitalist Transformations and State Restructuring

There are at least five sets of interrelated factors – technological, geographic, economic, geopolitical, and financial – related to the historical development of global capitalism which explain why states have expanded their role as promoter, supervisor, and owner of capital (Alami and Dixon 2024). First, technological factors. Capitalism is driven by a compulsion (fueled by inter-capitalist competition) to increase labor productivity via technological change. This is because the firms that control more advanced technologies can appropriate more surplus value and generate superior profits than their competitors. This makes capitalism a remarkably technologically dynamic system, with a fast-moving frontier of technological innovation. The sectors currently at the cutting edge of the technology and productivity frontier include advanced semiconductors, nanotechnologies, artificial intelligence, quantum computing, 5G, the Internet of Things, cloud computing, and intelligent robotics, among others. Importantly, many of these things are "general purpose technologies," meaning that they can be used in a wide range of production methods and innovation processes, as well as military applications (Rikap and Lundvall 2021). They therefore have the potential to impact entire economies. This makes them particularly strategic for states and firms alike. As a result, governments in advanced capitalist economies in the West and East Asia have developed new modalities of techno-industrial policies (encompassing spending on research and development, government procurement policies, subsidies, tax breaks) to coordinate the emergence of these technological frontiers. These states increasingly use policy banks and sovereign funds to provide credit and low-cost finance to small firms and national champions so they could develop or acquire these strategic technological capabilities. They also resort more and more to investment restrictions and trade defensive measures to protect critical firms, assets, and intellectual property.

Furthermore, these technological developments have enabled considerable progress in terms of automation, robotization, computerization, and digitalization. These have in turn allowed firms (especially the largest and most powerful ones) to reorganize labor processes in large-scale industries and logistical networks in ways that maximize exploitation across territorial borders (Charnock and Starosta 2016). Thus, the formation of increasingly complex regional and global value chains connected frontiers of natural resource extraction (largely located in Latin America, Africa, and Central Asia) to sites of labor-intensive manufacturing (predominantly situated in East and South East Asia), and to spaces of consumption in urban agglomerations in advanced capitalist economies, thereby transforming the geographic structure of the world capitalist economy (Arboleda 2020). This directs this text to the second set of factors explaining changing forms of state interventionism: this world-historic geographic reorganization of the global economy has required extensive state involvement, in the form of planning and territorial development agencies (in both the global North and the global South) and large-scale state-supported investment (often conducted by state enterprises, sovereign funds, and development banks) in energy grids, telecommunications networks, transportation infrastructure, and integrated systems of logistical connectivity (Schindler et al. 2023).

Taken together, these technological and geographic transformations contributed to an immense increase in worldwide manufacturing capacities, which, over time, have led to global industrial overcapacity, slower economic growth, and economic stagnation. This brings the chapter to the third set of factors, which are economic. Capitalism is a highly unstable economic system. A fundamental reason for that is that competition and the profit motive force capitalist firms to keep growing by producing more commodities. Expanding production capacities and investing in more efficient production methods is therefore rational from the perspective of individual firms. But as a whole, it creates problems, insofar as the production of commodities often expands to a point where markets become saturated and struggle to absorb what has been produced. Firms must then lower prices (after all, the commodities must be sold for profits to be realized), and cost-competition intensifies. This results in falling profit rates, which firms can compensate by producing even more, thereby reinforcing the cycle of overproduction, and resulting in a slowing pace of investment and low manufacturing-output growth. This is exactly what happened, particularly post-2010, across a wide range of industrial sectors from extraction to metallurgy, manufacturing, and energy production, pushing states to implement a range of policies to support their firms as they face this tense economic context. Hence the use of industrial policy and policy banks to help firms (including state enterprises) compete internationally and acquire competitors, and the deployment of sovereign funds to facilitate the flow of capital from sectors particularly affected by overproduction to more economically dynamic ones. In addition, states increasingly adopt trade and investment restrictions to protect firms and key markets from foreign competition.

The combination of these technological, geographic, and economic factors altered the geopolitical context in the mid-2010s onward, which in turn became an important determinant of state interventionism. The transformations in the geographic structure of the world economy discussed earlier led to a new multipolarity of power and economic activity, underpinning a certain reshuffling of geoeconomic force fields. At the same time, technological development and economic stagnation intensified competition between states in the realms of trade, investment, and technology. This triggered a certain hardening of geopolitics (consider, for instance, the changing relationships between advanced capitalist economies, China and Russia, but also many regional powers such as India, Turkey, South Africa, and Saudi Arabia), and a general turn toward assertive forms of economic nationalism (and extra-territorial outreach, i.e., China's Belt and Road) which collapse the distinction between economic interest and national security (Gertz and Evers 2020). In this context, states increasingly use sovereign funds and state enterprises to strengthen control over strategic sectors, critical resources, and key infrastructure. They resort more and more to economic diplomacy, for instance, by directly negotiating contracts for high-tech firms and opening markets abroad. They also increasingly deploy policy measures (such as tariffs or bans on foreign technologies) to penalize foreign competitors and adopt rhetoric which portrays economic competitors as threats to the sovereignty, autonomy, and integrity of the nation.

Finally, financial factors also played a key role in triggering experimentation with extensive forms of state interventionism. The material transformations discussed so far have been accompanied by the development of an incredibly sophisticated global financial system and a vast expansion of financial flows, many of which are highly volatile and speculative. This has not only rendered the poorer countries particularly vulnerable to repeated and brutal financial crises. Even advanced capitalist economies have experienced profound difficulties maintaining financial and political stability. This is because these financial transformations have made economies more fragile and vulnerable to shocks which quickly reverberate through the financial system and spread to the world economy (the COVID-19 pandemic, for instance, has triggered a massive financial shock which has thrown many developing countries into debt crises). States have had to adapt to this context of enhanced vulnerability. In addition to sizable rescue packages, bank recapitalizations, and selective industry bailouts in the aftermath of financial crises, states increasingly mobilize a range of policy tools to try and stabilize financial markets. Many sovereign funds and policy banks are used in a countercyclical way, that is, to provide credit and finance to economic actors when private finance contracts. In both the global North and South, central banks have also become incredibly powerful actors. They continuously develop new policy instruments to keep financial markets functioning, notably by guaranteeing cheap liquidity, including in noncrisis times (Musthaq 2021).

To sum up, the so-called "new state capitalism," or the expansion of the state's role as promoter, supervisor, and owner of capital over 15–20 years, is not a phenomenon contained within developing and emerging economies. It is a worldwide phenomenon fundamentally rooted in material transformations of global capital accumulation. What kind of future trajectories in state interventionism can economists envisage going forward?

Climate Change and Future Trajectories of State Capitalism

States are likely to respond to the challenge of catastrophic climate warming with renewed activism. Consider, for example, the technological, geographic, economic, geopolitical, and financial factors earlier discussed. Climate change will bear upon all of them and, in all likelihood, will heighten their salience. Insofar as high technologies such as advanced semiconductors, artificial intelligence, and the like are central to green transitions and renewable energy, states will likely develop further modalities of techno-industrial policy to support their development. High-tech competition will increasingly become a climate issue. It is also likely that climate change (and exogenous shocks) will increasingly disturb global value chains, therefore, prompting a partial reorganization of the geographic structure of the world economy. Here again, this would require significant state activism in the form of investment in infrastructure and planning (or denial of climate change and political repression). The convergence of climate and geopolitical imperative is already underway, catalyzing renewed state interventionism. A good example of this is the ongoing geopolitical competition between states to secure energy sources and critical raw materials such as rare earth metals (Kalantzakos 2021). Finally, in terms of finance, states may well be called to intervene further to mitigate climate change-induced financial instability. In short, in an age of catastrophic planetary warming and other crises, the "new state capitalism" is likely here to stay.

As should be clear by now, there is nothing inherently progressive about states accumulating vast amounts of capital in their own hands. State-owned or state-controlled capital can be, and often is, as environmentally destructive as privately owned capital. Think, for instance, about the vast quantities of fossil capital and non-renewable resources owned by states. Besides, workers are exploited in state enterprises often just as much as they are in privately owned enterprises, sometimes in particularly brutal ways. For example, 19 workers in the French telecom giant Orange committed suicide between 2007 and 2010, as a result of moral harassment by management in the context of successive plans to increase labor productivity (BBC 2019). Generally speaking, resurgent state activism has not aimed at transforming the social property relations and economic imperatives characterizing capitalist society. It has been geared toward maximizing capital accumulation and profits in the context of a competitive and geopolitically charged world capitalist economy.

That said, within these parameters, there is scope to influence what states will do with their newfound capabilities and resources. Indeed, as addressed at the beginning of this chapter, although state activities are conditioned by capital accumulation, they are also shaped by sociopolitical conflicts. State ownership and the muscular forms of statism described earlier are no exception. The key question is therefore the following: What sort of opportunities and constraints does the new state capitalism offer for emancipatory politics? In response to this, the remainder of this chapter argues that the new state capitalism generates openings for at least two types of strategies and political engagement with (and against) the state: a reformist and a transformative one (vs. regressive and repressive). It is worth bearing in mind that the line between the two is not always clear-cut, and the former would no doubt have a role in enabling the latter. Let the chapter start with the reformist one, which can be labeled as "democratizing and greening state capitalism."

Democratizing and Greening State Capitalism

The logic and objective of this strategy are relatively straightforward: since states are already doing all sorts of things in the economy and society, progressive movements can push them to use these newfound capacities and resources in ways that are, at a minimum, less socially and environmentally destructive, and, going a step further, in ways that actually empower workers and communities. There is a window of opportunity for this strategy: it is currently much harder for free-market ideologues to claim that states are incapable of doing meaningful things besides protecting property rights and waging war. The new state capitalism shows that states can, and indeed must, do more for the majority of the population, notably in terms of leading a green transition. Consider the following examples.

Central banks have demonstrated that they can mobilize incredibly powerful resources to maintain financial stability, prop up the value of financial assets, and influence the terms according to which states and firms fund themselves. This opens up the possibility that such financial and regulatory power can be harnessed for altering financing conditions in ways that encourage the channeling of financial capital away from fossil-fuel–based industries and into green sectors. Central banks could also contribute to offering low-cost finance to states, as they did during COVID-19, only this time to massively augment their investing firepower in low-carbon production systems, green transportation, ecosystem restoration, and renewable energy infrastructure. Similarly, state-owned banks have become again major economic actors, supporting firms and sectors deemed strategic. Why not drastically scale up their lending capacities to support rapid decarbonization pathways and vast transfers of resources from richer to poorer countries? (vs. fossil fuel corporate resistance). States also now directly or indirectly own vast amounts of capital, via their state enterprises and sovereign wealth funds, which are themselves invested in a wide range of firms and sectors. Here, too, there is potential for leveraging this increased state presence in the circuits of capital. Where relevant, this could mean forcing states to divest from carbon-intensive industries, or, on the contrary, forcing them to keep fossil fuels in the ground (Malm 2020). This could also mean making state enterprises and sovereign funds behave as "activist shareholders," that is, putting pressure on the firms where they hold shares to redirect their activities to less environmentally destructive ones. Moreover, if muscular forms of statism can be mobilized by powerful states to penalize foreign states and firms, then surely these coercive capabilities can be redirected toward enforcing strict regulations and robust tax systems to discipline carbon-intensive capital.

These efforts to green state capitalism would arguably only work in ways that benefit the majority of the population if they are pursued in conjunction with strategies of economic democratization. Pressure could be put on state-owned and state-controlled corporate entities so that they internalize public goals and values, such as strengthening local community democratic control, public accountability, and labor participation (Bloch and Hockett 2022). Moreover, putting powerful and democratically controlled and accountable economic institutions at the center of the economic systems could help reduce the influence of purely profit-maximizing financial actors and could help build working class power and mass popular support for decarbonization pathways.

Overall, then, "democratizing and greening state capitalism" can work to achieve a form of capitalism safer for humans and non-human natures, beyond neoliberalism. Yet this reformist project faces serious potential obstacles and limitations. One is of course the fierce political opposition of various segments of capital who stand to lose most from its realization, not least fossil fuel industries. Another is that there is a risk that power competition between nation-states undermines the potential positive effects of this project at the aggregate, planetary level (for instance, if gains for workers and citizens in one country are made at the expense of populations and non-human natures elsewhere, strengthening ongoing patterns of eco-apartheid and green imperialism) (Ajl 2021). Moreover, the liberal–democratic channels and mechanisms of parliamentary representation through which progressive forces have pushed for reformist projects in the past (trade unions and the broader labor movement, social democratic parties, collective bargaining institutions, etc.) have been seriously eroded over the past decades, and states in both the under- and the overdeveloped world have generally turned toward more coercive and authoritarian forms of rule, empowering repressive apparatuses to suppress dissent and quell various forms of mobilization, protests, and demonstrations (Alami et al. 2024).

Last but not least, and to put it as unequivocally as possible: even if these obstacles and limitations are overcome, there should be no illusion that this reformist project would address the fundamental structures of inequality (between classes and states, etc.) and the enduring forms of misery and alienation characterizing capitalism. The rhythms of social life would still be regulated by those of capital, including its tendencies to enter into destructive crises, and its voracious appetite for human labor and non-human natures. Capitalism is a system ruled by the profit imperative and the compulsive logic of accumulation. Anything else (the realization of human needs, the self-actualization of both individual and collective capabilities, the flourishing of nature–society relations) is always secondary and subordinated to them. Reformist strategies are therefore necessary in the here and now but can never be sufficient. Hence the need for transformative strategies, to which this chapter now turns.

Toward Democratic Planning and Alternative Forms of Ownership

From the perspective of reformist strategies, expansive state ownership and muscular modalities of statism offer a material and ideological opportunity for improving the world in its current (capitalist) form. But from the perspective of a transformative project, that is, one that aims to radically transform existing social relations in order to bring another world into existence (beyond capital and the state), the ongoing development of the new state capitalism offers something altogether different. It reveals fault lines and cracks in capitalist society. Researchers can identify the seeds of progressive future societal transformations, including alternative forms of *planning* and *ownership* of productive activities.

1. Capitalism is a system which exhibits a separation between the economic (the sphere of private market activity) and the political (the public sphere of the state). This separation is important because it allows presenting the capitalist market economy as an autonomous and apolitical entity which allocates resources solely according to criteria of efficiency. This allows emptying the capitalist economy of its social and political content, isolating it from broad-based democratic decisions, and portraying it as immutable (Wood 1995). But with the increased and more visible role of the state, the separation between the economic and the political collapses, and economic relations are re-politicized: the capitalist economy appears in plain sight for what it is, that is, a political construct that is fundamentally (and perhaps increasingly) underpinned by political power and public authority in the form of the state. This fissure therefore reveals the possibility of politically reconstructing economic relations, so that society does not experience them as an external, impersonal, semi-autonomous force (in the form of the movement of prices, markets, money, and so on), as its currently experienced. By contrast, economists could reconstruct them so that they are directly subordinated to collective decisions. This is not simply about delegating to the state more responsibilities for planning the economy and

governing markets. This crack offers a glance at a much more radical prospect of politicization of economic relations: that of directly and consciously organizing productive activities and regulating metabolic relations with nature following principles of voluntary association and cooperation, based on capacities and on collective identification of needs and desires to be fulfilled, while balancing goals of efficiency, justice, democracy, and equality (Sorg 2022).

2. Second, and relatedly, the new state capitalism reveals another fissure in contemporary capitalist society, this time around questions of ownership and control. Capitalism is based on a particular set of social property relations, where the majority is dispossessed of the means of reproducing ourselves. The means of production are owned or controlled by a small group of firms and individuals, who also own or control vast amounts of wealth, resources, and assets. With this comes tremendous power, that of deciding how social wealth is allocated, and where and how labor and non-human natures are put to work (or not): in short, the power to invest, withhold, or withdraw capital across sectors and geographies. Now, as argued earlier, there is no reason to assume that state ownership of capital is necessarily better than private ownership (although it can be). So, the point here is not simply to call for further expanding state ownership of the economy, as a means to complement or gradually substitute for private capital allocation. Rather, from the perspective of a radical project of transformation, what the new state capitalism shows is that social property relations are not natural or eternal, and the very power to allocate social wealth can be wrested away from the owners of capital and assets. In other words, this crack reveals the potential for democratic experiments with alternative forms of public ownership, through which communities can own, manage, and socialize the wealth they produce in ways that do not prioritize profits over social life and non-human natures, but rather favor objectives of human flourishing, sustainable nature–society relations, and planetary solidarity. What is at stake is nothing less than regaining power and control over the collective future (Buller and Lawrence 2022).

References

Ajl, Max, *A People's Green New Deal*. London: Pluto, 2021.

Akkerman, Mark, *Financing Border Wars*. Amsterdam: Centre Delas, *Stop the Wall*. Transnational Institute, 2021. https://www.tni.org/files/publication-downloads/financingborderwars-report-tni_2.pdf

Alami, Ilias, and Adam D. Dixon. *The Spectre of State Capitalism*. Oxford University Press, 2024.

Alami, Ilias, Jack Copley, and Alexis Moraitis, The Wicked Trinity of Late Capitalism, *Geoforum*. v. 24 2024. 1–20.

Alami, Ilias, and Adam D. Dixon, State Capitalism(s) Redux? Theories, Tensions, Controversies. *Competition & Change.* v. 24 (1), 2020. 70–94.

Arboleda, Martín, *Planetary Mine: Territories of Extraction Under Late Capitalism.* London: Verso Books, 2020.

Babić, Milan, State Capital in a Geoeconomic World: Mapping State-Led Foreign Investment in the Global Political Economy, *Review of International Political Economy.* v. 30 (1),2021. 201–228.

BBC (2016) France Télécom suicides: Prosecutor calls for bullying trial. BBC News, 7 July 2016. Accessed at: http://www.bbc.com/news/world-europe-36733572 on March 1, 2019.

Bloch, Fred and Robert Hockett (eds.), *Democratizing Finance.* London: Verso, 2022.

Bremmer, Ian, *The End of the Free Market.* New York: Portfolio, 2010.

Buller, Adrienne and Matthew Lawrence, *Owning the Future: Power and Property in an Age of Crisis.* London: Verso Books, 2022.

Charnock, Greig and Guido Starosta, *The New International Division of Labour: Global Transformation and Uneven Development.* London: Palgrave, 2016.

Clarke, Simon, *The State Debate.* London: Palgrave Macmillan, 1991.

Gertz, Geoffrey, and Miles M. Evers, Geoeconomic Competition: Will State Capitalism Win? *The Washington Quarterly.* v. 43 (2), 2020. 117–136.

Gilmore, Ruth Wilson, *Abolition Geography: Essays Towards Liberation.* London: Verso Books, 2022.

International Monetary Fund. State-owned enterprises: The other government. in *Fiscal monitor*, ed. IMF, 47–74. Washington, DC: IMF, 2020.

Jayasuriya, Kanishka, The Age of Political Disincorporation: Geo-Capitalist Conflict and the Politics of Authoritarian Statism. *Journal of Contemporary Asia.* v. 53 (1), 2023. 165–178.

Kalantzakos, Sophia, Rare Earths, the Climate Crisis, and Tech imperium, *LSE Blog.* 2021. https://blogs.lse.ac.uk/cff/2021/03/24/rare-earths-the-climate-crisis-and-tech-imperium/

Malm, Andreas, *Corona, Climate, Chronic Emergency: War Communism in the Twenty-First Century.* London: Verso Books, 2020.

Marois, Thomas, *Public Banks: Decarbonisation, Definancialisation and Democratisation.* Cambridge: Cambridge University Press, 2021.

Marx, Karl, *Grundrisse: Foundations of the Critique of Political Economy.* London: Penguin UK, 2005.

Musthaq, Fathimath, Unconventional Central Banking and the Politics of Liquidity, *Review of International Political Economy*, v. 30 (1),2021. 281–306.

Rikap, Cecilia, and Bengt-Åke Lundvall, *The Digital Innovation Race.* New York: Springer Books, 2021.

Schindler, Seth, Ilias Alami, and Nicholas Jepson, Goodbye Washington Confusion, Hello Wall Street Consensus: Contemporary State Capitalism and the Spatialisation of Industrial Strategy. *New Political Economy*, v. 28 (2), 2023. 223–240.

Sorg, Christoph, Failing to Plan Is Planning to Fail: Toward an Expanded Notion of Democratically Planned Postcapitalism. *Critical Sociology*, v. 49 (3),2022. 475–493.

Sperber, Nathan, The Many Lives of State Capitalism: From Classical Marxism to Free-Market Advocacy. *History of the Human Sciences*, v. 32 (3), 2019. 100–124.

Wood, Ellen Meiksins, *Democracy Against Capitalism.* Cambridge: Cambridge University Press, 1995.

14

SOME BASIC ELEMENTS OF A GLOBAL GREEN NEW DEAL

Robert Pollin

Introduction

Climate change necessarily presents a profound social, economic, and political challenge in our present historical moment. This is for the simple reason that we are courting ecological disaster by not advancing a viable global climate stabilization project. There are no certainties as to what ultimately will transpire by allowing the average global temperature to continue rising. But as a basis for action, we only need to understand that there is a non-trivial possibility that the very continuation of life on earth as we know it is at stake.

The severity of the risks we face has been documented scrupulously for decades by the Intergovernmental Panel on Climate Change (IPCC), the most authoritative global organization advancing climate change research. Thus, in its landmark October 2018 report titled *Global Warming of 1.5°C*, the IPCC presented an unequivocal case for urgent action to fight climate change, along with specific goals for moving onto a viable climate stabilization path. The report emphasized the necessity of limiting the increase in global mean temperatures to 1.5 degrees Celsius (1.5°C) above pre-industrial levels as of 2100. The previous climate stabilization target, of both the IPCC itself and a broader consensus of climate scientists, had been 2.0°C. But the IPCC concluded that lowering the target to 1.5°C will substantially reduce the risks of heat extremes, heavy precipitation, droughts, sea level rise, biodiversity losses, and corresponding impacts on health, livelihoods, food security, water supply, and human security.

The IPCC concluded in its 2018 report that to stabilize the global mean temperature of 2100 at 1.5°C, global net carbon dioxide (CO_2) emissions will have to fall by about 45 percent as of 2030 and reach net zero emissions by 2050. CO_2 is the most significant greenhouse gas contributing to climate

DOI: 10.4324/9781003366690-16

change, accounting for about 74 percent of all greenhouse gases. Methane and nitrous oxide, the other two major greenhouse gases, contribute about 17 and 6 percent, respectively, to the greenhouse gas total.[1]

The IPCC followed up its 2018 analysis with two major installments of its *Sixth Assessment Report*, in February and April 2022. The press release for its February 2022 study summarized its basic message as follows:

> Human-induced climate change is causing dangerous and widespread disruption in nature and affecting the lives of billions of people around the world, despite efforts to reduce the risks. People and ecosystems least able to cope are being hardest hit.

Hoesung Lee, Chair of the IPCC, further stated then that

> This report is a dire warning about the consequences of inaction. It shows that climate change is a grave and mounting threat to our well-being and a healthy planet. Our actions today will shape how people adapt and nature responds to increasing climate risks.

What are "our actions today" that are most critical for advancing a viable global climate stabilization project? As I use the term, the core of the Green New Deal, is exactly targeted at achieving the IPCC emissions reduction targets and to accomplish this in a way that also expands decent job opportunities and raises mass living standards for working people and the poor throughout the world. The global Green New Deal, in other words, is a climate stabilization program which fully recognizes that "people and ecosystems least able to cope are being hardest hit." As such, the global Green New Deal presents a robust alternative to neoliberalism, the dominant economic policy framework throughout the world over the past 40 years. Neoliberalism is a variant of capitalism in which the prerogatives of big capital and the rich dominate in all areas of economic policy. This has produced unprecedented increases in income and wealth inequalities throughout the world. For the first time throughout the entire era of industrial capitalism, average global temperatures have also risen steadily during the 40 years of neoliberal ascendency.

This paper reviews some of the major design features and challenges of a global Green New Deal and the potential outcomes that can result. It will focus on analytic and policy-design questions, and only briefly consider the related political challenges, even while these political challenges are enormous.

The global Green New Deal includes five major features. These are:

1. Phasing out global fossil fuel consumption by 2050.
2. Clean energy investments, averaging about 2.5 percent of global GDP per year, including both public and private investments.

3. A large-scale expansion of job opportunities globally, generated by the clean-energy investments.
4. Just transition support for workers and communities that are currently dependent on the fossil fuel industry.
5. Phasing out deforestation and industrial agriculture, to be replaced with afforestation and sustainable agricultural practices.

In the interests of space, this paper focuses on the first two issues only, on the phase out of the global fossil-fuel dominant energy infrastructure and its replacement by a zero-emissions clean-energy infrastructure. The other three areas, especially regarding, on a global scale, job creation through clean-energy investments, and just transition for fossil fuel-dependent workers and communities have been examined elsewhere. These areas of focus are summarized in Chomsky and Pollin (2020).

Fossil Fuel Phase Out

To have any chance of moving onto a viable global climate stabilization path, the single most critical project at hand is straightforward. It is to phase out the consumption of oil, coal, and natural gas, so that, by 2050, fossil fuel consumption for producing energy will have fallen to zero. CO_2 emissions from burning fossil fuel energy sources will have then, correspondingly, also fallen to zero by 2050.

As of the International Energy Agency's (IEA) figures for 2019 – this being the most recent full year prior to the COVID-19 lockdown for which we have data – global CO_2 emissions were at around 36 billion tons (International Energy Agency 2022). This represents a roughly 70 percent emissions increase since 1990 and a 14 percent increase since 2010. More to the point, according to the IEA's estimates for future emissions under alternative realistic scenarios, emissions will fall barely at all by 2030 and will not come close to achieving the zero emissions target by 2050.

The overarching challenge for climate stabilization then becomes clear: how to move onto a path to zero emissions by 2050 while recognizing that people still need to consume energy to light, heat, and cool buildings, to power cars, buses, trains, and airplanes, and to operate computers and industrial machinery, among other uses. As such, to make progress toward climate stabilization requires a viable alternative to the existing fossil-fuel dominant infrastructure for meeting the world's energy needs. Energy consumption and economic activity more generally need to be *absolutely decoupled* from the consumption of fossil fuels. That is, the consumption of fossil fuels will need to fall steadily in absolute terms, even while people will still be able to consume energy resources to meet their various demands.

As of 2019, total fossil fuel energy consumption amounted to 485 quadrillion British Thermal Units (Q-BTUs). As a matter of simple arithmetic, to bring fossil fuel consumption down to zero by 2050 would entail, in absolute figures, cutting consumption by average of about 18 Q-BTUs per year over 27 years, starting in 2023. This amounts to a 3.7 percent cut in fossil fuel consumption each year relative to the 2019 consumption level.

Economies can continue to grow – and even grow relatively rapidly, as in China and India – while still advancing a viable climate stabilization project as long as the growth process is absolutely decoupled from fossil fuel consumption. In fact, several European countries have managed over the past 20 years to absolutely decouple GDP growth from CO_2 emissions, including the United Kingdom, France, Germany, Sweden, Finland, Italy, Czechia, and Romania.[2] These decoupling patterns hold in terms of both production levels and the more stringent standard of consumption levels – that is, including in a country's total emissions figure the emissions content of the goods that they are importing. This is a positive development, but clearly, to date, only a small step in the right direction.

Clean Energy Investment Program

In fact, as a technical and economic proposition, it is entirely realistic to assume that a global clean energy infrastructure can supply close to 100 percent of global energy supply by 2050. By a higher-end estimate, it will require an average level of investment spending throughout the global economy of about 2.5 percent of global GDP per year, focused on two areas: (1) dramatically improving energy efficiency standards in the stock of buildings, automobiles and public transportation systems, and industrial production processes; and (2) equally dramatically expanding the supply of clean renewable energy sources, available at competitive prices relative to fossil fuels and nuclear power to all sectors and in all regions of the globe.[3] The primary clean renewable energy sources are solar and wind power. Geothermal, small-scale hydro and low-emissions bioenergy can serve as supplemental clean renewable sources.

It is critical to recognize that once investments in energy efficiency and renewable energy projects are installed and operating at scale, they will deliver significantly lower energy costs than our current fossil fuel-dominated system. Thus, the International Renewable Energy Agency (IRENA) reports that, as of 2021, fossil fuel-generated electricity ranged between 5 and 15 cents per kilowatt hour within the high-income economies. By contrast, the global average costs for generating a kilowatt of electricity from existing utility-scale onshore wind, at 3.9 cents, or solar photovoltaic technology, at 5.7 cents, were already at the low end of the fossil fuel-generated electricity cost range.[4] In addition, according to recent research, the average costs of achieving a kilowatt hour of energy savings through efficiency investments is between 2.5 and 3 cents – that is, roughly one-third the costs of even the midpoint figure for fossil fuel-generated electricity.[5] It is therefore reasonable to assume that, even with existing clean energy technologies, electricity can be delivered now at approximately half the costs of fossil fuel-generated electricity.

This is without taking account of any policy incentives to support clean energy investments or, for that matter, any environmental costs from continuing to burn fossil fuels. Further, the costs of renewable electricity have been on a sharp downward trajectory. The average cost of electricity from solar photovoltaics, in particular, fell by about 80 percent between 2010 and 2020. These cost declines are likely to continue through "learning-by-doing" as investment levels in clean energy scale up.

In calculating the total cost of the global clean energy investment project through 2050, it is realistically assumed that the project won't begin in earnest until 2024. The level of necessary investment in 2024 would amount to about $2.6 trillion. Investment spending would then average about $4.5 trillion per year between 2024 and 2050. Total clean energy investment spending for the full-scale 27-year investment cycle 2024–2050 would amount to about $120 trillion.[6]

These figures are for overall investment spending, including from both the public and private sectors. Establishing the right mix between public and private investment will be a major consideration within the industrial and financing policies framework. It is not realistic to expect that this can all be accomplished through private capitalist investments. But it is equally unrealistic to expect that public enterprises, on their own, can mount a project at this scale, and with the speed that is required. As a general proposition, it is reasonable to assume that clean energy investments should be divided roughly equally – that is, 50 percent public and private investments, respectively, on a global basis. For the first year of full-scale investment activity in 2024, this would break down to $1.3 trillion in both public and private investments. A major part of the policy challenge will be to determine how to leverage the public money most effectively to create strong incentives for private investors, large and small, while also maintaining tight regulations over their activities.

For 2019, global clean energy investment levels, including both energy efficiency and clean renewable investments, were estimated by the IEA to be about $600 billion, equal to about 0.7 percent of global GDP.[7] Thus, the increase in clean energy investments will need to be in the range of 1.8 percent of global GDP – that is, about $2 trillion assuming global GDP in 2024 is about $100 trillion. Clean energy investments would then rise in step with global GDP growth thereafter until 2050.

Raising energy efficiency levels will generate "rebound effects" – that is, energy consumption increases resulting from lower energy costs. But such rebound effects are likely to be modest within the context of a global project focused on reducing CO_2 emissions and stabilizing the climate. Among other factors, energy consumption levels in advanced economies are close to saturation points in the use of home appliances and lighting – that is, we are not likely to clean dishes much more frequently because we have a more efficient dishwasher. The evidence shows that consumers in advanced economies are likely to heat and cool their homes as well as drive their cars more when they have access to more efficient equipment. But these increased consumption levels are usually modest. Average rebound effects are likely to be significantly larger in developing economies. But it is critical that all energy efficiency gains will be accompanied by policies that will both discourage fossil fuel consumption and support clean energy investments. The transition from fossil fuels to renewable energy will allow higher levels of energy consumption without leading to increases in CO_2 emissions. It is important to recognize further that different countries at comparable levels of development presently operate at widely varying levels of energy efficiency. For example, Germany presently operates at an efficiency level roughly 50 percent higher than that of the United States. Brazil is at nearly three times that of South Africa. There is no evidence that large rebound effects have emerged as a result of these high-efficiency standards in Germany and Brazil relative to those of the United States and South Africa.

Clean Energy Challenges: Intermittency, Mineral Supply, and Land Use[8]

Three major sets of challenges arise in building a high-efficiency/renewable-energy dominant global energy infrastructure. These concern the issues of (1) intermittency with solar and wind energy; (2) mineral requirements as inputs for the clean energy infrastructure; and (3) land-use requirements for renewables, especially solar and wind.

Intermittency refers to the fact that the sun does not shine and the wind does not blow 24 hours a day. Moreover, on average, different geographical areas receive significantly different levels of sunshine and wind. As such, the solar and wind power that are generated in the sunnier and windier areas of the globe will need to be stored and transmitted at reasonable costs to the less sunny and windy areas. In fact, these issues around transmission and storage of wind and solar power will not become pressing for many years into the clean energy transition, probably for at least a decade. This is because fossil fuels, along with nuclear energy, will continue to provide a baseload of non-intermittent energy supply as these energy sectors proceed toward their phase out while the clean energy industry rapidly expands. Fossil fuels and nuclear energy now provide roughly 85 percent of all global energy supplies. Even with a phase out to zero by 2050 trajectory, with fossil fuel supply cut on average by 18 Q-BTUs per year, fossil fuels will continue to provide the majority of overall energy demand through about 2035. Meanwhile, fully viable solutions to the technical challenges with transmission and storage of solar and wind power – including around affordability – should not be more than a decade away, certainly as long as the market for clean energy grows at the rapid rate that is necessary. For example, IRENA estimates that global battery storage capacity could expand between 17- and 38-folds as of 2030.[9]

Building a global clean energy infrastructure will entail a massive expansion in demand for the set of minerals that are used intensively in clean energy technologies. The IEA estimates that demand for minerals needed in clean energy technologies will rise six-fold in order to meet the 2050 zero-emissions target. Some of the most heavily required minerals include lithium, graphite, cobalt, and nickel. Several rare earth minerals will also experience heavily increasing demand, including tellurium, used for solar cell production and neodymium, used in producing wind turbines and electric vehicles.

Short-term supply shortages will likely emerge with some of these minerals as demand for them expands rapidly. But none of the likely shortages should be insurmountable. One solution will be to greatly expand the industry for recycling the needed metals and minerals. At present, average recycling rates for these resources are below 1 percent of total supply. By contrast, recycling rates for aluminum throughout the world are at around 75 percent. Increasing recycling rates by even relatively modest amounts will make a substantial contribution toward overcoming supply shortages.

In addition to recycling, opportunities will also emerge to economize on the level of minerals and metals necessary to produce solar panels, wind turbines, and batteries, as production technologies improve along with the rapid expansion of the industry. Substitute materials can also be developed for those materials that remain in short supply. What happened with neodymium provides a valuable recent case in point. When the world price of neodymium peaked in 2010, producers found ways to economize on its use or eliminate it altogether as a necessary material. Demand for neodymium rapidly fell by between 20 and 50 percent as other materials were found to be adequate substitutes.

The issue of land use requirements is frequently cited to demonstrate that building a 100 percent renewable energy global economy is unrealistic. But these claims are not supported by evidence. Thus, the Harvard University physicist Mara Prentiss shows, in her 2015 book *Energy Revolution: The Physics and the Promise of Efficient Technology*, as well as her more recent follow-up discussions, that the US economy could run entirely on clean renewable energy sources by 2050 or earlier. Her arguments can be readily generalized to the global economy.

Focusing on Prentiss's discussions on land use, she shows that well below 1 percent of the total US land area would be needed through solar and wind power to meet 100 percent of US energy needs. Most of these land use requirements could be met, for example, by placing solar panels on rooftops and parking lots, then operating wind turbines on about 7 percent of current agricultural land. Moreover, the wind turbines can be sited on existing operating farmland with only minor losses of agricultural productivity. Farmers should mostly welcome this dual use of their land, since it provides them with a major additional income source. At present, the US states of Iowa, Kansas, Oklahoma, and South Dakota all generate more than 30 percent of their electricity supply through wind turbines. The remaining supplemental energy needs could then be supplied by geothermal, hydro, and low-emissions bioenergy. This particular scenario includes no further contributions from solar farms in desert areas, solar panels mounted on highways or offshore wind projects, among other supplemental renewable energy sources. However, if handled responsibly, all of these options are also viable possibilities.

It is true that conditions for renewable energy production in the United States are more favorable than those in some other countries. Germany and the United Kingdom, for example, have population densities 7–8 times greater than the United States and also receive less sunlight over the course of a year. As such, these countries, operating at high-efficiency levels, would need to use about 3 percent of their total land area to generate 100 percent of their energy demand through domestically produced solar energy. Using cost-effective storage and transmission technologies, the United Kingdom and Germany can also import energy generated by solar and wind power in other countries, just as, in the United States, wind power generated in Iowa could be transmitted to New York City. Any such import requirements are likely to be modest. Both the United Kingdom and Germany are already net energy importers in any case. Taking a global perspective, the most critical point with respect to Prentiss's calculations focused on the United States is that, in terms of both population density and the availability of sunlight and wind to harvest, average conditions for renewables throughout the globe are much closer to those in the United States than to Germany and the United Kingdom.

Providing Cheap and Accessible Financing

In principle, it should not be especially challenging to finance the global Green New Deal. To begin with, as of 2020, the Financial Stability Board estimates that the total value of global financial assets was $469 trillion.[10] The $2.6 trillion being proposed to channel into clean energy investments as of 2024 amounts to 0.6 percent of this total financial asset pool. As noted above, assuming that the overall global financing requirement would be divided equally between public and private sector financing sources. About $1.3 trillion would need to be raised in 2024 from public sector sources, 0.3 percent of total global financial assets in 2020.

For illustrative purposes, there are three large-scale funding sources to support public clean energy investments. Other approaches could also be viable.

These three funding sources are: (1) a carbon tax, in which 75 percent of revenues are rebated back to the public but 25 percent are channeled into clean energy investment projects; (2) transferring 10 percent of funding out of military budgets from all countries, but primarily the United States; and (3) a Green Bond lending program, initiated primarily by the US Federal Reserve and the European Central Bank, but also including the People's Bank of China, the Bank of England, the Bank of Japan, and the central banks of other high-income economies. Strong cases can be made for each of these funding measures. But each proposal does also have vulnerabilities, including around political feasibility. The most sensible approach is therefore to combine the measures into a single package that minimizes their respective weaknesses as standalone measures.

Carbon taxes have the merit of impacting climate policy through two channels – they raise fossil fuel prices and thereby discourage consumption while also generating a new source of government revenue. At least part of the carbon tax revenue can then be channeled into supporting the clean energy investment project. But the carbon tax will hit low and middle-income people disproportionately, since they spend a larger fraction of their income on electricity, transportation, and home-heating fuel. An equal-shares rebate, as proposed by James Boyce (2019), is the simplest way to ensure that the full impact of the tax will be equalized across all population cohorts.

Consider, therefore, the following tax-and-rebate program. Focusing, again, on 2024, the first year of the full-scale investment program, we begin with a tax at a low rate of $40 per ton of carbon. Given current global CO_2 emissions levels, that would generate about $1.3 billion in revenue. Focusing on gasoline prices, a rule-of-thumb for estimating the impact of a carbon tax on retail prices is that every one dollar in a carbon tax will add about one cent to the retail price per gallon of gasoline. Thus, starting the tax at $40 per ton will add about 40 cents to the price of a gallon of gasoline. As of mid-2022, the average retail price of gasoline globally was around $5.00, though there is substantial variation by country around this average price, due to differences in how gasoline is distributed and taxed in each country. Nevertheless, as an illustrative average only, the carbon tax of $40 per ton would increase the average global retail gasoline price as of 2022 by 8 percent.

If only 25 percent of this revenue is used to finance clean energy investments, that amounts to roughly $325 billion for investment projects. The 75 percent of the total revenue that is rebated to the public in equal shares would then amount to $975 billion. This amounts to about $120 for every person on the planet, or nearly $500 for a family of four.

Global military spending in 2021 was at $2.1 trillion. The US military budget, at about $800 billion, accounted for nearly 40 percent of the global total. There are solid logical and ethical grounds for transferring substantial shares, if not most, of each country's total military budget to supporting climate stabilization, to seriously take the idea that military spending is fundamentally aimed at achieving greater security for the citizens of each country. Russia's invasion of Ukraine in February 2022, and the subsequent massive disruption of global energy supplies, only reinforced this point. But to remain within the realm of political feasibility, assume that 10 percent of global military spending will transfer into supporting climate security. The 10 percent transfer of funds would apply to all countries on a proportional basis. The full amount of funds generated would be roughly $200 billion.

It was demonstrated during the 2007–09 Great Recession and again during the 2020–2021 COVID-19 lockdown that the Federal Reserve is able to supply basically unlimited bailout funds to private financial markets during crises. Thus, during the COVID-19 lockdown between March 2020 and December 2021, the Fed purchased more than $4 trillion in financial assets from Wall Street firms – about nearly 20 percent of US GDP – to prop up financial markets during the crisis. The policy interventions in other high-income countries followed broadly similar trajectories during the pandemic. The Bank of International Settlements (BIS) described these measures as "unprecedented" in "size and scope." The BIS estimated that these interventions exceeded 30 percent of GDP in Germany and Italy, over 20 percent in Japan, and around 15 percent in the United Kingdom and France (Epstein and Pollin 2021).

It may be proposed that the Fed supply $400 billion in Green Bond financing. This would amount to only 10 percent of its 2020–2021 bailout operations. The other large central banks could match these Fed injections, bringing the total level of support to $800 billion initially, then rising annually with overall economic growth. This support from the Fed and other major central banks could be injected into the global economy through straightforward channels. That is, various public entities, such as the World Bank, could issue long-term zero-interest-rate bonds. The Fed, for example, would purchase these bonds. The various public entities issuing these bonds would then have the funds to pursue the full range of projects falling under the rubric of the global clean energy project.

In short, these three sources – revenues from the carbon tax, transfers out of military spending, and green bond financing from major central banks – can readily generate the roughly $1.3 trillion in public financing that will be needed in 2024 to finance clean energy investments at the level needed to achieve a zero emissions economy by 2050. Through the simple illustrative example here, we would generate approximately $300 billion from the carbon tax, $200 billion from transferring funds out of military budgets, and $800 billion through central bank green bond programs, to reach the $1.3 trillion total. The level of funding will then rise in proportion to the increases in global GDP between 2024 and 2050.

It will also be critical to eliminate all fossil fuel subsidy programs in all countries. According to estimates by Fossil Fuel Subsidy Tracker, the average level of global fossil fuel subsidies between 2011 and 2020 was about $630 billion.[11] However, through keeping retail energy prices low, such fossil fuel subsidies act as a form of general support for all energy consumers. Lower- and middle-income households are then benefitting from fossil fuel subsidies, along with, of course, the fossil fuel corporations. The fossil fuel subsidies should be converted into clean energy subsidies that will then help lower-income consumers pay for clean energy. But using the roughly $600 billion per year in redirected subsidy funds to directly support consumers' clean energy purchases will also mean that the funds would not be available to directly finance clean energy infrastructure investments.

Ensuring Global Fairness

Where is all the money coming from and going to? The ability to answer this question clearly is important to ensure that the basic standards of fairness are built into the global Green New Deal. Three basic points need to be emphasized as background:

1. Starting with the early phases of industrial development under capitalism, what are now the globe's high-income countries, including the US Western Europe, Japan, Canada, and Australia, are primarily responsible for loading up the atmosphere with greenhouse gas emissions and causing climate change. They therefore should be primarily responsible for financing the global Green New Deal.
2. Moving from this historical perspective to the present, high-income people in all countries and regions have massively larger carbon footprints today than everyone else. As documented in a 2020 Oxfam study, the average carbon footprint of people in the richest 1 percent of the global population, for example, is 35 times greater than the average emissions level for the overall global population (Oxfam 2021).
3. The upfront investment costs of a global Green New Deal are real and substantial, at around 2.5 percent of global GDP annually, amounting, as discussed above, to about $2.6 trillion in 2024. But these investments will pay for themselves over time, by dramatically raising energy efficiency levels and providing abundant clean renewable energy at average prices that are at parity or lower today than fossil fuels and nuclear and falling.

Within this overall framework, how well do the financing proposals above measure up in terms of global fairness? First, under the simple tax-and-rebate proposal, everyone on the planet receives a $120 rebate. For the average person in the United States, this $120 will provide tiny 0.2 percent boost to their income. But for the average person in, say, Kenya, this additional $120 will raise their income by roughly 6 percent. The impact of transferring 10 percent of all global military spending, provided on a proportional basis relative to the current military budgets within each country, will also be strongly egalitarian. This is because, starting with the United States, military spending levels of the high-income countries are much higher in absolute amounts than those of middle- and low-income countries.

The Green Bond financing proposal will not take money out of anyone's pocket. It rather involves the world's largest central banks effectively printing money as needed. This would be just as they did during both the 2007 and 2009 global financial crisis as well as the COVID-19 recession, except on a far more modest scale than the largesse that the central banks showered on Wall Street and global financial elite twice within the little more than a decade. To be clear, it is not being suggested that the US Fed or European Central Bank should rely on this policy – what is technically known as "debt monetization" – on a routine basis. But we need to be equally clear that this is a fully legitimate option that the two major central banks have in their toolkit and that this option should indeed be brought into action as needed under crisis conditions. Note here that the funds will be generated by the central banks of high-income countries, but then distributed globally on an equitable basis, to underwrite the clean energy investment projects at scale in all regions of the globe.

Public investment banks in all regions, but especially in low-income countries, will then serve as primary conduits in moving specific investment projects forward. The public investment banks will be financing both public and private sector clean-energy projects, along with mixed public–private projects. We cannot know what the best mix should be between public and private ownership with any specific project in any given country. There is no point in being dogmatic and pretending otherwise. But, in all situations, it is important to stick with a basic principle: that with private-sector projects, it is not reasonable to allow private firms to profit at rates that they have gotten away with under 40 years of neoliberalism. If private firms are happy to accept large public subsidies to support their clean energy investments, they then also need to be willing to accept limits on their profitability.

As should be clear, the global Green New Deal project that I have outlined here will not replace capitalism with socialism. In fact, this variant of a global Green New Deal project will actually need to take root and flourish within the interstices of capitalism. We do not have the luxury of postponing a viable climate stabilization program until the uncertain time at which socialism will have been established worldwide as the prevailing social system. But the Green New Deal will end the 40-year reign of the neoliberalism era within capitalism, because the Green New Deal will have enabled the principles of ecological sanity and egalitarianism to gain ascendancy over capitalist acquisitiveness.

Notes

1 https://ourworldindata.org/greenhouse-gas-emissions.
2 https://ourworldindata.org/co2-gdp-decoupling.
3 Some analysts include nuclear energy, natural gas, and even petroleum and coal, operating with carbon capture technologies, as clean energy sources. For a range of reasons, I disagree with all such arguments. See Chomsky and Pollin (2020) for discussions on these points.
4 https://www.irena.org/publications/2021/Jun/Renewable-Power-Costs-in-2020.
5 https://emp.lbl.gov/publications/cost-saving-electricity-through; https://www.aceee.org/blog/2018/12/renewables-are-getting-cheaper-energy; https://emp.lbl.gov/publications/cost-saving-electricity-multi-program.
6 Pollin (2020) presents the full derivation as to how I generated these estimates. It is notable that the 2021 study by IRENA, *World Energy Transitions Outlook*, reached almost the identical figure for average annual spending to reach a 1.5°C stabilization point by 2050: they estimate an average of $4.4 trillion per year as opposed to my own average figure of $4.5 trillion per year (p. 100). The IEA's cost estimate for their Net Zero scenario is also close to my figure, at an average of $5.1 trillion per year through 2050.
7 https://www.iea.org/reports/energy-efficiency-2021/executive-summary; https://www.iea.org/reports/world-energy-investment-2021/executive-summary.
8 These issues are discussed in more detail in Chomsky and Pollin (2020), along with references to the research literature in all three areas.
9 https://www.irena.org/publications/2019/Sep/Enabling-Technologies.   See   also Prentiss, "The Technical Path to Zero Carbon," *The American Prospect*, https://prospect.org/greennewdeal/the-technical-path-to-zero-carbon/.
10 https://www.fsb.org/wp-content/uploads/P161221.pdf.
11 https://fossilfuelsubsidytracker.org/.

Bibliography

Chomsky, Noam and Robert Pollin, *Climate Crisis and the Global Green New Deal: The Political Economy of Saving the Planet*, London: Verso, 2020.
Epstein, Gerald and Robert Pollin, *Neoliberalism's Bailout Problem, Boston Review*, 2021. https://www.bostonreview.net/articles/neoliberalisms-bailout-problem/
Intergovernmental Panel on Climate Change (IPCC), Global Warming of 1.50C, 2018. https://www.ipcc.ch/sr15/Intergovernmental Panel on Climate Change (IPCC), 6th Assessment Report, 2022. https://www.ipcc.ch/assessment-report/ar6/
International Energy Agency (IEA), Net Zero by 2050: A Roadmap for the Global Energy Sector, Net Zero by 2050 – Analysis - IEA, 2021. *International Energy Agency (IEA)*, World Energy Outlook, 2022. https://www.iea.org/reports/world-energy-outlook-2022
International Renewable Energy Agency (IRENA), Enabling Technologies: Innovative Landscape Briefs, 2019. https://www.irena.org/publications/2019/Sep/Enabling-Technologies.
International Renewable Energy Agency (IRENA), Renewable Power Costs in 2020, 2021. https://www.irena.org/publications/2021/Jul/Renewable-Power-Generation-Costs-in-2020
International Renewable Energy Agency (IRENA), World Energy Transitions Outlook: 1.50C Pathway, World Energy Transitions Outlook: 1.5°C Pathway (irena.org), 2021.

Oxfam, Carbon Inequality in 2020, 2021. https://oxfamilibrary.openrepository.com/bitstream/handle/10546/621305/bn-carbon-inequality-2030-051121-en.pdf.

Pollin, Robert, An Industrial Policy Framework to Advance a Global Green New Deal, Arkebe Oqubay, Christopher Cramer, Ha-Joon Chang and Richard Kozul-Wright eds., *The Oxford Handbook of Industrial Policy*, Oxford, UK: Oxford University Press, 2020.

Prentiss, Mara, *Energy Revolution: The Physics and Promise of Efficient Technology*, Cambridge, MA: Harvard University Press, 2015.

Prentiss, Mara, The Technical Path to Zero Carbon, *American Prospect*, 2019. https://prospect.org/greennewdeal/the-technical-path-to-zero-carbon/

15

SOCIO-HISTORICAL ONTOLOGY, EXPLANATIONS, AND EMPIRICAL APPROACHES

Paulo L. dos Santos

Introduction

Ontological and epistemological considerations may seem an esoteric terrain for discussions about differences and controversies across traditions in economic analysis. Ontology, after all, is a branch of metaphysics in philosophy, tasked with grappling with the nature of things; while epistemology grapples with the nature, origins, and scope of knowledge about things. The controversies across different traditions in economics and political economy, on the other hand, involve conflicts and realities of a worldly nature. Yet lurking beneath many of the persistent disagreements between radical and conventional treatments of contemporary capitalism are very different appreciations of the very nature of capitalist economies, and of how we may come to understand their functioning.

Contending schools of economic thought are founded on distinctive philosophical appreciations of two crucial relationships shaping the nature of all economic formations: the relationship between individuals and social aggregates, and the relationship between economic functioning and historical development. The types of abstraction different traditions in economic analysis draw upon in theoretical development, the things they seek to explain and consider to be valid explanations, and the conceptual and empirical instruments they use in efforts to explain are all ultimately grounded on contending appreciations or characterizations of those two relationships.

Walrasian approaches dominant in contemporary economic thought are philosophically founded on forms of individualist reductionism: they typically reject the notion that there is anything in social aggregates beyond the characteristics and actions of economic individuals and look for economic

DOI: 10.4324/9781003366690-17

explanations based on detailed descriptions of those agents and their interactions. A focus on individual characteristics and behavioral imperatives, taken as given, tends to generate explanations that are asocial, ahistorical, and ultimately conservative in their discursive thrust.

Radical approaches to political economy, in contrast, recognize economic reality as irreducibly social and historical. They typically study capitalism as a system with specific origins, social relations, evolving regimes or periods, and with an eventual demise. And while not eschewing notions of individual agency or the relevance of subjectivity in social life, they look for explanations based on social categories like class, gender, race, monetary regimes, the world system, core and peripheral economies, etc. Those are understood to correspond to consequential social realities and schisms that directly shape the functioning of markets and the historical development of capitalism.

Careful consideration of these philosophical controversies offers a broad, critical perspective on the differences between conventional and radical approaches to economic analysis. Perhaps more importantly, in a world where the core individualist and ahistorical philosophical propositions sustaining mainstream economics resonate strongly with social prejudices and biases that are pervasive in contemporary thought, a clear understanding of the conceptual issues involved is crucial to the development of new radical approaches to economic analysis. At a minimum, it can help radical economists avoid echoing those biases and transcend the analytical and normative vices they create.

To make its case, this chapter starts with a discussion of key elements in philosophical debates about the nature, evolution, and analytical problems of complex, higher-order systems and their relationship with their constituent lower-order parts. It then turns to specifically socioeconomic systems, considering first forms of individualist reductionism and their influence over mainline economic analysis; then taking up the historical materialist alternative, its key conceptual foundations, and the irreducibly social and historical analytical concerns it defines. The chapter concludes by illustrating the differences between the two approaches by considering their contrasting theoretical treatments of prices and economic development, discussing how individualist reductionism shapes and limits statistical inference in economics, and how innovations in information theory may help develop statistical approaches in line with the social or systemic thrust of radical political economy.

Systems and Their Constituent Parts

The philosophical differences across currents in Economics and Political Economy involve longstanding controversies. By the time contemporary economic and social thought first confronted the relationship between individuals and the societies in which they exist, philosophers had been feuding over the nature of the relationship between systemic wholes and their individual constitutive parts since Aristotle's rejection of philosophical atomism in favor on an account of the emergence of human consciousness from distinctive arrangements of non-conscious matter (Caston 1997).

Reductionism, Dualism, and Emergence

The development of modern scientific enterprises brought new emphases and focus to those debates. Scientific progress proved to require the development of new, specialized fields of inquiry focused on what appeared to be deeply inter-related yet distinct domains of nature: fields like Physics, Chemistry, Biology, Ecology, etc., with distinct analytical categories, problems, and explanatory frameworks. Trying to understand the reasons for this proliferation of domains of inquiry and the boundaries between them, scientists and philosophers of science faced the problem of the relationship between "higher-level" entities or phenomena and the "lower-level" ones constituting them: chemical reactions and atoms; organisms and amino-acids; ecosystems and individual species; etc.

The relationship between high- and low-level entities is non-trivial and inter-esting whenever higher-level wholes are complex results of persistent arrange-ments, patterns of interaction, structural regularities, or of any other stable *relational* characteristics involving a number of their lower-level constituent parts (Lawson 2012). A crucial analytical question posed in those situations is the extent to which the properties and evolution of higher-level entities are autonomous or dependent on those of their constituent or lower-level ones. As noted by O'Connor, two antithetical philosophical stances can be identified in this connection: *reductionism* which rejects any notion of autonomy for higher-level entities; and *dualism*, which rejects their dependence on lower-level ones. Between these two polar stances lies the important notion of emergence (2021).

While introduced as a term by Lewes, a modern notion of emergence was already articulated by Mill, who identified higher-level, complex entities whose properties are not contained in the properties of their constituent parts (1875; 1843). Controversies about the precise nature of emergence, its relationship to notions of causality, and its implications for scientific inquiry have persisted in the philosophy of science since that time (Chalmers 2008). Most contemporary treatments recognize that emergent phenomena both entail definite mecha-nisms involving their constituent parts, and face observers with distinctively high-level features and properties.

Two types of emergence are recognized by philosophers of science – weak and strong. Chalmers defines weak emergence as settings where a, "high-level phenomenon arises from the low-level domain, but truths concerning that phe-nomenon are *unexpected* given the principles governing the low-level domain" (2008). Such phenomena are "amenable to high-level but not low-level expla-nation," forcing analysis to use concepts and taxonomies defined over states of the higher-level phenomenon as a matter of epistemic expediency.

Strong emergence, in contrast, occurs, "when the high-level phenomenon arises from the low-level domain, but truths concerning that phenomenon are *not deducible even in principle* from truths in the low-level domain" (Chalmers 2008). Here the adoption of high-level taxonomies and explanatory frameworks is more than a convenience; it reflects the very nature of higher-level phenomena with at least some properties and causal relations that are irreducible to lower-level mechanisms.

Constitutive Parts and Relational Interiority or Exteriority

Work on biological and social systems posed an important, converse problem in the relationship between higher-level systems and their lower-level parts: What is the nature of those constituent parts, particularly in relation to the regularities shaping the systemic whole? Here two broad possibilities arise, which have been termed *relational interiority and exteriority* (Deleuze and Parnet 2002).

Relational exteriority occurs when the intrinsic nature of lower-level entities does not depend on higher-level phenomena. The individual parts of the system exist and their properties are defined independently of relationships involved in the functioning of the higher-level system. In contrast, relational interiority occurs when the intrinsic nature of lower-level entities is defined by higher-level phenomena. The functioning of higher-level phenomena is internal to the very being of lower-level entities or parts.

The notion of emergence has often been associated exclusively with situations where higher-level wholes exhibit some irreducible properties, and lower-level parts also exhibit at least some measure of relational exteriority (de Landa 2011). If lower-level entities are entirely subsumed into the functioning of the whole, it may be generally possible to ignore those parts in analysis of the whole. In those cases, there is no emergence, and consideration of the properties of parts is simply a distraction from the identification of the correct level of analysis for those wholes.

Strong Emergence and Time

Despite its patent presence in a large number of systems (Laughlin 1998), strong emergence may be the most controversial element in debates about the relationship between high-level entities and their low-level constituents. It is often confused with dualist or even mystical rejections of the naturalistic or material foundations of emergent phenomena (Chalmers 2008). It also challenges reductionist biases pervading all fields of human inquiry (Jaynes 1989). This has ensured its continued contestation in a wide range of debates, including those about the nature of economic systems and the methodological approaches necessary to grapple with their functioning.

Lawson offers a compelling, materialist account of the strong emergence of higher-order entities or systems through processes of natural selection and evolution taking place over time or *diachronically* (2012).

All levels of reality see the continual reconfiguration of their elements or entities. While most reconfigurations have no lasting effects and dissipate, material reality is sufficiently rich that reconfigurations of numbers of lower-level entities or parts sometimes spontaneously result in orderings, arrangements, or structures that prove stable or persistent in their environments.[1] Those persistent relational schemes define new, emergent higher-order wholes existing as such over periods of time.

In those cases, the dynamic evolution of lower-order parts becomes bound up with the stability or reproduction of emergent wholes. Lower-order causal relations are of course not negated.[2] But the dynamic persistence of the emergent, higher-order whole involves new systemic causal relations that cannot be reduced to them. The system evolves as a whole. At any given point in time, its functioning involves relational realities beyond the properties of its parts, making it irreducible to them.

An important instance of processes of this kind involves systems whose members exhibit at least some measures of relational interiority in their evolution. In those cases, discernible regularities in the co-evolution of parts and wholes will generally be defined at the level of the whole and prove irreducible to the properties of the parts. Idiosyncratic properties may influence that co-evolution, but the dynamic functioning of the whole cannot be inferred, even in principle, from them alone.

Strong emergence is in all instances defined both by systemic relational schemes and by the flow of time. Irreducible systemic totalities are themselves irreducibly historical. In the presence of strong emergence, analysis of any given lower-order entity requires identification of the systemic totality of relations shaping its development. Understanding those relations, in turn, requires grappling with their own evolution over time. Systemic totality and evolution over time are fundamental and deeply intertwined analytical concerns.

Methodological Individualism

Modern social thought has been grappling with the relationship between wholes and parts in its object of study from its inception. Anticipating what was to become the dominant, *individualist* stance on that relationship in subsequent centuries, Thomas Hobbes counseled that, "it is necessary that we know the things that are to be compounded, before we can know the whole compound" (Hobbes 1973). The opposing stance was given early expression about a century later by Scottish Enlightenment thinkers like William Robertson, who proposed instead that the nature of individuals is fundamentally social and historical. In the hands of Karl Marx and Friedrich Engels, this was to become the integrated approach to the nature and development of individuals and societies known as *historical materialism*. This and the next section consider those stances in turn.

Individualist Reductionisms

In analysis of social and economic systems, the reductionist hypothesis is associated with notions of individualism. Even within the confines of social inquiry, the term individualism has a number of broadly related but distinct uses. It often denotes, for instance, a normative stance in political or economic inquiry, one where the evaluation of outcomes, "should be guided exclusively by the wishes of the individuals who are seen as the only bearer of values" (Schubert 2006).

Individualism can also refer to a methodological stance in approaches to socioeconomic systems. Lukes defines *methodological individualism* succinctly for all fields of social inquiry as, "a prescription for explanation, asserting that no purported explanations of social (or individual) phenomena are to count as explanations... or as [fundamental] explanations, unless they are couched wholly in terms of facts about individuals" (Lukes 1968).

This explanatory or epistemological stance needs to be distinguished from various forms of *ontological individualism* in the analysis of social phenomena. Proponents of ontological individualism contend that social properties are *exhaustively* determined by properties and interactions between individuals (Sudgen 2016). This often takes the form of the commonplace stance Lukes termed Truistic Social Atomism, the contention that since all economic and social life trivially involves the actions of individuals, it always *boils down* to those actions. Stronger forms of ontological individualism posit that social laws or regularities do not exist and that social aggregates are illusory abstractions (Lukes 1968).

Ontological individualism has two key corollaries. Even in cases where social categories are accepted as an analytical convenience, ontological individualism implies that all social properties *supervene* on individual ones: that is, social properties are understood to change only as a result of changes to individual ones (Sudgen 2016). It also implies relational exteriority for individuals in society. Taken together these stances define a strongly reductionist characterization of the evolution of social systems: historical change in social groups is reducible to changes in individuals, and changes in individuals are autonomous from their interactions, broader social relations, and institutions.

Canonical Reductionism

Mainstream economics is anchored philosophically on a specific blend of reductionist stances. Its substance and institutional dominance were described succinctly in a polemical intervention by Arrow, an often dissenting voice among leading 20th-century theorists,

> It is a touchstone of accepted economics that all explanations must run in terms of the actions and reactions of individuals. Our behavior in judging economic research, in peer review of papers and research, and in promotions, includes the criterion that in principle the behavior we explain and the policies we propose are explicable in terms of individuals, not of other social categories...The starting point for the individualist paradigm is the simple fact that all social interactions are after all interactions among individuals.
>
> *(Arrow 1994)*

Contemporary economics takes methodological individualism and Truistic Social Atomism as its fundamental epistemological and ontological stances.

Most economists will also recognize the existence of weakly emergent phenomena in economic life, and the notion that aggregate outcomes are often unexpected given individual actions and intentions. That is the thrust of Adam Smith's celebrated argument that competition ensures that the pursuit of selfish individual interests spontaneously yields socially desirable outcomes. It is also the substance of more recent prominent interventions like Schilling's work on how interactions over large numbers of individuals can give rise to aggregate outcomes that do not reflect the underlying intentions of any group of individuals (1978).

But this recognition is not taken to imply the existence of irreducibly social entities, facts, or causal relations. The dominant ontological view remains that "all social interactions are after all interactions among individuals." This is reflected in the conceptual structure not only of general-equilibrium and conventional game-theoretic analyses but also of the more general agent-based model scholars like Schilling advocate. Those approaches all seek to explain expected or unexpected social outcomes in terms of detailed descriptions of individuals, their circumstances and behavioral imperatives, and interactions.

Dissenting Individualisms

A few leading individualist scholars have sought to relax some of the strictures of ontological individualism, without transcending it entirely.

Arrow questioned the extent to which it is useful for economic theory to abstract from the nature and origins of institutions and particular forms of economic interaction. Pointing to the qualitative differences between the Cournot and Bertrand models of oligopolistic interactions, Arrow drew attention to the general lack of robustness game-theoretical exercises have across specifications of the rules of interaction. This underlines the importance of grappling with the nature and development of those rules. For Arrow, "the rules of the game are social," and, "[m]ore generally, individual behavior is always mediated by social relations. There are as much a part of the description of reality as is individual behavior" (1994).

Friedrich Hayek was skeptical about any observer's ability to grapple with the crucial details of individual economic behavior. For him, individual economic actions are irreducibly subjective and defined by beliefs and knowledge that are often inalienable. The search for economic explanations drawing on detailed descriptions of individual characteristics and actions is doomed, because some of the most important aspects of those characteristics and actions cannot be known by any external observer (Hayek 1943).

More importantly, the search for reductionist explanations of this kind misses entirely on the fact that, many of the institutions on which human achievements rest have arisen and are

> functioning without a designing and directing mind...and that the spontaneous collaboration of free men often creates things which are greater than their individual minds can ever fully comprehend.
>
> *(Hayek 1948)*

Institutions are historically emergent phenomena and irreducible to the characteristics of individuals. For Hayek, the price system in capitalist economies is the epitome of such emergent institutions, enabling societies to coordinate economic efforts in a world where no individual agent or observer can ever possess all the knowledge necessary for coordination.

Historical Materialism

Historical materialism offers a well-developed socio-historical alternative to all forms of individualist reductionism, based on the recognition that individuals are themselves irreducibly social and historical. The materialist approach to history follows directly from the consequent pursuit of this simple stance.

Historical materialism considers that "human essence is no abstraction inherent in each single individual. In its reality it is the ensemble of the social relations" (Marx and Engels 1969). To grapple with this essence, it advances an integrated conceptualization of individuals, social life, and historical development that places analysis of economic relations at the heart of all inquiry into the nature and evolution of human society.

Materialism proposes that all stable systems of economic organization or *modes of production* continuously draw from and reproduce irreducibly social relations and that those relations, in turn, shape all aspects of social life and the very nature of individuals, including their subjectivities,

> In the social production of their life, men enter into definite relations that are indispensable and independent of their will, relations of production

which correspond to a definite stage of development of their material productive forces. The sum total of these relations of production constitutes the economic structure of society, on which rises a legal and political superstructure and to which correspond definite forms of social consciousness. The mode of production of material life conditions the social, political, and intellectual life process in general. It is not the consciousness of men that determined their being, but, on the contrary, their social being that determines their consciousness.

(Marx 1977)

Echoing and developing on the early materialism of Scottish Enlightenment of thinkers like Robertson and Smith, Marx and Engels understood that a crucial social relation in all societies was that between classes – aggregate groups of individuals defined by definite roles in the production and distribution of the material things members of those societies have come to need (Meek 1954). Antagonisms and conflicts between social classes are understood not only to shape crucial economic outcomes but also to drive broader historical development. This is not to deny that individual agency influences economic and social outcomes. In fact, the agency of self-interested individuals in competitive factor markets is crucial to Marxist political economy. But Marxists generally understand its exercise in relation to class and historical realities, and its effects as emergent, social outcomes.

Within this historical-materialist stance, economic life appears as a determinant moment in the broader historical evolution of individuals and societies. Economic analysis is a lynchpin of social and historical inquiry, because and to the extent to which it can cast light on the ways relations of production and distribution shape the social, political, institutional, and cultural realities that condition the nature and historical development of human groups. This appreciation of economic analysis fundamentally shapes the analytical concerns and explanatory frameworks offered by Marxist political economy and related radical frameworks.

Profits and the Social Nature Capitalist Reproduction

Materialist approaches to capitalist economies grapple with the characteristic social relations defining their functioning and historical development. This requires seeing beyond immediate appearances in economies where self-regarding individuals interact voluntarily in markets and identifying how their functioning hinges upon and distinctively reproduces relations between social groups over time.

Since Adam Smith, all political economy has understood that the central driving force in capitalist economies is the pursuit of profits through the production of commodities – goods produced for sale in markets. Marxist political economy understands profit as irreducibly social, both in its nature and in its origins.

The nature of capitalist profit is bound up with the social role of money. In commodity economies, money is a distinctive form of social power (Lapavitsas 2005). Holders of money can command the products of social labor and social labor itself in markets. Profit is the characteristic form in which this social power reproduces itself, through the production and sale of commodities in ways that enable quantities of money to grow.

How capitalist economies sustain or reproduce social conditions under which profit-making is generally possible is a central concern for Marxist and radical approaches to political economy. Much like Adam Smith, Marx understood that profits are ultimately made possible by a system of property rights that defines two classes – capitalists in a position to mobilize capital goods to engage in production and workers with no direct, independent means to produce their means of subsistence and forced to sell their capacity to work to capitalists. The capitalist monopoly over control of the means of production defines two realities enabling profit extraction: it gives capitalists a crucial advantage in the bargain over the level of wages and gives them control over the organization and pace of production.

The class schism between wage earners and capitalists is not the only social relation early Marxist Political Economy recognized as crucial to the social reproduction of the possibility of profits. Marx and Engels themselves understood that capitalism relies directly on patriarchal systems and norms ensuring that the overwhelming proportion of household-reproduction and care labor is performed by women, without direct social reward. Marxist political economy also understands that patriarchal traditions and historically specific systems of social subordination by race, ethnicity, and regional origin play a crucial role in sustaining capitalist profits. Those social realities contribute to the development of what Marx termed *reserve armies of labor*, pools of workers with precarious and inferior conditions of employment that can be drawn upon to increase employment during upswings while moderating upward pressures on wages.

More recent Marxist and radical contributions have broadened the analysis of systems of social relations and institutions that sustain profit extraction. In any given national economy profit hinges on a large number of interrelated processes, including techniques of labor management (Braverman 1974), the forms taken by capitalist competition (Baran and Sweezy 1966), the reproduction of cultural norms and habits (Heilbroner 1985), the ways in which different goods and services are provided to wage earners (Lapavitsas 2009; dos Santos 2009), etc. As Aglietta argued, the evolution of these social relations, conventions, and institutions in specific national capitalist economies sees the historical, diachronic emergence of systems or regimes that prove stable in their ability to sustain profit extraction and accumulation over definite time periods (1976). Grappling with the nature and evolution of these social systems is a central analytical concern of contemporary Marxist and radical strains of political economy.

Diverging Ontologies: Theory and Practice

The philosophical differences between conventional and radical approaches to economic analysis are evident in their core theoretical frameworks, including their theories of price and conceptualizations of economic development. Individualist reductionism also defines the ways statistical inference is conventionally approached, creating significant social biases in much empirical work in economics. This concluding section briefly discusses these differences both to illustrate how pervasive they are in economic analysis and to motivate the need for explicitly socio-historical theoretical and empirical approaches in radical work on contemporary capitalism.

Prices, Scarcity, and Distribution

General-equilibrium analysis defines market prices with reductionist abstractions based on detailed descriptions of consumers' individual preferences, the production sets describing technically feasible combinations of productive inputs and outputs available to individual firms, and the "endowments" of factors of production taken as given to each individual consumer (Hahn 1980).

Scarcity and distribution are also conceived in individualist terms. Scarcity is defined in relation to the simple sum of individual endowments of labor and capital goods, individual production techniques, and individual consumption preferences. The distribution of produced goods depends on the distribution of endowed factors of production across individuals, and on equilibrium prices paid by firms for those factors of production. Individual endowments are taken as given and as idiosyncratic. And equilibrium factor prices are seen ultimately to reflect their scarcity and the specific forms taken by preferences and production sets (Garegnani 1990).

The difficulty with this abstraction is that it leads to explanations of market outcomes that hinge on things that are themselves the product of market and broader social interactions. Consumption preferences are social outcomes, shaped not only by the kinds of socio-referential processes considered by Veblen (2009) but also by the competitive efforts of capitalist enterprises themselves. The productive capacities of enterprises also reflect the history of competitive interactions (Smith 2000). And the distribution of labor skills and capital value across individuals is shaped not only by histories of social stratification of individuals by class, gender, race, and other categories (Mason 2023) but also by the social need to reproduce the capitalist monopoly over control of productive resources.

By abstracting from these social and historical processes in their explanations, Walrasian characterizations are conservative in thrust. Differences in economic outcomes that are irreducibly social in capitalist economies are cast as the result of given, idiosyncratic characteristics. The social nature and economic significance of the class schism between labor and capital disappear. It does not influence the governance and property rights of productive firms or income distribution. All individuals are socially equivalent, as consumers and as potential suppliers of both labor or capital goods, in line with their endowments and preferences.

Marx-Sraffa approaches offer a very different, social account of prices. They consider systems of *prices of production*, defined for abstract, long periods over which the competitive movement of all labor and capital across possible employments leads to an allocation of productive resources that equates wages and rate of return on investment. That allocation also defines a *productive system* consisting of input-output interrelations between sectors of a capitalist economy and the labor input required to produce each good (Foley 2008). Systems of prices of production are defined in terms of the long-period relationship between an economy's equilibrium wages, productive system, and rates of return on capital investment.

In this approach, scarcity, prices, and distribution are irreducibly social. Capital goods are not understood as scarce in themselves. They are outputs of the productive system, whose structure reflects the fundamental scarcities facing the economy. Prices reflect both the economy's production system and the distributional tradeoffs between labor and capital. And the functional distribution of income between labor and capital is influenced but not set by technological considerations. Its exact state is also shaped by social conflict over the net products of labor. Grappling with all moments of that conflict is cast as an integral part of economic analysis.

Historical Development and Underdevelopment

Conventional thinking about economic development is also deeply shaped by individualist reductionism. It does not start from the distinctive social realities shaping specific national economies, or from interdependences among national economies. Instead, development is typically cast as involving the same, universal set of transformations and stages in each individual national economy – bringing its characteristics in line with those of advanced economies (Rostow 1960). Differences in economic outcomes that are irreducibly global are again cast as the result of given, idiosyncratic, in this case national, characteristics (Solow, 1956). Acemoglu et al. offer a prominent, recent instance of this thinking, with an argument that differences in levels of development across national economies are primarily caused by differences in national institutions (2005).

Almost 50 years ago, Amin criticized this framing, under which,

The underdeveloped countries are seen as being like the 'developed' ones at an earlier stage of their development. In other words, the essential fact is left out, namely that the underdeveloped countries form part of a world system, that the history of their integration into this systems forged their special structure.

(1974)

Marxist and radical approaches to political economy consider capitalism as an irreducibly global system – an international division of labor composed of fundamentally interdependent national economies (Wallerstein 1974). The institutions, social structures, and broader regimes sustaining capitalist accumulation in each of those national economies reflect their specific position and relations within the wider, global whole. Capitalism exists as an evolving world system of interconnected, national varieties of capitalist accumulation.

This system is not equitable. Its development has consistently reproduced hierarchical patterns of subordination and resource extraction from less developed areas of the globe. Across the history of capitalism those patterns have involved direct control over resources in formal colonies; the export of capital from core economies (Hobson 1902, Lenin 1963); uneven international exchange (Prebisch 1950, Singer 1949); the integration of low-wage workers in poorer regions into international supply chains (Keaney 2022); and control over crucial institutions and conventions in international economic relations, including international monetary systems (Ali 2016; dos Santos and Dutt 2022; Vasudevan 2009).

As a result, advanced economies typically enjoy propitious conditions for accumulation, and for social compromise between domestic constituencies. Conversely, underdeveloped economies face systematic resource drains, international institutional realities that systematically disadvantage them, and much harsher tradeoffs in domestic politics and policy. As a result, stubborn patterns of underdevelopment and differences in labor productivity, living standards, and political power across national economies, have persisted across the history of capitalist development.

For radical political economy, those differences are a feature of global capitalism, not a "bug" due to the idiosyncrasies of developing economies (Bayliss et al. 2011). They are one of its core analytical concerns.

Beyond Representational Individualism

While the differences between mainstream and radical theoretical treatments of prices and economic development are widely acknowledged, the ways in which the philosophical differences between those two traditions shape formal statistical work are not generally understood – not even among radical scholars. Yet individualist reductionism also shapes how economists carry out work of statistical inference; in ways that reinforce individualist biases and prejudices. While the technical details are demanding, a simple example can illustrate how conventional approaches to inference do this, and how new tools from information theory can provide an alternative, social approach to statistical inference (dos Santos 2020, 2023).

Suppose researchers are interested in the determination of annual incomes across individuals in a population, and in the role economic characteristics (like education, experience, occupation) and elements of social identity (like gender, race, ethnicity, class background) play in those processes. Those processes are complex, involving the dynamic accumulation of effects over time, and irreducibly social (dos Santos and Wiener 2020). To investigate them, researchers draw inferences from what they can observe – individual measures of income (denoted by y_i), individual values for economic characteristics (denoted by E_i), and the elements of individuals' social identities (denoted by C_i).

In conventional approaches, the observed data is used to estimate parameter values in models like,

$$y_i = \beta_0 + \beta_1{}' E_i + \beta_2{}' C_i + \varepsilon_i$$

This common procedure is reductionist, involving a form of *representational individualism*: observed data is interpreted *as if* the complex social processes shaping individual incomes boil down to a single, linear relationship between individual characteristics. The above relationship is taken to hold independently for each and every individual in the system, casting the relationship between y, C, and E as varying across individuals only by an "error term" ε_i, assumed to be unrelated to all the variables.[3] All interactions and associations in processes generating incomes are reduced to values of parameters β_1 and β_2, measuring the average effects individual characteristics E_i and C_i have on incomes, within the terms of the model. Estimates of those parameters are calculated from individual values of the variables and their mean values across all individuals, ignoring other statistical properties in the data.

This procedure provides poor bases for analysis of interdependences or irreducibly social determinations, like those emphasized by Stratification Economics in relation to the economic effects of social systems of subordination and discrimination by gender, race, ethnicity, or class background (Mason 2023). What if the influence of occupations on incomes hinges on the proportion of members of subaltern social groups in that occupation? Or what if attributions of productivity to individual workers are systematically shaped by social expectations and stereotypes for the groups to which they are deemed to belong? In all such cases, conventional approaches cast differences due to irreducibly social realities in terms of individual characteristics. Here again, the political thrust of individualist analysis is conservative, as it tends to obscure the operation and consequences of pervasive systems of social subordination.

A body of recent work in mathematical political economy is drawing on concepts and tools from information theory to develop an approach to inference that transcends all forms of representational individualism. Instead of starting with models and making statistical inferences by treating the observed data as a series of autonomous individual values of the variables, the approach makes inferences based on the overall distributions $f(y, E, C)$ of the observed variables.

Distributions describe the share of observed individuals taking on each possible combination of values for (y, E, C). They are social properties of the collection of those individuals, taken as a whole, and are irreducible to individual values of the variables.[4] The concept of *entropy* and its generalizations can define a non-reductionist, social approach to statistical inference about the processes generating incomes from observed distributions $f(y, E, C)$.

Entropy is a measure of observer uncertainty implicit in any statistical distribution. The entropy in the distribution of income across all observed individuals, $f(y)$, measures, in informational units like binary bits, how much uncertainty somebody who can only observe that distribution has about individual incomes. The mutual information between income and a covariate like race measures how much of that total uncertainty is removed on average when it is also possible to observe each individuals' race, and to consider the distributions of income for each racial group separately. It is a formal measure of how much is learned about all individual values of y once income distributions are organized by race.

The mutual information between income and a characteristic like race (or any other element of C) is a total, social measure of association between income and race – including both indirect effects, where race is associated with economic covariates in E that in turn shape incomes, and direct effects of race on incomes. Its measure is a property of the observed distribution and is well-defined independently of the mechanisms and associations through which this total is established. As a result, learning more about the details of those mechanisms and associations does not challenge its validity. Multivariate generalizations of the mutual information define measures allowing researchers to consider those details, including measures of how much is learned about incomes from observation of an economic characteristic like occupation, when the race and gender of all individuals are already known, or measures of the informational intersection between income, occupation, and race across the population.

Crucially, all informational measures of association and interaction are systemic or social. They are properties not of individual values of the variables but of the social distributions $f(y, E, C)$, providing measures of statistical association and interaction in line with the radical understanding that the regularities in the functioning of capitalist economies are irreducibly social. Their use can help inform the development of explicitly social theorizations, not only of the relationships and interactions between income, economic, and social-identity characteristics considered in this example but of any other set of relationships and interactions in capitalist economies generating observable data. As such, they make a useful addition to the plural set of explanatory frameworks and empirical tools that radical political economics can draw upon as it works to see past the strictures and biases of individualist approaches to economic analysis, and grapples with the distinctive nature, social content, and dynamic evolution of contemporary capitalism.

Notes

1 This may involve persistence or stability of a system in self-contained equilibrium, like a crystal lattice; or far-from-equilibrium systems requiring constant external inputs, like biological organisms existing within broader ecological and physical systems.
2 As Engels put it, they are merely "pushed into the background by other, higher laws.".
3 Generalizations by hierarchical models or models with interaction terms do not fundamentally address the difficulties here. They merely relax the individualist strictures imposed on inference.
4 To see this, consider a simple one-variable example: A group of individuals where 23 percent are foreign born and 77 are native. Those population shares define a distribution of individuals across two values for their place of birth. The resulting distribution is a social property of the group of individuals, not of any given individual.

References

Acemoglu, Daron, Simon Johnson, and James Robinson, Institutions as a Fundamental Cause of Long-Run Growth. *Handbook of Economic Growth*. v. 1. New York Elsevier, 2005. 385–472. New York: Elsevier, 2005.

Aglietta, Michel, *A Theory of Capitalist Regulation*. London: NLB, 1976.

Ali, Mona, Global imbalances & asymmetric returns to US foreign assets: fitting the missing pieces of the US BoP puzzle. *International Review of Applied Economics*. v. 30 (2). 2016. 167–187.

Amin, Samir, *Accumulation on a World Scale – A Critique of the Theory of Underdevelopment*. New York: Monthly Review Press, 1974.

Arrow, Kenneth, Methodological Individualism and Social Knowledge. *The American Economic Review*. v. 84 (2). 1994. 1–9.

Baran, Paul and Paul Sweezy, *Monopoly Capital*. New York: Monthly Review Press, 1966.

Bayliss, Kate, Ben Fine, and Elisa Van Waeyenberge, *The Political Economy of Development*. London: Pluto Press, 2011.

Braverman, Harry, *Labor and Monopoly Capital*. New York: Monthly Review Press, 1974.

Bryant, Levy, Nick Srnicek, Graham Harman, *The Speculative Turn: Continental Materialism and Realism*. Melbourne, 2011.

Caston, Victor, Epiphenomenalisms, Ancient and Modern. *The Philosophical Review*. v. 106 (3). 1997. 309–363.

Chalmers, David, Strong and Weak Emergence. *The Re-Emergence of Emergence: The Emergentist Hypothesis from Science to Religion.* Oxford: Oxford University Press, 2008. 244–254.

de Landa, Manuel, Emergence, Causality, and Realism. *The Speculative Turn: Continental Materialism and Realism.* Melbourne, 2011.

Deleuze, Gilles and Claire Parnet, *Dialogues II.* New York, Columbia University Press, 2002.

dos Santos, Paulo, On the Content of Banking in Contemporary Capitalism. *Historical Materialism.* v. 17 (2). 2009. 180–213.

dos Santos, Paulo, Statistical Equilibria in Economic Systems: Socio-Combinatorial or Individualist-Reductionist Characterizations? *European Physical Journal Special Topics.* v. 229. 2020. 1603–1622.

dos Santos, Paulo, Information as a Probabilistic Measure of Generative Heterogeneity: Key Results and Applications to Complex Socioeconomic Systems. *New School for Social Research*, 2023.

dos Santos, Paulo and Devika Dutt, A Multilateral International Monetary System. *The New International Economic Order.* v. 16. Progressive International, 2022.

dos Santos, Paulo and Noe Wiener, By the Content of Their Character? Comparative Group Income Heterogeneity and Socio-Economic Discrimination. *Journal of Mathematical Sociology.* v. 44 (1). 2020. 12–41.

Engels, Friedrich, Ludwig Feuerbach and the End of Classical German Philosophy. *Selected Works.* v. 2. Moscow: Foreign Language Publishing House, 1958.

Foley, Duncan, The Long-Period Method and Marx's Theory of Value. *Manuscript.* New School for Social Research, 2008.

Garegnani, Pierangelo, Sraffa: Classical versus Marginalist Analysis. *Essays on Piero Sraffa.* London: Routledge, 1990.

Hahn, Frank, General Equilibrium Theory. *The Public Interest.* 1980. Reprinted in *National Affairs.* v. 57. 2023.

Hayek, Friedrich, The Facts of the Social Sciences. *Ethics.* v. 54 (1). 1943. 1–13.

Hayek, Friedrich, Individualism, True and False. *Individualism and Economic Order.* Chicago: University of Chicago Press, 1948.

Heilbroner, Robert. *The Nature and Logic of Capitalism.* New York: WW Norton & Company, 1985.

Hobbes, De Corpore. *The Light of Reason.* London: Fontana, 1973.

Hobson, John. *Imperialism: a Study.* New York City: James Pott & Company, 1902.

Jaynes, Edwin, Delaware Lecture. *E. T. Jaynes: Papers on Probability, Statistics and Statistical Physics.* New York City: Springer, 1989. 87–113.

Keaney, Michael, Book Review: Value Chains: The New Economic Imperialism. *Review of Radical Political Economics.* v. 54 (2). 2022. 255–258.

Lapavitsas, Costas, The Emergence of Money in Commodity Exchange, or Money as Monopolist of the Ability to Buy. *Review of Political Economy.* v. 17 (4). 2005. 549–569.

Lapavitsas, Costas, Financialised Capitalism: Crisis and Financial Expropriation. *Historical Materialism.* v. 17 (2). 2009. 114–148.

Laughlin, Robert, Fractional Quantization. *Nobel Lecture.* 1998.

Lawson, Tony, Ontology and the study of social reality: emergence, organisation, community, power, social relations, corporations, artefacts and money. *Cambridge Journal of Economics.* v. 36 (2). 2012. 345–385.

Lenin, Vladimir. Imperialism: The Highest Stage of Capitalism. *Lenin's Selected Works.* v. 1. Moscow, Progress Publishers, 1963. 667–766.

Lewes, George, *Problems of Life and Mind (1875).* Charleston: BiblioBazaar, 2009.

Lukes, Steven, Methodological Individualism Reconsidered. *British Journal of Sociology.* v. 19 (2). 1968. 119–129.

Marx, Karl, *A Contribution to the Critique of Political Economy (1859).* Moscow: Progress Publishers, 1977.

Marx, Karl and Friedrich Engels, Theses on Feuerbach (1845). *Marx and Engels Selected Works.* v. 1. Moscow: Progress Publishers, 1969.

Mason, Patrick, *The Economics of Structural Racism.* Cambridge: Cambridge University Press, 2023.

Meek, Ronald, The Scottish Contribution to Marxist Sociology, *Economics and Ideology and Other Essays.* London: Chapman and Hall LTD, 1954.

Mill, John Stuart, *A System of Logic, Ratiocinative and Inductive (1843).* Honolulu: University Press of the Pacific, 2002.

O'Connor, Timothy, Emergent Properties. *The Stanford Encyclopedia of Philosophy.* 2021.

Prebisch, Raul, *The Economic Development of Latin America and its Principal Problems.* Santiago: Economic Commission for Latin America and the Caribbean, 1950.

Rostow, Walt, *The Stages of Economic Growth: A Non-Communist Manifesto.* Cambridge: Cambridge University Press, 1960.

Schilling, Thomas, *Micromotives and Macrobehaviour.* New York: Norton, 1978.

Schubert, Christian, A Note on the Principle of 'Normative Individualism'. *Papers on Economics and Evolution 2005–17.* Philipps University Marburg: Department of Geography, 2006.

Singer, Hans, Economic progress in under-developed countries. *Social Research.* v. 16 (1). 1949. 1–11.

Smith, Adam, *The Wealth of Nations (1776).* New York: Modern Library, 2000.

Solow, Robert, A Contribution to the Theory of Economic Growth. *The Quarterly Journal of Economics.* v. 70 (1). 1956. 65–94.

Sudgen, Robert, Ontology, Methodological Individualism, and the Foundations of the Social Sciences. *Journal of Economic Literature.* v. 54 (4). 2016. 1377–1389.

Vasudevan, Ramaa, Dollar Hegemony, Financialization, and the Credit Crisis. *Review of Radical Political Economics.* v. 41 (3). 2009. 291–304.

Veblen, Thornstein, *The Theory of the Leisure Class (1899).* Auckland: The Floating Press, 2009.

Wallerstein, Immanuel, *The Modern World-System.* New York: Academic Press, 1974.

PART III
Post-Capitalist Futures

16

DEMOCRATIC PLANNED SOCIALISM

Moving Beyond Capitalism to Support and Promote Human Development

Al Campbell

Introduction

Two points of confusion immediately thrust themselves into almost all discussions on what socialism is. These two issues need to be addressed before one can even begin to meaningfully consider the question.

The simpler of the two issues is to indicate the common confusion between two different things that too often are, and must not be, conflated. The first of these is what this short chapter is intended as, an introduction to a clear statement of the general modern concept of socialism, as it has been (and continues to be) historically developed by its advocates for a better world. The second and very different thing is to look at the very broad spectrum of social systems in the real world, which at one time or another have self-declared that they were building socialism, and then try to define socialism from this spectrum of experiences. There are two reasons why the second approach will not be pursued in this chapter. The first and most mechanical reason is that to try to do so would require a book-length study, which is precluded for this chapter. There were almost 20 such countries which actually developed non-capitalist economies, plus a large number of other self-declared "socialist countries" at times, especially in Africa and Latin America, which in fact never eliminated their capitalist economies. All of these were different, and so all would need to be treated separately and in detail. Some politically simplistic labeling of them such as "not socialist because they were Stalinist and non-democratic" for those with non-capitalist economies, or "not socialist because they remained capitalist" notwithstanding their benefits for their poor for the others, would be no more than (correct) labeling, not a determination of the nature of socialism from their experiences. But the deeper reason for not trying to establish the

DOI: 10.4324/9781003366690-19

concept of socialism from real-world experiences is that it would be a blatant case of circular reasoning. One cannot evaluate what real-world practices contributed to or precluded the building of socialism until one has a concept of socialism to compare the real-world practices to, in order to evaluate their "socialist or anti-socialist nature." Even to carry out the simplistic labeling of real-world experiences suggested above requires that one have a concept of socialism to use to give those labels. This chapter will then avoid this common confusion and address only the necessary first step of giving the fundamental nature of today's concept of socialism, as it congealed originally in the nineteenth century and then has continuously evolved until today.

The second point of massive confusion concerning the consideration of "what is socialism," even once one has clearly established that one means "what is the concept of socialism," is that the definition of the concept of socialism is not like the definition of, for example, a quadratic equation. For such a concept, there is a universal social agreement as to the nature of the concept, to the extent that anyone advocating a different concept is considered "to have made an error." That is not the case for many concepts central to the debates in the various social sciences. There is a plethora of somewhat different concepts of socialism.

Among this large number of different concepts of socialism, however, many aspects of many of them overlap. This chapter will present a concept of socialism rooted in three different types of ideas about what a system must be like to be considered socialist, ideas common to the majority of modern concepts of socialism. The first ideas concern the concept of human nature, ideas that underlie why socialist systems are called "socialist." The second type of ideas about the definition of socialism concerns the plethora of socialism's goals. The final type of ideas determining the concept of socialism are the various organizational and operation principles people maintain would constitute a socialist system. Of the scores of these in the literature, this chapter will consider here as illustrations three that are widely considered central for a system to be considered socialist. The last of these three also brings up the important point concerning the common confusion between the concept socialism, the topic of this chapter, and a concept that builds on socialism but then goes beyond it, communism.

A fundamental division exists in the spectrum of concepts of socialism between those put forward by people who advocate for replacing the current organization of society with a social organization consistent with their concept of socialism and those put forward by people who have created negative concepts of socialism in order to defend capitalism against the changes advocated by socialism. Shared aspects of various different concepts of socialism of this latter type are familiar to anyone who has grown up in the extremely pejorative US news and educational environments: lack of personal choice concerning anything, lack of democracy and uniformity, lack of variety in all aspects of life, lack of material well-being, lack of freedom, and so on. These concepts of socialism share almost no basic aspects with the many different concepts of socialism of its advocates. As advocates use the word socialism, this "US brainwashing" is not "socialism." This "non-socialist concept of socialism"[1] will not be discussed in this chapter.

This still leaves a very broad spectrum of different concepts of socialism among its advocates. This chapter will elaborate on a meta-concept called Democratic Planned Socialism. Section 2 will briefly indicate two aspects of the concept of human nature inherent in the goals of Democratic Planned Socialism. Section 3 will indicate what the goals of Democratic Planned Socialism are, which are so fundamental to its nature. Section 4 will then indicate three general organizational and operational principles for Democratic Planned Socialism that further indicate what it is. The meta-concept of Democratic Planned Socialism differs from a number of other socially relevant meta-concepts in the spectrum of concepts of socialism.

Two Aspects of Human Nature

The first "background socialist assumption" on human nature is that humans by their nature are a *collective and social species-being*. Many of the goals and operational principles looked at in Sections 3 and 4 rest to differing degrees on this assumption. A somewhat extended quote from early modern socialist writings in 1844 gives a particularly clear example of this socialist assumption about human nature. It also highlights a number of the important negative consequences seen today which result from a social organization inconsistent with this aspect of human nature.

> Since *human* nature is the *true community* of men[2], by manifesting their *nature* men *create*, produce, the *human community*, the social entity, which is no abstract universal power opposed to the single individual, but is the essential nature of each individual, his own activity, his own life, his own spirit, his own wealth... as long as man does not recognise himself as man, and therefore has not organised the world in a human way, this *community* appears in the form of *estrangement*, because its *subject*, man, is a being estranged from himself... To say that *man* is estranged from himself, therefore, is the same thing as saying that the *society* of this estranged man is a caricature of his *real community*, of his true species-life, that his activity therefore appears to him as a torment, his own creation as an alien power, his wealth as poverty, the *essential bond* linking him with other men as an unessential bond,... and he himself, the lord of his creation, as the servant of this creation.
>
> *(Marx[3] 1844a: emphasis in the original)*

As a part of this discussion of socialism's understanding of the collective and social nature of humans, it is important to consider its view of the individual.

This is particularly important today, given the currently much-discussed important contribution of *hyper-individualism* to the social breakdown of "the modern world," for example, to the current social implosion of the United States.[4] With the birth of neoliberalism, Margaret Thatcher took this assumption to a new level of popular presentation in 1987 with her claim that there is no such thing as society, only individuals and families.

A standard attack on socialism by the defenders of capitalism is that it subordinates the interests of the *individual* to those of the *collective*, and effectively dissolves the individual into the collective. It will become apparent in the next section that the goals of socialism are exactly the opposite, to create a social system that supports and promotes the development of all individuals to their full potential. But socialism's understanding of the individual, and its understanding of the false concept of the individual that underpins capitalism, is conceptually deeper and richer than just this. Capitalism's "isolated individual"[5] consists of an individuality that not only exists independently of the existence of anyone else or society, but further, one where individual interests in general are opposed to society's interests. Equivalent to its understanding of human nature as inherently social, socialism to the contrary understands individuals as "social individuals." An obvious point concerning the concept of social individuals is that human individuals are individuals whose individuality is shaped in part by society. But a little reflection on human nature and human existence indicates the social nature of their individuality goes deeper than that. Given their innate species-abilities, if individual humans could not interact socially, they could not even survive in the world. Again, this issue of the relation of the individual to the collective was specifically and carefully addressed already in early modern socialist theory:

> Above all we must avoid postulating "society" again as an abstraction *vis-à-vis* the individual. The individual *is the social being*. His manifestations of life – even if they may not appear in the direct form of *communal* manifestations of life carried out in association with others – *are* therefore an expression and confirmation of *social life*. Man's individual and species-life are not *different*, however much – and this is inevitable – the mode of existence of the individual is a more *particular* or more *general* mode of the life of the species, or the life of the species is a more *particular* or more *general* individual life.
>
> *(Marx 1844b: emphasis in the original)*

The point is rather that private interest is itself already a socially determined interest and can be attained only within the conditions laid down by society and with the means provided by society and is therefore tied to the reproduction of these conditions and means. It is the interest of private persons;

but its content, as well as the form and means of its realization, are given by social conditions that are independent of them all.

(Marx 1857)

To understand what socialism is, its second assumption about human nature that must be understood is that a *differentia specifica* of humans is that they have some capabilities that no other animals have. Two of these understandings of human nature that are of central importance to the concept of socialism are that humans have the ability to imagine future states of reality different from the existing reality, and that humans have the capability to employ rational thought, or reason, to decide how they want to realize whatever future state is desired. Socialism holds that beyond the ability to act, which is common to most animals, *humans can act consciously*. These characteristics could be called "specifically human," or as in the second quote to follow, "truly human."

Although the direct topic in the following work from 1867 is human labor, this early modern socialist discussion brings out clearly this background assumption about human nature:

We are not now dealing with those primitive instinctive forms of labour that remind us of the mere animal. ... We presuppose labour in a form that stamps it as exclusively human. A spider conducts operations that resemble those of a weaver, and a bee puts to shame many an architect in the construction of her cells. But what distinguishes the worst architect from the best of bees is this, that the architect raises his structure in imagination before he erects it in reality. At the end of every labour process, we get a result that already existed in the imagination of the labourer at its commencement. He not only effects a change of form in the material on which he works, but he also realizes a purpose of his own ...

(Marx 1867)

All animals are active, and they even transform their environment in accord with their needs. A socialist understanding of human nature and one that is important to the goals and organizational principles of socialism, however, holds that only humans do so *consciously*, in that many of their actions are linked to thought, contemplation, and reason, in a way that no other animal is capable of.

While the following quote from 1878 indicates very specifically one of the goals of socialism that will be discussed in the next section, here it is being presented *not* to consider that goal of socialism, but rather only as a second quote to underline socialism's second fundamental belief about human nature, about the human capability for *conscious* action.

With the seizing of the means of production by society, production of commodities is done away with, and, simultaneously, the mastery of the product
over the producer. .... The struggle for individual existence disappears. ....
The whole sphere of the conditions of life which environ man, and which
have hitherto ruled man, now comes under the dominion and control of
man, who for the first time becomes the real, conscious lord of nature,
because he has now become master of his own social organization. ... Only
from that time will man himself, with full consciousness, make his own history – only from that time will the social causes set in movement by him
have, in the main and in a constantly growing measure, the results intended
by him. It is humanity's leap from the kingdom of necessity to the kingdom
of freedom.

(Engels 1987)

With these two background socialist assumptions on human nature established, which will be manifested repeatedly throughout the next two sections,
the chapter will now return to the direct consideration of the question "what is
socialism?" First, a fundamental determinant of the nature of any social system is its goals. Section 3 will consider the goals of socialism. But despite their
fundamental importance, the goals of a social system by themselves do not
fully determine its nature. What are envisioned as appropriate ways to achieve
those goals also determine the nature of the social system, and Section 4 will
consider three such organizational principles of Democratic Planned Socialism.

The Goals and the Goal of Socialism

In the quote by Engels above one sees three from among the plethora of broad
goals that were cited frequently in the 19th and 20th centuries (and still are
today). The first was that "man makes his own history." This is tied to the concept of human nature that was considered above that humans have the potential to act consciously, and from that gain increased collective self-determination
over their social existence. Two other common expressions of this same idea
are that "people collectively become the *subjects* of history as opposed to being
its *objects*," and that "people collectively become the masters of their own
fate." The second goal of socialism indicated in the quote by Engels is that
humans "become the master of [their] own social organization." Other expressions commonly used to indicate goals of socialism roughly equivalent to this
are "self-determination," "self-governance," "socialist democracy," or even
simply "democracy." The third commonly indicated goal of socialism in the
quote is "freedom," often expressed roughly equivalently as "liberty," or by the
act that freedom or liberty is obtained by, "self-emancipation."

While this last goal of socialism is often referred to simply as "emancipation," it is important for this chapter's focus on understanding socialism to
briefly pause in the listing of goals of socialism to underline why the prefix

"self" is needed for all goals that are actions for constructing socialism. It is a profound misunderstanding of socialism to see it as only concerned with material well-being and material equality. Cows have great material well-being in that the drive for maximum profits means they get all the food they want, immediate care for any medical problems, housing suitable to protect their health and well-being, and maybe even air conditioning for milk cows to boost their production if that passes a cost-benefit analysis. But "being materially taken care of" by Plato's philosopher kings or by "Father of the Nations" Joseph Stalin is inconsistent with the socialist goal that has been considered of collective self-determination, of becoming the collective masters of all the institutions that society consists of. Developing the potential to be more fully human definitionally (by the socialist definition of being human) requires being the collective active agents in determining everything about social existence, since such collective self-determination is, as previously seen, something specifically human. In contrast with the drivers of capitalism that are presented as acting on the isolated individual, emancipation must be collective self-emancipation, governance must be collective self-governance, and so on.

Other broad goals of socialism often used, many of them also connected to the previous points on socialism's assumptions on human nature, include human development (of each individual, and of the human species); becoming more fully human, or "truly human"; developing humans' potential, or abilities, or capabilities; meaningful work (that will develop us as individuals and as a species); free human activity; solidarity; equality; an end to oppression (a negative formulation of the goal of freedom); an end to exploitation; variety; maximizing individual choices consistent with the well-being of society; and many more. In addition to such general goals, there are many common more concrete goals, which could be thought of as supporting and promoting the more general goals just listed. These include universal health care, universal free education, abolition of child labor, humanly dignified housing, social control of production, various aspects of social security, and an additional plethora of other such concrete goals.

By the end of the 20th century, capitalism's operational goal of production for the purpose of expanding capital – roughly, "production for profit" – had initiated massive and rapidly escalating environmental destruction. In line with the goals of socialism being determined by humanity's drive to replace the practices of capitalism which harm humanity with non-harmful ones, protecting the environment and ecological sustainability have become additional standard goals of almost all concepts of socialism for the 21st century.

In line with these observations, it can be useful when talking about the desirability of socialism quite abstractly to think of it as having a single fundamental goal, with the plethora of goals just indicated then being thought of as subgoals. As subgoals of socialism, they still are goals that socialism is intended to achieve better than capitalism, but now instead of simply being postulated as goals of socialism, they obtain their justification as subgoals from being considered to contribute to achieving the single postulated fundamental goal. This author frequently refers to the central goal of socialism as "human development," as do numerous other advocates of socialism.

In practice, it makes no difference for using socialism's goals in order to evaluate some proposed policies if one talks of a plethora of goals or of a single goal with subgoals. If one were to consider the former and some policy supports and promotes them all, then that policy supports and promotes socialism. But a problem with having multiple goals arises when some policy supports one and harms another. A classic example for economists is the Federal Reserve's claimed dual goal of fighting inflation and maintaining full employment. In practice if some proposed policy promotes one goal and harms another, society then has to decide what it considers to be the tradeoff between the goals, how much gain for the one must result to offset the loss for the other. But talking of socialism as having a single broad goal such as human development, and hence posing the question whether the policy promotes or harms this single goal, does not avoid this problem in any way. To decide if human development is increased or decreased, one needs to decide if the policy's increased contribution to it from one subgoal contributes more or less than the loss to it from the other subgoal, which is obviously exactly the same social choice.[6]

Another dimension of looking at the goal of socialism as human development is to, in addition to seeing it as the goal of the desired better society, see it in relation to the history of humanity. Eric Fromm presented it concisely this way in 1961:

... the history of mankind is the history of increasing human development.
(Fromm 1961)

In an equally terse indication of this goal of human development in 1970 Paulo Freire also included the historical dimension, and then went beyond that to present the crucial dimension of the goal of human development as rooted in the very nature of being human – not only do we pursue being more human, but we do so exactly because it is part of the nature of being human to do so: it is

... man's ontological and historical vocation to be more fully human.
(Freire 1992)

Three General Organizational and Operational Principles for Democratic Planned Socialism

First, a comment on the nature of the ideas in this section of this chapter's discussion of what socialism is. It would be a violation of the fundamental socialist concept of collective self-determination to specify exact institutional and organizational details that members of society must implement to create a socialist society. Reducing members of society to being mechanical implementors of a predetermined script is the direct opposite of socialism's goal of empowering them to be the collective masters of their own fate.

Establishing *principles* for social organization (hereafter, "organizational principles") considered necessary to achieve the goals of socialism, however, does not suffer from that problem. A wide variety of institutional and organizational details would be consistent with these organizational principles, giving rise to a heterogeneity of socialisms, exactly as there is a heterogeneity of capitalisms. The nature of these principles are not "recipes" or "blueprints" for humans to follow in order to build and operate a socialist society. To the contrary, these principles are precisely part of the subject of this chapter, establishing what socialism is. To be concrete on what this claim means exactly, consider the first such principle that will be discussed, social planning of social production. This is not being put forward as "what the social agents must do." To the contrary, to generate socialism, the social actors must collectively decide for themselves how exactly they will organize and operate their society. If that choice is not consistent with the socialist organizational principle of social planning of social production, however, then what they have decided to create will not be socialism. These organizational principles are not scripts for action, but rather part of the specification of what socialism is, and what is not socialism.

In his detailed preface to his *Envisioning Real Utopias*, Erik Olin Wright clearly indicated the important "mid-level role" of such socialist organizational and operational principles in specifying what socialism is.

> … workable institutional principles that could inform emancipatory alternatives to the existing world. This falls between a discussion simply of the moral values that motivate the enterprise [of indicating possible emancipatory alternatives] and the fine-grained details of institutional characteristics.
>
> *(Wright 2010)*

The three general organizational and operational principles to be discussed here to further establish the concept of Democratic Planned Socialism are reflected in its name. The first is social planning of social production, and this will include discussions of social ownership of the means of production, and the contentious issues of markets and money in socialism. The second is democracy and will include discussions of classes and the much-debated nature of the state in socialism. The final is the principle of social organization and operation that differentiates the concept of socialism from the concept of communism.

Social planning of social production

The socialist argument for the necessity of social planning for social production is not an "economic reductionist" argument that this will raise human productivity and hence output of socially produced goods and services, though that is an expected result. To the contrary, the socialist argument is that this is necessary in line with socialism's goal of human development and socialism's understanding of human nature. Planning in one way or another is the specifically human way humans do everything in their lives. In capitalism, social production is determined by the mechanical summation of the decisions on what to produce (and how to do so, and how many people to employ, etc.) in pursuit of their profits by the minority of society that own the means of production.[7]

It was almost universally accepted by advocates of socialism in the 20th century who understood socialism as a system contrary to capitalism[8] that social planning of social production required social ownership of the means of production. This follows immediately because whoever owns the means of production is, by their property rights, empowered to plan how they will be used and hence determine social production.

Following the failure of the dominant attempts in the 20th century to build socialism without markets,[9] the century ended and the next one began with discussions of the possibility of using markets to build socialism. Using the socialist reason for social planning of social production just given, and understanding markets as any place where equivalents are exchanged, there is no theoretical reason one could not build "socialism with markets," using markets as tools for the distribution of intermediate goods in the process of production[10] and of final goods for consumption. The operational principle is that the economy be fully planned by society to attempt to produce what it decides to produce. Whatever tools are used are appropriate as long as they allow such planning and related control. Much of the opposition to using markets in socialism comes from a confusion of the concept of "markets as a site for the exchange of equivalents,"[11] with "markets required by the circuits of capital" in capitalism. Not only are these two different things, but the exploitation that occurs in capitalism, which is its *raison d'être*, doesn't actually occur in the market exchanges of equivalents in any case.[12] The many variants of what has become known as "market socialism," however, are driven by individual production units deciding what to produce to maximize the returns to themselves, with some subsequent redistribution by the government to reduce the inequality in revenue this inevitably produces. Unlike in "socialism with markets," social production under "market socialism" does not involve social planning, and so it is not socialism. The various models of market socialism are fundamentally just particular variants of left social-democratic capitalist production.

Note that accepting that socialism could use the tool of markets to organize parts of its social production and distribution is not an assertion that it has to, or even that doing so would necessarily be more efficient than any conceivable non-market system. With modern information technology, it would be possible to do what the old unsuccessful material balance systems could not do. The most worked-out presentation of this argument has been made over the course of three decades by Cockshott and Cottrell, beginning with its first comprehensive presentation in 1993 (Cockshott and Cottrell 1993). However, in direct opposition to the twentieth century, the issue of if one could have efficient material balance planning for socialism is socially moot today, in the sense that that the governments that have self-declared that they are working to build some form of socialism – China, Vietnam, Laos, and Cuba – have all rejected full material balance planning in favor a planned economy that includes major roles for markets.[13]

The idea that money is at the root of exploitation of the poor by the rich goes back to long before Jesus threw the money changers out of the temple. Its incarnation among modern anti-capitalists appeared already in the early 19th century in the work of many social critics such as Pierre-Joseph Proudhon, and it continues to this day. Socialists understand that any system of production that has any markets will generate a form of money appropriate for itself, different from money in any different system of production, in order to resolve the coincidence of wants problem inherent to markets. There is no conflict with any of its goals or operating principles that would prevent a socialist system from having money to facilitate exchange, and it would have to have money appropriate for its system if it had markets.

Socialist democracy

The socialist goal that "people become the collective masters of their social institutions" implies democracy, where democracy is understood broadly in the sense one finds in any standard dictionary definition of democracy along the lines of "a process in which all people in a decision-making group participate equally, directly or through representatives they select, in the determination of the group's choice and its implementation." Such a socialist democracy is understood to be more democratic than capitalist democracy (also called "bourgeois democracy") could possibly be for two different reasons. In the first place, under capitalism, "democracy stops at the 'factory gate'," where working people spend half their waking hours. Property rights in the means of production that are essential for the process of exploitation, which is the purpose and core of capitalism, mean that decisions on social production are made by the minority of society that owns capital, and not by the whole society, as required by democracy. It is not possible for capitalism to allow all production units to operate democratically, or the first act of the majority workers would likely be to choose to end their exploitation, and that would end capitalism. In the second place, for all to be able to participate equally in decision-making, there cannot be structural power differences among them. In all class societies the ruling class has vastly greater power than the subaltern classes. With its end of exploitation, socialism will be history's first classless society. As history's first classless society, socialism will be the first organization of society in human history that can realize this aspect of the greater democracy just defined.

Socialism's requirement of socialist democracy, combined with humanity's collective social species-nature, rejects the incorrect understanding that with socialism the state would "wither away." The correct insight contained within this misunderstanding is that because in any class society the primary function of the state is the oppression of the subaltern by the ruling class, the withering away of classes in socialism will necessarily cause "the state *as it has been*" to wither away. The state, however, also carries out many other roles that are of secondary importance to the ruling class in a class society, but nevertheless are essential for any society to function. Because humans have collective social interests at local, regional, national, and international levels, a socialist society will need to have socialist democratic institutions and procedures for determining and implementing social choices on all those levels. Such institutions *will constitute the various levels of a socialist state* necessary not only for the mechanical operation of a socialist society, but beyond that, for socialism to achieve its goal of making humanity the collective master of its own fate. The question then is what are the necessary social functions a socialist state will have, some of which will be transformations of some analogous necessary functions of capitalist states.

It became common at the end of the last century and into this century to identify the nondemocratic planned economies similar to that of the USSR as Bureaucratic Socialism (or more colloquially, Top-down Socialism), to counterpose them to the desired Democratic Socialism (or Bottom-up or Grassroots Socialism). With this understanding of Bureaucratic Socialism as some (undesirable) form of socialism, this different concept of socialism would correspond to its different goals, and organizational and operational principles.

The expressions Bureaucratic and Top-down Socialism make it clear that people using them favor the term Democratic Socialism. With the definition of the concepts of socialism presented in this chapter, however, planning alone does not make a system of social production socialist. With this understanding of socialism, a system of planned social production is not socialist without socialist democracy, and the terms Bureaucratic or Top-down Socialism are oxymorons. In line with some of the discussions in Post-Soviet Marxism, the term "Industrialization"[14] is appropriate to refer to this type of system of social production. This chapter defines this as "Bureaucratically Planned Industrialization" to appropriately reflect its planned but nonsocialist nature.

The principle of socialist distribution, and the difference from communism[15]

The socialist goals of equality, solidarity, and an end to exploitation determine the socialist principle of distribution of the social product: each person gets back from social production goods and services that take the same amount of social labor-time to produce as that person contributes social labor to social production. A common way envisioned for the last two centuries to effect this has been by giving people labor certificates to indicate how much social labor they contributed, which they then would redeem for any social goods and services created by that same amount of social labor. This concept of distribution is based on a sense of justice, or "fairness," that people coming out of capitalism can identify with: an exchange of equivalents, getting back from society what you contribute to it. Under capitalism, the exchange of a wage for ownership by the capitalist of what the hired worker produces seems to be fair, but in fact is the source of the exploitation which is the purpose of the capitalist structure of the society. In socialism, on the contrary, that exchange really will be equivalent, and hence fair in this sense. But despite this fundamental improvement, a moment's reflection from the perspective of human solidarity and our collective species-nature indicates the limitations of this sense of justice. Even in capitalist societies, humanity accepts that some people have greater abilities to contribute to society and some have less, and so to give them all claim on the social product in accord with what they contribute is unfair as measured by what they need as humans to survive and develop their human potential. Generally, contemporary culture considers this way already in (well-functioning) families which interact on the basis of human solidarity. No one would think of giving less food and shelter to a "handicapped" child (who could "contribute less" to the material survival of the family). To the contrary, the family generally expends more resources on those members less able to meet their material needs from their interactions with society outside the family. A communist organization of society then fundamentally distinguishes itself from a socialist society (and considers itself a "higher form of social organization" based on this, based on "more humanly developed humans") by expanding this inherent human behavior to society as a whole.

Socialism is a more just system than capitalism because people really do get back from society what they contribute to it, unlike capitalism where a part of what they contribute to society is seized by the capitalists for themselves. Communism builds on socialism to go further and achieves a higher, "more human," sense of justice; everyone gets what they need from society, regardless of their greater or lesser natural ability to contribute more or less to society with the same effort.[16]

Conclusion

A concept of socialism is determined by its conception of human nature, its goals, and the various organizational and operational principles on what is necessary to achieve those goals. Different concepts of socialism have enough in common to establish a broad concept of socialism, analogous to the concept of capitalism. The goals and organizational principles of socialism differentiate it from other ways of organizing social production and society like capitalism, and they also establish the "fuzzy boundaries" between different concepts of socialism. Both social planning of social production and a socialist democracy, that is more democratic than capitalist or bourgeois democracy, are integral to the concept of Democratic Planned Socialism.

Notes

1 The concept of socialism elaborated here is exactly the opposite of this characterization, in that it argues it will provide more freedom, more democracy, more material well-being, more variety, more personal choice, and so on.
2 The word "men" was almost universally preferentially used as a synonym for "people" or "humanity" until the end of the twentieth century, when the rise of awareness of, and concern with, the myriad ways society conceptualizes women as second class humans changed this usage.
3 On the one hand, Karl Marx and Frederick Engels were just two among thousands of advocates of socialism. On the other hand, over the course of the 20th century, they became its best-known advocates, notwithstanding that this author holds that the majority of people who considered themselves advocates of Marx and Engels' ideas of socialism and communism misrepresented their ideas, from slightly to fundamentally. This section emphasizes that these two "background socialist assumptions" have been present at least since the birth of modern socialist thought in the first part of the 19th century. This is the fundamental reason, in addition to its clarity, for referencing their work here. Given the extreme prestige of their work among many advocates of socialism, however, it is important to stress that their work is *not* being referenced as "the revealed truth concerning socialism," as their ideas are too often presented.
4 For one very readable documentation of the extensive breakdown of organizations promoting social connectedness in the United States over the last half century, see *Bowling Alone* (Putnam 2020).
5 Equivalently this can be referred to as "Robinson Crusoe individualism," for obvious reasons.
6 For a further discussion of this issue of if a policy promotes to a chosen goal when it supports one subgoal and harms another, in general and in the case of building socialism in Cuba, see Campbell (2021).
7 Note that capitalists being humans do plan their actions, with their goal being to maximize their individual profits. The mechanical summation of these decisions that establishes what social production will be, however, does not constitute social planning by society of what it wishes to produce.
8 This excludes people who often self-identify as "socialist" who advocate social democratic capitalism, municipal socialism, or other such particular systems of capitalism linked to particularly strong redistributive schemes.
9 Specifically, by a number of different variations of what became known as the "material balance" system.
10 As opposed to the tool of mandated delivery of material balances.
11 Markets have existed in the core of all except the very simplest modes of production throughout history: feudalism, Greece and Rome, imperial China, even in Sumer 5000 years ago.
12 Capitalist exploitation is the result of workers receiving less value in wages than the value of their production, the difference which the capitalists expropriate.
13 The Democratic People's Republic of Korea still uses a variant of twentieth-century materials balance planning and production system that, notwithstanding its economic successes in certain countries in certain time periods, is today nearly universally evaluated as inadequate and inappropriate for building socialism by socialists.

14 Productive systems where society's surplus labor is not controlled by society (all class societies) are generally named in accord with the use of that surplus – capitalism to expand capital, feudalism to maintain the feudal operation of society, and so on. The bulk of the social surplus in the USSR from 1930 to 1991 was used to promote a planned and non-capitalist industrialization. Hence this name. See, for example, Tikhonov (2021) on the discussion in Post-Soviet Russian Marxism on the Soviet system of social production.

15 As the modern concepts of socialism and communism developed over the course of the 19th century, the usage of those labels varied extensively between authors, and from one time period to another. The distinction indicated here was clearly established only in the early 1890s, after which it has been very widely, but not universally, used to the present.

16 For the first concise formulation of this difference between a human-centered classless society initially emerging from capitalism (socialism) and a still "more human" society (communism) to arise out of socialism, see Marx (1875: 86). Note that this understanding of the appropriateness for a human-centered society to distribute goods according to need (but without planning of social production or democracy) was already specifically elaborated long before the rise of modern socialist thought, in the first modern utopian work by Sir Thomas More in 1516 (More 1516).

References

Campbell, Al., Evaluating Against a Multi-Dimensional Economic Goal: A Sustainable and Prosperous Socialism, *International Journal of Cuban Studies*, v. 13 (1), 2021. 105–126. doi.org/10.13169/intejcubastud.13.1.0105.

Cockshott, Paul and Allin Cottrell, *Towards a New Socialism*. Nottingham: Russell Press Limited, 1993.

Engels, Frederick, *Anti-Dühring*. Reprinted in *Karl Marx Frederick Engels Collected Works (MECW)*. Progress Publishers, v. 25, 1987. 1–309.

Freire, Paulo, *Pedagogy of the Oppressed*. Reprint. New York: Continuum, 1992.

Fromm, Eric, *Marx's Concept of Man*. New York: Frederick Ungar, 1961.

Marx, Karl, *Economic and Political Manuscripts of 1844*. Reprinted in *MECW*. Moscow: Progress Publishers, v. 3. 1975 [1844a]. 229–346.

Marx, Karl, Comments on James Mill, *Élémens D'Économie Politique*. Reprinted in *MECW*. Moscow: Progress Publishers, v. 3, 1975 [1844b]. 221–228.

Marx, Karl, *Grundrisse*. Reprinted in *MECW*, Moscow: Progress Publishers, v. 28, 1987 [1857]. 49–537.

Marx, Karl, Critique of the Gotha Programme. Reprinted in *Karl Marx Frederick Engels Collected Works (MECW)*. Moscow: Progress, v. 24. 1989 [1875].

Marx, Karl, *Capital*. Reprinted in *MECW*. New York: International Publishers, v. 35, 1996 [1867].

More, Thomas, *Utopia*. Reprint. London: J. M. Dent, 1994 [1516].

Putnam, Robert, *Bowling Alone: Revised and Updated: The Collapse and Revival of American Community*. New York: Simon & Schuster, 2020.

Tikhonov, Vladimir, The Soviet Problem in Post-Soviet Russian Marxism, or the Afterlife of the USSR. *Historical Materialism*. v. 29 (4), 2021. 153–187.

Wright, Erik Olin, *Envisioning Real Utopias*. London: Verso, 2010.

17

WORKER COOPERATIVES AND POST-CAPITALISM

Erik K. Olsen

Introduction

Critics and advocates of capitalism agree that it has transformed societies and brought tremendous material development. But along with technological advances and rising living standards have also come new forms of subjection and exploitation, as well as precarity, despair among a significant part of the population, and an unfolding ecological disaster. Inequalities of income, wealth, and power remain, but in different arrangements. It is increasingly clear that these pathologies are not temporary growing pains of modern capitalist development but, rather, are predictable consequences of this way of organizing economic activity. One response is to accept these consequences as regrettable but intrinsic aspects of an efficient economic system and search for ways to reduce them. Another is to consider what feasible alternatives exist. This chapter explores one of these alternatives, the worker cooperative.

Thinking about going beyond capitalism, that is, to consider post-capitalism, requires an understanding of what capitalism is and what it is not. Many things often associated with capitalism – commodities, markets, money, money lending, credit, account keeping for calculating gains, contracts, and entrepreneurship – emerged and became routine thousands of years before the explosive and transformative growth of modern industrial capitalism in the eighteenth and nineteenth centuries (Hudson 2010). Even capital, in the form of merchant and finance capital, predates the capitalist transformation in the West. Because these things functioned for millennia in pre-capitalist societies, it is dubious to consider them defining features of modern capitalist social relations.

Marxist analysis recognizes that while these commercial and financial practices are important conditions of existence for modern capitalism, they are not

DOI: 10.4324/9781003366690-20

what distinguishes it from other forms of social production. Instead, Marxist social and economic analysis characterizes social sites, including societies, according to the prevalence of their economic class relations and class structures. From this perspective, going beyond capitalism requires changing class relations. Class, in Marxian theory, is not a simple taxonomy of people in society, grouping people by levels of income or wealth (upper, middle, and lower), hereditary titles and aristocracy, caste, or, more generally, social status. Instead, Marxist class analysis begins by identifying the relations between individuals in production.

Considered at the high level of abstraction necessary to characterize the vast complexity of the human experience, we find that prior to the emergence of capitalist production people labored for themselves as agricultural smallholders, in household production, or as craft workers, for others as slaves or serfs, or collectively in tribal groups, village communes, or similar communal arrangements.[1] Each of these ways of producing has their own sets of class positions and class relations that are different from those found in capitalist production (Resnick and Wolff 1986, 115-24; Wright 1985, 64-104). To simplify matters greatly, what distinguishes modern, industrial capitalist class relations is that production is organized in enterprises controlled by owners, while workers sell their time and capacity to work – their labor power – to the owners in exchange for a wage. In this way, human labor power itself becomes a commodity, and by selling their labor power to an employer, workers become employees. As employees, they take direction from their employer, who has invested in the enterprise and operates it for the employer's own benefit. The most basic class positions that emerge from the exchange of labor power for a wage are then owner and worker or employer and employee.[2] This class relation is exploitative because workers labor not only to provide for themselves and their families but also to produce profit for their employer, who appropriates the product of their labor and returns a portion of it to them as wages.

Almost since the emergence of industrial capitalism, radicals, social reformers, and ordinary working people have experimented with ways of organizing the workplace to eliminate the wage relation, end the dependence of workers on an employer for their livelihood, and produce for the benefit of the workers, their families, and their communities. These experiments have had mixed results, and none have formed an enduring challenge to the capitalist organization of production. But some of these experiments have changed the fundamental class relations in the enterprise and, in this sense, serve as potential models for postcapitalist forms of production.

A worker cooperative is a type of enterprise in which the people who do the work of the enterprise are also the ones who own and control it through democratic means. Unlike the employer–employee relationship of the capitalist enterprise, a worker cooperative is organized on the basis of *membership*. The enterprise is owned and democratically controlled by the workers in the cooperative, who are worker-members rather than employees. The specific rights and obligations of a worker cooperative are established by the policies adopted by the worker-members and the relevant laws they are subject to, but the three cardinal rights of ownership of the enterprise – control, claim on the residual income of the enterprise ("profit"), and ability to sell these rights – belong to the worker-members as a group, who exercise them through democratic processes on the basis of one member, one vote.

Like earlier communal and independent ways of working, the worker-members themselves control the labor process, collectively appropriate the product of their labor, and participate democratically in its distribution. A worker cooperative replaces the wage relation with membership and democratic control, and therefore the class relations are not capitalist, and the members of the cooperative are not exploited in the Marxian sense.

Because the class relations in the enterprise are not capitalist and the purpose of the enterprise is to enhance the wellbeing of the workers themselves (rather than the suppliers of capital), worker cooperatives are not capitalist enterprises.[3] Worker cooperatives are appropriately referred to as *postcapitalist* because they developed out of industrial capitalism, largely as a reaction to its effects, but they do not, in themselves, embody any of the well-known alternatives to capitalism. Socialism, for example, is typically envisioned as replacing private ownership of enterprises with state ownership, and, in some versions, replacing markets with central planning. Since throughout their history worker cooperatives have existed almost exclusively as private enterprises operating in markets, they bear little resemblance to traditional conceptions of state socialism. An exception to this was the economy of socialist Yugoslavia, which for decades was organized around publicly owned but labor-managed enterprises similar to worker cooperatives in a system of socialist self-management. These experiences indicate that worker cooperatives have no necessary association with either the state-led or private enterprise-led visions of economic organization.

Organizing an enterprise on either a capitalist or a cooperative basis has important implications for the people associated with it, and for society more generally. This chapter considers some of the obvious problems associated with capitalist firms as well as the possibilities and limitations of worker cooperatives as an alternative.

Capitalist Enterprises

Three cardinal economic rights are associated with the ownership of an enterprise in Western liberal economies: (1) the right to control the enterprise, including the ability to hire, direct, observe, and fire employees; (2) the right to the residual income ("profit") of the enterprise; and (3) the right to sell the ownership of the enterprise, either whole or in part.[4] Capitalist enterprises are created and operated for the benefit of their owners, who invest their capital with the objective of receiving profit income and increasing the value of their capital assets. Owners use their control rights in pursuit of this objective. In modern corporations, the owners' control rights are delegated to a board of directors appointed by them, and, further, to managers hired by the board, but these groups derive their authority from the owners' right to control the enterprise. Because managerial authority is derivative of the owners' control rights, for simplicity in this chapter, an owner is described as carrying out these functions even if it is their delegates who routinely do so.

Ownership and control of productive resources give employers power over workers. Employees take direction from employers, with little or no influence over the directions they take or control over the conditions they work under and can be dismissed for failing to follow direction. The employer's power over the employee derives from the ability to exclude them from the productive assets they need to provide their livelihood and the cost they face from losing access to these assets (Bowles and Gintis 1993). Employees are free to leave a job they find oppressive, but this will not improve their situation unless different employment conditions can be found elsewhere. If they can freely choose to exit one place of employment and directly enter an equivalent position, then leaving a job has no cost to the employee and the employer holds no power over them. But employer power is ubiquitous in capitalist economies, in part, because employers refrain from hiring when unemployment falls below levels that assure sufficient power over their employees. Macroeconomic policy also aims to maintain labor market conditions such that job loss results in a significant and costly period of unemployment (Boddy and Crotty 1975; Kalecki 1943).

Owners also use their control over the enterprise to increase their power over employees. They routinely choose production technologies that allow them to replace skilled employees who command higher wages with lower skill employees that do not, a process known as deskilling (Braverman 1974, 70-84; Gordon et al. 1982, 100-164). Deskilling not only replaces highly skilled and highly paid employees with low skilled and low paid ones, but also allows firms to locate anywhere labor costs are low, weakening the connection between enterprises and local economies, and making the market for labor global rather than local. When workers must compete for jobs with workers in other parts of the country or the world, employment becomes increasingly precarious, as employers can credibly threaten to relocate in search of lower labor costs.

It is clear from the definition of the rights of ownership that the capitalist enterprise is undemocratic. The capitalist workplace operates as a small command economy in which employees take direction without participating in determining the directions they are obligated to obey (Coase 1937, 387-88). Not only is this lack of democracy in enterprises odious for those who believe in the intrinsic virtue of democratic governance, but lack of democracy in the workplace affects democracy in society more broadly. Employees who lack autonomy and decision-making authority may perceive themselves as having low status and be less prepared to participate in democratic processes outside the workplace (Pateman 1970; Dow 2003, 34-38). A combination of perceived low social status, lack of autonomy, being subject to unaccountable power of an employer, precarious employment, stagnant or declining wages, and limited job opportunities has increasingly characterized the experience of workers in the United States without a college degree since the 1970s. Case and Deaton (2020) cite this decline of well-paying, relatively stable, unionized jobs, and the transition to low skilled and precarious employment as an important contributor to the growth of "deaths of despair" (primarily deaths by suicide, drug overdose, or alcohol abuse) in the United States. Growth in mortality from these causes began in the 1990s and continues unabated, resulting in an unprecedented decline in life expectancy for segments of the US working population. Dependence on employment in enterprises designed to serve the interests of capital owners does not just lead to unsatisfying working lives, it leads to millions of early deaths from self-harm.

The concentration of the ownership of enterprises in the hands of relatively few individuals and families also means this fundamentally important economic institution is directed to serve the interest of a small portion of the population.[5] This inequality in ownership contributes significantly to income inequality, and, consequently, to inequality in a range of income-dependent resources, like nutrition, education, health care, housing, safety, social connections, and status. This generates significant inequality of opportunity among citizens to participate as equals in governing the state as well as inequality of influence over political leaders (Dahl 1985, 54-55; Gilens and Page 2014).

For Marxists, capitalist class relations perpetuate inequality because they are, like feudalism and slavery before them, exploitative. While the exploitation of serfs and slaves resulted from overt compulsion, under capitalist class relations it results from the sale of labor power for a wage. In this exchange, the output produced by a worker exceeds the compensation received in return, and this surplus created in production becomes the property of the employer. As the appropriator of this surplus, the owner of the enterprise or their delegates distribute it in the interest of the enterprise and, thus, in the interest of the owners themselves. Because the workers who produce the surplus of the enterprise are not the people who appropriate or allocate it, they are exploited (Resnick and Wolff 1986, 20-22; Wright 1985, 73-77). One of the forms the surplus takes is profit, which provides income for the owners but brings no necessary reciprocation or obligation beyond the contractual wage payment. Seen in this light, the capitalist enterprise is just the latest institution that channels the benefits of economic activity to elites rather than a break from earlier exploitative class relations.

The Potential of Democratic Enterprises

Organizations like worker cooperatives have existed in the United States almost since its founding. In 1791, because of a labor dispute, journeyman carpenters in Philadelphia acted to collectively employ themselves in an early worker cooperative, followed in 1806 by journeyman shoemakers (Saposs 1966, 97, 127-130). Thousands of worker cooperatives have existed in the United States since that time, with notable clusters associated with the Knights of Labor in the 1870s, self-help cooperatives supported by federal agencies during the Great Depression of the 1930s, and an upsurge of development in the 1970s (Olsen 2013). This third wave of worker cooperative development in the 1970s was unusual in that it had no national organization or government support. Instead, it resulted primarily from the spontaneous initiative of groups of committed workers using their own resources to start new cooperative enterprises. The founding of the US Federation of Worker Cooperatives in 2004, which provides technical assistance to cooperative developers, helped start a fourth wave of worker cooperative development in the United States, leading to an estimated population of 900–1,000 worker cooperatives or democratic workplaces with roughly 10,000 employees by 2021 (Democracy at Work Institute 2021).

This US total is a small fraction of the number of worker cooperatives in some European and Latin American countries. Italy, for example, had nearly 24,000 worker cooperatives with over 500,000 worker-members, or 2.3% of all employment, in 2020 (Lomuscio et al. 2023). The cooperative sector in Italy is supported by public policies and a well-established association of cooperative businesses (National League of Cooperatives and Mutual Aid Societies or La Lega), which has operated since 1886. The most comprehensive and advanced support system for worker cooperatives is Mondragon, a federation of cooperative enterprises in the Basque region of Spain. Mondragon consists of over 90 separate worker cooperatives, operating in finance, manufacturing, retail, and information sectors. These cooperatives employ approximately 80,000 people and produce billions in annual income for their worker-members (Mondragon Corporation 2023). The Mondragon network of cooperatives has multiple representative bodies and a bank that coordinate and guide the activities of member cooperatives, including their formation and growth. This comprehensive system of support created what is arguably the most successful and dynamic worker cooperative network that exists, but this has yet to be replicated outside of Mondragon.

Despite their long history in the United States and elsewhere, the number of existing worker cooperatives is very small relative to the number of capitalist firms, never representing a significant fraction of national employment in any country. There is also considerable diversity in those that do exist, so it is not possible to fully extrapolate their potential from the behavior of these examples. But some conclusions can be drawn with a reasonable degree of certainty. Most prominently, because the worker-members jointly share decision-making authority, they make choices for their own benefit. The labor economist John Pencavel, who conducted the most rigorous econometric studies of worker cooperatives to date, concludes,

> ... members of the co-op place the well-being of the workers at the core of its ideals. For the typical capitalist enterprise, the well-being of its workers is achieved as a by-product of the firm's activities; for the co-op the well-being of its member-workers is a distinct and categorical goal. The master-servant relation that predates the employer-employee association in the capitalist firm is replaced in the co-op by one of self-employment and the democratic determination of issues.
>
> *(Pencavel 2013, 466)*

Unlike capitalist firms, the purpose of a worker cooperative is to provide well-paying and stable work under conditions of worker self-management. Compensation of worker-members consists of a regular paycheck and an equal share of the annual profit of the firm (an annual "dividend"). This residual income varies significantly, both across industries and because of cyclical or secular economic conditions beyond the control of the enterprise, but the annual dividend can be significant. Pencavel (2001, 42) finds that the income of workers in the cooperative plywood mills that were once numerous in the US Pacific Northwest exceeded that of comparable capitalist mills, usually by a large amount. Similarly, Meyers (2022, 97, 122) finds significant income premiums for the worker-members in both the cooperative bakery and cooperative grocery store she studied in the early 2000s. These enterprises likely drew the attention of Pencavel and Meyers because of their success, so we should refrain from drawing general conclusions about the income-generating potential of worker cooperatives under all circumstances from their findings, but it is clear they can and do create well-paying jobs in competitive industries.

Employment stability is another benefit that worker cooperatives provide under fairly general circumstances. In democratically controlled workplaces, worker-members routinely prioritize employment stability and maintain employment levels even in the face of adverse market conditions (Pencavel 2013). Because the compensation of worker-members consists of wages and a share of annual profits, cyclical declines in demand and downward pressure on output prices decrease worker income. But even when facing declining income, cooperatives typically choose to maintain employment levels. Facing similar conditions, capitalist firms typically respond by keeping the wage rate constant while reducing the number of employees, which directs more of the impact of an economic downturn onto laid-off employees who bear the cost of unemployment.

Democratic decision-making in worker cooperatives also results in a much more egalitarian distribution of income. It is common for there to be wage differentials in worker cooperatives, usually based on years of experience, skill levels, differences in occupation, or the necessity of retaining members with specialized skills or experience. But studies of cooperatives routinely find the ratio between the highest and lowest paid worker-members between 2-to-1 and 5-to-1 rather than the 300-to-1 ratio that is the average for large corporations in the United States (Herrera 2004; Democracy at Work Institute 2021). So, while income differentials do exist in worker cooperatives, they are a fraction of the differentials observed in capitalist enterprises.

Another important dimension of equality is power in the workplace. As discussed above, in a capitalist workplace, the exercise of authority is unilateral: employers and their surrogates give commands, employees obey those commands, and this agreement is enforced by sanctions. In contrast, control rights in a worker cooperative belong to the members collectively, and the structures chosen by the members to coordinate production and exercise authority are subject to democratic control. Individual members still face costly sanctions if they fail to abide by workplace policies, but the occupants of positions in any hierarchy adopted, or rules agreed by common consent, are subject to recall and renegotiation by democratic processes. A cooperative workplace cannot provide complete autonomy to individual workers, but, like a citizen in a democratic polity, the worker-member participates in making the rules they must abide by and in choosing those who exercise authority.

It is clear that worker cooperatives can provide important benefits for worker-members and their communities. Economists have also studied the potential costs, in terms of reduced productivity and performance, of democratic ownership and control. This line of research is constrained by the limited opportunities to study comparable populations of worker cooperatives and capitalist firms in operation, but the econometric research that has been done consistently finds that worker cooperatives suffer no productivity disadvantage relative to their capitalist competitors (Pencavel 2013). Several rigorous studies actually find higher productivity in worker cooperatives, and while this finding is not universal, there is clearly no indication of a productivity disadvantage.

A different line of empirical research into the effect of different ownership structures on firm performance studies the relative survival times of worker cooperative and capitalist firms. Inefficiency should result in shorter firm survival times as less productive enterprises are driven out of operation by the more productive, but research on relative survival times consistently finds that cooperatives survive at least as well as or better than capitalist firms (Olsen 2013). Taken together, the empirical research on productivity coupled with the research on firm survival convincingly refutes the proposition that worker-owned firms suffer a competitive disadvantage relative to capitalist firms and supports the conclusion that their productivity and performance meet or exceed that of capitalist firms. This evidence is multidimensional, repeated, and robust, so this conclusion should no longer be in dispute.

In sum, worker cooperatives can provide a well-paying job, a higher degree of employment stability, and a self-governing workplace that puts the wellbeing of the worker-members at the center of its mission and decision-making. Convincing evidence finds that this is more likely to enhance than compromise productive efficiency and competitiveness. This indicates the potential not only exists for a transformation of the workplace and the work experience but also poses an important question. If worker cooperatives have existed for centuries, and have such important advantages, why are they not more prevalent?

The Limits of Worker Cooperatives

For some time, economists have taken the ubiquity of capitalist firms as *prima facie* evidence of superior productivity relative to more egalitarian alternatives. But the prevalence of any economic institution is a result of historical processes that depend on the complex dynamics of creation (birth), growth, persistence, replication, and decline. Productive efficiency is only one aspect of this, and the capitalist firm has no productivity advantage over democratic enterprises. It is clear, however, that worker cooperatives have never existed in sufficient numbers to challenge the hegemony of capitalist firms. There is no consensus regarding why this is the case.[6] Much of the early literature addressing the question of why worker cooperatives are relatively rare searched for sources of inefficiency or competitive disadvantage, but these things can now be ruled out with a high degree of confidence, so attention needs to focus elsewhere. Space limitations require consideration here of just two important points, the low rate of creation of new worker cooperatives and limits to growth once created.

One obvious reason for the relatively small number of worker cooperatives is that few of them are created. Simply put, entrepreneurial activity in pursuit of individual gain, the primary way new businesses are created, does not lead to the creation of worker cooperatives. Even with their productivity and survival advantages, a self-interested individual with the resources to form a new enterprise will not choose to create a worker cooperative, which requires sharing profit broadly, when creating a capitalist business allows an entrepreneur to capture the residual income of the enterprise for themselves. Groups of workers, who might seek to improve their working conditions through collective entrepreneurship, are likely to be constrained by lack of assets. Forming a new enterprise typically requires an initial capital investment, but most US households have little savings and few assets to pledge as collateral for a loan, so most workers cannot choose to become self-employed, either individually or collectively. This leaves new business creation primarily to individuals who do have the means to employ themselves or others but are unlikely to use their assets to create an enterprise that shares profits broadly with its employees.

Once created, worker cooperatives also have more limited incentives for growth than capitalist firms. A capitalist firm has an incentive to hire new employees and expand if an additional employee generates profit for the firm. A worker cooperative, on the other hand, only has an incentive to add new members if the new worker-member generates more profit than existing members. This asymmetry exists because a capitalist firm normally has a fixed number of ownership shares, so any increase in the total profit of the firm increases profit per share. In contrast, increasing the size of a worker cooperative requires adding new members who have the same claim on profit as existing members. Consequently, adding new members who generate the same profit per capita as existing worker-members does not increase the annual dividend[7]. New members who generate less profit than existing members reduce the average dividend.

Furthermore, increasing the number of members in a worker cooperative increases the number of people who participate in decision-making. This dilutes the control existing workers have over democratic processes in the firm, and, if they value their ability to influence decisions, diminishing this influence would be perceived as a cost. Overall, it should be the case that in the long-run, worker cooperatives facing the same conditions as a capitalist firm will choose to operate with fewer workers and will not exploit opportunities for growth as extensively as capitalist firms (Vanek 1970, 27-34). This is especially true for enterprises, such as restaurants or retail stores, that grow by adding entirely new establishments.

These two constraints on worker cooperatives, very low rates of formation and limits on growth, are sufficient to explain why worker cooperatives are rare and capitalist firms predominate in developed economies even though capitalist firms lack productivity or competitive advantages. These limitations can be overcome, as has been demonstrated by Mondragon and La Lega. But this requires cooperative development and growth guided by the objective of making employment in worker cooperatives widely available rather than being guided purely by the interests of the current worker-members.

Conclusion

If large inequalities of wealth, income, and power, as well as exploitation, precarity, and despair, are unintended but necessary consequences of an efficient economic system, then efforts to alter the basic allocation of ownership and control require a trade-off between better outcomes for working people and economic performance. Trade-offs like this are typically resolved in favor of those with power, and, currently, this does not favor working people who depend on wages for their livelihood. But decades of economic research indicate that sharing ownership broadly does not adversely affect enterprise performance and, therefore, democratizing ownership and control does not require this trade-off of efficiency for equity. This research also indicates that capitalist firms do not predominate in developed economies because of superior efficiency. Economists, who are trained that market competition selects more efficient institutions over less, could have a difficult time reconciling these findings with the current economy where worker cooperatives are relatively rare. But market competition is not the only, or even the primary, selection mechanism at work determining why capitalist enterprises predominate. Despite their advantages, worker cooperatives will remain rare until they are created in significant numbers. But the mechanism that creates multitudes of capitalist firms – self-interested entrepreneurial activity – does not reliably create worker cooperatives, and the spontaneous initiative of motivated groups of workers who could benefit from them is constrained by lack of assets and other factors.

The creation of large numbers of these enterprises requires the sustained intervention of private and public cooperative developers, as well as access to new sources of funding for start-ups and the conversion of existing businesses to the worker cooperative model. Worker cooperatives also face different incentives for growth than do capitalist firms, and increasing their prevalence requires making increasing employment an objective for existing cooperatives alongside the economic wellbeing of current members. The primary purpose and appeal of a worker cooperative is that it gives the worker-members ownership and control of the firm, which makes the interests of the worker-members the objectives of the enterprise. But consideration of the growth dynamics of democratic firms suggest that acting solely in the interest of the current membership limits the potential of democratic firms to be a viable option for large numbers of working people.

The potential of this type of organization is then limited by this contradiction between the immediate economic interests of the existing working members and the benefit to potential members. In other words, for the benefits of this form of economic organization to have a significant impact broadly on society, worker cooperatives need to act in ways that may not advance the immediate interests of their existing members. But this contradiction can be overcome. Indeed, the successful networks of worker cooperatives and public policies in the Basque country and in Italy do precisely this. In return for financial, technical, and managerial support, cooperatives cede some of their autonomy. Making worker cooperatives a viable alternative for large numbers of working people likely requires the replication of these models of cooperative development and support. This should not dissuade aspiring cooperators or policymakers in the United States and elsewhere from participating in and supporting current efforts to create and grow independent worker cooperatives. Indeed, the realization of a cooperative sector with broad social impact depends on the success of these endeavors.

Advocating for increased prevalence of worker cooperatives is radical because it proposes profound change to a basic economic institution, the enterprise. Some find this proposal insufficiently radical because it falls short of their preferred ideal. But the relevant evaluative criteria is not whether institutional change fully realizes one's preferred ideal, it is whether it brings us closer to realizing the objectives embodied in that ideal. Worker cooperatives place the interests of those who perform the labor of the enterprise, rather than the interests of the providers of capital, at the center of organizational decision-making, and put the product of labor under the control of the people who produce it. Under the right circumstances, they provide competitive compensation, greater employment stability, and workplaces where the power of the enterprise is under the democratic control of those subject to it. None of these things should be in question. Even though what they can achieve is constrained by both competitive and macroeconomic pressures, worker cooperatives offer achievable improvement in the lives of working people. However, if the wellbeing of current worker-members is the only objective of the enterprise, the potential of worker cooperatives to address the economic and social problems associated with capitalist enterprises will not be realized. Furthermore, without some way of regulating and coordinating their behavior, an economy primarily composed of cooperatively owned and managed enterprises would still exhibit the kinds of collective action failures that prevent full employment, produce business cycles and price instability, and allow climate change to proceed. Solutions to these problems require more than just a change in the organization of enterprises, but extending democracy in the workplace offers the potential for a more vigorous political democracy that could more effectively address these challenges.

Notes

1 These predate capitalist production, but each is still found in some form today.
2 Marx uses the terms "bourgeoise" and "proletarian"; Resnick and Wolff refer to these as the "fundamental class positions" of capitalist class relations; Wright uses the term "basic classes".
3 On this point, there is agreement between both anti-Marxists (Ellerman 1992) and anti-essentialist Marxists (Gibson-Graham 2006, 65; Burczak 2006).
4 This is a simplification of Alchian and Demsetz's (1972) bundle of five rights of ownership in the "classic capitalist firm." Because an enterprise consists of a set of contractual arrangements that can be terminated by either party, it is an abstraction to say that an enterprise is truly "owned." But this term is used in this chapter as a shorthand way of referring to this set of legally enforceable rights (Dow 2003, 107-10).
5 Piketty (2014, Table 7.2, Figure 8.10) and Wolff (2017).
6 See Dow (2003) and Olsen (2013) for discussions.
7 More formally, if the total annual profit of the cooperative is π, and the number of worker-members is L, the annual dividend for each is π/L. If membership increases by a factor of t, and profit also increases t-fold, the dividend is unchanged ($t\pi/tL = \pi/L$), and existing members are no better off. Only if increasing membership t times results in profit greater than $t\pi$ would the dividend increase. In other words, adding members only increases the annual dividend when production is subject to increasing returns to scale. In contrast, with a fixed number of shares, the dividend to a

shareholder of a profitable capitalist firm increases under both constant and increasing returns, and even decreasing returns as long as an additional employee produces additional profit. This does not preclude cooperatives from choosing to become relatively large when they benefit from economies of scale or scope, but they have less incentive than capitalist firms to grow without them.

References

Alchian, Armen A. and Harold Demsetz, Production, Information Costs, and Economic Organization, *The American Economic Review*. v. 62 (5), 1972. 777–795.

Boddy, Raford, Crotty, James R., Class Conflict and Macro-Policy: The Political Business Cycle, *Review of Radical Political Economics*, v.7 (1), 1975. 1–19.

Bowles, Samuel and Herbert Gintis, The Revenge of Homo Economicus: Contested Exchange and the Revival of Political Economy, *Journal of Economic Perspectives*. v. 7 (1), 1993. 83–102.

Braverman, Harry, *Labor and Monopoly Capital*. New York and London: Monthly Review Press, 1974.

Burczak, Theodore A., *Socialism After Hayek*. Ann Arbor: The University of Michigan Press, 2006.

Case, Ann and Angus Deaton, *Deaths of Despair and the Future of Capitalism*. Princeton and Oxford: Princeton University Press, 2020.

Coase, Ronald H., The Nature of the Firm, *Economica*. v. 4 (16), 1937. 386–405.

Dahl, Robert A., *A Preface to Economic Democracy*. Berkeley and Los Angeles: University of California Press, 1985.

Democracy at Work Institute, 2021 State of the Sector. 2022. https://institute.coop/resources/2021-worker-cooperative-state-sector-report

Dow, Gregory K., *Governing the Firm*. Cambridge and New York: Cambridge University Press, 2003.

Ellerman, David, *Property and Contract in Economics*. Oxford U.K. and Cambridge U.S.: Blackwell Publishers, 1992.

Gibson-Graham, J.K., *A Postcapitalist Politics*. Minneapolis and London: University of Minnesota Press, 2006.

Gilens, Martin, and Benjamin I. Page, Testing Theories of American Politics: Elites, Interest Groups, and Average Citizens. *Perspectives on Politics*. v. 12 (3), 2014. 564–581.

Gordon, David M., Richard Edwards, and Micheal Reich, *Segmented Work, Divided Workers*. Cambridge and New York: Cambridge University Press, 1982.

Herrera, David, Mondragon: A For-Profit Organization That Embodies Catholic Social Thought, *Review of Business*. v. 25 (1), 2004. 56–68.

Hudson, Michael, Entrepreneurs: From the Near Eastern Takeoff to the Roman Collapse, in *The Invention of Enterprise*, David S. Landes, Joel Mokyr, and William J. Baumol eds. Princeton and Oxford: Princeton University Press, 2010.

Kalecki, Michael, Political Aspects of Full Employment. *The Political Quarterly*. v. 14, 1943. 322–330.

Lomuscio, Marco, Ermanno Celeste Tortia, Andrea Cori, Worker Cooperatives in Italy: Legislation, Prevalence and Recent Trends. *Journal of Participation and Employee Ownership*. 2023. https://www.emerald.com/insight/content/doi/10.1108/JPEO-10-2022-0023/full/html

Meyers, Joan S. M. *Working Democracies*. Ithaca and London: ILR Press, 2022.

Mondragon Corporation, About Us. 2023. https://www.mondragon-corporation.com/en/about-us/

Olsen, Erik K., The Relative Survival of Worker Cooperatives and Barriers to Their Creation, in *Sharing Ownership, Profits, and Decision-Making in the 21st Century*, Douglas Kruse ed. Emerald Group Publishing Limited, v. 14, 2013. 83–107.

Pateman, Carole, *Participation and Democratic Theory*. Cambridge U.K.: Cambridge University Press, 1970.

Pencavel, John, *Worker Participation: Lessons from Worker Co-ops of the Pacific Northwest*. New York: Russell Sage Foundation, 2001.

Pencavel, John, Worker Cooperatives and Democratic Governance, in *Handbook of Economic Organization*, Anna Grandori ed. Cheltenham U.K. and Northampton U.S.: Edward Elgar, 2013. 462–480.

Piketty, Thomas, *Capital in the Twenty-First Century*. Cambridge and London: Harvard University Press, 2014.

Resnick, Stephen A. and Richard D. Wolff, *Knowledge and Class*. Chicago and London: The University of Chicago Press, 1986.

Saposs, David J., Colonial and Federal Beginnings (to 1827), part I of *History of Labour in the United States*. v. 1, John R. Commons, David J. Saposs, Helen Sumner, E.B. Mittelman, H.E. Hoagland, John B. Andrews, Selig Perlman. New York: Augustus M. Kelley Publishers, 1966 [1918].

Vanek, Jaroslav, *The General Theory of Labor-Managed Market Economies*. Ithaca and London: Cornell University Press, 1970.

Wolff, Edward N., *A Century of Wealth in America*. Cambridge and London: Harvard University Press, 2017.

Wright, Erik Olin, *Classes*. New York and London: Verso, 1985.

18

THE MIDDLE WAY

Social Democracy as an Alternative to Laissez-Faire Capitalism

Geoffrey Schneider

Introduction

In 1936, Marquis Childs referred to Swedish social democracy as the "middle way" between the absolute socialization of the USSR and the laissez-faire capitalism in the United States. In the modern era, the social democracies of northern Europe are thriving examples of a humane economic system that works for the vast majority of people. About half of these economies are governed by the public sector, which has dramatically expanded the human rights of the population to include health care, childcare, dental care, education through college, housing, generous parental leave and access to training and employment. The other half of the economies of social democracies feature regulated capitalism which, ironically, is thriving thanks in part to an educated and well-trained workforce and remarkably effective state-led industrialization efforts.

While social democracies feature the highest levels of human development in the world, this model requires constant struggle to maintain against the forces of neoliberal global capitalism. Capitalist businesses push relentlessly for less regulations, lower taxes, and the ability to move operations to low-wage locations. There has been some reduction in the welfare states and labor protections in most social democracies in the face of such pressure. Only by resisting these pressures, and by creating a domestic environment that actively fosters domestic capital accumulation and growth, can social democracies preserve their advanced levels of human development.

DOI: 10.4324/9781003366690-21

What Is a Social Democracy?

It is useful at the outset to lay out the different types of economic systems that exist in the modern world. Traditionally, economists have contrasted laissez-faire capitalist economic systems, featuring minimal government intervention and economic decision-making vested almost entirely in the private sector, with communist economic systems where economic decisions are made via state-directed central planning bodies. However, in the modern world, all economic systems are mixed economies, with some economic decisions made by the state and other economic decisions made by a capitalist, corporate sector. The real issue is the balance of state and market that a particular society chooses.

We can group modern economic systems into three broad categories: market-dominated economies (MDEs), social democratic economies (SDEs), and communist (or socialist) economies (CEs).[1] In MDEs, economic decisions are primarily made by the private sector, especially corporations, in a largely unregulated market. In MDEs, the government plays a relatively minor role, usually in support of the corporate sector. In SDEs, social values take a leading role in directing the economy and determining the allocation of resources through the actions of a democratic government. Markets play a key role in producing consumer goods, but health and education are provided to everyone by the state, and the government plays a large role in strategically directing society's resources. In CEs, the state controls society's main economic resources and makes most of the important economic decisions. Markets are utilized when they serve society's interests but are otherwise severely constrained.

Figure 18.1 shows the range of economic systems. As you can see, SDEs are, quite literally, the "Middle Way" combining both state and market in relatively equal amounts.

The rationale for a "Middle Way" between ruinous laissez-faire capitalism and centralized communism was articulated by Marquis Childs (1936, 143-144), in the following passage:

> [In Sweden] the state, the consumer, and the producer have intervened to make capitalism "work" in a reasonable way for the greatest good of the whole nation...That this constitutes a...middle course seems to me obvious;

The Size of Government in Select Economies.

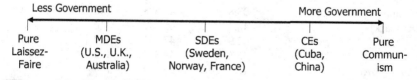

FIGURE 18.1 The Size of Government in Select Economies.

it is a course between the absolute socialization of Russia [under the USSR] and the end development of capitalism in America. In Russia...the rulers of the state attempted to make all of life conform to an idea, an ideal. In the United States the profit motive was put above every other consideration and it worked to the end of blind self-destruction.

The philosophy guiding social democracies is based on a skepticism regarding unregulated markets, which are viewed as exploitative, unstable, and environmentally destructive, as well as a distrust of overly centralized power that could devolve into dictatorship and oppression. With the fall of the Soviet bloc in 1990, most developed countries in the modern world can be classified as either MDEs or SDEs, so it is worthwhile to compare the two in more detail.

Table 18.1 displays some important characteristics of MDEs and SDEs. First, MDEs maintain a much smaller government sector compared with SDEs, with tax revenue averaging only 30% in MDEs versus 43% in SDEs. Much of this is due to the fact that SDEs spend on average 27.5% of GDP on social expenditures, which includes health, welfare, unemployment, job assistance, and childcare, whereas MDEs only spend 18.7% of GDP on these public services.

TABLE 18.1 Data on Select Market-Dominated and Social Democratic Economies

Selected Market-Dominated Economies (MDEs)	GDP Devoted to Social Expenditures, 2019 (%)	Tax Revenue, % of GDP, 2019	Real GDP per Capita, 2019 ($)	Growth in Real GDP per Capita, 1971–2019 (%)	Poverty Rate, % 2017
Australia	16.7	28.7	57,071	112	12.4
Canada	18.0	33.5	51,589	113	12.1
United States	18.7	24.5	55,670	141	17.8
New Zealand	19.4	32.3	38,993	93	10.9
United Kingdom	20.6	33.0	43,688	144	11.7
MDE average	*18.7*	*30.4*	*49,402*	*120*	*13.0*
Selected Social Democratic Economies (SDEs)					
Norway	25.3	39.9	92,556	186	8.4
Sweden	25.5	42.9	57,975	118	8.9
Germany	25.9	38.8	47,628	140	10.4
Denmark	28.3	46.3	65,147	116	5.8
Belgium	28.9	42.9	47,541	139	10.1
France	31.0	45.4	44,317	120	8.1
SDE average	*27.5*	*42.7*	*59,194*	*136*	*8.6*

Source: Schneider (2022, 154), from OECD data.

Social expenditures in SDEs are paid for via tax revenues, so SDEs average significantly higher tax rates (42.7%) than MDEs (30.4%).

Although most laissez-faire economists argue that higher tax rates reduce growth and lower tax rates stimulate growth, actual data on MDEs and SDEs indicate that both MDEs and SDEs in the developed world are rich. Real GDP per capita tends to be as high or even higher in SDEs, something that is particularly striking with the consideration that workers in SDEs typically take more vacations and work many fewer hours than workers in MDEs. Similarly, from 1971 to 2019 economic growth in real GDP per capita in SDEs has been similar to and sometimes higher than in MDEs. Despite similar levels of per capita GDP and growth, however, there are vast differences in poverty levels, with MDEs featuring 51% more poverty than SDEs on average.

So, the data tell us that SDEs are able to achieve some of the highest levels of GDP in the world, and they are able to do this while keeping poverty and inequality low and providing their entire population with first-rate health care, education, and welfare. Next, the chapter will examine how SDEs are able to achieve such impressive economic outcomes. Because Nordic countries are among the most successful SDEs in the world, the next sections focus primarily on their model of social democracy.

The Expansion of Human Rights in Social Democratic Economies

The social democratic model began with labor movements and social reformers organizing to push for an expansion of human rights, including the right to the basic necessities of life. For example, Sweden established a Poor Law of 1847 featuring a mandatory public relief fund and housing for the poor. In the 20th century, this was followed by laws providing support for children, sick benefits, social security for the elderly, national health insurance, and national dental care. The right to free, high-quality education, including infant care, pre-school, and even college, was added subsequently.

Most of these reforms were a direct product of highly mobilized and unionized labor movements that organized Politically to push for worker-friendly reforms. Indeed, labor unions still play a prominent role in modern social democracies. It is no accident that the developed countries with the most generous and efficient welfare states are also those with the highest unionization rates. According to the OECD, in 2019, Nordic social democracies had unionization rates ranging from 50.4% in Norway to 66% in Denmark and Sweden to 90.7% in Iceland. Meanwhile, the percentage of workers in unions in MDEs ranged from 9.9% in the United States to 23.5% in the United Kingdom and 26.1% in Canada.[2]

The power of unions in Nordic SDEs resulted in organizational structures that are very worker-friendly. Wages are influenced by centralized wage bargaining between employers, unions, and the government, known as a *corporatist* organizational structure. Firms feature a co-determination structure in which workers play a prominent role in major corporate decisions and are represented on corporate boards of directors. And labor-backed political parties frequently control the government in SDEs, where they work to establish a robust safety net for all citizens.

Given that citizens are supported from the time they are infants all the way until the end of life, this means that SDEs feature a "cradle-to-the-grave welfare state" designed to support citizens' needs whenever they need it. Note also that the state benefits are available to everyone, rich or poor. Thus, one crucial feature of SDEs is the establishment of the *universal human right to all of the necessities of life*. It is not left up to the market system to determine whether or not you should receive health care, food, shelter, or other basic needs. It is the government's job to ensure that all citizens have these things.

Another human right featured in social democracies is work-life balance. In 2021, workers in the United States averaged 1791 hours of work per year, whereas Norwegian workers averaged 1427 hours, Swedish workers averaged 1444 hours, and Danish workers averaged 1363.[3] US workers average 428 hours more per year of work than their Danish counterparts – which is 10.7 additional full time (40-hour) weeks of work! And yet, Danish citizens have higher annual incomes on average. Some of this difference in work hours is a product of the amount of vacation days workers receive. Danish workers are guaranteed 5 weeks of paid vacation and 11 paid public holidays, whereas US workers are not guaranteed any paid vacation or paid holidays. After one year of employment, most US workers are granted two weeks of paid vacation and some paid holidays, but some US workers get no paid vacation time at all.

Gender equity and support for families is another essential feature of social democracies. *The Economist*'s Glass Ceiling Index attempts to measure the role and influence of women in the workforce, by comparing higher education access, labor force participation rates, gender-wage gaps, childcare costs, paid leave for mothers, paid leave for fathers (which allows mothers to work), and women in top positions in corporations and parliament. Topping the index in 2022 are Sweden, Iceland, Finland, and Norway, followed closely by Belgium and France, whereas MDEs rank much lower, with the United Kingdom ranking 17th and the United States 20th.

The system of support for families includes generous parental leave for both mothers and fathers. Countries such as Sweden and Norway grant new parents more than a year of parental leave at 80% pay, and they require that some of that leave be taken by fathers so that parenting responsibilities and career opportunities are more balanced than might otherwise be the case. The United States only guarantees new mothers 12 weeks of unpaid leave and no paternity leave is guaranteed. The United States is the only OECD country that does not require paid maternity leave. Nordic social democracies also require firms to hold positions for workers who decide to take extended family leave, guaranteeing that they can return to their job when they are ready. And, in Nordic SDEs, men and women are guaranteed equal pay for equal work (or work of equal value), which limits pay inequality to levels far below those found in MDEs.

Additional support is provided to new parents in social democracies via free or heavily subsidized childcare, often provided by the government. In MDEs such as the United States, childcare is generally paid for privately by parents and is very expensive.

One direct result of the greater level of support for women in social democracies is a much higher labor force participation rate. According to the OECD (Figure 18.2), between 76% and 85% of women are employed in Nordic social democracies, whereas only 68% of women in the United States are employed. Generous family leave policies play a direct role in allowing women to work and have a family in social democracies, which in turn allows these countries to tap into a greater percentage of the workforce, thereby increasing productivity and GDP.

In order to help women break through the "glass ceiling" that limits women's opportunities at the highest level, Nordic social democracies pioneered regulations requiring the representation of women in parliament and on corporate boards of directors. In 2008, Norway implemented the world's first law requiring that company boards of directors be constituted by at least 40% women. Since then, numerous other social democracies have enacted similar laws. The idea is to gradually break down gender barriers in corporate ranks, and eventually to see more gender balance among corporate leaders. These laws caused an explosion in the representation of women on corporate boards, doubling or even quadrupling the representation of women in SDEs

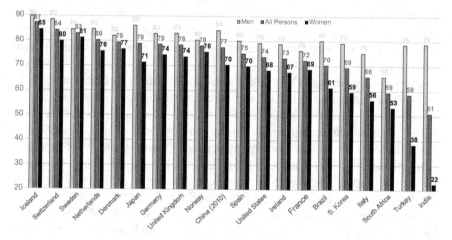

FIGURE 18.2   Labor Force Participation Rates, Select OECD Countries, 2018.

(The Economist 2018). It will be interesting to see how corporate hiring and practices will change once women are more ensconced in corporate leadership. Meanwhile, MDEs that prefer not to regulate corporate behavior experience a much larger degree of gender inequality.

Gender equality is part of the general push in social democracies toward greater equality and the idea that all citizens should have the right to basic necessities as well as economic opportunities. All social democracies feature progressive tax rates with the rich paying higher tax rates than the poor. This contrasts starkly with the tax system in the United States where the richest people actually pay a slightly lower tax rate than the very poor. In 2018, the richest 400 families in the United States paid only 23% of their income in taxes (of all types), whereas the poorest 10% of the population paid 25.6% (Schneider 2022, 730). Thus, the various taxes imposed by the US government actually increase inequality, whereas SDEs use taxes to reduce inequality.

In addition, the support for workers in terms of education, training, and job creation is particularly impressive in Nordic social democracies, much more so than in MDEs. This is a topic taken up in the next section.

Active Labor Market Policies and Industrial Policies

One of the most impressive aspects of the most efficient and dynamic SDEs is their active labor market polices. The most emulated program is the "Flexicurity" system originally designed in Denmark and now adopted in various forms in many social democracies. The system is based on two core principles: (1) flexibility in hiring and firing for firms so they can adjust production based on market conditions, and (2) high-income security for workers, which is achieved via generous unemployment benefits and mandatory active labor market policies that move workers quickly into employment in new jobs. Workers in Denmark not only are guaranteed the right to generous levels of support but also have the duty to participate in training and to accept appropriate offers of employment. Failure to fulfill one's duties can result in government sanctions.

Interestingly, firms in Denmark have a similar level of flexibility as firms in the United States regarding the adjustment of their labor force, resulting in similar turnover rates (Kreiner and Svarer 2022, 84). But the countries differ vastly regarding state support for those who become unemployed. Danish workers receive two years of unemployment compensation at 83% of their previous pay versus 57% of pay for 6 months in the US. Danish workers can continue to get support beyond the second year, if necessary, whereas US support for the long-term unemployed is negligible (Kreiner and Svarer 2022).

Even more striking is the set of programs available to Danish workers. The unemployed in Denmark are provided with job-search assistance, education programs, and retraining. The right to free or heavily subsidized education through college is instrumental in creating more opportunities for those who start out life at the bottom. Adult students receive income payments to ensure that they can complete their studies. This means that workers newly unemployed or just starting out will receive a steady income while they pursue the training and education they need to find employment.

In Sweden, active labor market policies are matched with a very sophisticated "triple helix" model of industrial development. The Swedish government works with local industries to identify promising sectors for economic development, such as biotechnology or aeronautics. The government provides the appropriate infrastructure for the industry in question, while the local university develops research programs to generate cutting-edge technologies and to stimulate innovation. The university also creates training programs to give workers industry-appropriate skills. People seeking employment are funneled via active labor market policies to the appropriate training programs, often with a job waiting for them upon completion of the program. The combination of training, technology development, and infrastructure results in an impressive increase in labor productivity. Private businesses are quite happy to invest in such partnerships given the level of state support. The result has been to push Sweden to the forefront in several key industries, and to establish Sweden as one of the most innovative economies in Europe (Schneider 2007).

Some of the proof of the success of the Nordic model of social democracy can be found in the labor force participation rates as displayed in Figure 18.3. A much larger percentage of the labor force works in the Nordic countries than is the case in the United States.

Additional evidence can be found in the Great Gatsby curve as depicted in Figure 18.3. The Great Gatsby curve, so named by Alan Krueger in 2012, plots inequality, as measured by the Gini coefficient, against intergenerational earnings mobility, which is the extent to which earnings of children are affected by the earnings of their parents. A society that is a true "land of opportunity" would tend to see a large number of children of poor parents able to move up to a higher income bracket. Figure 18.3 shows that the Nordic SDEs (Sweden, Finland, Norway, and Denmark) are all significantly more equal than MDEs (Great Britain, the United States, Ireland, Australia, Canada, and New Zealand), and the SDEs all experience significantly more intergenerational earnings mobility. A Danish child from the poorest 25% of the population has a 23.5% chance of staying poor and a 22% chance of getting rich (making it to the richest 25% of the population), whereas a US child from the poorest 25% has a 41.8% chance of staying poor and only an 8.5% chance of making it to the top (Schneider 2022, 546). Relative to MDEs, social democracies appear to be the actual lands of opportunity.

Another component of the effort of social democracies to generate a wealth of opportunities for their populations is their slate of policies to stimulate innovation and entrepreneurship. One of the factors typically overlooked by

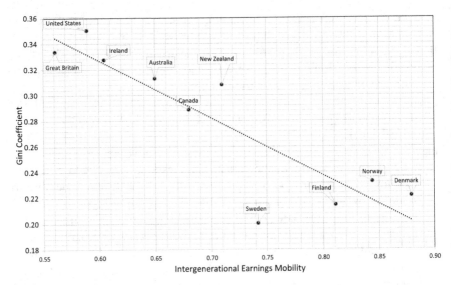

FIGURE 18.3 The Great Gatsby Curve: Inequality (Gini) versus Intergenerational Mobility, 2018.

mainstream economists is the role of the state in creating an environment that is conducive to innovation and growth. It is no accident that the most rapidly growing economies over the last 50 years have utilized high levels of state involvement.

For example, governments fund scientific research to generate break-throughs, provide early-stage financing for high-risk endeavors, supply infrastructure to improve efficiency, provide education and training to improve productivity, and much more. One of the quintessential examples of state leadership in innovation is the triple helix model described above, which was pioneered in Sweden and imitated in most other European social democracies.

There is also substantial support for entrepreneurs in Nordic social democracies. Rates of start-up creation are among the highest in the world in Nordic SDEs: Norway has more entrepreneurs per capita than the United States does, and Sweden generates more patents per capita than the United States (Lakey 2016). It turns out that entrepreneurs in Nordic countries are more willing to take risks because of the generous safety net, which means that if their business idea does not work out they will still have an income from the state and retraining until they find a new job. The fact that education and health care are free and childcare is heavily subsidized means that many college graduates start their working life debt free, which makes them more willing to take a chance on a startup (Semuels 2017). Then, there is substantial direct support for entrepreneurs. Norway offers free courses on starting a company, and local governments across the region provide direct support in the form of training and infrastructure, including some of the fastest internet speeds in the world. This, coupled with some of the world's best educational systems that emphasize technology from an early age, has resulted in a burgeoning tech sector in the Nordic countries (e.g., Spotify, Skype, and Angry Birds).

Some countries, such as South Korea, have gone even further, establishing a *developmental state* in which the government intervenes directly in industrial planning (Schneider 2022). The South Korean government would determine an industry in which it could be competitive, construct a supportive infrastructure for the industry to succeed, develop education and training programs to provide skilled workers for the industry in question, and provide government research assistance and funding to large conglomerates to develop cutting edge technologies and products. Furthermore, the government protected infant industries until they had time to develop but insisted that support for corporations was conditional on meeting clear performance goals, including job creation and hitting export targets. South Korea used this approach to target one industry after another, beginning with simpler industries like energy and textiles, then moving into steel and electronics, and then into cars, shipbuilding, and advanced technologies. The result was stunning. In 1960, South Korea was one of the poorest countries in the world. In 2022, South Korea was a wealthy country with a higher GDP per capita than most EU countries and the second-fastest rate of economic growth over the last four decades (behind only China). Clearly, an efficient government with vision can establish an economic system that is remarkably dynamic.[4]

Another key element to a successful modern economic system is environmental sustainability. Economists project that environmental damage from climate change and eco-system destruction will reduce economic growth by 2% per year by 2060 (Schneider 2022, 461). Not only will economies that emphasize sustainability experience less damage, but they will be better poised to take advantage of the world's need for sustainable products and manufacturing techniques.

Perhaps not surprisingly, social democracies are leading the world in efforts to reorient their economies to be sustainable. The Environmental Performance Index, produced by the Yale Center for Environmental Law and Policy, ranks countries on climate change performance, environmental health, and ecosystem vitality (Wolf, et al. 2022). The results are displayed in Table 18.2. Nordic SDEs Denmark, Finland, and Sweden rank in the top 5, whereas Norway ranks 20th, brought down by their massive oil export industry. The United States and Canada rank particularly poorly, 43rd and 49th, respectively, thanks to lax environmental regulations, a continuing focus on fossil fuels for energy and transportation, poor public transportation options, and notoriously dirty industrial farming systems that have a huge carbon footprint. Interestingly, the United Kingdom stands out as an MDE with a strong environmental performance record recently thanks to an emphasis on reducing emissions and

TABLE 18.2 Environmental Performance Index, 2022

Country	Score	Ranking
Denmark	77.9	1
United Kingdom	77.7	2
Finland	76.5	3
Sweden	72.7	5
Netherlands	62.6	11
France	62.5	12
Germany	62.4	13
Australia	60.1	17
Norway	59.3	20
United States	51.1	43
Canada	50.0	49

switching to renewable energy. This indicates that, although social democracies tend to be more environmentally focused, it is possible for MDEs to be more sustainable if they are willing to engage in stricter industrial regulations than they have historically used.

The economic record of social democracies is quite impressive in terms of human rights, work-life balance, equality, opportunity for workers, economic growth, and sustainability.

Social Democracies as a Step Toward Full Socialism

Despite the many achievements of social democracies, radical political economists generally see them as less desirable than full socialism. Social democratic systems still feature a significant degree of poverty and inequality. Work is still alienating for many. Also, some progress has been made, but there are still significant environmental problems in SDEs.

And the incessant attacks on the welfare state by capitalist interests make social democracy inherently unstable. For example, the Swedish social democratic system was gradually weakened in the 1980s and 1990s under pressure from global competition. Inequality increased substantially, and the generosity of the welfare state was reduced. This led Rudolf Meidner, one of the architects of the Swedish model, to declare that it was being systematically dismantled and destroyed (Meidner 1998). Other social democracies have faced similar reductions of social safety nets, as well as reductions in regulations and taxes on corporations.

The relentless pressure from capitalists to undermine social democracy led the Swedish social democrats to advocate a gradual move to full-fledged socialism. Swedish economist G. Adler-Karlsson made the following appeal:

Let us look upon our capitalists in the same way as we have looked upon our kings in Scandinavia. A hundred years ago a Scandinavian king carried a lot of power. Fifty years ago he still had considerable power. According to our constitutions the king still has equally as much formal power as a hundred years ago, but today he is in fact powerless. We have done this without dangerous and disruptive internal fights. Let us in the same manner avoid the even more dangerous contests that are unavoidable if we enter the road of formal socialization. Let us instead strip and divest our present capitalists of one after another of their ownership functions. Let us give them a new dress, but one similar to that of the famous emperor in Hans Christian Andersen's tale. After a few decades they will then remain, perhaps formally as kings but in reality as naked symbols of a passed and inferior development stage.

(Adler-Karlsson 1970, 95–96)

It is an intriguing vision. Could the foundation provided by social democracy, where half of the economy is already run by the government for the benefit of the people, and the other half is directly influenced by government policy designed to foster job creation and innovation, provide a jumping-off point for true socialism?

Given the experiences of the modern world, it appears to be quite possible for a socialist system to exist and to be productive and efficient. In the last several decades, the most rapid economic growth rates in the world have tended to be in government-directed economies such as China and South Korea (Schneider 2022).[5] The Mondragon Cooperatives of Spain have demonstrated repeatedly over the last 70 years that workers can efficiently run and direct businesses and even out-perform standard capitalist ventures (Sackrey, Schneider and Knoedler 2016).[6] A carefully designed market socialist system that was democratically controlled might therefore be able to improve the outcomes of social democracies, especially when it comes to the experiences of workers and the environment. Such a system could still be competitive with market capitalist economies due to the emphasis on productivity and innovation.

Ultimately, despite the flaws in social democratic systems, and the decline in the generosity of social democratic welfare states in recent decades, social democracies remain some of the most humane, sustainable, and equitable economies in the modern world. In fact, given their places among the leaders of the World Happiness Index, the OECD Better Life Index, the World Innovation Index, the Environmental Performance Index, and measures of GDP per capita, modern social democracies appear to be remarkably successful relative to other types of economic systems, and especially MDE systems. That makes them worthy of study and, perhaps, of emulation.

Notes

1 See Schneider 2022 for more discussion of these categories. Note that Schneider defines Social Democracies as Social Market Economies due to the relatively even split between government (social values) and markets found in such systems.
2 Source: OECD.Stat. Accessed 12.15.2022.
3 Source: OECD.Stat. Accessed 12.8.2022.
4 South Korea had favorable conditions that allowed it to implement a developmental state. Many poor countries in the modern era do not have the same options. Most heavily indebted poor countries (HIPCs) have extremely high levels of foreign debt, which forces them to depend on funding from the World Bank and the International Monetary Fund. These international financial institutions (IFIs) loan money to HIPCs under strict conditions. IFIs insist on the adoption of neoliberal policies, fiscal austerity, and open markets. These conditions make it impossible for poor countries to invest in education, infrastructure, industrial development, and protectionist policies. Meanwhile, elites in the HIPCs enrich themselves via their ownership of extractive industries. Sadly, if the power of the IFIs were directed toward the structural transformation of poor countries via robust investment in the establishment of a developmental state, HIPCs would be much more likely to escape the poverty traps in which they find themselves.
5 See Chapter 33.
6 See Chapter 10.

References

Adler-Karlsson, Gunnar. *Functional Socialism: A Swedish Theory for Democratic Socialization.* Stockholm: Bokforlaget Prisma, 1970.

Childs, Marquis, *The Middle Way.* New Haven: Yale University Press, 1936.

Kreiner, Claus Thustrup and Michael Svarer, Danish Flexicurity: Rights and Duties. *Journal of Economic Perspectives.* v. 36 (4), 2022. 81–102.

Lakey, George, *Viking Economics.* Brooklyn, N.Y.: Melville House 2016

Meidner, Rudolf, The Rise and Fall of the Swedish Model. *Challenge.* v. 41 (1), 1998. 69–90.

Sackrey, Charles, Geoffrey Schneider, and Janet Knoedler, *Introduction to Political Economy,* 8th Edition. Boston: Dollars and Sense, 2016.

Schneider, Geoffrey, Sweden's Economic Recovery and the Theory of Comparative Institutional Advantage, *Journal of Economic Issues.* v. 41 (2), 2007. 417–426.

Schneider, Geoffrey, *Economic Principles and Problems: A Pluralist Approach.* London: Routledge, 2022

Semuels, Alana, Why does Sweden Have So Many Start-Ups? *The Atlantic,* 2017.

The Economist, Ten Years on from Norway's Quota for Women on Corporate Boards. *The Economist,* 2018.

Wolf, M. J., J. W. Emerson, D. C. Esty, A. deSerbinin, Z. A. Wendling, et al. 2022 *Environmental Performance Index.* New Haven, CT: Yale Center for Environmental Law & Policy, 2022. epi.yale.edu

19

ECONOMIC DEVELOPMENT IN THE 21ST CENTURY

Concepts, Constraints, and Possibilities

Jayati Ghosh and C. P. Chandrasekhar

Contexts and Concepts of Development

Development, however differently it may have been defined, has been central to the study of economies for centuries. But the emergence of the distinct academic sub-discipline of development economics can be traced to post-Second World War wave of decolonization, when there was heightened attention on the prospects for development in underdeveloped countries.

Very different concerns underlay that interest in different circles. Governments in the newly independent countries and others that had experienced the fallout of the Great Depression were aspiring to accelerate development and "catch up" or reduce their economic distance from the developed countries by designing and pursuing "national" strategies that involved delinking from foreign capital and markets. That seemed imperative because past experience indicated that there were limits to significantly raising exports at remunerative prices within the prevailing international economic order. These less developed countries saw the experience of rapid development in the Soviet Union despite relative isolation by Western powers and its resilience and role during the Second World War as providing the rudiments of an alternative economic trajectory. That inspired a turn to "development planning" (Chandrasekhar 2016).

The governments in the industrialized West worried that extreme poverty in the underdeveloped world could drive the majority to push for more egalitarian, "socialist" strategies with reduced roles for markets and private initiative, thereby encouraging them to befriend the Soviet Union. So, there was a concerted effort on the part of the West, especially the United States, to use "development aid" and technical assistance to retain their influence in these countries,

DOI: 10.4324/9781003366690-22

many of which were former colonies of one or other Western power.[1] Meanwhile, the Soviet Union found the need to build alliances to dilute its own political encirclement, expand the "socialist bloc" following Soviet-style policies and strategies of development and increase trade integration with and influence in the less developed market economies. The concept of economic development and the strategies devised to pursue trajectories that facilitated catch-up were influenced by this mix of concerns and interests. Economic development was sometimes seen in terms of universal trajectories involving the structural transformation of economies as their per capita incomes increased, along the lines of the Kuznets Curve (Kuznets 1955). But there was also the recognition that developing countries could differ in significant ways from industrial economies in their economic logic, whether expressed in the idea of economic dualism put forward by W. Arthur Lewis (1954) or through Paul Rosenstein-Rodan's (1943) theory of the co-ordination failures inherent in less developed economies. Kalecki (1976) argued that the most critical difference between the two types of economies arose from the nature of unemployment: in developed capitalist economies, unemployment was seen to be linked to the inadequacy of effective demand; in developing economies, it was seen as structural, resulting from shortages in capital equipment and supply bottlenecks in the production of necessities such as agricultural wage goods. These varying perspectives were also associated with sometimes conflicting approaches to growth strategy: balanced growth strategies dependent on central co-ordination through development planning (Mahalanobis 1955) versus unbalanced "big push" strategies for industrialization advocated, for example, by Albert Hirschman (1958).

Import Substitution

Given the experience of being subordinate players in the unequal international order that prevailed in the interwar years, governments of underdeveloped countries of reasonable geographical size wanted to match their newly won political freedom with a substantial degree of independence from foreign capital and Western "aid". Since relying on foreign markets for growth would dilute such independence, they were committed to protecting their home markets for domestic producers and growing those markets to serve as drivers of growth. Import substitution backed by trade protection was a commonly adopted policy. Countries that did not have the size to rely solely on internal markets looked for opportunities to link with more fortunate, less developed countries and grow in tandem with them, rather than depend on the West.

The focus of development was to reduce the gap separating rich and poor countries, so the main metric used to measure progress was increasing per capita income relative to advanced market economies. This required increasing investment rates (as shares of GDP), which in turn required suppressing domestic consumption and lifting the extremely low saving rate in many of these countries (United Nations 1951), in order to generate internal resources for investment. In addition, structural change (expressed as a shift of workers away from low to high-productivity sectors) was seen to be essential, through diversification away from agriculture and other primary production to manufacturing, where the potential for rapid increases in productivity was high. Industrialization was seen as the core process in any development agenda. This made development synonymous with economic growth, industrialization, and the building of industrial and then post-industrial societies similar to those of affluent countries. It was only several decades later that wider and more nuanced concepts of development, which included human development and the enhancement of people's freedoms and capabilities, came to be recognized. Even then, income growth and sectoral diversification remained the central goals of economic development policy.

However, the complexities inherent in this process soon became apparent. First, there was the issue of the required surplus for industrialization: both the size and the composition of this surplus matter. This requires, for example, a marketed surplus of the essential goods required for workers' subsistence, such as food and other basic necessities (otherwise referred to as "wage goods") or the ability to import them. This means that the issue of financing development has a real economy aspect, in addition to enabling the purely financial flows required. This problem became evident as countries seeking to increase investment came up against not only domestic savings constraints but also wage goods constraints and foreign exchange constraints.

Another complexity arose from the institutional and political economy conditions of the development project. Most countries operated within the framework of a "mixed economy", with a significant role for markets and the private sector along with public intervention. Since market economies are by nature demand-constrained systems, it was necessary to relax the demand constraint as well, simply to induce private investment. "Making markets" was a crucial requirement—and one device for that was a policy of import substitution that reserved the domestic market for domestic producers. However, if the domestic market itself did not grow, further expansion would be inhibited once domestic supply had substituted for the earlier imports. Growing the domestic market in turn required two strategies, which very few countries could undertake successfully. First, there was a need for significantly enhanced public expenditure (which was important both for improving infrastructure and other supply conditions and for expanding the domestic market), preferably financed with taxation. Second, it was important to reduce asset and income inequalities, to create a larger base of mass consumption, which (given the structure of these economies at that time) had to include measures to break down monopolies of land ownership through land reform.

The political economy configurations in most countries of the Global South did not really allow for such measures to be undertaken, as governments balked at the prospect of taking on powerful vested interests among the rich and landed classes. This obviously impacted the ability to reduce social and economic deprivation, and it also held back the growth of the home market and made economic diversification more difficult. Persisting inequality also led to demands from elites for inessential manufactures or imports associated with conspicuous and luxury consumption, creating a disjunction between the nation's capacity to produce and the desire to consume of those who had the incomes to effectively demand goods they desired. Over time, this generated pressures for opening up the economy to both trade and finance (Chandrasekhar and Patnaik 1995).

The Era of Liberalization

Notwithstanding internal political economy pressures, the emergence of an alternative policy to far-reaching institutional change depended on greater access to international finance starting in the late 1970s. The removal of regulations on international trade and finance inevitably widened current account deficits, at least in the short run. These need to be financed with foreign exchange. The oil price shocks in the 1970s had generated large hard currency surpluses for the oil exporters, which flowed into the private international financial system and increased pressures on private financial institutions to find new targets to lend to and invest in. Concurrently, record trade and current account deficits in the United States increased dollar liquidity in global markets. Financial liberalization in the advanced economies, together with the slowdown in real economy growth, particularly in the United States in the 1970s, strengthened this tendency. Such enhanced access to foreign capital through debt and equity markets ensured that external liberalization in the developing countries could be sustained for relatively long periods, despite periodic balance of payments crises. Even when the process was halted because of unsustainable deficits, debt rescheduling and fiscal adjustment under IMF surveillance paved the way for new rounds of capital inflow.

This was associated with growing demand for the transformation of the economic policy regime in less developed countries. This was broadly in line with the "Washington Consensus" on the set of policies promoted by the IMF and the World Bank, especially from the 1980s onward (Wiliamson 2002). Instead of relying on domestic markets for growth, export-led growth became the new orthodoxy. It was combined with the argument for internal deregulation, on the assumption that unfettered markets would generate competition to restructure inefficient productive capacities, while foreign investment would use developing countries as locations for world market production. Deregulation of domestic investment and other economic activities and markets, along with relaxation of restrictions in external transactions, was supposed to encourage economic activities that reflected "comparative advantage" and induce greater economic "efficiency". All these would encourage exports to become an engine of growth.

The new export obsession ignored the fact that the countries that did succeed in an export-led growth strategy (such as those in East Asia) were those that largely avoided these deregulated strategies of deregulation and blanket liberalization. Instead, they relied on a combination of export orientation and import substitution, directed by proactive developmental states. Furthermore, the success of the first phase of late industrializers in East Asia was linked to one exceptional factor: the special relationship with the United States, as "frontline" states in the Cold War fought by proxy between the two superpowers of that time. China, the more recent exceptional performer, also had a government that actively intervened to regulate, govern, and shape markets and investment. Countries that were not incorporated into the US sphere of influence in the ways in which South Korea, for example, was, or which did not have governments that could adopt an independent developmental stance because of special social and historical conditions, but merely opted for integration through liberalization, were not successful in realizing sustained export-led expansion. The very fact that ever since the Second World War, and especially after the widespread adoption of export-oriented strategies, there were very few cases of export-led success in market economies (Japan, South Korea, Taiwan (China) as well as the city-states of Hong Kong and Singapore), and one significant success in a "hybrid", socialist-market economy (China), is evidence of the wider failure of the strategy of export-led industrialization.

The period of globalization was certainly driven by the push from international financial institutions and global capital's efforts to enter new markets. But, in addition, the desire of the dominant classes and elites in the less developed countries to exploit the opportunity offered by easier access to foreign capital was also important. Such capital, by enhancing liquidity and fueling an expansion of domestic credit, contributed to increases in demand that raised GDP growth for short periods, even if it mostly did not result in productive diversification in recipient countries.

However, financial liberalization, based on the mistaken notions of "efficient financial markets" and self-regulation of large players, has generated a series of speculative bubbles that have ended in crises, within advanced and developing countries as well as in the world as a whole. In the developing world, the consequences of not holding global reserve currencies make the implications of such crises particularly severe, as they result in domestic financial fragility, banking crises, and real economic slumps that can alter previous growth trajectories in fundamental ways (Chandrasekhar and Ghosh, eds. 2009). In addition, exposure to external finance affects domestic economic policies because of the fear of capital flight, constraining fiscal and monetary policies that could promote industrialization. Even the most "successful" economies of the developing world did not gain much in financial terms from capital market integration. This is because of the global currency hierarchies mentioned earlier: economic agents in the United States and other rich nations (especially those holding global reserve currencies) can borrow relatively cheaply, while financial investments in low- and middle-income countries are perceived as inherently more "risky", even when that is not borne out by experience. As a result, returns on assets held by foreign residents in such countries tend to be much higher than the return on assets held abroad (including central bank reserves held in assets like US Treasury Bills) held by residents of these countries. This difference between rates of return on foreign assets and liabilities is known as seigniorage gains or losses. Several apparently dynamic Asian economies, like Malaysia and Thailand, lost so much in such seigniorage costs that these outweighed all forms of net inflow put together (Ghosh 2023).

Meanwhile, various aspects of the global trade architecture put in place in this century have served to diminish the possibilities of autonomous industrialization. There was an explosion in the treaties, agreements, and other mechanisms whereby global capital imposes rules, regulations, and modes of behavior upon governments and their citizenry—from the GATT that created the World Trade Organization, to various bilateral and plurilateral trade agreements and investment agreements (Ghosh 2015). These have also operated to constrain domestic industrial policies. For example, the Agreement on Trade-Related Investment Measures (TRIMS) prevents local content specifications, which serve to increase linkages between foreign investors and local manufacturers and generate more domestic upstream production in inputs and ancillaries and were widely used in the past by rich countries during the course of their own industrialization process. Similarly, foreign exchange balancing requirements and restrictions on foreign exchange use by foreign investors can play a very important role in preserving scarce foreign exchange and enabling developing countries to make the best use of it for purposes of industrialization, but this possibility is also effectively denied by TRIMS.

The Agreement on Trade-related Intellectual Property Rights (TRIPS) allows for the concentration and privatization of knowledge in the hands of major private companies and severely restricts the imitative innovation, or emulation, that was used by all currently rich countries for their own industrialization. This has become a major impediment for enabling domestic production in low- and middle-income countries, which emerged as a major problem for public health during the COVID-19 pandemic, and is likely to become a major barrier in global strategies for climate change mitigation and adaptation. The Agreement on Agriculture (AoA) contains fine print that effectively allows developed countries to continue with their massive subsidization and protection of their own agriculture and agri-businesses, but it prevents developing countries from doing even a small fraction of this. Other "economic partnership" agreements signed since then often go even further in such restrictions, even as they continue to be entered into by lower-income countries for the elusive goal of greater exporting access to rich country markets.

Meanwhile, global tax arrangements, caught in a time-warp for more than a century, continue to operate as if multinational corporations and tax havens do not exist, enabling the shifting of profits, incomes, and assets by both corporations and rich individuals to low-tax or no-tax jurisdictions. These—and the consequent illicit financial flows—mean a significant loss of fiscal revenues for developing countries, which they can ill afford to lose (Ndikumana and Boyce, eds. 2022). International agreements that would remedy this continue to be biased in favor of rich countries who dominate the negotiations, preventing the tax cooperation that would provide more fiscal space for development.

The period of loose money policies in advanced economies after the Global Financial Crisis, with massive increases in liquidity and very low, sometimes even negative, interest rates, led to large inflows of "hot money": private financial capital driven not so much by developing countries' economic outlook as by developed countries' macroeconomic policies. Capital inflows triggered higher interest-rate spreads and currency appreciation, generating asset bubbles in recipient economies. It also made these economies especially vulnerable to capital flight and to possible debt crises when the flow of finance halted. By the early 2020s, tighter monetary policies had the inevitable effect of causing debt crises and serious problems in financing both public and private investments, in scores of developing countries. The inability or unwillingness of the global system to provide rapid and effective debt relief to lower-income sovereign debtors has become yet another major drag on their economic development potential.

All of these processes reflect the significance of power—and of power imbalances—both within and between countries, as large corporations and rich elites have influenced the economic policies of their own governments and determined the legal codes that frame the global economic and financial architecture (Pistor 2019). As a result, the pursuit of neoliberal economic policies has led to significant increases in both spatial and vertical inequalities of assets and incomes, extreme concentration of wealth and public impoverishment, increasing material insecurity of working people in rich and poor countries alike, and the intensification of social deprivation.

There are some important exceptions—most notably, the spectacular rise of China over the first two decades of the 21st century. It is now increasingly recognized that this success was not based on neoliberal policies but on active state intervention in making and then shaping markets, and strategically using export orientation based on significant economies of scale along with active import substitution and domestic technology development. This model is hard to replicate, not least because China's very success becomes a barrier for other countries wishing to adopt the same strategy, given the sheer size and productive capacity of China's economy. For example, India—which is frequently but wrongly compared to China—has been much less successful at productive transformation and shifting the bulk of the workforce to higher value-added activities, despite apparently relatively high growth rates of economic activity. It is true that China is now a significant player in the global geopolitical and economic landscape, and some larger and more populous economies, including the group now included in the expanded BRICS (which includes Brazil, Russia, India, China, South Africa, and recent entrants Egypt, Ethiopia, Iran, and the United Arab Emirates) also have a bigger role than earlier, especially in combination. Nevertheless, the basic power imbalances and constraints posed by the international regulatory context remain strong.

The important conclusion is that neoliberal policies within countries and the thrust of the substantial changes in international trade and finance have sharply eroded the possibilities of autonomous development in much of the world. This has resulted from several factors. Deregulation gives a greater role in markets that are not benign because of the differential power of agents who participate in markets. The international financial institutions have failed to meet their obligations as originally proposed in the Bretton Woods agreement and instead have in effect served the interests of large capital to the detriment of people in the affected countries. As a result, the dependence on global finance and the intervention of the IMF and World Bank in the context of crises have led to inadequate public resource mobilization despite regressive tax policies, cuts in public spending cuts, reducing both necessary public investment and redistributive social expenditure. Neoliberalism is a strengthening of the class project favoring large capitalists and elites, involving privatization of public assets, favors to large private capital such as land grants, permission to exploit nature, budgetary transfers and access to low-cost intermediates, and fiscal policies that subsidize the rich at the expense of the poor. All of these policies together engineer a redistribution of incomes in favor of the rich. The flip side of that is a loss of employment and livelihood opportunities for the bulk of people, with increases in precarious low-wage employment and self-employment and declining wage shares in national income.

Recent years have seen an intensification of these unequal economic processes. Uneven fiscal responses during and after the COVID-19 pandemic, between rich economies on the one hand and low- and middle-income countries on the other, accentuated existing imbalances. Since then, the implications for developing countries of financial liberalization and inadequate re-regulation in the advanced economies have become even more apparent. Just as in the late 2000s, people in developing countries have been devastated by dramatic increases in global food and fuel prices that have resulted not from changes in real demand and supply, but by profit margin increases of global corporations and financial speculation in commodity markets. Meanwhile, rapidly accelerating climate change has created ever greater needs for climate finance, even as it has been almost non-existent, even compared to promises. In sum, the development prospects for much of the world in the third decade of the 21st century look bleak. Yet rapid shifts in geopolitics and the fragmentation of cross-border trade create new possibilities even as they generate greater uncertainty.

The Need to Re-imagine Development

While this presents a depressing, even tragic, picture, none of this is inevitable. It is not just possible but necessary to reconceive development—and therefore the construction of economies—to fit the needs of people and the planet, rather than the more common reverse tendency of subordinating people's needs and nature to the supposed demands of the market-driven economy. While economic diversification is still required and necessary for development, it must be sought along very different principles from those that currently hold sway. Some of the basic principles are described below.

Obviously, economic arrangements should go beyond being oriented to the simple expansion of aggregate incomes and profits as the most significant goals. It is deeply irrational to be obsessed with GDP growth as the prime indicator of even material progress. GDP as a measure was created in the mid-20th century and is clearly not fit for purpose to evaluate progress or development now. It leaves out too much, such as the essential and often unpaid care work that constitutes the bedrock on which societies and economies rest. It includes too much that is socially undesirable, such as heavily polluting activities, gains from financial speculation, and the production of weapons of mass destruction. Recognizing that expansion of monetary incomes is not the sole purpose of economic life makes other goals matter for economic policy: reasonable living conditions for all, health for all, development of people's capabilities and space for their creativity, decent employment opportunities, and safe and clean environments. A major goal of economic policy must be to ensure that access to the essentials of life—food, water, basic housing, and so on—is not determined by the ability to pay but treated as a human right, with these basic goods and services made available to all in an affordable way. The right to decent employment must be seen not just as a fundamental right but also as a central goal of economic policy. At the same time, the recognition of unpaid work—specifically but not only in care activities—is an essential element of this. This also requires explicit public policies to recognize, reduce, redistribute unpaid care work and adequately reward, and represent all care workers. Ensuring the dignity of all work must be a central part of the focus of economic decision-making.

This requires a different attitude toward how markets should function. Market forces that help in achieving social goals should be encouraged, while those that operate to reduce the standards of living and quality of life of ordinary people must be regulated, restricted, or even abolished. Extreme inequalities should not be tolerated. Systems of taxation and distribution, as well as methods of monitoring and regulating pay and other returns, should ensure that material differences between people do not grow too large. Social discrimination and exclusion of all kinds must be actively discouraged and sought to be done away with, while ensuring equality of opportunity, social protection, and dignity for all.

This also requires much greater social respect for nature. Economic activities need to be monitored and assessed for the damage they do to nature, with a focus on reducing this as much as possible. Unsustainable patterns of production and consumption are now deeply entrenched in the richer countries and are aspired to in developing countries, even as billions of citizens of the developing world still have poor or inadequate access to the most basic conditions of decent life, such as minimum physical infrastructure including electricity and transport and communication links, sanitation, health, nutrition, and education. Ensuring universal provision of this in some countries will require greater per capita use of natural resources and more carbon-emitting production. But both sustainability and equity require a reduction of the excessive resource use and carbon emissions of the rich, especially in developed countries, but also among the elites in the developing world.

Ensuring these changes requires a reshaping of the priorities of national governments, away from the failed neoliberal agenda, the free market rhetoric of which is actually associated with state intervention to engineer a redistribution of incomes and wealth in favor of the rich. What is required instead is intervention aimed at regulating the functioning of capital, especially finance, and the mobilization of resources through taxation of the incomes and wealth of the rich to pursue a redistributive agenda that also generates a market for mass consumption goods and relaxes binding supply constraints. That in turn requires a transformation of the state, ensured through mass support and social sanction for an alternative agenda.

These policies at the national level obviously require an international context that would permit, enable, and even encourage them. A fundamental change required is a reshaping of the international economic order, where currently power play not only constrains structural change and development in low- and middle-income countries but also drastically reduces their fiscal space and capability to address climate change and realize the United Nations' sustainable development goals. Several trade agreements would need to be renegotiated, in particular, the WTO's TRIPS, TRIMS, and AoA, as well as various bilateral and plurilateral agreements. A viable and speedy mechanism for sovereign debt restructuring and relief that involves all public and private creditors is essential. Private financial flows both within and across national borders clearly need to be subject to greater regulation to bring them into alignment with social and planetary goals. The pressing challenges posed by climate change cannot be addressed without a global response based on the principles of global public investment, which could be implemented by using the frame already provided by international financial institutions to provide much-needed financial resources for public spending by countries where such investments are most required. International tax cooperation that would enable the fair taxation of multinational companies and wealth taxes on the extremely rich in all countries is also important.

It is clear that such changes would require significant political pressure within the developed countries as well as greater solidarity among low- and middle-income countries, which would strengthen their voice in international negotiations. The fact that the world is increasingly multipolar, with the attrition of the superpower status of the United States and the rise of China, could mean some amplification of the voices of less developed countries. But to be effective in bringing about the change in the international order, those voices must speak in unison and reflect the needs of their people rather than their elites. Ultimately, this means shifts in national and international political forces.

Note

1 See Rosen 1985 for an interesting narrative on how this worked.

References

Chandrasekhar, C. P.. 2016. "Development planning", in Reinert, Eric S., Jayati Ghosh and Rainer Kaitel (eds.), *Handbook of Alternative Theories of Economic Development*, Cheltenham, UK: Edward Elgar.

Chandrasekhar, C. P. and Prabhat Patnaik. 1995. Indian economy under structural adjustment. *Economic and Political Weekly*, Vol 30 No 47.

Chandrasekhar, C. P. and Jayati Ghosh, eds. 2009. *After Crisis: Adjustment, Recovery and Fragility in East Asia*. New Delhi: Tulika Books.

Ghosh, Jayati. 2015. The creation of the next imperialism: The institutional architecture. *Monthly Review*, Vol 67 No 3.

Ghosh, Jayati. 2023. "Macroprudential policies in Asia: A consideration of some Asian experiences", in Esteban Perez-Caldentey, (ed.), *Financial Openness, Financial Fragility, and Policies for Economic Stability: A Comparative Analysis Across Regions of the Developing World*, Santiago, Chile: ECLAC.

Hirschman, Albert. 1958 *The Strategy of Economic Development*, New Haven, Conn.: Yale University Press.

Kuznets, Simon. 1955. Economic growth and income inequality. *American Economic Review* 45 (March): 1–28.

Kalecki, Michal. 1976. *Essays on Developing Economies*, London: Harvester Press.

Lewis, Arthur. 1954. Economic development with unlimited supplies of labour. *The Manchester School*, Vol 22, No 2.

Mahalanobis, P. C. 1955. 'The approach of operational research to planning in India', *Sankhya*, Vol 16, Parts I and 2.

Ndikumana, Leonce and James Boyce. Eds. 2022. *On the Trail of Capital Flight from Africa: The Takers and the Enablers*. Oxford University Press.

Pistor, Katharina. 2019, *The Code of Capital*, Princeton: Princeton University Press.

Rosen, George. 1985. *Western Economists and Eastern Societies: Agents of Change in South Asia*. Baltimore: The Johns Hopkins University Press.

Rosenstein-Rodan, P. N. 1943. Problems of Industrialisation of Eastern and South-Eastern Europe. *The Economic Journal*, Vol 53 No 210/211.

United Nations. 1951. *Measures for the Economic Development of Underdeveloped Countries: Report by a Group of Experts Appointed by the Secretary-General of the United Nations*, New York: United Nations.

Wiliamson, John. 2002. "What Washington means by policy reform", *Petersen Institute for International Economics*, November 1. https://www.piie.com/commentary/speeches-papers/what-washington-means-policy-reform

20

GOOD SCIENCE, BAD CLIMATE, BIG LIES

Climate, Class, and Ideology in the Capitalocene

Jason W. Moore and John Peter Antonacci

Introduction

You've been lied to. Whenever you read, view, and hear the conventional description of the climate crisis, it's something like this: "Human society causes climate change" (Intergovernmental Panel on Climate Change 2022). (From the IPCC's most recent report.) Climate change is anthropogenic. (Made by Humans.) The phrase is repeated. *Anthropogenic.* On an endless loop. *Anthropogenic.* By academics. By journalists. By the major environmentalist organizations. By the leading institutions of the transnational bourgeoisie, like the World Economic Forum. What sane person, upon examining the evidence, would say otherwise?

Very few, it turns out. In striking testimony to the power of bourgeois naturalism, the hegemonic view on the left holds that climate change is indeed the result of "human activity" (Angus 2016). There's a sort of naïve empiricism in such statements, which smuggle bourgeois humanism and naturalism into radical assessments of the climate crisis.

To be sure, the radical view condemns capitalism. But the interpretive architecture inverts – rather than transcends – the neo-Malthusian scheme. Rather than an abstract Humanity, with "too many people" driving the planet toward "overshoot," an abstract capitalism creates "anthropogenic rifts" that define the climate crisis (Ehrlich 1968; Catton 1980; Clark and Foster 2016; Foster 1994). In both instances, capitalism – when not disappeared entirely – manifests as a subset of a general category, Humanity. In a breathtaking instance of the "ideological unconscious," even many socialists accept Man and Nature as innocent descriptive categories (Althusser 1977). They are anything but. These are fetishes, ahistorical and asocial ideological constructs, "ruling ideas" invented

DOI: 10.4324/9781003366690-23

through capitalism's becoming a biogeological force – and refined ever since (Marx and Engels 2010; Patel and Moore 2017). Man and Nature – the upper-case is deliberate – drip with blood and dirt; far from merely cultural *expressions*, they have been crucial instruments of bourgeois ideology and the endless accumulation of capital from the very beginning.

The resulting model of historical change is one of *collision* between discrete essences: of Man and Nature. On this, the mainstream and ecosocialist Anthropocenists agree – even if the latter give *their* Limits-to-Growthism a shiny new coat of bright red paint (Chakrabarty 2021; Foster 2002b; Moore 2011; Bonneuil and Fressoz 2015). The collisionist divergence with historical materialism – defined by its emphasis on the active, interpenetrating dialectics of "historical man" and "historical nature" within specific socio-metabolic relational "ensembles" – is impossible to miss (Marx and Engels 2010). But this is precisely what's happened with the "Capitalism in the Anthropocene" discourse (Foster 2022; Saito 2022). This is no academic quibble. The questions of geohistorical method and proletarian strategy are dialectically joined (Lukács 1971). Externalist models of capitalist limits necessitate radically different political strategies than dialectical frameworks, for which the limits emerge through relations that unify the inside, the outside, and the in-between (Moore 2015).

The differences between collisionism and dialectics are philosophical, historical – and pregnant with tectonic political implications for climate justice politics. Here we distinguish the Popular Anthropocene from its strictly geological forms. The former is a discourse surrounding the origins, development, and contemporary features of the climate crisis; the latter is focused on stratigraphical signals. The distinction is, however, blurred by its scientific practitioners, who along with many ecosocialists wish to eat their cake and have it too (e.g. Crutzen 2002; see Moore 2017a). The Popular Anthropocene's collisionism reduces the climate crisis to a conflict between Man and Nature, and to externalist limits premised on substances (fossil capital, Stop Oil, ecological footprints, etc.). Layering capitalism upon this substantialism, ecosocialists have accomplished two things. They have affirmed the independence of capital accumulation from its socio-ecological conditions of reproduction, insisting that capitalism can survive "until the last tree is cut" (Foster 2002a; Moore 2017d). In so doing, they have embraced philosophical substantialism: the primacy of substances over relations, a key element of Cartesian – that is, *bourgeois* – materialism (Watts 2005; Harvey 1974; Moore 2017c).

This produces a curious situation. After centuries of class struggle *against* reactionary substance fetishisms – from eugenics to environmental determinism to blood and soil nationalism – and *against* "natural law" justifications of inequality, the dominant radical view of climate justice has embraced both (Chase 1977; Robertson 2012; McNally 1993; Moore 2021a). Moreover, as if to move from the frying pan into the fire, it has done so in exceedingly deceptive fashion, smuggling reactionary premises into radical-sounding interpretations, and denouncing alternative readings of Marx's materialism as objective "enemies of socialism" (Foster 2016).

Anthropogenic phraseology serves double duty for much of the Green Left. It works descriptively, advancing a naive empiricism. To the degree that a philosophical anthropology is offered, readers are served up a philosophy of history that turns on a self-referential, even tautological, conception of human nature: "The struggle for freedom represents the *inner*-human need to be free in terms of self-activity and human development" (Foster 2022). For Marx, as we'll show, the struggle for freedom is not limited... limited to humans – "the creatures, too, must become free." Nor does it derive from an "*inner*-human need" (Marx and Engels 2010). In contrast, Marx underlines that the *relational essence* of "human need" is "outside itself" (Marx 1975b). That relational essence of human experience is grounded in "modes of life" that are *irreducible* to the interaction (collision) of acting units: human groups and ecosystem units. Rather, these must be grasped through an underlying labor-metabolic *relation* (Marx and Engels 2010). Thus: "labor created man" (Engels 1987). Through the metabolic labor process, historical man's conditions of possibility emerge, entwining a "physical life-process" and a "historical life-process" (Marx and Engels 2010). Modes of life and modes of production are constituted through social relations of environment-making within environments that are at once, and unevenly, producers and products of those social relations (Marx and Engels 2010; Moore 2015; Levins and Lewontin 1997). At the same time, given geographical conditions – Marx and Engels call them "natural bases" – *necessarily exceed* the narrow confines of a particular mode of production. For instance, volcanic and solar activity has heavily influenced the course of civilizational history, regardless of mode of production (Brooke 2014). This dialectical approach counteracts one-sided determinations – social reductionism and environmental determinism – through geohistorical reconstruction. In sum, to use a fashionable expression, the *human* "struggle for freedom" is a multi-species affair – situated in modes of production that co-produce environments, even as they are subjected to biospheric and cosmological events of unimaginable proportions. The philosophical recognition of this problem is frequently alienated from geohistorical method; the Capitalocene addresses this disconnection (Moore 2017c). Far from denying these geographically external events in the pulse of civilization, the philosophy of internal relations allows for discerning how they influence the course of history (Ollman 1993).

Marx's critique of the bourgeois conception of anthropogenesis – between "man in general" and "historical man" – was fundamental to elaborating historical materialism (Marx and Engels 2010). Let's recall that Marx's militant observation – that "philosophers have only *interpreted* the world in various ways; the point is to *change* it" – directly builds upon his critique of Feuerbach's contemplative conception of the "essence of man" as "abstract[ed] from the historical process" (Marx 2010). For good reason, socialist projects always insisted on a new politics of human nature: socialist construction depends on a radical break with bourgeois humanism and its folk concepts. One may generatively disagree over the contours – and balance sheets – of revolutionary projects to create a "new socialist man" – from Bogdanov to Che. But one can scarcely doubt that the socialist clarion call for collective solidarity and mass mobilization in the interests of revolutionary transition is a minor point.

And yet, in affirming bourgeois Man, this is exactly what ecosocialist Anthropocenism has done. Nor does the problem end there. Its fetishized view of the human essence serves as an explanatory gateway drug for manifold social and substance causations – everything from population to fossil fuels to racism and colonialism (e.g., Haraway 2016; Malm 2016). All are significant, abstracted from their connective geohistorical tissues – and therefore dialectical syntheses – the celebration of one or another flavor-of-the-month factor obfuscates capitalogenic processes in the making of the climate crisis. Such obfuscation through the celebration of causal pluralism is a pillar of the Western intelligentsia's neoliberal realignment since the 1970s, crucial to manufacturing consent to bourgeois hegemony (Moore 2022b).

In relation to climate studies, the Anthropocene–Industrial Complex has been remarkably successful. Installing the fetish of bourgeois Man as its point of departure, the Anthropocene obscures and sublimates these capitalogenic forces. One cannot move from a bourgeois fetish to a dialectical conception. One *can*, however, easily move from the ideologized binary of Man and Nature toward a chaotic hodge-podge of concepts (Marx 1973). This is the hallmark of all Popular Anthropocenic tendencies. These include not only the mainstream and ecosocialist tendencies but also the "critical" Anthropocenes, of which the race-reductionist Plantationocene, with its substantialist defense of Latour's Earthbound epistemology, has become fashionable (Latour 2014; Wolford 2021). Across this Cene Craze, causal pluralism and its cognates have won the day (Moore et al. 2022d; Chwałczyk 2020).

For socialists, this marks an unsettling return to the Second International's "'factorial' approach." In this movement, quasi-independent factors (today, ecology, economy, race, gender, etc.) are separated and "thereby emptied of any effective socio-historical content" (Colletti 1972). The result is more than a series of epistemic rifts that "divorce" accumulation from the web of life, exploitation from domination, ideology from scientific knowledge, oppression from class (Colletti 1972). These dualisms seriously affect socialist climate justice efforts to cohere political unity. Meaningful unity cannot be organized based on a smorgasbord of class orthodoxy, oppressed groups, and economic fetishes (e.g., growth/degrowth) – all abstracted from their geohistorical relations, patterns, and historical crises (e.g., Foster 2022; see Moore 2022a). Unity-in-difference is meaningless when severed from capitalist geohistory.

Why should all this be so *unsettling*? Let us recall that such intellectual fragmentation preceded European social democracy's support for war in 1914. At a time of Green New Dealism, the return of inter-imperialist war, and other looming specters of green austerity for the Global South, we ignore the historical relations of national chauvinism, imperial knowledges, and de-historicizing fragmentation at our peril.

And yet to focus narrowly on this moment would surrender to one-sided doomism (Moore 2024). The Cene Craze is more than an ideological barrier to dialectical interpretations of the climate crisis and capitalism in the web of life. It is also a vital opportunity for how we might build out an interpretation of capitalism as a world-ecology of power, profit, and life (Moore 2015; Patel and Moore 2017; Antonacci 2021). Only a dialectical materialist approach to socio-ecological totality is sufficient to grapple with – and interpenetrate – the combined and uneven relations between geohistorical assessments of capitalism's drive toward the planetary inferno and the political questions they imply.

The Capitalocene: From Geopoetics to Geohistory

This is the strategic contribution of the Capitalocene thesis. We'll focus on two of its elements: geopoetry and geohistory.

The Capitalocene is a species of argument called geopoetics: literally, *earth poetry* (Last 2017). It directly provokes the imperialist cosmology of Man and Nature, fundamental to Civilizing Projects from Columbus onward (Patel and Moore 2017; Moore 2022a). Critics call the Capitalocene an inelegant formulation. Perhaps. But Anthro-po-cene? Shakespeare it ain't.

The Capitalocene is, first and foremost, a challenge to an ideology of Nature that operates through Good Science. New Left thinkers called this "scientization" to denote the ideological laundering of contentious political issues into techno-scientific prescriptions (Habermas 1987). Good Science was indeed a major institutional and ideological node of American postwar hegemony (Selcer 2018). But Scientism was hardly a Cold War invention. It crystallized during the great climate crisis of the seventeenth century – this was the Cartesian Revolution – and was reproduced and reinvented across a long Malthusian cycle that commenced at the turn of the eighteenth century (Moore 2021a). The Anthropocene is its latest expression.

The relations between science and scientism are deeply embedded in the world histories of capital and empire. As Marx underlines, science and industry work hand-in-glove to produce capitalism's historical natures. To defend the Anthropocene (and its cognates) on narrowly scientific grounds, to pretend that it is somehow innocent of questions of capital, ideology and class power is to take capitalism's structures of knowledge at face value. (Not least its claims to value neutrality.) When *marxisante* Anthropocenists make such arguments, they ignore Marx's warnings about the class character of modern science, which "has invaded and transformed human life all the more practically through the medium of industry" (Marx 1975a).

Marx's insight reaches well beyond science as a productive force and incorporates *scientism* in its effective sublimation of class struggle. Man and Nature become scientific "folk concepts" whose common sensibility is so robust that they are effectively immunized from ideological critique on an analytical or policy sphere. "Environmental problems" are correspondingly *preconceptualized*, inducing an extraordinary Cartesian habitus premised on a structural misrecognition, at the level of everyday life, of capitalism's manifold class antagonisms (Haila and Heininen 1995). These are transmogrified through the alchemy of the Cartesian Revolution: the class struggle is rendered an externalist collision between Man and Nature (Bourdieu and Wacquant 1992; Dundes 2007).

This means something crucial: analytical contestation will not suffice when it comes to Man and Nature. These are not ideas but *belief structures* (Moore 2022e). They operate through plastic but sinewy and durable webs of folk concepts, intellectual frameworks, and political assumptions. They are *de facto* religious dogmas, secularized by capitalism's "rational mastery of the world," sanctified by Civilizing Projects (Weber 1951). The Anthropocene and its cognates operate through an affective dimension that resists analytical and empirical critique. It is akin to the widely-reported phenomenon of climate denialism: under conditions of dualism ("black-and-white thinking"), there is a strong psycho-social tendency to deny uncomfortable facts that might require a very different way of reckoning the world (Shapiro 2023). The more that critique builds, the stronger the denialism. From this standpoint, the Capitalocene unfolds an aesthetic and affective mode of critique, alongside its philosophical and geohistorical claims. It understands that *unthinking* the Anthropocene can only occur by *feeling* its conceptual violence, practically joined to the long history of Civilizing Projects and class war in which it's embedded. The unthinking must proceed simultaneously at the levels of folk concept, academic fashion, and ruling ideology.

The Capitalocene's geopoetics unfolds through geohistory: *Earth poetry and earth history*, mediated through the metabolic labor process, are joined in this reconstruction. In and through these geopoetic and geocultural arguments, the Capitalocene grounds its interpretations in a definite geohistorical line of march. World-ecology understands geohistory's point of departure as Marx and Engels put it in *The German Ideology*: human social relations are defined by their "twofold relation," social and natural, and both determine and are determined by "natural bases" (e.g., climate), "anthropological nature" as socio-ecological ensemble, and their "subsequent modification" (Marx and Engels 2010; Marx 1975a). The geohistorical movement is clear: successive phases in the development of class society and capitalism must be interpreted through this totality of the "twofold relation." Every era of class society, and capitalism, is a product and producer of the web of life.

The Capitalocene thesis refuses to indulge the idealist fantasy of theory for the sake of theory; the Capitalocene is geohistorical, or it is nothing. Eschewing neo-Smithianism, resource determinism, and Anglo-centric property formalism, the Capitalocene thesis identifies the origins of capitalism and capitalogenic environment-making in the labor/landscape revolutions between 1450 and 1750

(Moore 2003; 2017c; 2018). In these centuries, capitalism became a biogeological force, creating a modern Pangea of biological flows through the globalizing infrastructures of capital, empire, and class formation. In its slaving-induced genocides, this twofold relation of power and profit in the web of life added a critical increment of capitalogenic forcing to the "long, cold seventeenth century": the coldest moment of the Little Ice Age, itself the coldest period of the past 8,000 years (Cameron et al. 2015; Ladurie and Daux 2008; Lewis and Maslin 2015). After 1450, the scale, scope, and speed of environmental change across the Atlantic world outstripped anything seen in the halcyon days of Europe's High Middle Ages. The difference was often an order of magnitude – a tenfold difference, give or take. The *speed* of early modern transformation was distinctive, and it remains crucial to capitalogenic environment-making in the twenty-first century. Only capitalism's ability to advance frontiers of Cheap Nature – expanding opportunities for the appropriation of the unpaid work of "women, nature, and colonies" – enabled it to outrun the exhaustion of the socio-ecological conditions necessary to resolve overaccumulation crises and enable capital's expanded reproduction (Mies 1986; Moore 2018).

The Capitalocene's geohistorical method bears directly on one's political conception of today's climate crisis. For world-ecology, the unfolding climate crisis can only ever be grasped adequately through a penetrating reconstruction of its origins in the rise of capitalism. For us, the Little Ice Age and the first capitalogenic contributions to climate crisis in the long, cold seventeenth century were *fundamental* to the rise of capitalism – a dramatic contrast to ecosocialist narratives (Moore 2021a). The development of planetary crisis tendencies therefore cannot be adequately explained through population and scarcity "abstract[ed] from the historical process" (Marx 2010). Rather, these operate only through the history of capitalism, whose mediations establish evolving "special laws" of population, capital, and other conditions necessary to world accumulation's evolving technical, social, and cultural requirements (Marx 1977). To this end, the Capitalocene foregrounds not only the "original" transition debate – from feudalism to capitalism – but also the periodic ruptures within, and reinventions of, the capitalist world-ecology through its successive developmental phases: waves of industrialization and imperialism above all. Then, and only then, can the *unfolding* "transition debate" – over the contours of the climate crisis and the character of the possible civilizational transitions ahead – be meaningfully discussed in a way that draws on Marx and Engels' understanding of "scientific socialism" and the communist horizon (Moore 2021b).

In sum, the Capitalocene is a family of *geohistorical propositions* whose theory develops through "empirically verifiable" world history: its geohistorical interpretations may well be partial, one-sided, or incorrect (Marx and Engels 2010). But any "theoretical" critique levied against it is idealist insofar as it remains theoreticist; a *materialist* critique must take seriously capitalism's world-historical emergence, developmental patterns, and crisis formation. World-ecology offers this. So far, the ecosocialist critique has not. It has remained silent on these questions, indulging in theoreticist theory, in the process revealing its bourgeois tendencies: the "flight from world history" (Moore 2022b).

Name the System! Anthropogenesis, Capitalogenesis, and "Historical Man"

World-ecology prioritizes the dialectical unification of world-historical processes and relations that are frequently dualized and fragmented, by scholars no less than political actors – even those on the left. Here geopoetics entwine with geohistorical reconstruction in the critique of ideology and knowledge. These are not merely expressions, but socially necessary cultural dynamics and productive forces. As we are seeing, the Capitalocene critique foregrounds the demystification of bourgeois fetishes: Humanity, Nature, Society, Economy, Race, and Gender above all. You'll notice the uppercase. This denotes fetishes that rise to the level of *ruling abstractions*, hegemonic ideas that run across capitalism's *longue durée* (Patel and Moore 2017). These practically guide and inform bourgeois projects that ideologically justify, and instrumentally enable, the endless accumulation of capital. By their nature, such fetishes are ahistorical and dehistoricizing (Bhaskar 1979). Bourgeois science is especially crucial in making sense of the history of capitalism – including the history of these fetishes. Every great capitalist era has relied on science as a force of production, power, and destruction, and – through the "double transference" – as an ideological force of justification and mystification (Foster and Clark 2008).

Among the most corrosive assumptions in climate discussions today is the idea that capitalism is a subset of "human activity." Here's NASA: "Human activity is the cause of increased greenhouse gas concentrations" (NASA 2023). Socialists use identical language (Angus 2016). This is not a matter of parsing words. Quite the opposite! The phrase's ubiquity indicates an acceptance of Man/Nature thinking so deep, and so pervasive, that to underline its ideological roots invites ridicule. Such is the power of folk concepts under bourgeois hegemony. But it's hardly a footnote to capitalism's ecologies to implicate a bloody and violent history of symbolic and material dispossession sublimated in the language of Man and Nature. These are words formed through the emergence of a new mode of thought, taking shape as a key moment in worldwide primitive accumulation – no less, during the climate crisis of the long seventeenth century (Williams 1983; Parker 2013).

Man and Nature are consequentially far from innocent. They intellectually cleanse and reproduce the ideological violence inscribed in Christianizing, Civilizing, and Developmentalist Projects since 1492. This has not persuaded the ecosocialist left. On the dominant left view, the climate crisis results from "anthropogenic rifts" abstractly connected to a plurality of capitalist processes – but without any sense of how capitalism's *internal* contradictions develop Foster and Clark 2016. Indeed, it should come as little surprise that internal contradictions are minimized, given the vaguely Schumpetarian and market-centered definitions of capitalism on offer (Foster et al. 2010). On this view, capitalism "will continue until the last tree is cut" – an expression derived from the German Green Party and before that, Max Weber (Foster 2002a). Such externalist conceptions of capitalism are hallmarks of bourgeois thought, and a far cry from Marx's emphasis on the metabolic labor process as a class struggle in the web of life.

The Capitalocene charts a radically different approach to anthropogenesis and capitalogenesis. As we've suggested, the ideological power of "man in general" and "nature in general" is essentially precognitive and plays out at the level of folk concepts. These are "unthought categories of thought" – they "delimit the thinkable and predetermine the thought" (Bourdieu and Wacquant 1992). The ideological unconscious is difficult to dislodge because ideologies are not mere beliefs; they are *belief structures*. They are "material forces" (Marx 1978). (The resulting appearances are not narrowly false, but enter into the historical "reality" of an entity or process.) In this instance, folk concepts reshape not merely peoples' minds, but their *brains*, in ways broadly similar to the influence of advertising (Carr 2010). In the well-traveled expression of neuroplasticity studies: neurons that fire together, wire together. Centuries of bourgeois thought-policing in service to empire and the law of value have installed Man and Nature as innocent and rational descriptions – and rewired our brains accordingly.

But innocent, Man and Nature are not. They are twin pillars of bourgeois ideology, embedded in successive Civilizing Projects, reproducing legitimate forms of geocultural domination: racism, sexism, and Prometheanism Moore 2022g. Abstract naturalism animates each, advancing "abstractly material" ideologies on the basis of "abstractly material" science (Marx 1975a). This is Good Science: "natural law" as justification of capitalist inequality and bourgeois domination. The double transference in play, from ideology to "abstract material" science and back to ideology. The Man/Nature cosmology is revealed not merely as an ideological farce, but as an instrumental force to advance the forces of production.

For two centuries, Marxists have pushed back against this ideologization. As we've seen, historical materialism emerges in opposition to the passive materialism of "man in general" and abstract naturalism. Marx and Engels prioritized the mutual formation of "historical man" and "natural history," mediated through modern class structure and its first order alienation. In this "*industry* is [the bearer of] the *actual*, historical relationship of nature, and therefore of natural science, to man" (Marx 1975a). Modes of production possess a "twofold character" – social and natural in their concrete historical forms. They are at once producers and products of webs of life that necessarily exceed the limited capacities of even the greatest civilizations. Thus, Engels' famous geopoetics of the "revenge" of webs of life in revolt against the bourgeoisie's Promethean conquests (Engels 1987).

In these early formulations, a definite thesis emerges. First, undialectical concepts – "chaotic concepts" such as Man and Nature – do not yield dialectical reconstructions of human history (Marx 1973). Fetish in, fetish out. To the degree that they rise to the status of ruling abstractions – Man, Nature, and Civilization above all – society must attend not only to their one-sided character but to their class basis. Every ruling class must either directly or indirectly set in motion a stratum of "conceptive ideologists" (Marx and Engels 1975). Today, these comprise the intellectual cadres associated with the professional-managerial class, whose task is to produce "scientific" (value-neutral) categories of perception and interpretation (Moore 2021b, 2022c).

Second, capitalism is not a derivative specification of "man in general." Marx and Engels' point of departure is not "man in general" but "historical man." This does not entail the reduction of the human species to its social "ensembles" – long a contentious *problematique* for historical materialism (Geras 1983). It *does* recognize that the historical character of biologically modern humans over the past 300,000 years or so – Braudel called this the "time of the sages" – admits only broad observations about modern hominins, mostly involving language, culture, and consciousness within enormously plastic forms of sociality (Braudel 2009). Any *geohistorical* claim must proceed through the concrete specification of socio-ecological "ensembles": *historical man*, not "man in general."

For Marx, anthropogenesis signifies the geohistorical process of creating "historical man" through a metabolism, grasped as a contradictory unity of labor processes that flow through the nexus of the "soil and the worker" (Marx 1977). *Historical man* is therefore an "ensemble" of socio-ecological relations – including the given geographical conditions and their "subsequent course of modification" by specific modes of production. Thus, the geohistorical tension between given "natural bases" (e.g., mountain ranges) and "anthropological nature." *Historical man* is emphatically not the idealist Man of the Anthropocene. It is, rather, the active materialist expression of a specific mode of production. In the capitalist era, the ontological conflict is not between Man and Nature but a class struggle whose "first order" pivot is the metabolic labor process (Mézáros 1970) – one that comprises, as Marx and Engels underscore, the relations of production *and* the reproduction of "fresh life in procreation" (Marx and Engels 1975; Seccombe 1992).

Why 1492 Matters: Cheap Nature, the Capitalocene, and Industrial Revolutions

The Capitalocene thesis challenges the philosophical claim that Humanity is a geohistorical agent, rather than a specific fetish that took shape in and through the global conquests following 1492. The "discovery" of the Americas found its ideological expression in the "discovery of mankind" (Abulafia 2009). It was an ideological invention of the greatest significance. Nature and Humanity emerged through the activation of new "means of mental production" (Marx and Engels 1975). From it issued a new, epoch-making ruling idea: Humanity. Through it, the vast majority of humankind – female, pigmented, Celtic and Slavic, and countless others – were banished to Nature: such domination was not "othering" but rather *overing*, the specifically bourgeois assertion of geo-cultural power in service of geo-profiteering.

In this conjuncture, Humanity was produced as an epoch-making fetish. For Wynter, this was a decisive moment of ideological "over-representation" (Wynter 2003). The imperial bourgeoisie imagined itself as the "best of all mankind" – to quote JFK's Moon Speech – and made sure that everyone behaved accordingly. Everyone else was not, or not yet, Human; only grueling, often unpaid and frequently deadly work would bring Light to the Savages, for whom Christianizing, Civilizing, and Developmentalist Projects promised Salvation (Patel and Moore 2017). The Capitalocene argument's first priority is, consequentially, to unsettle the assumptions (Man and Nature, but including further fragmentation and taxonomization) that obscure the deadly relation between capital and its political, cultural, and class conditions of possibility.

The ruling abstractions of Man and Nature have been central to world accumulation. Recognizing with Luxemburg the centrality of geographical expansion to the (always-temporary) resolution of overaccumulation crises, the Capitalocene thesis joins the three moments – endless accumulation, endless domination, and endless conquest – to highlight capitalism as a logic of Cheap Nature (Luxemburg 2003). The history of Cheap Nature is a proposition about how capitalism works. A strategy and logic – not a thing – the history of Cheap Nature reveals capitalism's prioritization of the "endless" identification and thence extra-economic appropriation of the Four Cheaps: labor-power and unpaid work, food, energy, and raw materials. Every great wave of world accumulation has depended upon a critical mass of these Four Cheaps, without which the surplus capital problem intensifies, and devalorization of capital threatens.

We can trace the lineages of Cheap Nature – and its fetishes of Society and Nature – to early capitalist ideology: bourgeois naturalism and its Civilizing Projects. In the first great era of capitalogenic climate crisis (c. 1550–1700), the new empires proceeded to "fix" the crisis through new imperialist advances that consolidated new labor regimes, many centered on plantations, from Ireland to the West Indies. It marked the crystallization of the Civilizing Project and the violent redefinition of colonized peoples as "savage." This combination generated what has been called the capitalogenic trinity: the climate class divide, climate apartheid, and climate patriarchy (Moore 2021a).

The Project's horrific genius was the redefinition of humankind's vast majority as part of Nature; such bourgeois naturalism quickly and terribly gave rise to globalizing patriarchy and successive world color lines. Why? In a word, to facilitate the creation of the Four Cheaps and thereby to advance the rate of profit, to counteract the overaccumulation tendency. Can that be reduced to the "immanent laws" of capitalism? *No.* And that's the point. The Civilizing Project and the invention specifically of Nature as a *ruling abstraction* became a world-historical lever of cost-reduction for capital. Nature, to paraphrase von Werlhof, became everything the new bourgeoisies did not want to pay for (Werlhof 1988). The world-ecological alternative does not argue that Society and Nature do not exist; *they emphatically do exist.* Man, Nature, Society, Civilization, are all ruling abstractions, pillars of bourgeois naturalism, and imperial projects over the *longue durée*.

The Capitalocene emerged through the climate–class crisis of feudalism in the long fourteenth century Moore 2003, 2021a. It was an epochal crisis characterized not merely by manifold biophysical problems but also by the world-historical defeat of feudalism's ruling strata by the era's semi-proletarian and peasant forces. The result, in successive moments of crisis (political, class, economic, and cultural), was a reorientation of late medieval Europe's dominant strata toward a new form of frontier-making that would immediately subordinate eastern Europe, Ireland, and the Americas to an audacious form of imperial rule, dominated by the logic of Cheap Nature.

This strategy of Cheapness fused the logic of capital (valorization) with a new, binarized geocultural logic: devaluation. Thus, the centrality of the Civilizing Project and its ruling abstractions. At its core was the securing of "socially-necessary" unpaid work via extra-economic means. This was accumulation by appropriation (Moore 2018). Those appropriations would – directly and indirectly – advance labor productivity within an exceedingly narrow sphere: the cash nexus. The new value-oriented technics – crystallizations of tools and ideas, power, and nature – allowed the prodigious appropriation of uncommodified work/energy, advancing labor productivity (as Marx observes, the appropriation of "natural fertility" functions like fixed capital) (Marx 1973). The great leap forward in the scale, scope, and speed of landscape and biological transformations in the three centuries after 1450 – stretching from Poland to Brazil, from the North Atlantic's cod fisheries to Southeast Asia's spice islands – may be understood in this light. From 1492, the imperialist bourgeoisies "discovered" not just new continents to exploit and appropriate, but an entirely novel socio-ecological logic of power, profit, and life: Cheap Nature.

Despite all the significant differences between the 1492 and 1830 theses, both prioritize the rise of capitalism. For Malm, it's an Anglo-centric story shaped by the geographies of class struggle, technical innovation, and the coal revolution (Malm 2016). For us, it's the epoch-making land/labor revolution after 1492, producing a capitalist world-ecology. Neither seeks to substitute human for geological history. Both are staunch critics of economism, insisting on the centrality of political power in establishing and reproducing the necessary conditions of endless accumulation. The two differ, however, on the conception of capitalism as metabolic regime. For world-ecology, substances *become* resources through the "activation of potentialities slumbering within nature"; for Malm, the relations of capital move *around* coal, rather than activating and incorporating coal's potentialities as significant moments of Marx's circulating constant capital (Marx 1977).

This is no quibble. There are significant points of agreement and differences between the 1830 and 1492 Capitalocene theses: over capitalism, the class struggle, the generative possibilities of the *oikeios* as a multi-layered and creative pulse of life-making, the role of bourgeois ideology, and the power of the fetishes of Nature and Society. Simply put, for Malm, the class struggles in early nineteenth-century English mill towns propelled the bourgeoisie to reconcentrate industrial production, powered by steam engines, in major cities like Manchester. Thus "fossil capital" was born and became a weapon in the bourgeoisie's class victory over an increasingly militant industrial proletariat (Malm 2016). For the 1492 thesis, Malm's fossil capital argument is one crucial element in a longer story.

We disagree with Malm's periodization not because the long nineteenth century was epiphenomenal. It wasn't. The fossil capital thesis denies, however, the constitutive geohistorical relations – from the Baltic to Barbados – that prefigured and accompanied large-scale industry before and after 1800. These are front-and-center for the 1492 argument: the connective tissues between the plantation complex, its trans-Atlantic class dynamics, and its contributions to capital formation in industrializing Britain (Genovese 1979; Blackburn 1997; Rediker and Linebaugh 2000; Williams 2022). The world-ecology position does not deny the significance of the productive forces. But we understand these differently, painfully aware of a longer history in which the "idea of mechanical progress... [presents itself] not merely as a necessary development but as an end in itself, almost as a kind of religion" (Orwell 1937). (As Orwell underlines, such a religious view hobbled socialist strategy no less than it enhanced bourgeois power.) From this perspective, we view the productive forces as configurations of capital, class, and technique – Mumford's *technics* – and situates these within the imperialist dynamics of accumulation (Mumford 1934; Moore 2018). The productive forces are, in this conception, technological movements that comprise "software" alongside "hardware" – cartographic and calculative technologies alongside machinery (Moore 2023).

Simply: coal and steam were nothing without cheap cotton, and cheap cotton was nothing without the cotton gin, the second slavery, and the dispossession of indigenous peoples alongside the imperialist de-industrialization of India and Ireland. How the *technics* of coal mining, textile manufacture, and the cotton gin fit together is worth integrating into the assessment of the climate crisis. We have mentioned, climate apartheid as a creation of the sugar plantation system in the long seventeenth century. At the turn of the eighteenth century – in another climate downturn (the Dalton minimum) – the world color line was again reinvented through a new mass commodity with a new repertoire of agro-industrialization.

The geographical locus of industrialization was never England as such. It depended on imperial deindustrialization and agro-industrialization from India to Ireland to Mississippi. This world-historical dynamic rendered the cotton gin a strategic technical node in the era's modest – but significant – industrialization. Marx thought as much when he reckoned that only the dramatic cheapening of cotton made large-scale industry possible (Marx 1971).

Anthropocene and fossil capital are not problematic because they assert turning points: of the early nineteenth century or the mid-twentieth century. They are problematic because they preconceptualize the problem into potted histories. These stylized narratives masquerade as history; in reality, they are ideological claims dressed up as history. "Great Acceleration" narratives cleave world accumulation, inter-imperialist rivalry, and worldwide class struggles (from above and below) in favor of a world-historical approach that scales out from the Anthropocene's aggregated "trajectories" (McNeill and Engelke 2016). Fossil capital, for its part, scales out and up from regional class struggles and technical developments in the early nineteenth century. In both instances, these potted histories implicate crucial moments of socio-ecological crisis formation while unnecessarily reducing the narrative to one moment of a richer world-historical process. Such one-sided histories derive from a series of more or less conscious reductionisms that stem from methodological nationalism fused with substance fetishism (fossil capital), or an abstracted methodological economism fused with neo-Smithian market fetishism (the great acceleration).

Such potted histories are pivotal to the formation of social theory, economic history, and Green Thought: all locate "the" Industrial Revolution as their lodestar. This is the Industrialization Moore 2003. That so many ecosocialists accept the transition of the long nineteenth century as *the* origin of capitalism cannot be explained by some rigorous ecosocialist investigation of – and debate over – the world-historical origins of today's epochal crisis. The centrality of historical debate over the origins of capitalism and the tasks of the socialist movement (such as it is) has been buried by Anthropocenists and ecosocialists alike.

Good Science, Big Lies: Capitalocene Vistas, Socialist Possibilities

The Popular Anthropocene is only the most recent slogan of Imperial Environmentalism. Indeed, the Popular Anthropocene recapitulates practically everything about its predecessor: Spaceship Earth. Both Environmentalist super-concepts aimed to contain a dangerous possibility: radicals might join their critique of work and power with a program for a broadly defined environmental justice. This is why the Capitalocene is a dangerous idea (Moore 2022a).

Dangerous ideas have a way of escaping from the rulers' prisonhouses in times of crisis. Even Greta Thunberg, until now a well-behaved and rather conventional Environmentalist, now flirts with anti-capitalist critique – one that resonates with a significant generational shift across the rich countries, against capitalism and for socialism (Thunberg 2022). No matter that both the critique of capitalism and openness to socialism are ill-defined and flimsy. One would expect nothing less after a half-century of worldwide class war by the rich against the world's working class and peasant majority; the overthrow of state socialisms; and three decades of American unipolar regime change and counter-insurgency politics across the Global South. And one would expect nothing less after a half-century of the Environmentalism of the Rich – since the first Earth Day (1970) a pillar of neoliberalism, with its hyper-individualized market-oriented virtue signaling and well-documented hostility toward the working class. The long arc of this neoliberal Environmentalism – marketed through its super-concepts of Spaceship Earth and the Anthropocene – is coming to an end (Moore 2022a).

We are therefore at a conjuncture, a new transitional moment, greater than any since the first agricultural revolution in the early millennia of the Holocene. Will the transition be "decadent," with the One Percent re-engineering planetary life in service to a new, new, hierarchical and exploitative, but non-capitalist, civilization? Or will it be revolutionary, one in which the associated producers and reproducers seize the means of mental and material production, and reinvent these on the road to planetary socialism (Amin 2018)? The answer is of course unknowable. But the revolutionary path will remain utopian so long as we continue to indulge the ahistorical and bourgeois modes of thinking – resting on Man, Nature, and Civilization – that enabled the climate crisis. Without a return to world history – to be sure a necessary but insufficient movement – struggles for planetary justice will remain fragmented and divided, existing solutions stained by bourgeois and professional virtue signaling and managerialism. It is to these dangers that the Capitalocene thesis speaks.

For centuries, the bourgeoisie's "conceptive ideologists" have delivered a clear message to the dangerous classes (Marx and Engels 2010): "Listen to the science." It is a central theme in a post-1968 environmentalism defined by such scientism. Even earlier, the science/scientism nexus was paramount. One cannot tell the story of postwar capitalism without addressing the centrality of Good Science in the interwoven history of world power, world accumulation, and world nature. The scientific development of "natural law" has, emphatically since 1945, converted the *political* problems of monopoly capitalism into techno-scientific "issues." Not just biological and geophysical problems but also "social" problems were to be "managed" by enlightened technocrats and scientists.

Listen to the science. A world of difference turns on a single three-letter article: *the*. Listen to *scientists*? Of course! Listen to *the science*? That's another matter entirely. Big Science is not only a force of production, an enabling condition of prodigious extraction and exploitation. It's also Good Science, the "fraternal code of the world's accumulators of capital. It [justified]... both their own activities and the differential rewards from which they benefited" (Wallerstein 1983). Every superpower, and every great phase of capitalism, depended on one or other version of this Civilizing Project, fusing Big Science as force of production and legitimating code. Man and Nature must be managed scientifically and rationally by scientific and rational institutions: states, markets, and firms.

It underscores the Big Lie, repeated since the birth of capitalism. It says: the problems created by *capitalism* are not capitalism's fault; they are the fault of human nature, as if modern genocide and ecocide is simply a matter of humans being human, like zebras will be zebras, or salamanders will be salamanders.

We have now come full circle. The Capitalocene depends on successive Civilizing Projects that seek to create new profit-making opportunities through Cheap Nature: a strategy of (economic) valorization and (geocultural) devaluation. Since 1492, Civilizing Projects have turned on a Nature that includes most humans. That *Nature* is a ruling abstraction at the core of manifold Christianizing, Civilizing, and Developmentalist Projects.

The immanent critique of capitalism as world-ecology must necessarily speak to the revolutionary possibilities. And they can be no more than possibilities at this conjuncture. To invoke the Capitalocene in the spirit of Marx and Engels is to implicate socialist internationalism and planetary justice. Such justice means the liberation of all life from the tyranny of capitalist work – or it is nothing. It is a vision for a biotarian socialism, for a *Proletarocene* (Salvage Collective 2021). It demands the emancipation of proletariat, femitariat, and biotariat – the interpenetrating relations of work and power that re/produce the work, paid and paid, human and extra-human, necessary for the endless accumulation of capital. In the climate crisis, a biotarian socialism grasps the web of life as a class struggle, such that an injury to one is an injury to all (to borrow a slogan of the American labor movement).

Intellectually, the Capitalocene thesis – and the world-ecology conversation in which it's embedded – invites a revolutionary reimagination of Man, Nature, and Civilization. To unthink the Anthropocene we must unthink the substantialism with us since the Cartesian Revolution, and how it has been fundamental to reactionary and imperial politics since the long, cold seventeenth century. In this reimagining – and unthinking – we can embrace and unfold an ethic of synthesis that strives to conceptualize and clarify the rich totality of many determinations that characterize and make modernity as a capitalist world-ecology.

Such intellectual revolutions are not the be-all and end-all of movements for climate justice. Nor are they incidental. Marx's point about philosophy and changing the world was not about the insignificance of philosophy, but the centrality of an active – dare we say *proletarian*? – materialism. It recognizes, and speaks to, the unevenness of the conditions for planetary socialism. This is precisely why the dialectical imagination is more crucial than ever: the surficial fragmentation of planetary and everyday life into the silos of nation, race, gender, and sexuality – abstracted at every turn from the unifying threads of capital and class in the web of life – has and will continue to produce a politics of accommodation to late capitalism and its planetary managers. The flight from world history will prevent us from seeing – and targeting the weak links of – the capitalogenic trinity. The climate class divide, climate apartheid, and climate patriarchy are not the results of climate change today, but pivotal to a long history of capitalogenic environment-making.

This world-historical recognition is fundamental to forging a socialist vision premised on the internationalism of the direct re/producers and the liberation of planetary life: *"the creatures, too, must become free."* Marx's condemnation of capitalism's degradation of the "soil and the worker" affirms its revolutionary possibilities. For Marx, the essence of proletarian revolution is found in the relations joining the inner and outer moments of work, life, and struggle under capitalism. The "social metabolism" is the terrain of class struggle in the Capitalocene. The bourgeoisie ignores this.

They believe their Big Lie. We don't have to.

References

Abulafia, D., *The Discovery of Mankind*. New Haven: Yale University Press, 2009.

Althusser, L., *For Marx*. London: New Left Books, 1977.

Amin, S., Revolution or Decadence, *Monthly Review*, v. 70 (1). 2018. 17–23.

Angus, I., *Facing the Anthropocene*. New York: Monthly Review Press, 2016.

Antonacci, J. P., Periodizing the Capitalocene as Polemocene, *Journal of World-Systems Research*, v. 27 (2). 2021. 440–467.

Bhaskar, R., *The Possibility of Naturalism*. Atlantic Highlands: Humanities Press, 1979.

Blackburn, R., *The Making of New World Slavery*. London: Verso, 1997.

Bonneuil, C. & Fressoz, J. B., *The Shock of the Anthropocene*. London: Verso, 2015.

Bourdieu, P. & Wacquant, L. J. D., *Invitation to Reflexive Sociology*. Chicago: University of Chicago Press, 1992.

Braudel, F., History and the Social Sciences, *Review*, v. 32 no. 2. 2009. 171–203.

Brooke, J., *Climate Change and the Course of Global History*. Cambridge: Cambridge University Press, 2014.

Cameron, C. M., Kelton, P., & Swedlund, A. C., *Beyond Germs*. Tucson: University of Arizona Press, 2015.

Carr, N. G., *The Shallows*. New York: W.W. Norton, 2010.

Catton, W. R., *Overshoot*, Urbana: University of Illinois Press, 1980.

Chakrabarty, D., *The Climate of History in a Planetary Age*. Chicago: University of Chicago Press, 2021.

Chase, A., *Legacy of Malthus*. New York: Alfred E. Knopf, 1977.

Chwałczyk, F., Around the Anthropocene in Eighty Names, *Sustainability*, v. 12 (11). 2020.

Colletti, L., *From Rousseau to Lenin*. London: New Left Books, 1972.

Crutzen, P. J., Geology of Mankind, *Nature*, v. 415. 2002. 23.

Dundes, A., *The Meaning of Folklore*. Logan: Utah State University Press, 2007.

Ehrlich, P. R., *The Population Bomb*. New York: Ballantine, 1968.

Engels, F., The Part Played by Labor in the Transition from Ape to Man, In *Collected Works*, Karl Marx and Frederick Engels, v. 25. New York: International Publishers, 1987. 452.

Foster, J. B., *The Vulnerable Planet*. New York: Monthly Review Press, 1994. 30–37.

Foster, J. B., Capitalism and Ecology, *Monthly Review*, v. 54 (4). 2002a. 6–16.

Foster, J. B., *Ecology Against Capitalism*. New York: Monthly Review Press, 2002b.

Foster, J. B., In Defense of Ecological Marxism, Climate and Capitalism. 2016.

Foster, J. B., *Capitalism in the Anthropocene*. New York: Monthly Review Press, 2022.

Foster, J. B. & Clark, B., The Sociology of Ecology, *Organization & Environment*, v. 21 (3). 2008. 311–352.

Foster, J. B., Clark, B., & York, R., *The Ecological Rift*. New York: Monthly Review Press, 2010.

Foster, J. B., & Clark, B. (2016). Marxism and the Dialectics of Ecology. *Monthly Review*, v. 68(5), 1–17.

Genovese, E. D., *From Rebellion to Revolution*. Baton Rouge: Louisiana State University Press, 1979.

Geras, N., *Marx and Human Nature*. London: Verso, 1983.

Habermas, J., *Toward a Rational Society*. Cambridge, UK: Polity, 1987. 249.

Haila, Y. & Heininen, L., Ecology: a New Discipline for Disciplining? *Social Text*, v. 42. 1995. 153–171.

Haraway, D. J., *Staying with the Trouble*. Durham, NC: Duke University Press, 2016.

Harvey, D., Population, Resources, and the Ideology of Science, *Economic Geography* v. 50 (3). 1974. 256–277.

Intergovernmental Panel on Climate Change, Climate Change 2022. Cambridge: Cambridge University Press. 2022.

Ladurie, E. L. R. & Daux, V., The Climate in Burgundy and Elsewhere, From the Fourteenth to the Twentieth Century, *Interdisciplinary Science Reviews*, v. 33 (1). 2008. 10–24.

Last, A., We are the World? Theory, *Culture & Society*, v. 34 (2–3). 2017. 147–168.

Latour, B., Agency at the Time of the Anthropocene, *New Literary History*, v. 45 (1). 2014. 1–18.

Levins, R. and Lewontin, R., Organism and Environment, *Capitalism, Nature, Socialism*, v. 8 (2). 1997. 95–98.

Lewis, S. L. & Maslin, M. A., Defining the Anthropocene, *Nature*, v. 519. 2015. 171–180.

Lukács, G., *History and Class Consciousness*. Cambridge, MA: MIT Press, 1971.

Luxemburg, R., *The Accumulation of Capital*. New York: Routledge, 2003.

Malm, A., *Fossil Capital*. London: Verso, 2016.

Marx, K., *Theories of Surplus Value*, v. 3. Moscow: Progress Publishers, 1971.

Marx, K., *Grundrisse*. New York: Vintage, 1973.

Marx, K., *Economic and Philosophic Manuscripts of 1844*, In *Collected Works*, Karl Marx and Frederick Engels, v. 3. London: Lawrence & Wishart, 1975a. 229–348.

Marx, K., On the Jewish Question, In *Collected Works*, Karl Marx and Frederick Engels, v. 3. London: Lawrence & Wishart, 1975b. 146–174.

Marx, K., Theses on Feuerbach, In *Collected Works*, Karl Marx and Frederick Engels, v. 5. London: Lawrence & Wishart, 2010. 3–5.

Marx, K., *Capital*. New York: Vintage, 1977.

Marx, K., Contribution to the Critique of Hegel's Philosophy of Right, In *The Marx-Engels Reader* (Second ed.). New York: Norton, 1978. 53–65.

Marx, K. & Engels, F., *The German Ideology*, In *Collected Works*, Karl Marx and Frederick Engels, v. 5. London: Lawrence & Wishart, 2010. 19–593.

Marx, K. & Engels, F., *Manifesto of the Communist Party*. New York: Penguin, 2002

McNally, D., *Against the Market*. London: Verso, 1993.

McNeill, J. R. & Engelke, P., *The Great Acceleration*. Cambridge: Harvard University Press, 2016.

Mészáros, I., *Marx's Theory of Alienation*. London: Merlin Press, 1970.

Mies, M., *Patriarchy and Accumulation on a World Scale*. London: Zed, 1986.

Moore, J. W., Nature and the Transition from Feudalism to Capitalism, *Review*, v. 26 (2). 2003. 97–172.

Moore, J. W., Transcending the Metabolic Rift, *Journal of Peasant Studies*, v. 38 (1). 2011. 1–46.

Moore, J. W., *Capitalism in the Web of Life: Ecology and the Accumulation of Capital*. London: Verso, 2015.

Moore, J. W., Confronting the Popular Anthropocene, *New Geographies*, v. 9. 2017a. 186–191.

Moore, J. W., Metabolic Rift or Metabolic Shift? Dialectics, Nature, and the World-Historical Method, *Theory & Society*, v. 46 (4). 2017b. 285–318.

Moore, J. W., The Capitalocene Part I, *Journal of Peasant Studies*, v. 44 (3). 2017c. 594–630.

Moore, J. W., World Accumulation and Planetary Life, *IPPR Progressive Review*, v. 24 (3). 2017d. 175–202.

Moore, J. W., The Capitalocene Part II, *Journal of Peasant Studies*, v. 45 (2). 2018. 237–279.

Moore, J. W., Empire, Class & The Origins of Planetary Crisis: The Transition Debate in the Web of Life, *Esboços*, v. 28. 2021a. 740–763.

Moore, J. W., Opiates of the Environmentalists? *Abstrakt* (November). 2021b https://www.polenekoloji.org/opiates-of-the-environmentalists-anthropocene-illusions-planetary-management-the-capitalocene-alternative/.

Moore, J. W., Anthropocene, Capitalocene & the Flight from World History, *Nordiav*. 51 (2). 2022a. 123–146.

Moore, J. W., Power, Profit, & Prometheanism Part I, *Journal of World-Systems Research*, v. 28 (2). 2022b.

Moore, J. W., Waste in the Limits to Capital, *Emancipations*, v. 2 (1). 2022c. 1–45.

Moore, J. W., There is No Such Thing as a Technological Accident, In *Technological Accidents*. Leiden: V2 Publishing, 2023.

Moore, J. W., Beyond Climate Justice, In *The Way Out of the Climate Crisis…*. Berlin: Hatje Cantz Verlag. 2022f, 105–130.

Moore, J. W., How to Read Capitalism in the Web of Life, *Journal of World-Systems Research*, v. 21 (1). 2022e. 153–168.

Moore, J.W., "Power, Profit & Prometheanism, Part I," *Journal of World-Systems Research* v. 28(2), 415–426.

Moore, J. W., El Hombre, La Naturaleza, y El Ambientalismo del Ricos, *Pensar la Ciencia de Otro Modo*. Caracas: Ministerio del Poder Popular para Ciencia y Tecnología, 2022d. 55–82.

Moore, J.W., Between the Devil and the Deep Blue Marble: Capitalism, Nature and the Promethean Gaze, from Mercator to the Space Age, in *Image Ecology*, Kathrin Schönegg and Boaz Levin, eds., *C/O Berlin* (Leipzig: Spector Books, 2023), 66–75.

Moore, J. W., "The Fear and the Fix: Environmentalism Serves the Powerful," *The Baffler* (May 15, 2024), online. https://thebaffler.com/latest/the-fear-and-the-fix-moore

Mumford, L., *Technics and Civilization*. London: Routledge and Kegan Paul, 1934.

NASA, The Causes of Climate Change. 2023. https://climate.nasa.gov/causes/

Ollman, B., *Dialectical Investigations*. New York: Routledge, 1993.

Orwell, G., *The Road to Wigan Pier*. London: Victor Gollancz Limited, 1937.

Parker, G., *Global Crisis*. New Haven: Yale University Press, 2013.

Patel, R. & Moore, J. W., *A History of the World in Seven Cheap Things*. Berkeley: University of California Press, 2017.

Rediker, M. & Linebaugh, P., *The Many-Headed Hydra*. London: Verso, 2000.

Robertson, T., *The Malthusian Moment*. New Brunswick, NJ: Rutgers University Press, 2012.

Saito, K., *Marx in the Anthropocene*. Cambridge: Cambridge University Press, 2022.

Salvage Collective, *The Tragedy of the Worker*. London: Verso, 2021.

Seccombe, W., *A Millennium of Family Change*. London: Verso, 1992.

Selcer, P., *The Postwar Origins of the Global Environment*. New York: Columbia University Press, 2018.

Shapiro, J. P., The Thinking Error That Makes People Susceptible to Climate Change Denial, *The Conversation*. 2023.

Thunberg, G., How Can We Undo Our Failures if We Are Unable to Admit That We Have Failed? In *The Climate Book*. New York: Penguin, 2022.

Wallerstein, I., *Historical Capitalism*. London: Verso, 1983.

Watts, M. J., Nature: Culture, In *Spaces of Geographical Thought*, eds. P. Cloke and R. Johnston. London: Sage, 2005. 142–175

Weber, M., *The Religion of China*. Glencoe, IL: Free Press, 1951.

Werlhof, C., On the Concept of Nature and Society in Capitalism, In *Women: The Last Colony*, Mies, Maria, Veronika Bennholdt-Thomsen, and Claudia Von Werlhof London: Zed, 1988.

Williams, E., *Capitalism and Slavery*. New York: Penguin, [1944 original].

Williams, R., *Keywords*. Oxford: Oxford University Press, 1983.

Wolford, W., Plantationocene, *Annals of the American Association of Geographers*, v. 111 (6), 2021. 1622–1639.

Wynter, S., Unsettling the Coloniality of Being/Truth/Power/Freedom, *New Centennial Review*, v. 3 (3), 2003. 257–337.

INDEX

Printed in the United States
by Baker & Taylor Publisher Services